THE BIRTH OF A NATION

THE BIRTH OF A NATION

NATION

The Cinematic Past in the Present

Edited by Michael T. Martin

INDIANA UNIVERSITY PRESS

This book is a publication of

Indiana University Press
Office of Scholarly Publishing
Herman B Wells Library 350
1320 East 10th Street
Bloomington, Indiana 47405 USA

iupress.indiana.edu

Manufactured in the United States of America

Cataloging information is available from the Library of Congress.

ISBN 978-0-253-04235-4 (pbk.)

1 2 3 4 5   24 23 22 21 20 19

*To our ancestors—people of color and whites—
who labored against
The Birth of a Nation and its legitimizing nod to white rule.*

*To Charlottesville's antiprotestors,
who challenged
all manner of white supremacy in real time.*

And to the late Chuck Kleinhans, social activist and educator.

CONTENTS

Preface   ix

Acknowledgments   xi

Revisiting (As It Were) the "Negro Problem" in
The Birth of a Nation: Looking Back and in the Present /
Michael T. Martin   *1*

Part I   National/Transnational in Historical Time

1   *The Birth of a Nation*'s Long Century /
Cara Caddoo   *33*

2   *Great Moments from The Birth of a Nation*: Collecting
and Privately Screening Small Gauge Versions /
Andy Uhrich   *46*

3   D. W. Griffith's *The Birth of a Nation*: Transnational
and Historical Perspectives / Melvyn Stokes   *76*

4   Defining National Identity: *The Birth of a Nation* from
America to South Africa / Peter Davis   *107*

5   Comment: Is *The Birth of a Nation* a Western? /
Alex Lichtenstein   *123*

Part II   Representational and Rhetorical Strategies

6   Serial Melodramas of Black and White: *The Birth of a
Nation* and *Within Our Gates* / Linda Williams   *137*

7   The Rhetoric of Historical Representation in Griffith's
The Birth of a Nation / Lawrence Howe   *164*

Part III Cinematic Iterations in the Present

8 Something Else Besides a Western: *Django Unchained*'s
Generic Miscegenations / Paula Massood *191*

9 *12 Years a Slave* and *The Birth of a Nation*:
Two Moments in Representing Race / Julia Lesage *207*

10 Engineering Different Equations in the Wake of
The Birth of a Nation: Blackface and Racial Politics
in *Bamboozled* and *Dear White People* /
Anne-Marie Paquet-Deyris *239*

11 Race, Space, Sexuality, and Suffering in *The Birth of a
Nation* and *Get Hard* / David C. Wall *259*

12 Anger or Laughter? The Dialectics of Response to
The Birth of a Nation / Chuck Kleinhans *282*

Index 305

PREFACE

THE CONTENTS OF THIS BOOK ORIGINATED IN A two-day symposium organized and hosted in 2015 by the Black Film Center/Archive at Indiana University, Bloomington.[1] The conference, "From Cinematic Past to Fast Forward Present: D. W. Griffith's *The Birth of a Nation*—A Centennial Symposium," was not intended for the entertainment or amusement of film aficionados or as a learned exercise among film scholars and media professionals about the film's aesthetics, cinematic innovations, and production values (extraordinary though they were for their time). In consideration of the relational concerns of representation and diversity in media that the hashtags #HollywoodSoWhite and #OscarsSoWhite infer and of larger societal concerns, programmatic enunciations, and mobilizing work of Black Lives Matter, the symposium was imminently practical, calling attention to *The Birth of a Nation*'s legacy, afterlife, and ideological project and to the hegemonic structures in the American social formation that support and maintain white supremacy and social inequality.

Nor was the symposium a discrete event. Its impetus and occasion certainly had the film's centennial in mind, as other formal convocations did elsewhere in the United States and abroad. Such assemblies that addressed the film's centenary occurred at the University College London (UK), Film Forum (New York City), George Eastman House International Museum of Photography and Film (Rochester, NY), Old Dominion University (Norfolk, VA), Black Cinema House (Chicago, IL), International Slavery Museum (Liverpool, UK), Denver Silent Film Festival (Denver, CO), Kansas City Silent Film Festival (Kansas City, KS), Virginia Film Festival (Charlottesville, VA), and in 2017, Independent Lens's screening of *Birth of a Movement* (PBS).[2]

The symposium featured two keynotes by distinguished scholars Linda Williams, Professor Emerita, University of California, Berkeley, and Melvyn Stokes, Reader, University College London. Three panels engaged with *The Birth of a Nation*'s cultural, political, and transnational resonances, and a roundtable discussion was devoted to a consideration of the film's utility for teaching. The symposium also featured a screening of the full-length 186-minute 35 mm print preserved by the Museum of Modern Art (New York City) at Indiana University's state-of-the-art theater, IU

Cinema, and was accompanied by an extraordinary virtuoso piano-solo version of a musical score performed by Maestro Rodney Sauer of the Mont Alto Motion Picture Orchestra.[3]

MICHAEL T. MARTIN is Professor at The Media School, Indiana University, and Editor-in-Chief of *Black Camera: An International Film Journal*. He is editor with David C. Wall and Marilyn Yaquinto of *Race and the Revolutionary Impulse in* The Spook Who Sat by the Door.

Notes

1. The symposium was sponsored by the Black Film Center/Archive, a premier national research center and repository for the study of filmmaking in the African diaspora, on November 12–13, 2015.

2. Available websites for the listed events:
   University College London: http://www.ucl.ac.uk/birth-of-a-nation
   Film Forum: https://filmforum.org/events/event/the-birth-of-a-nation-introduced-by-don-perry-event-page
   George Eastman House International Museum of Photography and Film: https://www.eastman.org/event/film-screenings/birth-nation
   Old Dominion University: https://www.odu.edu/news/2015/9/_birth_of_answer_dra#.W8DOJvYnbcs
   Denver Silent Film Festival: https://www.denverpost.com/2015/04/22/the-denver-silent-film-festival-is-screening-the-birth-of-a-nation/
   Kansas City Silent Film Festival: http://www.kssilentfilmfest.org/kssff2015/notes.html#birth
   Virginia Film Festival: http://virginiafilmfestival.org/films/the-birth-of-a-nation/Independent Lens: http://www.pbs.org/independentlens/films/birth-of-a-movement/

3. The full score by the orchestra is available on the Kino Lorber release of *The Birth of a Nation* on DVD and Blu-ray. For a brief history of musical accompaniments during the period of early cinema and that of *The Birth of a Nation*'s, see "The Birth of a Nation," *Mont Alto Cue Sheet*, http://www.mont-alto.com/recordings/BirthOfANationScore.html.

ACKNOWLEDGMENTS

L IKE ANY PROJECT OF THIS SCOPE, THIS BOOK was made possible by the essential support of several people and entities.

Among institutional supporters, many thanks to the Black Film Center/ Archive. It is an extraordinary research center at Indiana University, where the labors of archivists to recover, preserve, and document the cinematic history, practices, personages, and traditions of filmmaking in the black diaspora is legendary.

To the center's staff of professionals and graduate research assistants, I am indebted to you—most notably to Ja Quita Joy Roberts and Brian Graney, the archive's associate director, for their essential assistance organizing the symposium from which this book derived. In no small measure, thanks also to Amanda Fleming, Mark Hain—and especially to Rachelle Pavelko, Yalie Kamara, and Katie Johnson—who were indispensable in preparing the manuscript for production. A special thanks to Zachary Vaughn for managing the editorial process, particularly the copyediting stage.

I am also indebted to Jon Vickers, founding director of Indiana University Cinema, for hosting several of the panels and plenary addresses during the symposium and for arranging the screening of the full-length, digitally restored version of *The Birth of a Nation*. Several academic units cosponsored the symposium, among them Cinema and Media Studies, The Media School, the Poynter Center for the Study of Ethics and American Institutions, departments of African American and African Diaspora Studies, American Studies and History, and the Center for Research on Race and Ethnicity in Society.

Additional financial support for the symposium and publication of the book was obtained in grants from the College of Arts and Humanities Institute, the Ostrom Program, and the New Frontiers in the Arts and Humanities Program at Indiana University.

Of no less importance, my thanks to the scholars, especially David Wall, who traveled afar and from abroad to participate in the symposium and who contributed chapters to this collection.

Last, my gratitude to Janice Frisch, Acquisition Editor at Indiana University Press, and staff at the Press, particularly Kate Schramm, who provided expert editorial and production assistance to render this collection publishable.

Until the next project then.

Michael T. Martin
Editor

THE BIRTH OF A NATION

REVISITING (AS IT WERE) THE "NEGRO PROBLEM" IN *THE BIRTH OF A NATION*

Looking Back and in the Present

Michael T. Martin

I N THE WEEKS FOLLOWING BARACK OBAMA'S SUCCESSFUL PRESIDENTIAL run in 2008, there was much talk and fanfare in the media of a "postracial" America. That this claim was deeply problematic was apparent to anyone with even the most cursory understanding of US society, and its egregious absurdity stood in stark and violent relief during Obama's presidency—and does so even more in the post-Obama era. In counterpoint to such an assertion of an inclusive and color-blind United States, consider that African Americans are routinely subject to intimidation, unprovoked violence, and even murder by law enforcement agencies across the country and are disproportionately victimized by the criminal justice system.[1] Consider, too, Donald Trump's dog-whistle racist evocation of Mexicans as "wetbacks," "rapists," and "drug smugglers"—an arguably significant factor and ploy in his successful bid for the presidency—in addition to his widespread characterization of all Muslims as "terrorist sympathizers" along with the corresponding calls for a wholesale banning of Muslims from entering the country. Indeed, mimicking Richard Nixon's 1968 "Southern Strategy," Trump's bigotry and racist vitriol appealed to and mobilized many white voters and, in no small measure, contributed to his election.

Far from having disappeared, then, it would seem that racism and xenophobia are given free rein to return to the very central mainstream of US political and social life.[2] Such current political developments amplify and legitimize stereotypical and demeaning depictions of African Americans in popular culture, circulate among the polity, and embody raced discourses and practices of foundational institutions that regulate society.[3] No less than it did in 1865, 1965, or 2005, race matters to economic and educational opportunity, wealth and income inequality, residential segregation, racial profiling, immigration, and particularly criminal justice and voter suppression as modes of disenfranchising African Americans and others of basic rights.[4]

With the resurgence of popular mass protests in recent years against racial injustices and economic inequality—not least in the Black Lives Matter and Occupy movements—and growing challenges to reassertions of a white patriarchy demanding class obeisance and heteronormative conformity, I can't think of a more timely film that conjoins the past in the present of raced denial and class divide than the photoplay *The Birth of a Nation* by D. W. Griffith.[5] Although lauded for its remarkable visual and narrative innovations and a box office hit with white film audiences, *The Birth of a Nation* is an unrivaled work of historical fiction and racial affront that, in defiling African Americans, provoked their indignation and protest when it was first screened in theaters in 1915.

No ordinary film for its time, consider film historian Melvyn Stokes's estimation that *The Birth of a Nation* "changed the history of cinema":

> It was the first to be shown mainly in regular theaters . . . the first to be shown at the White House, the first to be projected for judges of the Supreme Court and members of Congress, the first to be viewed by countless millions of ordinary Americans. . . . In many ways, in fact, *Birth of a Nation* was the first "blockbuster": It was the most profitable film of its time (and perhaps, adjusted for inflation, of all time), it helped open new markets (including South America) for American films, and it may eventually have been seen by world-wide audiences of up to 200,000,000.[6]

If place, time, and circumstance are consequential to a film's reception and salience (as essays in this collection contend), then one account for *The Birth of a Nation*'s popularity at the time of its release and its ever-present controversy to this day is suggested by Davarian Baldwin, who described the film as "a cinematic history of its present: a tale of 1915 and the forces of urbanization, migration, and American empire that swirled around the early twentieth century."[7] The period Baldwin refers to and that *The Birth of a Nation* gestures toward is marked by political upheaval and indeterminacy in both the United States and the wider world. Correspondingly, it was profoundly shaped by innovative artistic invention as new technologies and modes of communication evolved to blur the distinction between entertainment, information, and propaganda. To borrow from Michael Rogin,

"*The Birth of a Nation*, by appropriating history, itself became a historical force."[8]

Moreover, and contrary to Enlightenment[9] precepts of reason from a century earlier and science in the conduct of Western civilization, this moment foregrounded elitist conceptions of human nature prefigured and informed by cultural precedents of racial disparagement expressed across the entire landscape of culture—from literature, popular lore, minstrelsy, and the ramblings and rants in newspapers and periodicals that constituted the general racialist discourses of the day to the widely accepted doctrine of scientific racism (figs. 0.1, 0.2, and 0.3).[10] These memorialized artifacts of popularized beliefs in the cultural marketplace of the early twentieth century framed debates about polygenetic notions of progress and posited the worldly order of things on biological, class, and cultural distinctions that endure to this day in the national psyche.[11]

During this period, the most egregious practices of Jim Crow happened, disenfranchising African Americans of their right to vote and other legalized exclusionary prohibitions; appropriating their labor (particularly in the South) under conditions of debt peonage; and practicing systemic violence as thousands of African Americans succumbed to public lynching (figs. 0.4 and 0.5). Such "racial terror" and "acts of torture," intended to regulate the new order through intimidation, hastened their migration by the millions "from the South into urban ghettos in the North and West during the first half of the twentieth century."[12]

From the end of the Civil War to the early decades of the twentieth century, state power was aggressively and deliberately consolidated on behalf of white privilege. Native peoples of the continental United States had long been culled, warehoused on reservations, and even exterminated. Indigenous peoples of Puerto Rico, Haiti, Cuba, Hawaii, and the Philippines were variously subject to military conquest and territorial occupation as the United States established its nascent imperial dominance.[13] Immigrants from these colonies and migrants from Southern Europe converged on American shores in great numbers,[14] causing consternation and apprehension among (Anglo-Saxon) elites as they swelled the ranks of labor in the increasingly industrialized North and Midwest, beginning what would become a labor movement and struggle for workers' rights against capitalism's exploitive, dehumanizing, and often brutal practices.[15] Together, such claims in the wake of "manifest destiny" projected America's outsized view of itself and its place in world affairs and, along with the denial of the

Figure 0.1 "The Freedman's Bureau! An agency to keep the Negro in idleness at the expense of the white man. Twice vetoed by the president, and made a law by Congress. Support Congress & you support the Negro. Sustain the president & you protect the white man." *Courtesy Library of Congress, Rare Book and Special Collections Division.*

Figure 0.2 Postcard from 1900s. *Public domain.*

Figure 0.3 Actor Thomas Rice as Jim Crow, nineteenth century. *Public domain.*

Figure 0.4. Black lynching in Marion, Indiana, 1930.

Figure 0.5. Imaginary black lynching by Adele Stephenson. *Courtesy of Adele Stephenson.*

franchise to African Americans, proffered a conception of the nation by racial lineage—and the social hierarchy that spawned it—sacrosanct and immutable. "For most of us, slavery is but a word, explained by other words, themselves barely understood: middle passage, chains, auction block. . . . The racial situation today is not much different from what it was when *The House of Bondage* was first published [1890]. Then, as now, the nation was in transition."[16] And it is to the past in the present that this book revisits and remarks on *The Birth of a Nation*.

* * *

Like all forms of cultural production, film masks ideology while rendering it apparent. With cinema constituting a distinctive cultural form of modernity and particular mode of storytelling, *The Birth of a Nation* serves as Griffith's filmic manifesto, an affirmative declaration of the legitimacy of white (read: Anglo-Saxon) rule through his vision of an America partitioned by race, gender, ethnicity, and class, poised for national greatness as it turned the corner and stumbled with great fanfare into the twentieth century. *The Birth of a Nation*'s importance is not only that it, as Stokes says, "changed the history of cinema" but also that it labors to naturalize a social order that masks the principles it claims to uphold: life, liberty, and the pursuit of happiness—the sine qua non of US democracy.

Visually commanding, *The Birth of a Nation* reframes and conjures the way history itself and collective remembrance are read in the trauma and afterlife of slavery and, therefore, "is fundamentally a film about memory . . . that relies upon the nature and function of memory to perform its emotive and seductive work . . . to provide a shared, yet wholly personal experience of whiteness, one that would be immediately and intimately familiar and recognizable to its intended audience . . . to provide a collective memory, rooted not in nationality or region but in race."[17]

A useful way of situating *The Birth of a Nation* in a regime of historical memory is to consider its location among four organizing classes of *cine-memory* that David C. Wall—a contributor to this collection—and I have developed in order to discern a film's ideological significations and purpose. We contend that *The Birth of a Nation* exemplifies a type of Class I memory that works:

> to affirm received assumptions and discourses about the past. It confirms the ideological certainties of the implied viewer, valorizes the beliefs, and conforms to the expectations of the audience. In doing so it functions to portray

the hegemonic order as being a consequence of nature rather than one of culture. Yet the past it represents hides ideological assumptions and values that normalize the "reality" it claims to express. Events appear to be fixed in time, discrete, simplistically framed, and analytically wanting. Hollywood has pioneered this form of historical reconstruction [in *The Birth of a Nation*], de-historicizing events both in relation to the period in which they occurred and in relation to the present. Films of this ilk and their stock of memories attempt to bring closure to historical trauma. They are also committed to a wholly personalized vision of history, in which trajectories of class and race are elided through the personalization of cultural narratives within the individual [or family]. This removes the individual from the processes of history, thus making him/her entirely responsible for his/her personalized circumstances rather than the product or consequence of historical forces ranged both beyond and before the individual.[18]

With this concept of cine-memory in mind (and further discussed in Lawrence Howe's chapter in this volume), it begs the following questions: In precisely whom did Griffith intend for *The Birth of a Nation* to provoke trauma? And who did he imagine would be demeaned and traumatized by the film?

Intuitively, we associate the aggrieved as African Americans, but I would argue that Griffith's project was to traumatize and incite white audiences against blacks, whom he portrayed, with the exception of the "faithful souls," as the purveyors of all things that threaten all manner of "whiteness" (figs. 0.6a and 0.6b). This is rendered apparent in scenes that legitimize the triumphant Ku Klux Klan as the only righteous and necessary means of self-defense against the barbarous blacks led by Silas Lynch—the mulatto—and his dream of a "black empire." This terrifying prospect of black power was designed by Griffith to evoke such horror in the white imagination that it would be seen as a violation of God's will and, for added measure, natural law. *The Birth of a Nation*'s call for justice and redemption serves, then, as a mediation for the trauma outside the film and in the actuality of raced experience (figs. 0.7 and 0.8).

Situating *The Birth of a Nation* within the genre of "trauma cinema" is appropriate, allowing as it does for the drawing of similar comparisons with the Western and war genres discussed in the chapters by Peter Davis and Alex Lichtenstein.[19] In *The Birth of a Nation*, the variant this form of trauma portrays is familial but signifying and emblematic of the nation and threat to whiteness rendered in the apocalyptic where power is inverted ("black empire") and miscegenation licensed. Along this trajectory, *The Birth of a Nation* may be the first iteration of what we now refer to

Figure 0.6a. Gus rape scene in *The Birth of a Nation*. *Screen capture by author.*

Figure 0.6b. Gus stalking Flora in *The Birth of a Nation*. *Screen capture by author.*

Figure 0.7. Silas Lynch accosting Elsie Stoneman in *The Birth of a Nation*. *Screen capture by author.*

Figure 0.8. The Ku Klux Klan prepares to lynch Gus in *The Birth of a Nation*. *Screen capture by author.*

as trauma cinema—no less fantastical and dystopic than science fiction or horror movies are today, in which race (or its multiple symbolic embodiments) works as protagonist and/or subtext of the story.

* * *

Does *The Birth of a Nation* contribute to the intelligibility of the past or obfuscate it? Neither seen nor heard in the film (by design) are two historical factors in play that refute the veracity of its claims. The first factual omission relates to Davarian Baldwin's earlier statement about *The Birth of a Nation*'s "cinematic history of its present" and reference to "American empire." Unlike analysis of the exhibition and reception history of the film in the United States, *The Birth of a Nation*'s relationship to the broader contexts of US imperialism remains understudied. As the United States pursued imperial interests, the territories it obtained embodied distinctive cultural traditions and racial traits, and the population groups from these regions migrated, as noted earlier, mostly to urban sites, where African Americans increasingly settled. As their presence and numbers increased, thus threatening white (read: Anglo-Saxon) cultural sensibilities and the presumption of superiority, they contested institutions of rule. It was a circumstance not unlike today, when migrants traverse Central America at great peril to *El Norte* and thousands arrive at the southern shores of "Fortress Europe" to Greece, Spain, and Italy or by the inland routes from Eastern Europe to escape poverty, civil wars, and environmental degradation. As it does in the present, such migration—particularly for those population groups whose bloodlines were not of "Aryan" stock—invoked virulent nativist sentiments and prohibitions (figs. 0.9 and 0.10). In *The Birth of a Nation*, Griffith's calculated schematic was to simplify race relations for white audiences to a black/white binary—a feature noted earlier of Class I cine-memory, which frames the social world as fixed in time and discrete. In this manner, *The Birth of a Nation* differentiates between black and foreign nationals, selectively inciting against the former to mitigate the combined threat of foreign nationals, who conceivably might discern similar class and economic interests and ally with them.

The second omission or misrepresentation of history concerns the disposition of wealth obtained by slavery. While *The Birth of a Nation* rejects slavery for the ills it brought upon the nation, it elides the matter of how the commerce in slave trading in the North and the labor it provisioned plantations with in the South generated great wealth on which both a planter aristocracy and industrial bourgeoisie arose and prospered and that enabled

Figure 0.9. Laboring European immigrants in textile mills. *"Sadie Pfeiffer, Spinner in Cotton Mill, North Carolina," by Lewis W. Hine, 1910.*

Figure 0.10. "Three women working in shoe factory—Lynn, Massachusetts." *By Frances Benjamin Johnston, no date. Courtesy Library of Congress Prints and Photographs Division.*

Figure 0.11. Black sharecroppers. "Black woman and young girls picking cotton," by Louise Boyle, 1937. *Southern Tenant Farmers Union Photographs, 1937 and 1982. Courtesy the Kheel Center for Labor Management Documentation and Archives, Cornell University, CC BY 2.0.*

Figure 0.12. White sharecroppers. "Frank Tengle, Bud Fields, and Floyd Burroughs, cotton sharecroppers, Hale County, Alabama," by Walker Evans, 1936. *Courtesy Library of Congress Prints and Photographs Division.*

both shipping and banking sectors of the economy to become pillars of American capitalism. Why did Griffith mask such developments in his narrative of America's renewal? It is fair to say that, along with the film's racist and historical fictions, *The Birth of a Nation* elides the workings and contradictions of capitalism, thus naturalizing the social order and foundations on which its ruling class presumed privilege, dispensed power, and accumulated wealth. This, then, raises another critical question: Is *The Birth of a Nation* an untold story about class and class conflict, where race serves to divide and rule those who have similar economic and political interests (figs. 0.11 and 0.12)? And, subsequently, is the persistence of racism in the present, deeply ensconced as it is in US culture and institutions, a symptom and abiding consequence of capitalist relations of production?

An ever-vexing conundrum is the relational salience of social class and race in *The Birth of a Nation*. For political theorists and activists alike, debates about the determinations of class and race proliferate to this day, and particularly among Western Marxists. In this schema, race is subordinate to class divisions, as are ethnicity, gender, and religion. In cinema studies, however, conversations, let alone debates, about this relationship are curiously infrequent, analytically wanting, and woefully undertheorized.

Raced representations of class begin with the general premise that class correlates with economic factors. For Sean Griffin, "class is a term used to categorize people according to their economic status. It frequently involves a consideration of income level, type of profession, inherited wealth and family lineage and a diffusely understood idea of social standing."[20] A defining construct in the organization of society, I understand class to be a formation whose temporality evokes distinctive iterations in cinema and the social world. However imprecise, representations of class illumine and prompt social consciousness, or obfuscate its historicity, as it regulates and legitimizes the order of things. In contrast to normative formulations, I propose a more expansive reading of class that engages with social theorist Pierre Bourdieu's concept of *habitus*, in which patterns of behavior inscribed in the embodied common sense enable the social reproduction of status and standing.[21]

In certain genres of Hollywood fare, class is differently constituted for racial groups. For whites, representations align largely with economic factors; for blacks, they are, for the most part, constituted by noneconomic criteria. Traces of this racial bifurcation of class have precedence in Hollywood's formation itself. Although portrayals of African Americans occurred as early as 1894 in such films as Lucy Daly's Pickaninnies' *The Watermelon Contest* (1896; 1900), *Chicken Thieves* (1897), *Sambo and Aunt Jemima: Comedians* (1900), and *The 'Gator and the Pickaninny* (1900), the elaboration of a black social hierarchy was first masterfully rendered in *The Birth of a Nation*.[22] Like no other photoplay of its time, *The Birth of a Nation* codifies and elaborates with extraordinary specificity a racially inflected class formation. For whites, class was constituted by (cultural) pedigree and economic criteria without calling attention to itself and the inequality it sustains. Conversely, for blacks, Griffith fashioned something altogether different by aggregating black archetypes into a rudimentary social hierarchy constituted (a) by racial features, sexual exchange, and proximity to whiteness among the planter aristocracy and Northern elite and (b) by habitus, marked by dress codes, tastes, speech mode and intonation, and bodily gestures of persons who occupy a social space in a particular "field"—plantation South or industrial North. In this way, race operates as "cultural capital," masking the determinations of economic factors.

The constituents of Griffith's racial order (not to be confused with caste) comprise features of several archetypes. Consider the Cameron household domestics—the "faithful souls"—who display attributes of the Mammy and Uncle Tom; the Coon, lazy and dull-witted; Buck, sexually voracious; the "black beast," who lusts after white women (and who, Linda Williams asserts in her chapter, was first evinced in *The Birth of a Nation*); and Jezebel, mixed-raced, amoral, and promiscuous. In the pecking order of things, light-complexioned male mulattoes are superordinate. Silas Lynch, opportunist and the alpha male groomed to be the leader of blacks, is accorded higher standing by his handlers, the Northern political class. But Lynch is also cast as the "black beast," who covets the sexual favors of Stoneman's daughter, Elsie, while he manically connives to create a "black empire" with her as queen consort (note the allusion to royalty, anathema to democracy, and the myth of a classless America).

Next in the lineup is that "deadly social virus," the mulatta women who conspire with Lynch to advance their station by ingratiating themselves and exchanging sexual favors for the patronage of Northern carpetbaggers, whom Griffith would have us believe are sadly mistaken to uphold the newly obtained rights of former slaves. More generally, the mulattoes—both female and male—are distinguished from the dark-skinned blacks who labor in the fields and populate the bottom rung in the hierarchy and who, because of their mixed parentage, display intelligence and gesture—what

Figure 0.13. "Faithful souls" in *The Birth of a Nation. Screen capture by author.*

we might think of as an example of Bourdieu's cultural capital—in ways that mimic the white gentry. Self-serving, the mulattoes' social standing is conferred by physical proximity to and association with whiteness. In Griffith's characterization, they neither share an affinity nor identify with laboring blacks but use them instead as cannon fodder to advance their own interests. Curiously, the "faithful souls" constitute a distinct stratum in the slave regime, marked by their location in the master's household; their status rests on an unflinching loyalty to the Cameron family and the patriarch's goodwill and fortune, thus their identification with all things white (fig. 0.13).

In the larger frame of Griffith's schema of race solidarity is the organizing principle for the nation's renewal, trumping all other social divisions (including class and region). His genius was to elevate white supremacy to existential cause—immutable, insoluble, and permanent. In the drama of the historical epic that is *The Birth of a Nation*, Griffith rejects a class-based hierarchy while affirming patriarchy and the reign of the planter aristocracy in which everyone occupies their natural place and to which everyone is expected to adhere. Griffith accomplishes two devilish objectives that

Figure 0.14. The nation as protagonist. A 1915 handbill advertising D. W. Griffith's *The Birth of a Nation*.

signify the ideological project of *The Birth of a Nation*: First, precipitated by the crisis of the Civil War and its aftermath, race is parsed to fashion a black social class, unlike that for whites and for which traces endure to this day in the cinematic. Second, America's renewal pivots on white supremacy and patriarchy, despite momentary discord among fraternal relatives, because, for Griffith, the personal is inseparable from the familial, which is to say, the nation (fig. 0.14).

* * *

Praise for *The Birth of a Nation* and its popularity among white film audiences did not go unchallenged.[23] Indeed, when it was first shown in theaters and during the decades that followed, the film provoked protests as civil rights organizations and African American communities challenged derogatory depictions in the film and the received assumptions from which they are derived. The National Association for the Advancement of Colored People mobilized to boycott and censor scenes that were particularly offensive to blacks (fig. 0.15); however, these efforts had limited success. William Monroe Trotter, the influential activist and editor of the *Boston Guardian*, who had earlier prevented the staging of Thomas Dixon's novel

Figure 0.15. Protestors at a screening of *The Birth of a Nation*. "NAACP members picketing outside the Republic Theatre, New York City, to protest the screening of the movie "Birth of a Nation," close-up view of demonstrators and sign reading "Birth of a Nation revives KKK," 1947. *Courtesy Library of Congress, Prints and Photographs Division, visual materials from the NAACP Records.*

The Clansman, labored through editorials, speeches, and rallies to mobilize against *The Birth of a Nation*'s exhibition in Boston.[24] And protests in the United States "spread to Canada, the [Panama] Canal Zone, and would even reach places like France," contends film historian Cara Caddoo.[25] In her opening chapter in this collection, Caddoo chronicles the "mass black protest movement" against the film's release and racist presumptions in 1915. Drawing from her earlier work, *Envisioning Freedom: Cinema and the Building of Modern Black Life*, in which she maps the initial and later protests to *The Birth of a Nation*, Caddoo asserts, "By 1917, the national movement had engaged hundreds of organizations across the country, involved tens of thousands of black protestors, and established demands for visual self-determination that endured well into the twenty-first century."[26]

Although African Americans had been making movies since the earliest days of cinema, filmic opposition to *The Birth of a Nation* was first manifested in the ambitious but "disastrous" *The Birth of a Race* (1918). Plagued at the start by financial and production problems and, later, a compromised storyline, it was nevertheless, contends film historian Marc Ferro, the "first historical *counter-film* in American cinema in which African Americans incarnate a new vision of history."[27] In the sphere of black filmmaking and outside Hollywood's orbit, consider that, from 1909 to 1948, more than 150 independent companies made, distributed, and exhibited "race movies"— that distinctive aggregate of films crossing genres that oriented toward, and were shown in, segregated theaters and featured all-black casts. Such films engaged with the spectrum of black life and experience and comprised a range of visual and narrative styles and artisanal practices, all while anticipating and contributing to an African American cinematic tradition. Among the few successful companies in the "race film business" were the Lincoln Motion Picture Company, the Micheaux Film Corporation, and the Norman Manufacturing Company.[28]

Just as those early pioneering black filmmakers had to resist (implicitly and explicitly) the powerful violence to which *The Birth of a Nation* subjected black America, so, too, the film continues to work its violence in the current racial and political climate. And in that context and against the backdrop of extremist evangelical Christians, police violence, and myriad white supremacist terrorist organizations committed to keeping the United States as an Anglo-Saxon culture, it's no wonder that *The Birth of a Nation* might resonate among a contemporary alt-right audience as it illumines the opposition against immigrants and black equality and civil rights. As a critical aperture to America's past and a means to examine early cinema as technology, cultural form, and ideological apparatus and through its defamation of African Americans, *The Birth of a Nation* nods to and anticipates the present moment. And as Caddoo asserts, "In light of ongoing antiblack police violence, the continued exclusion of black Americans' rights to public space, and the systemic valuation of private property over black lives, the history of *The Birth of a Nation* is just as much a story about our present as it is of our past."[29]

* * *

Organized in three parts, this collection comprises original essays derived from the 2015 symposium and another by Lawrence Howe commissioned by the editor after the event. Three distinct organizing principles frame the chapters in the book:

- *The Birth of a Nation* as text, artifact, and cultural legacy
- *The Birth of a Nation* in historical time—then
- *The Birth of a Nation* in historical time—now

Figure 0.16. The triumphant Ku Klux Klan in *The Birth of a Nation. Screen capture by author.*

In developing their essays, contributors were asked to consider six research questions, particularly regarding the national and transnational contexts of *The Birth of a Nation*'s exhibition and reception histories as well as the intersectionality of race and patriarchy and their representations in popular culture.

- How does *The Birth of a Nation* contribute to the intelligibility of the past? For example, are enactments consequential to readings of historical claims?
- By what cultural and political means is *The Birth of a Nation*'s ideological mission refashioned and manifest in the present?
- For whom does *The Birth of a Nation* signify constructs of agency and mobilization (fig. 0.16)?
- Are there traces of *The Birth of a Nation* in contemporary Hollywood fare?
- Under hegemonic conditions, how is art repurposed and aesthetic strategies constituted in the service of politics?
- Is *The Birth of a Nation* relevant to understanding the present (fig. 0.17)?

Part I is devoted to a discussion of *The Birth of a Nation* in national and transnational contexts in historical time and contains five chapters situating

Figure 0.17. Protestors and antiprotestors in Charlottesville, Virginia, August 12, 2017. *Photo by Anthony Crider, CC BY 2.0.*

the film's reception in the United States and correspondence within the national politics where it was exhibited abroad.

Of *The Birth of a Nation*'s reception and exhibition in the United States, Caddoo's and Andy Uhrich's chapters provide critical insights and documentation. Caddoo asserts that African American women "were at the forefront of the protests" against the film and that working-class blacks supported protests precisely "because the movement encompassed many of their most urgent material, cultural, and political concerns." In this important regard, her essay contributes to the literature of not only African American history but also social movements. She challenges ensconced views that "elites" within a subjugated class or social group rise to leadership rather than, in Gramscian terms, a bottom-up approach, where ordinary folk mobilize and draw leadership from among their own ranks. Such protests also illustrate a feature of some redress movements when the interests of aggrieved groups, seemingly discrete, galvanize and coalesce against commercial and institutional entities that are perceived as being aligned against them.

Uhrich's chapter and novel contribution to the discussion, which is derived from dissertation research, engages with the presence and varied formats and iterations of *The Birth of a Nation* in white film collectors' holdings and its screenings in "domestic and nontheatrical" venues such as schools, homes, and repertory theaters between the late 1930s and the late 1970s. Uhrich distinguishes between the multiple small gauge versions shown for the home market and the debates that ensued among collectors to rationalize such screenings. Purposefully narrow in scope and focus, Uhrich foregrounds the significance of this nontheatrical market of "specialized publics" to consider the "role of whiteness in film fandom" in the determination of American cinema classics. Ironically, his research reveals that at least one cultural black organization in 1971, the Grassroot Experience, reconstituted a screening of *The Birth of a Nation* accompanied by musical scores of the jazz greats John Coltrane and Pharoah Sanders. Speculating on the motive for the film's cultural appropriation and repurposing by blacks, Uhrich suggests that the "screening might have been intended as a sort of exorcism of the lasting, pernicious power of *The Birth of a Nation* or perhaps a clash between icons of black art and white cinema." To document the different versions of *The Birth of a Nation* screened in nontheatrical venues, he examines David Bradley's collection and discerns that, among the nearly 3,900 films Bradley had amassed, six were various versions of *The Birth of a Nation*. What this and Uhrich's detailed chronology reveal of the film's numerous iterations is "the range of companies and individuals that were distributing and exhibiting the film, and the transformations—textual, material, and paratextual—that the film underwent as it traveled the collector and nontheatrical circuits." Uhrich's examination of collectors' views about *The Birth of a Nation* notes that some opinions were favorable and others were less so and critical, which raises anew the long-standing debate about the relationship of art and ideology, recalling one of the five research questions above: "Under hegemonic conditions, how is art repurposed and aesthetic strategies constituted in the service of politics?"

The Birth of a Nation's exhibition and reception histories abroad varied, as the next three chapters address. Melvyn Stokes's authoritative account of the film's origins, production, exhibition, and reception makes for a compelling read. He discusses Griffith's intent to extend *The Birth of a Nation*'s promotion in the United States to international markets and documents how the film was altered to appear less inflammatory to Canadian audiences, noting that the "entire so-called rape sequence . . . was required to be cut." Stokes also notes that protest against *The Birth of a Nation* was "almost entirely black-led" in Canada. In Britain, and in contrast to Canada, Stokes claims that, with few exceptions, scholars agreed that the opposition to the film's exhibition there was minimal. Conversely, in France, the film was denied a visa by the Central Commission of Control in 1917; it was screened seven years later in 1923 and, after four performances, was banned by the government largely because of objections by "influential black politicians in the National Assembly." Further, a factor in *The Birth of a Nation*'s exhibition success abroad were "road shows" in Britain, South America (Argentina, Chile, Peru, Bolivia, Uruguay, and Brazil), Japan (though it was shortened to little more than half the length shown in the United States), and Australia and New Zealand. As in France, Germany the exhibition of *The Birth of a Nation* in Germany was delayed in the immediate aftermath of World War I because of the racialist international campaign "Black Horror on the Rhine," against the presence of French African troops in the country. In South Africa, where the film was not shown until 1931, Stokes draws comparisons between *The Birth of a Nation* and *De Voortrekkers* (1916), describing their shared anxieties ("sexual paranoia") and false claims to nationhood that blacks challenged.[30] Stokes concludes this exacting study noting omissions in *The Birth of a Nation*'s reception in those countries where it was exhibited in Latin America, Japan, Scandinavia, the Caribbean, and Britain's African colonies, with the exception of South Africa.

Next, Peter Davis's brief but informative chapter draws comparisons between *The Birth of a Nation* and South African productions *De Voortrekkers* (*Winning a Nation*, 1916) and *They Built a Nation* (1938).[31] He argues that the "assertion of white supremacy and black menace," the projection of political power, and, more important, nationalism inscribed in these films share similarity with *The Birth of a Nation*. Although not shown in South Africa until 1931, the film, Davis contends, played an "indefinable role" in the formation of Afrikaner solidarity and national identity and that an earlier film by Griffith, *The Zulu's Heart* (1908), "shows an awareness" by Griffith of the "parallel history with the United States," evoking the travails of a pioneer family under seize by Indians in the American frontier. In *They Built a Nation*, Boer society is mythologized as genteel and stable, later reconciled between Afrikaner and Anglo, similar to Griffith's portrayal at the end of *The Birth of a Nation* between Northern and Southern whites. In both films, Zulus and blacks are cast as aggressive and treacherous but, curiously, in *They Built a Nation*, not a sexual threat to white masculinity—unlike in *The Birth of a Nation*, where the sexual threat, arguably, works as the central organizing motif.

Alex Lichtenstein's compelling chapter is comparative as it is synthetic, putting these contributors' essays in productive conversation with one another. First, he notes that South Africa and the United States are settler societies obtained by conquest and occupation and that *The Birth of a Nation* is "a parable of settler colonialism" as, too, *They Built a Nation* is.[32] Together, the two films signify what Lichtenstein contends is a feature of settler societies, "the persistence of white nationalist mythology" manifest in the cinematic genre of the Western.[33] Second, he makes two critical claims that the films' evocation of white nationalist mythology is repurposed, reenacted, and convened across place, circumstance, and time in racialized discourses of the nation. However racialist the films are, Lichtenstein calls for a more nuanced and complex reading of *The Birth of a Nation* and *They Built a Nation*, asserting that, above all, both films are "fundamentally nationalist in character." In this claim, Lichtenstein nods to Davis and proffers an expanded reading of *The Birth of a Nation* as a war film while asserting black complicity in propagating received views about Reconstruction up to and during the 1950s, until the historiography of the period radically changed during and following the civil rights movement.

Part II contains two chapters that look beyond *The Birth of a Nation*'s formal innovations in visual storytelling to consider its rhetorical and representational strategies that signify the film's ideological project. Several consequential subjects are addressed in Williams's essay: African Americans' response to the film, the importance of Oscar Micheaux's reworking of melodrama in *Within Our Gates* (1919) to reinscribe African Americans in the narrative of America's racial history, and the uneven and problematic black portrayals in some race movies before and after *The Birth of a Nation* in what she refers to as the "American melodrama of black and white." But what stands out and is most compelling is Williams's claim that, in *The Birth of a Nation*, Griffith introduced a novel stereotype of the "black marauders" to shift "racial sentiment away from the sufferings of Uncle Tom and toward the sufferings of an embattled White South."[34] As such, and in consideration of the mobilizing activities of white supremacists at the time, the introduction of such a threatening—indeed, incendiary—stereotype in the narrative of race was most problematic for white film audiences because it provoked anxiety that miscegenation infers to this day.

In correspondence to Williams's take on the "melodrama of black and white," Howe's chapter and close reading argues that *The Birth of a Nation*'s historicism works as a rhetorical strategy in and out of the frame to "couch the film's racist polemics" as factual and, therefore, objective. Emphasizing Griffith's use of historical enactments, Howe notes that such facsimiles project a seemingly credible authenticity for "the authority of history." He observes three distinct forms of historical reconstruction in *The Birth of a Nation*: scenes of battle, "tableaux of momentous [defining] national events," and a third form that is illustrated by the enactment of Lincoln's assassination. The two essays in Part II reveal the means by which Griffith constituted and signified the ideological project of *The Birth of a Nation*: to direct blame for America's social ills not on the social order that caused and sanctioned injustice and inequality but on the presence of blacks who dared challenge it.

Part III considers various cinematic iterations a century after *The Birth of a Nation*'s release and the film's ideological aftereffects in the context of discourses that claim the United States as a postracial nation. Four of the five chapters in this section examine correspondences between more recent films and *The Birth of a Nation*, and the final chapter dismisses the film's relevance in the present.

First in the lineup is Paula Massood's chapter, which situates *The Birth of a Nation* in what Ed Guerrero has named the "plantation genre." Focusing on Quentin Tarantino's "cinematic style"[35] in the genre-bending *Django Unchained* (2012), she argues that the film, like the conventions of plantation literature, aligns more with than against aspects, for example, of interracial violence in *The Birth of a Nation*. Massood describes how the film anticipated the genre conventions of the Western, blaxploitation, and action movies, along with those of the plantation genre. Noting how both films deploy historical fiction, spectacle, and melodrama to portray the Ku Klux Klan as an "intimidating and invincible force," Massood foregrounds the irony of their contradictory significations: in *The Birth of a Nation*, the Ku Klux Klan is portrayed as "heroic" and in *Django Unchained* as "an overwhelming and terrifying force." Further, Massood delineates the symbolic purpose of lynching in both films to regulate racial and sexual divides, and she concludes—contrary to Tarantino's claim that in *Django Unchained* is to be found a new genre—that the film constitutes a "generic mash up that lacks a cohesive identity."

Next, Julia Lesage's chapter puts Steve McQueen's *12 Years a Slave* (2013) in conversation with *The Birth of a Nation*. In the former, it is metonymy, whereas the latter evokes the rescue narrative by the Ku Klux Klan's unfettered vigilantism as a "legitimate" mode of intervention for societal dysfunction in the wake of the Civil War. Lesage proffers a materialist reading of *12 Years a Slave* as a "realist" narrative in counterpoint to a psychoanalytic one for *The Birth of a Nation*'s "melodramatic structure." For example, in emphasizing the "Southern rape complex" as metaphor for a vanquished South, Lesage claims that *The Birth of a Nation* is a "projective fantasy" and likens the cabin scene to a "besieged vagina" rather than the site of a reconstituted (white) nation.[36] Unlike other interpretations of the cabin scene, Lesage advances a new reading that is novel and provocative by its sexual inference and associations. No less intriguing an analysis and particularly cogent is Lesage's materialist approach to *12 Years a Slave*. She deconstructs the director's aesthetic strategies that gesture toward social space—a space where power relations are manifest and differentiated by gender, race, and class. In doing so, Lesage foregrounds an ethos of freedom where the protagonist, Solomon Northup, evinces in captivity agential authority to "develop both material and inner resources, act, plan, create values, choose many aspects of his daily routines, and forge short- and long-term goals" in such liminal spaces under conditions of bondage—marking the slave's assertion "to maintain a sense of self." Last, in the rich details of the analysis, Lesage points to *12 Years a Slave*'s power of affect, showing "what slavery felt like."

Anne-Marie Paquet-Deyris's chapter discerns resonances between *The Birth of a Nation* and Spike Lee's *Bamboozled* (2000) and Justin Simien's *Dear White People* (2014). Like other contributors to this collection, she refutes the claims of a postracial America, asserting that both of the more recent films, unlike *The Birth of a Nation*, labor most directly to challenge normative accounts of America's racial history. Contrary to Chuck Kleinhans's assertion in the concluding chapter against *The Birth of a Nation*'s importance today, Paquet-Deyris contends that "the impact of *The Birth of a Nation* is still so strong that the film's current reception summons very specific and passionate reactions about the staging of race and inequality today." For comparisons with African Americans' response to *The Birth of a Nation*, she notes similar reactions of French students to representations of Syrian and African migrants on French television. Regarding *Dear White People*, Paquet-Deyris argues that it serves as a counterpoint to *The Birth of a Nation*'s racial discourse by reclaiming black identity in the present and inverting the representation of whites along the lines of Griffith's depictions of blacks. And for *Bamboozled*, she distinguishes Lee's representational strategy to recycle "grotesquely stereotyped" black bodies to illustrate how racism operates in the present.

David Wall's chapter and novel account of black masculinity in Etan Cohen's interracial buddy film *Get Hard* (2015) reads a reconstitution of the deep sexual and racial anxieties that shape *The Birth of a Nation* so profoundly. Further, considering the relationship between a film's formal structure and its ideological assertions, Wall draws on linguist Mikhail Bakhtin's notion of the "dialogic," by way of situating meaning making as a process that is to be constantly renegotiated in time and place and in relation to a viewer's subject position. In a theorized and complex approach, Wall meticulously unravels the spatial matrix in which race and the black body are situated in each film to make sense of their shared meaning, however renegotiated and reconstituted. His reading of *Get Hard* demonstrates that the film "labors to convince viewers of its knowing postracial sensibility while mired in the trammeled racial representations it purports to undermine" and, in doing so, recalls *The Birth of a Nation* and the whiteness they share.

Last in the queue is the late Chuck Kleinhans's provocative and partly autobiographical chapter. Contrary to the contributors before him, Kleinhans posits that *The Birth of a Nation* has neither meaningful importance today nor should it evoke or "deserve an angry response." Indeed, he asserts the film is "laughable" and that it merits "ridicule." First, he situates the fiftieth anniversary of *The Birth of a Nation* in the context of the mid-1960s—the era that spawned the formalization of film studies—arguing that "within cinema studies, this historical epic was canonized, often with praise that neglected the film's racism, even during the civil rights era."[37] Contending that *The Birth of a Nation*'s shelf life as propaganda has expired and is no longer effective for audiences today because "the film's style and politics are outmoded" and "new forms of social media . . . uses snark and sarcasm to speak truth to power."[38] Kleinhans counsels, "We don't need to fear it" or let it evoke our anger, because the "best response [is] dismissive laughter."

Notwithstanding its "overt politics" and simplistic assumptions on behalf of ideological aims, the efficacy of *The Birth of a Nation* in galvanizing hatred and prejudice is not lost to racists and nativists today as we turn another corner and find ourselves stumbling into the next century burdened by the same issues that inspired Griffith to realize *The Birth of a*

Nation. It is with these developments in the present in mind that one hopes this collection has meaning and utility.

MICHAEL T. MARTIN is Professor at The Media School, Indiana University, and Editor-in-Chief of *Black Camera: An International Film Journal.* He is editor with David C. Wall and Marilyn Yaquinto of *Race and the Revolutionary Impulse in* The Spook Who Sat by the Door.

Notes

1. Ava DuVernay's documentary *13th* (2016) not only explains the multiple ways in which African Americans are unfairly targeted by the justice system because of their race but also makes a powerful argument for these processes as deliberate efforts to maintain disciplinary control over black bodies that was lost after the end of slavery.

2. See "The Trump Effect: Spreading Hate at School, at Church, and Across the Country," Southern Poverty Law Center, February 16, 2017, http://www.alternet.org/right-wing /trump-effect-spreading-hate-school-church-and-across-country; and Steven Rosenfeld, "A United States of Hate Has Exploded under Trump," *Alternet*, February 15, 2017, http://www .alternet.org/print/election-2016/united-states-hate-has-exploded-under-trump. Consider that the almost uniform conservative response to Obama was driven in no small measure by coded racial anxiety. Recall the campaigns of 2008 and 2012, in which race, citizenship, and nationality were strategically deployed to mobilize conservative white voters and discredit Obama's eligibility to hold office. The "birther" stratagem was intended to discredit—indeed, invalidate—Obama's eligibility for the presidency as an African and foreign national, foregrounding race and alien status. See Michael Eric Dyson, "Barack Obama, the President of Black America?" *New York Times*, June 24, 2016, https://www.nytimes.com/2016/06/26 /opinion/sunday/barack-obama-the-president-of-black-america.html; Paul Mason, "Globalisation Is Dead, and White Supremacy Has Triumphed," *The Guardian*, November 9, 2016, https://www.theguardian.com/commentisfree/2016/nov/09/globalisation-dead-white -supremacy-trump-neoliberal; Andrew O'Hehir, "Trump, Sanders and Tribalism: Why the Donald's Dark Allure Goes Deeper Than Racism and Xenophobia," *Alternet*, September 13, 2015, http://www.alternet.org/print/election-2016/trump-sanders-and-tribalism-why -donalds-dark-allure-goes-deeper-racism-and-xenophobia; and Juan Cole, "Yes, Trump, Some Americans Also Murder: Some Are Your White Supremacists," February 6, 2017, *Reader Supported News*, http://readersupportednews.org/opinion2/277-75/41804-yes-trump -some-americans-also-murder.

3. See Matthew Pratt Guterl, *Seeing Race in Modern America* (Chapel Hill: University of North Carolina Press, 2013).

4. Numerous studies substantiate such claims. See Michael K. Brown, Martin Carnoy, Elliott Currie, Troy Duster, David B. Oppenheimer, Marjorie M. Shultz, and David Wellman, "Race Preferences and Race Privileges," in *Redress for Historical Injustices in the United States*, ed. Michael T. Martin and Marilyn Yaquinto (Durham, NC: Duke University Press, 2007), 55–90; and the more recent studies by Daria Roithmayre, *Reproducing Racism: How Everyday Choices Lock in White Advantage* (New York: New York University Press, 2014)

and David Dante Troutt, *The Price of Paradise: The Costs of Inequality and a Vision of a More Equitable America* (New York: New York University Press, 2014).

5. *The Birth of a Nation* was adapted from the novel *The Clansman* by Thomas Dixon, which, as the film does, glorifies the Ku Klux Klan. The film was used to recruit for the Ku Klux Klan until the 1970s. Xan Brooks, "The Birth of a Nation: A Gripping Masterpiece . . . and a Stain on History," *The Guardian*, July 29, 2013, http://www.theguardian.com/film /filmblog/2013/jul/29/birth-of-a-nation-dw-griffith-masterpiece.

6. Melvyn Stokes, *D. W. Griffith's* The Birth of a Nation (New York: Oxford University Press, 2007), 3.

7. Davarian L. Baldwin, "'I Will Build a Black Empire': *The Birth of a Nation* and the Specter of the New Negro," *Journal of the Gilded Age and Progressive Era* 14, no. 4 (2015): 599.

8. Michael Rogin, "'The Sword Became a Flashing Vision': D. W. Griffith's *The Birth of a Nation*," *Representations* 9 (1985): 186.

9. Such Enlightenment tenets, however, excluded European imperialism and relations between the races in Africa, among other regions of the world inhabited by peoples of color. See Emmanuel Chukwudi Eze, ed., *Race and the Enlightenment—A Reader* (Cambridge, MA: Blackwell, 1977).

10. For example, see the *Encyclopeadia Britannica*'s 1895 entry, which contains several explicit references, such as the anatomical features of the "Negro" approximating that of the gorilla, "enabling the Negro to butt with the head and resist blows which would inevitably break any ordinary European's skull." The entry also describes "premature ossification of the skull, preventing further development of the brain, many pathologists have attributed the inherent mental inferiority of the blacks, an inferiority which is even more marked than their physical differences." *Encyclopaedia Britannica*, American ed., vol. 17 (New York: Werner, 1895), 316–320.

11. See W. Fitzhugh Brundage, "Working in the 'Kingdom of Culture': African Americans and American Popular Culture, 1890–1930," in *Beyond Blackface*, ed. W. Fitzhugh Brundage (Chapel Hill: University of North Carolina Press, 2011), 1–42.

12. Lynching, as a systemic practice, took place from the Civil War to World War II. See the Report Summary of *Lynching in America: Confronting the Legacy of Racial Terror* (Montgomery, AL: Equal Justice Initiative, 2015), 3.

13. In counterpoint to empire, recall the rise of antisystemic movements by workers, racial minorities, and women in the United States and, internationally, the Mexican and Russian revolutions in play, for example.

14. Consider that, while immigrants from Southern Europe were accepted, others were denied entry from Asia, marking the closure of America's borders as anti-Asian sentiments and movements emerged, beginning as early as 1882.

15. Along with the racial terror in the South, the formation of the factory and mass production under industrial capitalism was also cause for why African Americans migrated North and to the Midwest at the turn of the century in pursuit of employment and opportunity.

16. Frances Smith Foster, introduction to *The House of Bondage or Charlotte Brooks and Other Slaves*, by Octavia V. Rogers Albert (New York: Oxford University Press, 1988), xxix.

17. Michael T. Martin and David C. Wall, "The Politics of Cine-memory: Signifying Slavery in the History Film," in *A Companion to the Historical Film*, ed. Robert A. Rosenstone and Constantin Parvulescu (Malden, MA: Wiley-Blackwell, 2013), 446–447.

18. Ibid., 448–449.

19. In Janet Walker's study, the focus is on incest and the Holocaust. See Walker, *Trauma Cinema* (Berkeley: University of California Press, 2005).

20. Sean Griffin, "Class," in *Schirmer Encycloypedia of Film*, vol. 1, ed. Barry Keith Grant (New York: Thompson Gale, 2007), 303.

21. For Bourdieu these include social, cultural, and symbolic capital manifest in social relations.

22. For elaboration, see Anna Everett, *Returning the Gaze: A Genealogy of Black Film Criticism, 1909–1949* (Durham, NC: Duke University Press, 2001), chap. 1.

23. See Stokes, *D. W. Griffith's* The Birth of a Nation, chap. 6.

24. See Dick Lehr, *The Birth of a Nation: How a Legendary Filmmaker and a Crusading Editor Reignited America's Civil War* (New York: PublicAffairs, 2014). For a comprehensive account of the film's reception and opposition to it, see Stokes's masterful work, *D. W. Griffith's* The Birth of a Nation, chap. 6.

25. See Ashley Clark, "Deride the Lightning: Assessing *The Birth of a Nation* 100 Years On," *The Guardian*, March 5, 2015, http://www.theguardian.com/film/2015/mar/05/birth-of-a-nation-100-year-anniversary-racism-cinema. A consideration of Caddoo's important study is suggested for context of the African American response to *The Birth of a Nation*. See Cara Caddoo, *Envisioning Freedom: Cinema and the Building of Modern Black Life* (Cambridge, MA: Harvard University Press, 2014), 140–162, 163–169.

26. See Caddo, *Envisioning Freedom*, 140.

27. Marc Ferro, *Cinema and History* (Detroit, MI: Wayne State University Press, 1988), 152. Italics appear in the original. For the backstory, see Thomas Cripps, *Slow Fade to Black* (New York: Oxford University Press, 1993), 70–76.

28. See Barbara Tepa Lupack, foreword to *Richard E. Norman and Race Filmmaking* (Bloomington: Indiana University Press, 2014) ix–x.

29. See Cara Caddoo's essay in this volume. See also Linda Williams's essay in this collection for a discussion of how race films resisted or were complicit in propagating such stereotypes.

30. The film *De Voortrekkers* chronicles the Boers' migration from Cape Colony during the 1830s to escape British rule.

31. The title *They Built a Nation* is the literal English translation of the film, but it is also common to see the film referred to as *Building a Nation*.

32. Direct quotation from original abstract with essay.

33. Direct quotation from original abstract with essay.

34. Direct quotation from original abstract with essay.

35. Direct quotation from original abstract with essay.

36. See Rogin, "The Sword," for an alternative reading.

37. Direct quotation from original abstract with essay.

38. Direct quotation from original abstract with essay.

PART I

NATIONAL/TRANSNATIONAL IN HISTORICAL TIME

By Adele Stephenson.

1

THE BIRTH OF A NATION'S
LONG CENTURY

Cara Caddoo

"Two [officers] that had me by the throat were choking me in such a manner that I couldn't remember anything," Aaron William Puller, the minister of the People's Baptist Church, testified in a Boston municipal court shortly after his arrest. One officer held Puller by the throat and another held him by the back of the neck as they dragged him for at least fifteen city blocks. "I wasn't conscious of much of anything that was taking place, but I think the officers who had me by the neck and throat let go at Boylston Street," he explained to the court (fig. 1.1).[1]

Puller was one of nearly a dozen individuals the Boston police force arrested in the proximity of the Tremont Theater on the evening of April 17, 1915. "Army of Police Nip Theater Riot in Bud," the *Sunday Post* exclaimed the next morning, with a photograph of Aaron Puller dwarfed by a larger image of Boston's police force. The officers stand in a row, shoulder to shoulder, in identical uniforms. Most of those arrested had directly clashed with this "army" of police, including James L. Dunn of West Newton, Massachusetts; Stephen Massey, a driver; James T. Bivens, a railroad porter; a woman named Lugenia Foster; and Clara Foskey, a thirty-year-old black Canadian married to a railroad porter, who was charged with assaulting an officer.[2]

The confrontations between Boston's police officers and the local black population occurred during the protests against D. W. Griffith's photoplay *The Birth of a Nation*. By early March 1915, black Americans had already organized demonstrations against in the film in cities such as Los Angeles and New York. Soon tens of thousands of black protesters, including those

Figure 1.1. Aaron William Puller, the minister of the People's Baptist Church, and Boston's police force. *From* Boston Globe, *April 18, 1915.*

in Boston, had joined the broad-based, concerted battle against the film. The campaigns engaged hundreds of organizations and unfolded in more than sixty cities in the United States, the Panama Canal Zone, Hawaii, and Canada. By the end of World War I, the fight against *The Birth of a Nation* had transformed into the first mass black protest movement of the twentieth century.[3]

What can the protests against *The Birth of a Nation* teach us today, more than a century later? Since Thomas Cripps's groundbreaking study *Slow Fade to Black*, scholars have described the campaigns against the film as a vivid example of black agency and resistance during the nadir of race relations. Historians have acknowledged that the protests helped activists gain experience and build institutions but have wondered whether the efforts were ultimately counterproductive: they did, after all, provide free publicity for Griffith's film and draw resources away from other causes and from black film production.[4] Interpretations of the success of the campaigns are based on assumptions that they were primarily legal battles, solely interested in film censorship and spearheaded by middle-class organizations such as the National Association for the Advancement of Colored People (which is given the lion's share of credit for organizing protests). Curiously little attention is paid to the people on the ground. Yet it was their demands and desires and their long engagement with the motion pictures that made the mass movement possible.

A broad swath of black Americans campaigned against *The Birth of a Nation* because the movement encompassed many of their most urgent material, cultural, and political concerns. Black communities had early and substantial engagements with moving pictures. Nearly two decades before the debut of Griffith's film, black Americans had forged their own cinema. Individuals' interactions with the motion pictures varied, but as a whole, black Americans had invested in the medium as an industry, a communication tool, and a form of leisure. This history fueled the campaigns against *The Birth of a Nation*, but as protesters interacted with one another—and the white supremacists who defended the film—the mass movement took on new dimensions. In cities such as Philadelphia and Boston, the local campaigns came to emphasize issues of pressing local concern, including police brutality and the role of law enforcement in the protection of private property. As we reflect on the centennial of *The Birth of a Nation*, the protest movement continues to offer important insights into our historical present.

* * *

On the day of Puller's arrest, the bespectacled fifty-six-year-old minister had arrived at the Tremont Theater shortly after 7:30 p.m. with the intention of purchasing a ticket to D. W. Griffith's photoplay *The Birth of a Nation*.[5] Across the city, reports of the film's exhibition at the Tremont had sent black Bostonians and their supporters into an uproar. Puller, as a "representative of the local colored people," had petitioned the mayor's office to block certain objectionable scenes from the film's exhibition in Boston. He was curious whether the request was carried out, and, hoping to see for himself, he approached the box office and requested a ticket. "There are no tickets to be sold," the employee of the theater told the minister. "I started to leave the lobby," Puller explained, "and when nearing the street I stumbled. A policeman gave me a slight shove which hastened me to the sidewalk. Outside were about 25 other colored people, all of the better class. Dr. Thornton, who had a ticket in his possession and who was about to go in with me, was pushed out when I was. While we were standing there in the street along came Dr. Lattimore, another prominent colored man, who said to us 'They are selling tickets.'"

When a scuffle broke out between a police officer and several protesters, Puller interceded by writing down the badge number of the officer involved in the incident. Without warning, a plainclothes police officer knocked the minister to the ground. In the chaos, Puller recalled Sergeant King directing the officers to "lock that nigger up." Meanwhile, inside the lobby of the Tremont, a group of protestors gathered to watch W. Monroe Trotter, editor of the anti-accommodationist black newspaper the *Guardian*, as he attempted to purchase tickets to the show. When ticket booth vendors refused to sell Trotter a ticket, he protested, and a crowd rushed into the theater to his defense. Trotter was then struck in the jaw by a plainclothes police officer and subsequently arrested for "disturbing the peace."[6]

Skirmishes continued throughout the night between the black public and the police. James L. Dunn of West Newton, Massachusetts, a town about half an hour by train from Boston, was arrested outside the Tremont Theater and charged with using profanity toward an officer. He later testified that he had been swept into the commotion by police officers who were indiscriminately harassing black people in the vicinity of the theater. Dunn explained that he traveled to Boston on Saturday night to shop with four female acquaintances, including his niece Lillian Lawson. After police officers outside the theater demanded he quickly move from the area, Dunn bristled. According to his testimony, he quipped, "My Lord, man, how do you expect for me to move any faster than I am." The officer, in response, "grabbed him and twisted his wrist, which [was] still sore" more than week later.[7]

Police officers provided conflicting accounts of the events that unfolded on the night of April 17. Despite the inconsistencies between the recollections of the police and the people who were arrested, both sides' testimonies pointed to the question at the heart of the conflicts: Who protects the rights of black citizens? Black protesters and passersby complained that the patrol officers ignored their rights to public space and fair access to public accommodations while defending the interests of their white counterparts. During the trial, Dunn and his niece depicted Dunn as an upstanding citizen, teetotaler, and a trustee of his Baptist church. They framed his response— "My Lord"—as a bit huffy but far from incendiary. In contrast, two white police officers described Dunn as physically confrontational and verbally abusive. According to Sergeant King and Officer William G. Carnes, Dunn made "gestures" and swore at the officers. "He said he was a citizen and that the 'cops' were 'foreign — — white trash," King told the court.[8] Had Dunn lodged these insults at Sergeant King, a second-generation Irish American, and the white officers outside the theater, his invectives would have been vehement declarations of Dunn's claims to his rights as a citizen, even if they pivoted on nativist presumptions.[9] In any case, both versions of the events illuminate the fact that issues such as fair access to public space were equally as, if not more, important to the protests than just the content of Griffith's motion picture.

In essence, at the same time protesters participated in the broader transnational movement, they were mobilizing around issues of pressing local concern. Such interactions raised issues that, at first glance, might seem far removed from the campaigns against Griffith's film. In Boston, police violence remained at the forefront of the demonstrations against *The Birth of a Nation*. When more than one hundred people showed up to testify in defense of the protesters during a special session of the municipal court, many specifically focused on the actions of the police. Witnesses testified that officers had indiscriminately targeted the black populace while ignoring the illegal actions of the white theater management. When Mary E. Moore of 36 Warwick Street, Roxbury, took the stand, she testified that the box office had sold white patrons tickets before and after her but refused to sell to her. When she asked Sergeant Martin King why William Monroe Trotter was arrested, King told her to "shut up." Others testified that they had witnessed or personally sustained injuries from the police.

Violent encounters between black protesters and police officers also marked the Philadelphia campaign against *The Birth of a Nation*. On September 21, 1915, shortly before 10:00 p.m., a brick crashed through the glass window above the entrance of Philadelphia's Forrest Theatre. Instantly, the streets erupted into a "bloody scene" of the "wildest disorder." Police charged with batons and revolvers. The crowd, which consisted mostly of black demonstrators, scattered. A few dashed for the building's main entrance. Hundreds more fled up Broad and Walnut Streets, the police at their heels. "Those who could not run fast enough to dodge clubs received them upon their heads."[10] Two protesters threw milk bottles at the officers pursuing them. At the corner of Walnut and Broad, someone hurled a brick at Officer Wallace Striker. On Juniper Street, either a rioter or a police officer fired shots into the air. By night's end, more than a score were injured, several arrested, and the theater defaced. Nineteen-year-old Arthur Lunn, a farmer from Worcester County, Maryland, was charged with inciting the riot. Dr. Wesley F. Graham, pastor of Trinity Baptist, sustained "severe injuries." Lillian Howard, a caterer; William A. Sinclair, the financial secretary of Douglass Hospital; and a thirty-three-year-old laborer named Lee Banks received severe lacerations.[11]

It was no coincidence that these protests occurred at the cinema. By 1915, black institutions, industries, and cultural practices were entwined with the motion pictures. Cinema in the early twentieth century was ubiquitous. Even those black urban dwellers who avoided the theater were confronted daily with its presence: churches hosted film exhibitions as fund-raisers, black newspapers published film reviews, and motion picture houses lined the streets black urbanites walked on their way to work or school. While white American film producers constructed their own cinema—which by World War I had grown into a powerful transnational industry—black Americans produced and exhibited their own films, and black cinema was an essential aspect of black urban leisure in the Jim Crow city.[12]

Neither were the protests against *The Birth of a Nation* the first time a site of leisure had become a battleground for social and cultural power. In fact, we might consider Philadelphia's Forrest Theatre a fitting location for the events that unfolded in that city. The Forrest's namesake was actor Edwin Forrest, the American Shakespearean whose feud with "elitist" performer William Macready sparked the Astor Place Riot in 1849.[13] The riot, as scholars Sean Wilentz and Eric Lott have demonstrated, expressed the growing social and cultural divisions among New York's laboring and middle classes in the antebellum period.[14] Like the events of 1849, the protests against Griffith's film emerged from a realm of cultural life entwined in the social and political landscape of a quickly growing arena of mass culture.

News of the protests circulated by word of mouth and through the black press. The oft-quoted W. H. Watkins of the Montgomery Business Men's League brought news of his experiences in Boston back to Alabama. "I saw this film in Boston," he explained. "In leaving the theatre after the production I heard a number of men remark, I would like to kill ever negro in the United States.' As I walked down the street, I hung my head for I felt as if the whole world was down on me."[15] In turn, news of Watkins's experiences and campaign in Montgomery was reprinted in black newspapers across the country, including the *Indianapolis Freeman*. In Chicago, the *Defender* printed stories of how Watkins linked Griffith's film to lynchings in Alabama and Georgia.[16]

Black newspapers published news of the protests of *The Birth of a Nation* as protesters launched new campaigns from the Panama Canal Zone to Halifax, Canada. The protesters learned strategies and tactics from one another as they cited the film's libelous representations of the race, its ability to incite violence, its showings in racially discriminatory theaters, and the undue political power of its white producers. Through the protests, they staked claim to their rights as citizens. Criticisms of the film pointed to the growth of the Hollywood film industry. As one correspondent for a black newspaper reported, the "moving picture trust, gorged in wealth it has filched from the people through their patronage of its efforts," had become "strong enough and powerful enough to entrench itself behind special legal barriers."[17]

* * *

The campaigns against *The Birth of a Nation* not only enabled protesters to link local issues to the larger movement; they also enabled the participation of a broad swath of black Americans with different interests and tactics. The voices of nonelite, working-class blacks were largely absent from middle-class publications such as the *The Crisis* and from legal proceedings against Griffith's film. Nonetheless, working-class black protesters still participated in the protests, often by targeting discriminatory public accommodations. Despite the efforts of the Tremont's management to block black patrons from entering the theater on the night of April 17, nearly two hundred black men and women had managed to sneak inside, including a waiter named Charles P. Ray.[18] As the film was exhibited, demonstrators hissed and exploded about twenty "stink pots," forcing members of the audience to cover their faces from the choking odor. At ten o'clock in the evening, Ray threw a "very ancient" egg at the screen.[19] In Cleveland, protesters, including "a number of city employe[e]s and saloon loafers," threw stones at a Jim Crow streetcar after police blocked their demonstration in front of the local opera house.[20] In other cases, the battle against *The Birth of a Nation* was more surreptitious. Bennie Johnson, a former janitor of the Cecil Theater in Mason City, Iowa, for example, was arrested for breaking into the theater's operating room, stealing the several reels of *The Birth of a Nation*, and throwing them into the incinerator.[21]

Black women, too, were at the forefront of the protests. With the headline "Colored Women Run Birth of a Nation Out of Philadelphia," the *Chicago Defender* lauded the actions of black women who hurled stones at the police-protected Forrest Theatre.[22] When Clara Foskey was accused of assault and battery of a police officer, at least one woman acquaintance and several men came to her aid after she clashed with an Officer Van

Lanningham. According to Officer Thomas H. Dowling, Foskey "elbow[ed] her way through the crowd of theater patrons" and attempted to use her "hat-pin" as a weapon. When Van Lanningham ordered her to move away from the theater, Foskey refused. Van Lanningham attempted to "force her to go along"—perhaps by pushing her or stepping on her feet.[23] Foskey reportedly struck Van Lanningham and was placed under arrest. Protestors Stephen Massey, James T. Bivens, and Lugenia Foster ran to help Foskey and were charged with attempting to rescue a prisoner. In other cities, members of elite black women's organizations, including the National Association of Colored Women's Clubs and local chapters such as the Arizona Colored Women's Clubs, abstained from engaging in physical altercations. Yet these women registered their discontent with *The Birth of a Nation* and actively participated in the campaigns by organizing petitions, lectures, and fund-raisers—activities that comfortably fit with their middle-class sensibilities.[24]

Indeed, participation in the campaigns could take many forms. When thousands of blacks and several hundred white allies gathered in front of Boston's Faneuil Hall after the April 17 Tremont Theater demonstration, tens of thousands of African Americans followed the story in the black press. They learned that the crowds sang "We'll Hang Tom Di[x]on to a Sour Apple Tree" and that black women passed around hats to collect money for the fines levied against the protestors.[25] Other forms of direct action have likely escaped the historical record because the protesters deliberately disguised their identities or worked clandestinely.

* * *

On April 26, 1915, more than a thousand black protesters in Boston adopted a resolution that linked the objectionable film to police brutality and discrimination. The resolution criticized local police who had behaved as agents of the theater managers:

> To the Mayor and Police Commissioner of Boston
>
> Whereas, To act as ticket sellers or ticket takers for a theater is not the proper function of a policeman who[se] salaries are paid by public taxation; and,
>
> Whereas, For a policeman to stop a citizen in the entrance lobby of a theater is illegal and for a policeman to demand to see and scrutinize the theater ticket and to check a citizen at the door is a violation of personal liberty.[26]

The final declaration read:

> Resolved, That we protest such action by the Boston police at the Tremont Theater during the run of "The Birth of a Nation," and that we demand a cessation of such invasion of public rights, and that any place which is deemed to make such police action necessary be stopped at once.[27]

The resolution, which directly linked police brutality to the campaign against *The Birth of a Nation*, articulated both older and new conceptions of black citizenship. Reverend Herbert Johnson told the audience that they could not win "by force" but reminded them of their power as a political constituency. "There are, understand, some 18,000 or 20,000 colored voters," he explained. "With the political parties as closely divided as they are, you have very nearly a balance of power if you will stand together and support the man, irrespective of color or creed, who stands by you." Aaron Puller, the minister who was violently arrested by the police during the demonstrations outside the Tremont Theater, counseled "race unity, race agitation and race sacrifice as the weapons available for fighting the issue." Minister Samuel A. Brown asserted that these rights extended beyond the law. "If no law is made which has teeth in it to stop this infamous thing," he explained, "I believe that white and colored people of Boston will make such a demonstration as will make unprofitable to exhibit the filth known as 'The Birth of a Nation.'"[28] "The mayor will not grant us our rights and we propose to take them into our own hands."[29] It is important to note that this report of the April 26 meeting in Boston was published in the *Washington Bee*, a black newspaper published by Calvin Chase in Washington, DC.

At the same time, protestors used the language of basic rights to criticize Griffith's film and to stake claims to self-representation on behalf of the race. In St. Paul, Minnesota, black residents admitted they had only been able to eliminate a few scenes from the film but believed their demonstrations "showed that we do not intend to have our rights utterly ignored or ruthlessly trod upon without protest."[30] The *Chicago Defender* was especially vocal on the issue of rights in regard to *The Birth of a Nation*. In a classic call to action, the paper argued that the film's mischaracterizations of the race threatened the freedom of black Americans. "Let us always register our protest, often unheeded, against violation of our natural rights, and the despoliation of the privileges of our citizenship," the paper announced.[31] A correspondent for the *Indianapolis Freeman* similarly saw Griffith's film as a strike against the civil rights of black citizens. "'The Birth of a Nation,'" the writer lamented, "is meant as the Negroes' civil death."[32] Framed as a "natural" or "civil" right, these demands for on-screen self-representation helped fuel the simultaneous emergence of a new black film production industry.

The protests against Griffith's film reveal the many ways that cinema—as a place, a medium, and a set of practices—overlapped with the experiences of black people in the early twentieth century. For the black men and women who protested the film, *The Birth of a Nation* was more than a projected image. It was part of a fast-growing racially exclusive industry promoted by white supremacists and exhibited, for the most part, in segregated theaters that were protected by the police. John B. Schoeffel, the manager of the Tremont Theater, relied on the Boston police force to protect its private property while it explicitly broke Boston laws. Evoking anxieties about black male criminality, the manager explained that he had learned a "certain gang of colored men" planned to "raid the theatre and destroy the picture and booth." "In pursuance of this information the management arranged with Supt of Police Michael H Crowley for police protections" because of a fear that the men would be "engaged in the attempt to destroy property" that would cause "serious damage to property," therefore "police protection was sufficient to keep order as far as we know." "All through the night, however, a police guard was maintained outside and inside the theatre, to prevent any breaking of windows or an attack on the films."[33] Within the campaigns were critiques ranging from police harassment and brutality to theater discrimination, economic privilege, state-sanctioned violence, and demands for the right to access public space and leisure venues.[34]

Through the summer of 1915, the protests in Boston continued. They were not as spectacular as the events that had unfolded in April, but they nonetheless demonstrated a sustained movement against Griffith's photoplay. According to the *Boston Daily Globe*, a group of sixty protesters, "a majority of them women," walked in pairs along Tremont Street in front of the theater. Among those arrested were Evelyn B. Washington, age 26, of 77 Sterling Street, Roxbury; James H. Kingsley, 47, of South Trumbull Street, South End; Carl T. Prinn, 22, of Gay Hear[t?] Street, Roxbury; Jacob Johnson, 33, of 42 Hammond Street, Roxbury; Augustus Granville, 45, of 53 Hammond Street, Roxbury; Estelle E. Hill, 36, of 309 Columbus Avenue; Raven W. Jones, 34, of 38 Cunard Street, Roxbury, and Jane W. Posey, 35, of 63 Ruggles Street, Roxbury. "Dr. John B. Hall of 60 Windsor St., Roxbury, furnished bail for the prisoners and they were released."[35] In Philadelphia, middle-class religious leaders such as Wesley F. Graham, who was beaten by police outside the Forrest Theatre, would continue to criticize police violence. In 1918, after police response to antiblack riots in Philadelphia once again brought these issues to a head, he and other ministers formed the Colored Protective Association.

Recent centennial reflections on *The Birth of a Nation* have cast the film as a powerful symbol of the past, as evidence of a shameful history of racism that US society has overcome. Yet if we consider the goals, demands, and desires of the men and women who fought against the photoplay, a different lesson comes into view. For the protesters, the significance of *The Birth of a Nation* extended beyond its text. It was inseparable from a system that privileged the film's white producers, distributors, theater proprietors, and audiences. For instance, publicly funded institutions such as the police not only refused to protect the rights of black Americans who faced discrimination in theaters where the film screened but also attacked black protesters who asserted their rights to occupy public space during the campaigns.[36] In light of ongoing antiblack police violence, the continued denial of black Americans' rights to public space, and the systemic valuation of private property over black lives, the history of *The Birth of a Nation* is just as much a story about our present as it is of our past.

A century after the protests of *The Birth of a Nation*, on June 27, 2015, a young woman named Bree Newsome climbed a thirty-foot flagpole outside the South Carolina state capitol and removed the Confederate flag. She was promptly arrested. Less than two weeks had passed since a white supremacist murdered nine African Americans at the Emanuel African Methodist Episcopal Church in nearby Charleston.

Like the men and women who gathered to protest *The Birth of a Nation*, Newsome's act targeted a broader system of racial injustice and antiblack violence. She understood the flag as a symbol of racial hatred, but its significance lay not only in the object itself but also in its location—placed at the steps of the state capitol. "It is important to remember that our struggle doesn't end when the flag comes down," she later wrote. "The Confederacy is a southern thing, but white supremacy is not. Our generation has taken up the banner to fight battles many thought were won long ago. We must fight with all vigor now so that our grandchildren aren't still fighting these battles in another 50 years. Black Lives Matter. This is non-negotiable."[37]

CARA CADDOO is Assistant Professor of History at Indiana University. She is author of *Envisioning Freedom: Cinema and the Building of Modern Black Life*.

Notes

1. "Birth of Nation" Causes Near-Riot: Alleged Plot to Destroy Film, *Boston Daily Globe*, April 18, 1915, 1; "Roughly Used by Police Negroes Testify in Court," *Boston Journal*, May 4, 1915, 4.

2. *New York Age*, September 23, 1915, 1.

3. Aspects of this chapter draw from my book *Envisioning Freedom* (especially chapter 6), and from "The Birth of a Nation, Police Brutality, and Black Protest," *Journal of the Gilded Age and Progressive Era* 14, no. 4 (2015): 608–611.

4. Thomas Cripps, *Slow Fade to Black: The Negro in American Film, 1900–1942* (New York: Oxford University Press, 1993), 41–69; Janet Staiger, *Interpreting Films: Studies in the Historical Reception of American Cinema* (Princeton, NJ: Princeton University Press, 1992), 139–153; Jane Gaines, *Fire and Desire: Mixed-Race Movies in the Silent Era* (Chicago: University of Chicago Press, 2001), 219–257; Melvyn Stokes, *D. W. Griffith's* The Birth of a Nation (New York: Oxford University Press, 2007), 129–170.

5. A. B. Caldwell, *A History of the American Negro, South Carolina Edition* (New York: A. B. Caldwell, 1919).

6. Ibid. Two men were ejected from the theater that evening for throwing rotten eggs at the screen. *Baltimore Sun*, April 18, 1915.

7. *Boston Evening Transcript*, April 28, 1915, 2.

8. Ibid.

9. Martin H. King, United States Federal Census Year 1920, Boston Ward 17, Suffolk, Massachusetts, roll T625_737, page 7B, enumeration district 446, image 590.

10. "Film Play Cause Hurt to Divines," *New York Age*, September 23, 1915, 1.

11. Ibid.; "Colored Women Run Birth of a Nation Out of Philadelphia," *Chicago Defender*, September 25, 1915, 1; *Harrisburg Telegraph*, September 21, 1915, 3; *Trenton Evening Times*, September 21, 1915, 7; Cara Caddoo, *Envisioning Freedom: Cinema and the Building of Modern Black Life* (Cambridge, MA: Harvard University Press, 2014).

12. Philip C. DiMare, *Movies in American History: An Encyclopedia* (Santa Barbara, CA: ABC-CLIO, 2011), 873; Ellis Paxson Oberholtzer, *The Morals of the Movie* (Philadelphia: Penn Publishing, 1922), 13.

13. Lawrence Levine, *Highbrow/Lowbrow: The Emergence of Cultural Hierarchy in America* (Cambridge, MA: Harvard University Press, 1990).

14. Sean Wilentz, *Chants Democratic: New York City and the Rise of the American Working Class, 1788–1850* (New York: Oxford University Press, 1984), 359; Eric Lott, *Love and Theft: Blackface Minstrelsy and the American Working Class* (New York: Oxford University Press, 1993), 66–67.

15. "Birth of a Nation Brings Out Protest to City Commission. Dr. W. M. Watkins Says Famous Film Has Been Misnamed," *Montgomery Advertiser*, February 2, 1916, 12.

16. "Birth of a Nation Opposed," *Chicago Defender*, February 12, 1916, 1.

17. "Birth of a Nation Run Out of Philadelphia," *Chicago Defender*, September 25, 1915, 1.

18. *New York Times*, April 18, 1915, 15; *Indianapolis Freeman*, May 8, 1915, 6; *Boston Sunday Globe*, April 18, 1915, 3.

19. According to census records, Charles P. Ray lived with his mother and appears to have struggled financially. Department of Commerce, Bureau of the Census, *Fourteenth Census of the United States: 1920—Population* (Washington, DC: Government Printing Office, 1920); Department of Commerce, Bureau of the Census, *Fifteenth Census of the United*

States: 1930—Population (Washington, DC: Government Printing Office, 1930), http://www
.ancestrylibrary.com; Department of Commerce, Bureau of the Census, *Thirteenth Census
of the United States: 1910—Population* (Washington, DC: Government Printing Office, 1913),
http://www.ancestrylibrary.com; "Say Box Office Discriminated: Two Witnesses Heard in
Negroes' Behalf," *Boston Daily Globe*, May 1, 1915, 8.

20. Caddoo, *Envisioning Freedom*, 160; *Moving Picture World*, April 28, 1917, 658;
Cleveland Gazette, April 14, 1917, 1; *Cleveland Gazette*, January 9, 1915, 3; *Cleveland Gazette*,
August 17, 1918, 3.

21. *Moving Picture World*, December 25, 1915, 2408; *Chicago Defender*, December 18,
1915, 7.

22. "Colored Women Run Birth of a Nation Out of Philadelphia," *Chicago Defender*,
September 25, 1915, 1.

23. *Boston Globe*, April 18, 1915, 1.

24. "Mrs. White Presides," *Chicago Defender*, April 15, 1916, 6. Like other black
organizations, the Colored Women's Clubs joined other local civic and religious
organizations—including the Christian Methodist Episcopal Church, the African Methodist
Episcopal Church, the Baptist Church, and the Colored Men's Protective League—to fight the
film. In Baltimore, over a thousand people gathered at the Bethel Church in Druid Hill at the
tenth annual session of the Federation of Women's Clubs to listen to Ruth Bennett, president
of the Chester, Pennsylvania, branch speak of her organization's struggle against *The Birth of
a Nation*. "Federation of Women's Clubs Elects Mrs. Mary Talbert Press," *Chicago Defender*,
August 19, 1916, 3.

25. *Savannah Tribune*, April 24, 1915, 1.

26. "1000 Negroes Hear Speakers Rap Photo-Play," *Washington Bee*, May 8, 1915, 6.

27. Ibid.

28. Ibid.

29. "Film Offends Negroes: 'Movie' Based on 'The Clansman' Causes Riot in . . . ,"
Baltimore Sun, April 18, 1915, 1.

30. *St. Paul Appeal*, October 30, 1915, 3.

31. *Chicago Defender*, June 5, 1915, 8.

32. *Indianapolis Freeman*, May 29, 1915, 4.

33. "'Birth of Nation' Causes Near-Riot," 1.

34. Caddoo, *Envisioning Freedom*, 159; Robert Gregg, *Sparks from the Anvil of Oppression:
Philadelphia's African Methodists and Southern Migrants, 1890–1940* (Philadelphia: Temple
University Press, 1993), 63.

35. "Arrest Eight of Objectors," *Boston Daily Globe*, June 8, 1915, 1.

36. Caddoo, *Envisioning Freedom*, 159; Gregg, *Sparks from the Anvil*, 63.

37. Goldie Taylor, "Exclusive: Bree Newsome Speaks for the First Time after
Courageous Act of Civil Disobedience," *Blue Nation Review*, June 29, 2015, http://archives
.bluenationreview.com/exclusive-bree-newsome-speaks-for-the-first-time-after-courageous
-act-of-civil-disobedience/.

2

GREAT MOMENTS FROM THE BIRTH OF A NATION

Collecting and Privately Screening Small Gauge Versions

Andy Uhrich

A *New York Times* article from 1965 titled "Classics on Home Screen" is a reminder, in our saturated home media present, of the comparative rarity of being able to own personal copies of films in the decades before home video. The author, Jacob Deschin, writes, almost amazed, that "Any amateur who owns an 8 mm projector can now put on a movie show of old-time classics on his own screen at home. Yes, even David Wark Griffith's *The Birth of a Nation*, the 50th anniversary of which occurred last week. The 12-reel film costs $65 [which is just under $500 today] and takes about three and one-half hours of screen time."[1]

To contextualize why the release of classic films to the domestic market made the news and to better understand how *The Birth of a Nation* was exhibited and watched in private settings on film prints before home video, this chapter describes the domestic and nontheatrical distribution and reception of *The Birth of a Nation* from the late 1930s to the end of the 1970s. By focusing on the nontheatrical market in general and private film collectors in particular, this chapter adds to previous studies on the film's circulation and versioning by scholars such as Melvyn Stokes, John Cuniberti, and J. B. Kaufman.[2] The chapter surveys the variety of spaces the film was shown in beyond the commercial movie theater, presents a necessarily incomplete list of the multiple versions that were released for the

Figure 2.1. Opening title card of the 1953 short produced by Blackhawk Films, *Great Moments from The Birth of a Nation*. Print from the Bradley, mss. *Courtesy of the Lilly Library, Indiana University, Bloomington.*

home market on small gauge film formats, discusses one of these derivative versions of *The Birth of a Nation* in greater detail, and presents the debates collectors engaged in around their various justifications for screening the film (fig. 2.1).

In this discussion, I explore the following questions: What was the role of private individuals in circulating and exhibiting *The Birth of a Nation*? How did the specifics of nontheatrical exhibition spaces—homes, classrooms, school auditoriums, community spaces, and private screening rooms—and the different textual and material versions of the film—8 mm or 16 mm, sound or silent, black-and-white or color, full-length or excerpted short—alter the experience and context of watching it? How did one subset of American cinephiles address issues of Hollywood's racism in their canonization and appreciation of cinema as an art form? Building on that last point to widen the scope of this analysis, how have collectors—and by implication archivists, historians, scholars, and viewers—balanced a desire to restore and exhibit films with a responsibility for a greater social good?

The Birth of a Nation and "the Privacy of One's Home"

To be fair, many of these questions would not have been the driving force for someone who purchased one of the films mentioned in the *New York Times* piece; presumably their motivation would have been to own an old film. This was not always an easy task. Film prints were hard to come by. What was available was often a poorly copied print or a short depicting only one scene or a condensation of the original. Showing a film required a high degree of technical knowledge in order to operate a film projector or edit and repair prints. And new prints, when they could be found, could cost up to a few hundred dollars per title.

At that time, from the 1930s to the 1970s, the major Hollywood studios had, for the most part, ignored the domestic market. Earlier efforts in the 1910s and 1920s to make the small gauge projector the successful home media follow-up to the phonograph, and thus a platform with which production companies could sell or lease film prints, had failed.[3] Until the adoption of VHS, the home market was essentially ceded to specialized film companies. Distributors such as those mentioned in the *New York Times* article—Blackhawk Films, Entertainment Films, Griggs Moviedrome— were small enough that they could make a profit from selling films in the public domain, or they were willing to break copyright law by duplicating newer, more popular titles. A few of these companies, such as Blackhawk Films, which was one of the largest distributors of commercially produced films for the home from the 1950s through the 1970s, were respectable businesses with several employees and a large and well-cultivated library of films for sale. Some, like Griggs Moviedrome, were collectors who ran films out of their homes and were primarily motivated by a love of cinema, and while they might have duplicated or traded films obtained outside of official circuits, they did so from a desire to preserve and share old films. Others exemplified the worst characteristics of media pirates, dealing in bootlegs and defrauding their customers.

This uncertain marketplace was one additional reason that the home audience for prepackaged films was limited. The audience for home cinema was, as Deschin described in the *Times*, primarily "collectors of old films and those serious amateurs who want to improve their techniques through occasional study of the great film achievements of yesterday."[4] In both cases, there was an element of functionality to buying old films; the former bought them to build a collection, while the latter used them as a resource to lift camera angles, shots, and other cinematic signifiers.[5] The effort and cost it took to acquire film prints usually required additional interests or socializing to justify the expense. Collectors and amateur filmmakers were, then, representative of what Greg Waller describes as the "specialized publics" of nontheatrical film. The fantasy, however skewed, of an undifferentiated audience coming together to see the same film in a movie theater was replaced with a "pragmatically targeted filmmaking."[6] The films did not attract a mass audience, as was the case with the commercial movie theater, broadcast radio, and television networks, but rather a number of different, interrelated, minor audiences. Sponsored, industrial, and educational films were made to meet a precise need among a necessarily limited number of people looking to buy a tractor, attending a job training session, or learning about chemistry or social studies. Or, in the case of the discussion here, various prints of *The Birth of a Nation*, a film made for the largest public possible, were circulated by and to select groups of cinephiles and film historians.

Showing how specialized these nontheatrical publics could be, I want to emphasize that when discussing the role of film collectors in circulating *The Birth of a Nation*, the focus of this chapter is on collectors of European descent and not the important African American collectors and film historians discussed in articles by Leah Kerr in *Black Camera* and by Jacqueline Stewart in "Discovering Black Film History: Tracing the Tyler, Texas Black Film Collection."[7] My decision to focus on the relationship of *The Birth of a Nation* to prominent white film collectors is an effort to begin thinking about the role of whiteness in film fandom and in the creation of what became canonized as the classics of American cinema and about practices of film preservation in the mid-twentieth century.

Along with specialized publics were specialized exhibition sites. Or, as Deschin describes the impetus for screening small gauge versions of film classics, "group entertainment in the privacy of one's home."[8] The copies of *The Birth of a Nation* that are analyzed here played in many places besides the living room, including private cinemas, classrooms, film societies, and repertory theaters. Thus, the word *private* does not adequately describe the specialized audiences to whom these prints were shown or the atmosphere of the screenings. However, it does suggest the insider nature of many of these screenings, replete with alternative and adjacent exhibition strategies and spectatorial positions to commercial moviegoing. The intent of many of these nontheatrical film programmers, or private individuals showing films in their homes, was not, for the most part, to specifically traffic in offensive images; it was to project films that could not be seen elsewhere due to commercial imperatives, copyright restrictions, or censorship.

For example, in a 1967 letter to members of the new Film Society of the School of Visual Arts, film historian and noted collector William K.

Everson stated why he did not want members to promote the screenings to outsiders. He requested that members: "do *not* spread the word among friends outside of SVA, nor discuss the films openly—particularly at places like the Museum of Modern Art where listening ears are always on the alert for private screenings. Many of the films we show are not legally available, and while there is no specific copyright or other infringement involved in these specific screenings, still it is diplomatic to publicize them as little as possible" (emphasis in the original).[9]

Thus, many of these screenings, by design, escaped, or were ignored by, the public eye. This has a particular resonance for *The Birth of a Nation*, which was regularly protested against by the National Association for the Advancement of Colored People at many of the film's more prominent screenings. Not that there were never protests against nontheatrical or collector screenings of the film. Yet, due to the secretive nature of these specific film cultures and the technical affordances of small gauge film, such as portability and relative ease of use, *The Birth of a Nation* was exhibited in contexts outside the more controlled setting of the commercial movie house. This offered nontheatrical film programmers a way to show the film despite possible pushback by civil rights groups. In program notes announcing an upcoming screening of *The Birth of a Nation* in the late 1950s, Everson assures attendees that if the arranged location at a high school is shut down, "we'll be going 'underground' to a little private theatre in New Jersey, so nobody need to be afraid of making the trek [from New York City] for nothing."[10] Additional examples of similar screenings are examined later in this chapter.

The availability of small gauge film projection also meant programmers and audiences could present a more complicated stance, if not outright contestation, to the film. Though not indicative of a larger approach to exhibiting *The Birth of a Nation*, in July 1971, the black theater group Grassroot Experience screened the film as the last part of a weeklong film series on representations of black America on film; Griffith's film was accompanied by jazz records by John Coltrane and Pharoah Sanders.[11] Details are scarce in the newspaper report announcing the event, but the pairing of the music of the two jazz greats with Griffith's film suggests the screening might have been intended as a sort of exorcism of the lasting, pernicious power of *The Birth of a Nation* or perhaps a clash between icons of black art and white cinema. However it was actually presented, that it was shown at a live venue working to fulfill the "need for black theatre in the community" and to stage plays with characters "that Black people can identify with"[12] reveals a use of the film very different from that of white New York cinephiles.

While the focus of this chapter is on how collectors, cinephiles, and amateur film historians recirculated small gauge versions of *The Birth of a Nation*, more research is required to chart how the Ku Klux Klan and other white supremacist groups used 16 mm and 8 mm prints of the film. The threat that substandard copies of the film posed as a recruiting tool for the Klan was addressed in a December 1970 op-ed piece by historian and political columnist Garry Wills. After recounting how the expanding list of titles available for home viewing allowed him and his mother-in-law to watch *Intolerance* (dir. D. W. Griffith, 1916), he noted the "the greatest of D. W. Griffith's films [*The Birth of a Nation*] cannot be bought, or taken out of the local library. And for a very good reason." Due to the film's promotion of the Ku Klux Klan, "it could be used in private showings, by the Klan or other bigot groups, to fan race hatred." However, while Wills supported a ban on the film in private screenings because they could not be monitored, he argued against attempts to stop its exhibition in public theaters. If a very small percentage of white racists might be inspired by the film, most of "any normal audience watching *The Birth of a Nation*" would be exposed to the country's past horrors and would be better armed to confront current-day forms of the Klan and white racists.[13] Private screenings were dangerous because they could not be policed by the common sense of the mass audience.

Historical precedents for how the Klan might have screened small gauge editions of *The Birth of a Nation* are covered in Tom Rice's *White Robes, Silver Screens: Movies and the Making of the Ku Klux Klan*. During the 1920s, and after the film's extended theatrical run, Klan chapters in Ohio, Texas, Illinois, Indiana, and elsewhere began circulating preexisting 35 mm prints of *The Birth of a Nation* on their own. If, during the late 1910s, Klan members would show up in full garb for screenings of the film put on by mainstream commercial theaters, in the following decade they exhibited it themselves "in smaller theaters—some owned by the Klan—and other kinds of spaces. As the Klan reappropriated the film . . . it pulled, stretched, and deepened the divides occasioned by the film's initial release."[14] Though the gauge of film and historical period is different from those covered in this chapter, Rice's example amplifies the larger argument that access to films and the ability to screen them changes their physical and textual shape, and thus their reception.

Still to be confirmed is whether the greater availability of *The Birth of a Nation* after its entry into the public domain in 1975 was responsible for its increased use by the Klan, which was then led by a newer generation of white supremacists, including David Duke. More research is needed to determine which formats they acquired and how the transportability of small gauge prints, and later home video, might have allowed them to screen the film in new spaces that 35 mm prints could not reach. However, a spate of Klan-produced screenings of the film demonstrates the importance that *The Birth of a Nation* continued to hold on the group's social identity and inflammatory public acts.[15] For example, a San Bernardino chapter hoped to rehabilitate views of moderate whites toward the Klan by forming a local bowling league, opening a bookstore, and, paradoxically due to the film then being over sixty years old, "sponsor showings of the film *The Birth of a Nation*."[16] On June 3, 1978, Klan members in Fairview, Kentucky, screened the film "to paying customers . . . at an undisclosed location" when they could not gain a permit to burn crosses.[17] Later that summer, a Klan screening held in a community center in Oxnard, California, was contested by antiracist groups who clashed with police.[18] A 1979 Klan screening in China Grove, North Carolina, was met by a protest that started a simmering dispute between the Klan and antiracist groups that culminated in the Greensboro Massacre later that year.[19]

An Incomplete Survey of Small Gauge and Nontheatrical Versions

To provide a sense of the variety of home and small gauge versions that existed of *The Birth of a Nation*, and which would have been projected at these types of nontheatrical screenings, this chapter now turns to a discussion of the many copies of the film owned by one collector. David Bradley was a filmmaker who started making amateur movies as a teenager, including Charlton Heston's first film, 1941's *Peer Gynt*. Bradley turned professional with a brief career as a director at MGM releasing one feature, *Talk About a Stranger* (1952), and later made a number of B pictures and cult films, including *Dragstrip Riot* (1958) and *Madmen of Mandoras* (1963, later reissued in 1968 as *They Saved Hitler's Brain*). Bradley started collecting films as a teenager in the 1930s and by the time of his death in 1997 had assembled one of the largest private film collections in the United States.

Bradley used index cards to document the date when he bought a film, how much he paid for it, and the venues to which he loaned a film. This record-keeping system allows for an analysis of how his collection grew over time, when certain titles became available on the collector's market, and, for the purposes of this study, a view of one collector's role as purchaser and circulator of private copies of *The Birth of a Nation*. Out of Bradley's collection of about 3,900 film titles on 16 mm, he had six versions of *The Birth of a Nation*. The chronological order in which he acquired them is as follows: The first two copies he owned of the film were shorts. One was a three-minute reel of excerpts that he acquired in 1943; the other was a nine-minute condensation with new narration called *Great Moments from Birth of a Nation* from 1953. The latter will be analyzed in greater detail later in this chapter. In 1955, Bradley was finally able to obtain a complete version of the film when he purchased a twelve-reel black-and-white copy of the feature. In 1969, he acquired another black-and-white full-length print. Bradley purchased three reels of outtakes and trims from *The Birth of a Nation* in 1972. Finally, in 1975, he bought a color version of the feature.[20]

Unfortunately, Bradley did not record where or from whom he located these prints in his catalog records. Perhaps he omitted the information to protect sources that engaged in illegal film piracy. His copies of *The Birth of a Nation* appear to be a mix of legitimate reissues approved by the copyright holder, gray-market releases produced by small distributors such as Griggs Moviedrome, and, potentially, bootleg copies, or dupes, produced by film collectors with the assistance of a film lab willing to break copyright. Reconstructing a history of the production origins of Bradley's prints of *The Birth of a Nation* involves a mixture of following archaeological clues from the prints themselves and from the advertisements that distributors placed in magazines for the nontheatrical, educational, and collecting markets such as *Home Movies*, *Educational Screen*, and *Classic Film Collector*.

What follows is a chronological account of all the versions of the film intended for nontheatrical or the home markets from before 1980 that were uncovered in the research for this chapter. Undoubtedly there are more, especially considering all the dupes that were made by and privately traded among collectors. Information about the source and specifics on how Bradley or other collectors used their personal copies are given along with the details about the prints of *The Birth of a Nation*. The intent is to acknowledge the range of companies and individuals that were distributing and exhibiting the film, and the transformations—textual, material, and paratextual—that the film underwent as it traveled the collector and non-theatrical circuits.

In 1937, the F. C. Pictures Corporation was distributing a 35 mm sound print of *The Birth of a Nation* to the educational market.[21] F. C. was a small distribution company in upstate New York that sold films to school, itinerant exhibitors, and other nontheatrical sites. In 1940, the previous owner of F. C. Pictures, Charles Tarbox, was running another company, Film Classic Exchange, which was circulating a bootlegged copy of *The Birth of a Nation* that had apparently expurgated the most outrageously racist scenes in the film, such as the attempted rape of the Little Sister by Gus.[22] Later, Film Classic Exchange was selling yet another version of the film on 8 mm to the collectors market.[23]

The same year, the Museum of Modern Art Film Library was distributing *The Birth of a Nation* "to museums, colleges, and film study groups throughout the country" as one of eight films in its fall series.[24] The film is still available for rental from the Museum's Circulating Film and Video Library in four different versions on 16 mm.[25]

In 1938, the Stone Film Library advertised sound and silent versions on 16 mm to the educational market. An ad in the February issue of *Educational Screen* reads, "In 1915 TEACHERS AND STUDENTS traveled miles to see it. In 1938 IT COMES TO YOU! **THE BIRTH OF A NATION**" [capital letters and bold type in the original].[26] The Stone Film Library was started in 1908 by one of the earliest known film collectors, Abram Stone, as one of the first stock footage companies (fig. 2.2).

In the summer of 1942, the Intercontinental Marketing Corp. released two excerpts in either 8 mm or 16 mm: *The Assassination of Lincoln* and *Civil War Battle Scenes*. The text of a 1942 ad for these excerpted versions, printed under a patriotic image of the nation's capitol, which was also the cover of the box they were sold in, reads: "Think of seeing, in your own living room, the mighty battle scenes that have held millions spellbound! Think of unreeling the stirring scenes of American heroism as vast armies charge and retreat—as big cannons roar—as shot and shell rain death and destruction! Think, too, of beholding the great patriotic scenes from American History" (fig. 2.3).[27]

At a moment when the United States had been militarily involved in World War II for just over six months, the distributor of these shorts made a sales pitch based on a patriotic appeal by selecting two scenes from *The Birth of a Nation* that embodied national sacrifice while still being

EXCERPTS FROM
D.W. GRIFFITH'S IMMORTAL MASTERPIECE...
"BIRTH OF A NATION"
GREATEST OF ALL PICTURES!

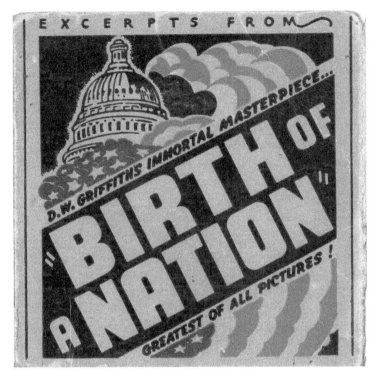

Figure 2.2. Advertisement for the Stone Film Library's version of *The Birth of a Nation*. Found on page 60 of the February 1968 issue of *Educational Screen*.

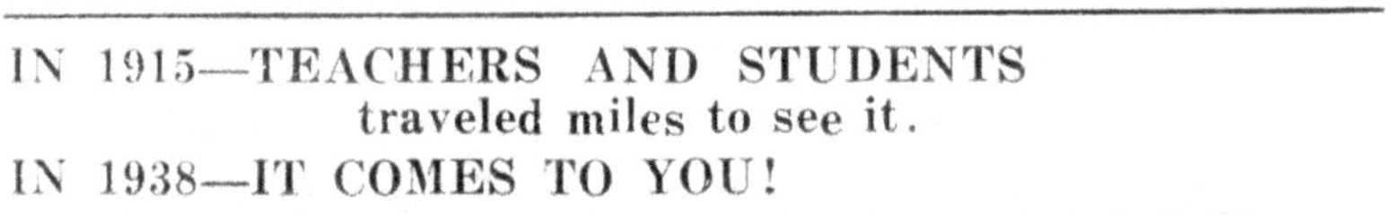

IN 1915—TEACHERS AND STUDENTS
traveled miles to see it.
IN 1938—IT COMES TO YOU!
THE BIRTH OF A NATION
Available at last: 16mm sound or silent
STONE FILM LIBRARY, INC., 444 W. 56 St. NYC.

Figure 2.3. Front cover of the two excerpted versions of *The Birth of a Nation* released in 1942 by the International Marketing Corp. The titles of the films that would have been sold under this cover were *The Assassination of Lincoln* and *Civil War Battle Scenes. From the author's private collection.*

entertaining. The evidentiary nature of Griffith's footage as representative of what actually happened in the past is expanded on in the description of *The Assassination of Lincoln*: "The authentic story of one of the greatest tragedies in our history."

Although this text is part of the International Marketing Corp.'s sales pitch, it does hint at the ways that *The Birth of a Nation* was occasionally screened as a factual visualization of US history. For example, in February 1976, the film was shown at McMurry University in Abilene, Texas, as part of a film festival recounting the history of the country. *The Birth of a Nation* was the second film in the series, after *1776* (dir. Peter H. Hunt, 1972), and was used to depict the South's view of the Civil War.[28]

Of the two shorts, only *The Assassination of Lincoln* was discovered in the research for this chapter; a copy exists in the Herb Graff collection at the Yale Film Study Center. It recounts the main points of the scene from the arrival of the president at Ford's Theatre to Booth's escape. Because the excerpt is just over three and a half minutes, it appears to be cut down from the original length of the scene. The other noticeable alterations are the opening and closing titles, the former reading "The Assassination of Lincoln" and the latter "The End." For each, the font is generic and does not match the title card lifted from *The Birth of a Nation* or the other original intertitles found in the short. The added credits do not include other information such as the name of the distributor or a date of rerelease, suggesting these two excerpts were illicitly produced without the consent of the copyright holders: *The Birth of a Nation*'s producers, Roy and Harry Aitken.

As an example of how collectors would recirculate and transform the titles they collected, in 1947 David Bradley duped his personal copy of *Civil War Battle Scenes*, making six new copies for Theodore Huff's filmmaking class at New York University for an assignment in which the students had to reedit a preexisting film.[29]

Even more illegitimate seeming were the 8 mm and 16 mm versions of *The Birth of a Nation* "with original sound score" that were advertised by an unknown source in the classified ads of *Popular Photography* in 1948 and in 1949 issues of *Home Movies*. The only identifying characteristic of the company selling these versions was a post office box in Philadelphia.[30]

In 1953, Blackhawk Films released a nine-minute summary of the film with new narration called *Great Moments from The Birth of a Nation*. The short was released at a time when the home market was not large enough to support releasing full-length feature films. This cut-down version was a way for the then owners of the film, the Aitkens, to continue to financially profit

Figure 2.4. Personalized end credit added to a copy of *Great Moments from the Birth of a Nation*. Print from the Bradley, mss. *Courtesy of the Lilly Library, Indiana University, Bloomington.*

from *The Birth of a Nation*.[31] *Great Moments* will be examined in detail in the next part of this chapter.

Showing the ways that collectors left their imprint on films in their collection, the reel of this short in the Bradley collection has an end credit added by the collector noting to whom it belongs, not unlike an ex libris stamp in a rare book (fig. 2.4).

The twelve-reel, black-and-white print that Bradley purchased in 1955 is harder to source. An article in the November 1954 issue of *Home Movies* on ways to add music to home screenings of silent films mentions a twelve-reel version that was "available with records of the original organ score." Unfortunately, it does so without naming the company selling this version, but it does describe the print as one of the few silent films with added sound tracks that were then commercially available.[32]

That same year, Bradley attempted to buy a full-length print from the New Jersey company Movie Classics, but he was served notice from Harry Aitken, the copyright holder of the film at the time, that the sale was illegal.

Around the same time (the exact year is not known), actor and film collector John Griggs released a version on 16 mm to a select number of other collectors. His print of the film included a new score that Griggs produced

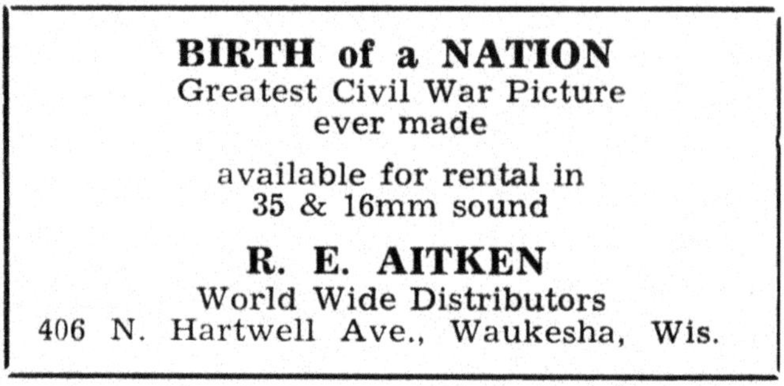

> ## BIRTH of a NATION
> Greatest Civil War Picture
> ever made
>
> available for rental in
> 35 & 16mm sound
>
> ## R. E. AITKEN
> World Wide Distributors
> 406 N. Hartwell Ave., Waukesha, Wis.

Figure 2.5. Advertisement for a version of the 1930 reissue of *The Birth of a Nation* marketed to schoolteachers by one of the film's original producers, Roy Aitken. Found on page 628 of the October 1962 issue of *Educational Screen*.

of improvisations based on historical songs and played on organ, piano, and drums. An undated letter from Everson to the curator of the George Eastman House film collection, James Card, describes the film's score in a sales pitch to the museum: "One of the best things about it is the spontaneous flavor. Before-hand, it was predetermined of course that the Clan [*sic*] call would be an oft-used motif, that 'The Perfect Song' would be used for Gish, and so on, but no definite cue-sheet was worked out. Johnny [Griggs] relayed instructions to Taubman [the organist Paul Taubman] via a microphone, and Taubman really seemed to get lost in the picture."[33]

Griggs's personal print of the film was included in the films that Yale University purchased from his estate in 1968, and which later became the genesis for the Yale Film Study Center.[34]

Roy E. Aitken, the film's producer, continued to rent it out on 35 mm and 16 mm in a sound version that was likely based on the 1930 sound reissue. A 1962 ad on page 628 of the October issue of *Educational Screen* shows that he was marketing it to teachers for classroom screenings. No direct evidence of Aitken selling the print to the home market has been uncovered; however, Ingmar Bergman gained permission from the rights holder to acquire a copy of *The Birth of a Nation* for his personal collection (fig. 2.5).[35]

In 1965, Blackhawk was selling an 8 mm black-and-white print of the film, as mentioned in the *New York Times* article discussed earlier in this chapter.[36] Around the same time, Minot Films was selling a silent version of the 1930 sound reissue on 8 mm.[37]

In August 1975, a ruling by the Second Circuit Court of Appeals on a lawsuit between film distributor Raymond Rohauer and television producer

Paul Killiam over the disputed copyright status of *The Birth of a Nation* declared the film to be in the public domain.[38] The ruling unleashed film distributors that had previously withdrawn home versions or were wary of releasing copies of the film due to the risk of a lawsuit from Rohauer. By the fall of that year, Thunderbird Films was selling 16 mm and Super 8 mm versions of the film in color for $600 and $200, respectively (which, after inflation, would be about $2,600 and $880 in 2016). Thunderbird also released a black-and-white version in 16 mm, Super 8, and 8 mm at the same time (fig. 2.6).[39] The color print from Thunderbird was sourced from a 35 mm print originally released in 1921 that had been tinted and toned. That print had been owned by collector Lawrence Landry and was later used as the source for the restoration of *The Birth of a Nation* that was made in the early 1990s by David Brownlow and David Gill of Photoplay Productions.[40] The next year, Thunderbird added a new sound track created by the company's owner, Tom Dunnahoo, to its 16 mm version of the film. The addition of the sound track increased the price by $100, making the cost of the color and sound version worth just under $3,000 in today's dollars. Reinforcing the complex exhibition and reissue history of the film theatrically, and how those multiple "original" versions shaped and were altered by companies selling the film to the home and nontheatrical market, Thunderbird also offered a 16 mm version of the 1940 reissue, not the first 1930 sound reissue.[41]

By 1976, Griggs Moviedrome, now operated by Robert Lee of the Essex Film Club after Griggs's death in 1967, was selling almost as wide an array of versions of *The Birth of a Nation* as Thunderbird. According to an ad on pages 46 and 47 of the summer 1976 issue of *Classic Film Collector,* the distributor was offering these products: 16 mm or Super 8 black-and-white silent prints; a 16 mm reduction print of the 1930 rerelease; *The Prologue to The Birth of the Nation*, an introduction by Griffith for the 1930 sound reissue; a trailer for the 1930 version with "a nondescript announcer reading inaccurate copy"; and a sound track of piano music on reel-to-reel or audiocassettes to accompany the silent version. Looking to differentiate their black-and-white version from the color copy available from Thunderbird, Griggs Moviedrome argued that its print was more authentic to the look of the initial theatrical experience of *The Birth of a Nation*. "There are no false color tones or tints added by printing on color stock, adding additional generations to the release prints [and thus degrading the photographic quality of the print], as we have kept it as close to the original as possible."

LEGALLY DECLARED PUBLIC DOMAIN!

NOW OWN A PRISTINE COLOR PRINT OF THE WORLD'S MOST DESIRED FILM!

REPRODUCED FROM THE ONLY 25mm COLOR REPRINT KNOWN. COLOR TINTED AND TONED - AS ORIGINALLY SHOWN!

FINEST QUALITY!   GUARANTEED!   13 REELS!

A THUNDERBIRD EXCLUSIVE!

16mm
Color
$600

16mm
Blk. & Wht.
$250

SUPER 8mm
Color on
Pre-mag
Stripe film
$200

SUPER 8mm
Blk. & Wht.
$100

STD 8mm
Blk. & Wht.
$100

D.W. GRIFFITH'S

"The BIRTH of a NATION"

A Picture With A Thousand Thrills

The picture that millions have seen again and again, that more millions will see; that you MUST see; that you are sure to want to see again even if you have already seen it once, or even twice, before.

Griffith's Classic Of The Screen

THUNDERBIRD FILMS
P.O. Box 65157
Los Angeles, Calif. 90065
Phone: 213-256-1634

Figure 2.6. Advertisement announcing the release of multiple versions of *The Birth of a Nation* from Thunderbird Films. Found on page x-5 of the Fall 1975 issue of *Classic Film Collector*.

In 1979, Blackhawk added a color version on Super 8, in silent and magnetic sound versions and running 158 minutes, to its existing line of black-and-white prints that it had been selling for a number of years.[42]

What Were the Great Moments from *The Birth of a Nation* According to *Great Moments from The Birth of a Nation*?

These multiple home and small gauge editions of *The Birth of a Nation* are an especially vibrant example of a business practice of Hollywood studios that Barbara Klinger describes as "recycling."[43] Aftermarkets such as television broadcasts, viewing in hotels and in airplanes, and various evolving home media formats offer production companies a way to extend the profitability of a title past its original theatrical run. As the history of nontheatrical and small gauge versions of *The Birth of a Nation* illustrates, recycling can also be a way for nonproducers, fans, and alternative modes of distribution to reuse what copyright holders have neglected to monetize. As more companies and individuals become involved with the recirculation of a film, and as distributors send the film into specialized screening spaces for specialized audiences with different forms of exhibition technologies, it undergoes a material transformation: 35 mm prints are reduced to 16 mm or Super 8, full-length films are excerpted, sound tracks are added, and so on. As Klinger states, "the history of home exhibition has been at the same time a history of textual transfiguration."[44] To better understand some of the alterations common to these nontheatrical circuits, this section presents a close analysis of the previously mentioned cut-down version titled *Great Moments from The Birth of a Nation*.

As previously stated, Blackhawk Films released *Great Moments* in 1953 under license from the copyright holders, Roy and Harry Aitken. Releasing a short version of *The Birth of a Nation* was a way to maximize the still-nascent market for commercially produced film prints. A shorter run time meant less film stock, which made the reel more affordable. Additionally, that it was not the complete feature lessened the chance of a home release cutting into any box office returns from a theatrical rerelease. This later became a fairly common practice for Hollywood studios in the 1960s and 1970s. Select titles would be edited down to anywhere from five to thirty minutes, most often with a condensed narrative, but sometimes focusing around a famous scene from a film. For example, in 1978 Universal 8, the small gauge division of Universal Studios, sold seventeen-minutes summaries of *Psycho* (dir. Alfred Hitchcock, 1960), *Frenzy* (dir. Alfred Hitchcock, 1972), and *Airport* (dir. George Seaton, 1970) while also offering a four-minute version of what were promoted as each films most spectacular scene, which was the shower scene, a rape and murder sequence, and a bomb explosion, respectively.[45]

However, *Great Moments from The Birth of a Nation* was neither a summary nor a selected scene from its parent film. Instead, the short was presented as a shared reminiscence of a decades-old but still important film both for the development of cinema and as a national event in its own right. The narrator led the audience through highlights of the film, recalling trivia about its production, the film's stars, and its cultural and artistic impact. In doing so, the narrator engenders the remembering of certain elements from the film, such as its romance, historical sweep, and daring cinematic achievements. However, the choice over which scenes were left out—the attempted rape of Flora by Gus and his subsequent murder, and Lynch's assault on Elsie—assists in the forgetting of some its most offensive racial stereotypes. As such, it acts almost as an updated defense of the film by its original producers. Despite its limited circulation primarily to collectors, *Great Moments from The Birth of a Nation* is an important piece of evidence in understanding the film's reception, and the continued debate that surrounded it, in the early 1950s.

The didactic nature of the nine-minute short, and its intent to safeguard *The Birth of a Nation*'s place in history, begins at its very beginning. Common to releases by Blackhawk Films, *Great Moments* begins with a contextualizing introductory text that describes the importance of the film. For *The Birth of a Nation* these are split into two parts. The first is economic and covers the size of its budget, its unprecedented ticket price, and its unprecedented box-office success. The second is aesthetic offering praise for Griffith's direction and Billy Bitzer's cinematography.

The main body of the short is a selection of nine clips organized around the topic of the "many different reasons" audiences "who saw *The Birth of a Nation* back in the silent days" would still remember it in 1953. The first is a nostalgic appreciation of the film's stars starting out with Lillian Gish and Henry Walthall. While the narrator's text is limited to naming the two actors and their roles, the footage depicts the two in a romantic embrace; the short regularly relies on the visuals of the film to rehabilitate its reputation with only slight prompting from the narrator. *Great Moments* continues this section with a focus on two other actors: Mae Marsh as Flora, or the Little Sister, and Wallace Reid as Jeff. For both, it is the fact they soon went to fame after their appearances in *The Birth of the Nation* that the narrator reminds viewers of, not anything to do about the plot of the film itself. In fact, it is during the segment on Reid that the disparity between the new narration and original footage becomes most apparent. While the voiceover mournfully recalls Reid's "untimely and tragic passing in the early twenties" the clip from *The Birth of a Nation* show his character almost gleefully engaging in violence against the men in the saloon that are hiding Gus from the posse looking for vengeance.

The next segment of *Great Moments* moves from the film's actors to the formal elements of the original. As the narrator states, "Many remember the film for its magnificent camera work. Such scenes as these were striking innovations for their time and had a profound effect on the photographic development of the motion picture." The shot under discussion starts with a medium shot of a mother and children huddled together as the camera pans to the right reveal a battle scene in the distance, before panning back to the family.

In the following section, the theme of the film's depiction of the Civil War becomes the focus. According to the narrator, "Many Hollywood directors, even today, feel that in the battle scenes Griffith achieved a realism and effectiveness that has never been excelled."

The next two segments focus on *The Birth of a Nation*'s use of male melodrama through showing the Civil War's effects on soldiers. One focuses on the impact an unknown extra supposedly had on the film's original audiences. According to *Great Moments*, "One of the most famous scenes in *The Birth of a Nation* was this one at a makeshift military hospital in Washington where a moonstruck sentry cast a wistful glance at Lillian Gish. Thousands of letters were written asking for the name of this extra but he had vanished from the Hollywood scene." The other follows the Little Colonel's "return home only to find the once beautiful and gay Piedmont. His family almost reduced to a state of want."

This is followed by two sections on the film's ability to represent, faithfully according to its narrator, important moments from American history. These are the Confederacy's surrender to Grant by Lee at the Appomattox Court House and Lincoln's assassination at the Ford Theater. Besides signaling the historical veracity and accuracy of these scenes, *Great Moments* again focuses on the actors that went on to become well-known actors and directors, including Donald Crisp as Grant and Raoul Walsh as John Wilkes Booth.

Figure 2.7. Closing title card of the 1953 short produced by Blackhawk Films, *Great Moments from The Birth of a Nation*. Print from the Bradley, mss. *Courtesy of the Lilly Library, Indiana University, Bloomington.*

The final two sections of *Great Moments* move to scenes from the second half of *The Birth of a Nation*. While explicitly acknowledging the controversy surrounding the original film, if only briefly, the short has the effect of amplifying the racist messages of Griffith's feature. It addresses then quickly erases the debates over *The Birth of a Nation*. The penultimate segment of *Great Moments* covers the scene in the South Carolina statehouse with the voiceover, "Also to be remembered was the coming of the carpet baggers and with them a virtual state of anarchy in South Carolina and much of the South. The mulatto Lieutenant Governor of South Carolina, played by George Siegmann, led the carpet bagging legislature that created all sorts of indignities for the white minority." As the shot fades on the black politician's impropriety in the state capitol building, there is a cut to a rider calling the hidden Ku Klux Klan out of the woods. Visually the short film ends with the ride of the Klan. The dialogue spoken over the Klan members riding furiously on horseback is worth quoting in full for the way it conflates film history and national history, and southern White racism with national patriotism (fig. 2.7).

And here in the birth of the Ku Klux Klan, the South waged a new revolution and *The Birth of a Nation* got its most spectacular and its most controversial ingredients. This great film was adapted from *The Clansmen* by Thomas Dixon. At a special showing on the night of February 20th, 1915, as the final scene faded out, Dixon shouted to Griffith, "*The Clansmen* is too tame a title. Let's call it *The Birth of a Nation!*" And as *The Birth of a Nation* it opened at the Liberty Theater in New York on March 6, 1915. *The Birth of a Nation*, on the way to becoming the most famous motion picture of all time.

Collectors' Views on *The Birth of a Nation*

Great Moments relied on a nostalgic appeal to sell a significantly shortened version of Griffith's film to the limited home market that existed at the time. The narrator's use of the second person plural to address the audience— "Those of you . . . " and "Some of you . . . "—allows for a reconstruction of the type of viewer Blackhawk and the Aitkens imagined might be watching the short. Based on the "great moments" the shorts replays and comments on for its audience, the viewer was envisioned as a white person old enough to have seen *The Birth of a Nation* in the silent era and who, almost forty years later, wanted to relive the excitement and spectacle of Griffith's film as a foundational work of cinematic art and a mass media sensation. It is easy to imagine, looking back at this short film from 2016, that some reactionary viewers might have seen *Great Moments* as fulfilling a revanchist dream, where the riding of a previous version of the Klan acted as a model for groups fighting to maintain a repressive culture of Jim Crow laws against the burgeoning civil rights movement.

But did this imagined viewer of *Great Moments* match the collectors who owned the short, or other nontheatrical versions of *The Birth of a Nation*? In some ways, yes. Most film collectors at the time were male, white, adult, and were film buffs interested in studying and rewatching the development of the cinematic art form. But what about agreeing with the argument presented in *Great Moments*? Can we assume it represents collectors' opinions on the film as an artistic achievement, cultural force, and purveyor of antiblack sentiments? Could they have, perhaps, purchased the short film as it was the only, legally, available version of the feature for the home market at the time? Could they have disagreed with the short's message, even while appreciating, if in a complicated manner, Griffith's film? To widen this series of questions out, does ownership of a cultural product imply a shared worldview? Or does collecting act to suture the ideologies of the collector and the producer? To align this inquiry with the questions animating the larger reevaluation of *The Birth of a Nation* at its centenary and beyond, why the continued preserving, restoring, exhibiting, repackaging, and purchasing of a film that worked to cement racist stereotypes into the core visual language of cinema?

Based on the massive popularity of the film during its initial release and subsequent rereleases and its status as the origin point for feature filmmaking in America, it is no surprise that collectors often expressed strong praise for the film. For example, in 1972, a collector refused to sell his copy of the film even though it had reached a higher monetary value due to being removed from the market because of the copyright struggles over the film that lasted from 1965 to 1975. "He considers the epic probably the greatest movie ever filmed despite the controversy over its scenes depicting slavery and the Ku Klux Klan."[46] That same year, another film collector called it "his favorite film of those he owns." This second collector justified his appreciation of the film based on its long-term box office success, the recent Academy Award presented to Lillian Gish, and the accolades from scholars and film critics.[47]

Other collectors were more critical of the film. The television screenwriter Samuel Peebles wrote a monthly column on film collecting for the journal *Films in Review* from 1965 until 1977. He regularly offered advice to collectors on how to find film prints, how to avoid violating copyright laws, and the best way to screen old films for one's friends and family. In a November 1976 column, Peebles laid out his theory on what constitutes "an ideal or representative film collection." He argues, "If you seriously collect old movies, there are many you *should* have not only for study but to screen for others interested in the history of films" (emphasis in the original). This suggests a dispassionate, rational, and studious approach to collecting films. Under Peebles's selection process, one would collect films based on their reputation and cultural significance. To understand cinema, one would have certain types of important films regardless of individual opinions. Film history happened, and a refined collection reflects the important milestones, advances, and filmmakers of cinema.

However, collecting according to this model does allow for a degree of individual choice when choosing a title that acts as a synecdoche for a larger filmmaking era, style, or oeuvre. As Peebles states, "If possible, choose one title to represent a particular thing: e.g., if I were limited to one film by

D. W. Griffith, I'd choose *Intolerance*. It holds much of his greatness, and though not a financial success, it is a recognized classic; less controversial, even today, than *The Birth of a Nation*."[48] A serious film collector needs a Griffith, but it does not need to be *The Birth of a Nation*. Peebles does not expand on the controversial nature of *The Birth of a Nation* or his discomfort with the film. Yet he implies that building a film collection is a personalized act of canonization that is a negotiation between common assumptions about film history—"greatness" and "classic"—and present-day politics and taste. An ideal film collection must acknowledge the past but is not entirely bound by it; collections are built to address current standards and to screen for current audiences. The repression of African Americans and promotion of the Ku Klux Klan in *The Birth of a Nation*, in Peebles's view, removed it from automatic inclusion into his collection.

Collector and repertory theater owner John Hampton took an alternative approach to *The Birth of a Nation*. As the co-owner and programmer of the Silent Movie Theatre in Los Angeles from 1942 to 1979, Hampton played an important part in keeping silent films in the public view before the rise of videotape. Hampton supplied the films, which played for week-long runs, from his extensive film collection, projected the films himself, and supplied the musical accompaniment from his collection of 78 rpm phonographs. The Silent Movie Theatre housed repertory screenings put on by Cinefamily until its closure in 2017, and Hampton's collection of rare films, which includes a number of unique prints of otherwise lost silent features, is owned by the Packard Humanities Institute, one of the major backers of film preservation in the United States.

Hampton regularly screened his personal print of *The Birth of a Nation* at his theater to large audiences. It is the first title in a listing of "the theater's staple presentations" in a short 1980 update on the Silent Movie Theatre in the *Los Angeles Times*. (The other staples included *Intolerance* [dir. D. W. Griffith, 1916], *King of Kings* [dir. Cecil B. De Mille, 1927], the Clara Bow vehicle *The Plastic Age* [dir. Wesley Ruggles, 1925], and *Sparrows* [dir. William Beaudine, 1926].)[49] It was also described as one of the theater's "consistent hits" in 1977.[50] The film played for a week run starting on Wednesday, June 28, 1967, preceded by a "Laurel and Hardy patriotic short."[51] *The Birth of a Nation* is included in a 1966 article in Hampton's response to a reporter's question about the theater's "biggest favorites—box office wise?" The collector answers, "Those that were popular in the old days seem to remain popular."[52] Griffith's film takes the lead in a description of "Mr. Hampton's choicest items" in an article from 1960.[53] In another article from the same year, Hampton recalls the popularity of *The Birth of a Nation* in 1948, the first time he publicly screened it. "'Why people lined up clear to Melrose Ave. [more than 500 feet away] to see the first show,' he says."[54] An article appearing in the *New York Times* in October 1948 describes that run as "drawing vast audiences" and doing "turnaway business." Indicating, though not explicitly naming, the protests that regularly accompanied public screenings of *The Birth of a Nation*, according to the journalist, "no untoward incidents marred the week's run."[55]

That same 1948 article from the *New York Times* provides insight into Hampton's view on the film and his justification for screening it on what became a yearly basis. His mission for the theater was to create a shrine for silent cinema, but in a way that countered the more serious-minded, high-art approach to screening silent films developed by the Museum of Modern Art and other film societies.[56] Hampton was "much more interested in recreating a program of film entertainment as it was enjoyed some twenty-five or thirty years ago, complete with a two-reel comedy, a serial, a cartoon and a feature picture."[57] However, recreating the exhibition strategies of the past did not automatically equal reconstructing the ideological and racist inflections of the films themselves. If Hampton's project was built on a nostalgia for filmmaking before the arrival of sound, he argued that it was possible to separate the cinematic style from the message when rescreening old films. As a supporter of the Committee on Racial Equality, Hampton stated that, while he disagreed with the virulently racist stereotypes in *The Birth of a Nation*, "silent films which used such types should be viewed with intelligent understanding of their place in film history." Further, he believed his audience, as silent film aficionados, was sophisticated enough to appreciate Griffith's artistry while categorically rejecting the director's worldview. However, Hampton expressed uncertainty whether general audiences would be able to do the same, implicitly pointing out the differences between private or semipublic screenings and the manner in which a mass audience, less educated about film history, might be more susceptible to its propagandistic appeals.[58]

This ability to bifurcate a film's artistry and ideology was central to collector and historian William K. Everson's explanation for screening *The Birth of a Nation*. As a prolific author of books and articles about silent cinema, Westerns, and B pictures; a collector who regularly interacted with leading film archives; a professor at New York University and the School of Visual Art; and programmer with the New York–based Theodore Huff Memorial Film Society, Everson grappled with the place of *The Birth of a Nation* in film history and the value and purpose of showing it decades after its release. His unpublished notes based on the lectures he gave on the film around 1972 condense his arguments for doing so. Interestingly, these notes themselves reflect the split between cinema as form and as message that he argues for, because Everson wrote notes only on the section of his lecture on this justification for screening and studying the film and not on the opening part of his lecture about its "technical and artistic aspects."[59]

Everson based his argument around four major points. First, while conceding that *The Birth of a Nation* appeared racist to viewers in 1972, Everson contended it was more representative of a generalized "condescension" that Griffith, as a Southern white man inculcated in what were the norms of white supremacy at the time, felt toward African Americans across his films rather than the outright "race-hatred" expressed by Dixon in *The Clansman* and *The Leopard Spots*.[60] For the former, Everson points to the faithful servant motif regularly employed by Griffith as proof of the director's patronizing view of African Americans; for the latter, Everson argues that Griffith largely replaced Dixon's "bigoted diatribes which seem to exist only to dispense racial hatred" with moments of cinematic spectacle and grandeur.[61]

Second, Everson argued that Hollywood had made "many, *many* films from all periods (and dealing with races other than blacks) that have been FAR more racist than *The Birth of a Nation*" (emphasis in the original). According to Everson, movies such as *Square Shooter* (dir. David Selman, 1935), *Golden Dawn* (dir. Ray Enright, 1929), and *The Mask of Fu Manchu* (dir. Charles Brabin, 1932) had not received the same degree of opprobrium as Griffith's film because they were not reissued and screened as regularly and were not as integral to the common assumptions about the development of the medium.[62] While this line of defense may not be convincing—arguing the other films are more harmful does not necessarily vindicate Griffith's representation of black America—it does, perhaps unintentionally on Everson's part, raise the larger issue of what it means to be a fan, cinephile, or collector of an art form like Hollywood cinema, which so regularly relied on racial stereotypes. I raise this point not to accuse this specialized film culture of collectors, but to suggest the ways that studying the nontheatrical reception and private ownership of *The Birth of a Nation* opens up a discussion of the politics of collecting, and also of film archiving and film history.

Everson's third justification for screening and studying *The Birth of a Nation* revolved around the power of Griffith's filmmaking over its original audiences, who were unaccustomed to cinema's visual storytelling. Everson states: "The impact of the film at the time was incredible, since it brought a whole new language with it; it was as though audiences that had known literature only through comic books were suddenly introduced to the works of Tolstoy and Dickens. Audiences were swept away by the dynamism of the film, and didn't understand that film can be cut so that shot A plus shot B can lead to a shot C that may have a totally different meaning."[63] Although this argument relies on an assertion that historical viewers were naive and that current spectators are more cultivated, a move based perhaps more on assumption than historical evidence, Everson's point seems to be that the film would have been less controversial if the original audiences had been more media literate. If they had not succumbed to Griffith's visual power, if they had been able to understand the intent behind cinematic signifiers such as a pan, iris, or cut, they would have been able to discount the director's social message and historical revisionism while appreciating his artistic skill.

Despite describing present-day viewers as sophisticated readers of cinematic technique, Everson still proposed that the film should be screened only when properly contextualized. This is his fourth justification for exhibiting it: that it be presented in controlled settings. Everson disapproved of *The Birth of a Nation* being "shown today for racial purposes, or even commercially where [its] influence would be widespread." Instead, it, and other offensive films need to be "studied dispassionately as records of racist attitudes of another day." This is possible by adopting an "aloof" model of spectatorship, where a viewer, informed by the historical circumstances of a film's production and reception, can, almost paradoxically, sidestep the cultural, political, and racial messages of a film to examine its artistic intent.[64] This act of knowing and then placing aside allows a viewer, in Everson's postulation, to escape the emotional influence of a film. According to Everson, film studies provides a defense for the viewer and defangs a film of its ideological power by helping students understand how a filmmaker might employ cinematic techniques and style to communicate, persuade, and propagandize.

Figure 2.8. Advertisement placed before a streaming version of *The Birth of a Nation* on Hulu. *Screen capture by author.*

Conclusion: What's So Important about the Development of Film Art?

After almost forty years of home video on VHS, DVD, Blu-ray, and online streaming, the idea of films in the home is no longer news. *The Birth of a Nation* today is easier to see, in better-quality and more faithful versions, than at any time since its original release in 1915. After being released on VHS as early as 1980, *The Birth of a Nation* is currently available on DVD from multiple distributors, including Kino, VCI Entertainment, two versions by Reel Classic DVD, Image Entertainment, and many budget companies dealing with films in the public domain. It is currently on Blu-ray in different restored versions from three companies: Kino, Eureka, and the British Film Institute's home media imprint. Additionally, as of February 2016, the film can be found uploaded on YouTube by more than twenty different users, though the quality and provenance of many of these is questionable at best. And *The Birth of a Nation* can be streamed on Hulu, in a restored version from Kino. The streaming platform monetizes viewing by selling ads before the film, which when reviewed in researching this chapter was, through the random serendipity of the algorithms controlling online advertisements, a 2015 ad for Gain detergent (fig. 2.8).

Equally common is the idea that the film's artistry can be understood, and even appreciated, in spite of its role in defining and amplifying black stereotypes on film. In a recent online article describing the restoration of *The Birth of a Nation* on Blu-ray, a conservator involved in a recent home media release of the film argues that a century of debates over the nature of the film and the impact of its racist messaging should not stop modern-day audiences "from acknowledging the part it played in the development of the American film industry, or, crucially, the rise of cinema as art." Moreover, "the only way to fully appreciate what it was that so electrified audiences in 1915 is to actually see the film—and to see it properly presented. Yet since the advent of sound there have been few opportunities to see *Birth* as its maker originally intended."[65] The author is implicitly critiquing the silent, reedited, black-and-white, and poor-quality versions that circulated on small gauge film prints in the mid- and late twentieth century, and which this article has attempted to place with the larger distribution and reception history of *The Birth of a Nation*. Without a doubt, this current restoration is a feat of archival, editorial, artistic, and technical skill, expertly building off an earlier restoration in the early 1990s as well as reflecting in-depth research on the original nitrate prints and negatives held at the Library of Congress.

However, the question I would like to close on is this: When a collector saves a rare print, or an archivist preserves a film, or a film programmer screens a title from the past, and the intent is to create an experience something like that which a historical audience would have experienced, which audience from the past are we talking about, and who might we be ignoring? If *The Birth of a Nation* electrified some audience members in 1915, it clearly shocked others. Can a film be restored and exhibited to recreate both responses?

ANDY UHRICH is a PhD candidate in Communication and Culture at Indiana University and film archivist at the Indiana University Libraries Moving Images Archive.

Notes

1. Jacob Deschin, "Classics on Home Screen," *New York Times*, February 14, 1965, X23.

2. See Melvyn Stokes, *D. W. Griffith's* The Birth of a Nation: *A History of "the Most Controversial Motion Picture of All Time"* (New York: Oxford University Press, 2007); J. B. Kaufman, "*The Birth of a Nation*: Non-Archival Sources," in *The Griffith Project*, ed. Paolo

Church Usai, vol. 8, *Films Produced in 1914–1915* (London: British Film Institute), 107–112; and John Cuniberti, *The Birth of a Nation: A Formal Shot-by-Shot Analysis Together with Microfiche* (Woodbridge, CT: Research Productions, 1979).

3. For more on earlier efforts to market cinema to the home, see Ben Singer, "Early Home Cinema and the Edison Home Projecting Kinetoscope," *Film History* 2 (1988): 37–69; Moya Luckett, "'Filming the Family': Home Movie Systems and the Domestication of Spectatorship," *Velvet Light Trap* 36 (1995): 21–32; and Haidee Wasson, "Electric Homes! Automatic Movies! Efficient Entertainment! Domesticity and the 16 mm Projector in the 1920s," *Cinema Journal* 48, no. 4 (Fall 2009): 1–21.

4. Deschin, "Classics on Home Screen."

5. For an in-depth discussion of the construction of the figure of the serious amateur filmmaker, see Charles Tepperman, *Amateur Cinema: The Rise of North American Moviemaking, 1923–1960* (Berkeley: University of California Press, 2014).

6. Greg Waller, "Free Talking Picture—Every Farmer Is Welcome: Non-theatrical Film and Everyday Life in Rural America During the 1930s," in *Going to the Movies: Hollywood and the Social Experience of Cinema*, ed. Richard Maltby, Melvyn Stokes, and Robert C. Allen (Exeter, UK: University of Exeter Press, 2007), 266.

7. Leah M. Kerr, "Collectors' Contributions to Archiving Early Black Film," *Black Camera* 5, no. 1 (2013): 274–284; Jacqueline Stewart, "Discovering Black Film History: Tracing the Tyler, Texas Black Film Collection," *Film History* 23, no. 2 (2011): 147–173.

8. Deschin, "Classics on Home Screen."

9. William K. Everson, Announcing a New Film Society at the School of Visual Arts, 1967, Series I: Correspondence, Subseries A: Alphabetical, William K. Everson Collection, George Amberg Memorial Film Study Center, New York University.

10. William K. Everson quoted in Bruce Goldstein, "Adventures of the Huff Society," *Film Comment* 33, no. 1 (January/February 1997): 71.

11. "Film Events: 'Citizen Kane' to Be Shown," *San Mateo Times*, July 14, 1971, 38.

12. "Hill Theatre Group Offers Diverse Summer Programming," *Potrero View*, July 1, 1971, 3.

13. Garry Wills, "American Past of Racial Violence Should Be Aired," *Indianapolis News*, December 25, 1970, 13.

14. Tom Rice, *White Robes, Silver Screens: Movies and the Making of the Ku Klux Klan* (Bloomington: Indiana University Press, 2015), 3.

15. Some of these screenings are mentioned by Janet Staiger, Melvyn Stokes, and Frank Beaver in Janet Staiger, *Interpreting Films: Studies in the Historical Reception of American Cinema* (Princeton, NJ: Princeton University Press, 1992), 139 and 152–153; Melvyn Stokes, *American History through Hollywood Film: From the Revolution to the 1960s* (New York: Bloomsbury, 2013), 259n37; and Frank Beaver, "A Film That Won't Go Away," *Michigan Today*, February 15, 2015, http://michigantoday.umich.edu/a-film-that-wont-go-away/.

16. Rick Martinez and Jan Cleveland, "KKK Alive and Well in the Inland Empire," *San Bernardino County Sun*, June 25, 1978, 1 and 3.

17. "Klan Holds Service Near Davis' Birthplace," *Kokomo Tribune*, June 5, 1978, 13.

18. "300 Protestors Battle Police as Klan Sees 'Racist' Film," *Des Moines Register*, July 31, 1978, 1.

19. "National and International News in Brief," *Philadelphia Inquirer*, July 9, 1979, 3; Eric Hodge, Rebecca Martinez, and Phoebe Judge, "Criminal: Birth of a Massacre," *WUNC* 91.5, May 20, 2016, http://wunc.org/post/criminal-birth-massacre#stream/o.

20. Information on the failed 1954 sale is from David Bradley to William Donnachie, February 2, 1954, Series III: Correspondence, Box 94, William Donnachie: 1951–1966 folder,

Bradley mss., 1902–1997, Lilly Library, Indiana University. The rest is from Series XIV: Miscellaneous, Box 126: Distribution records, index cards, A–G, of the same collection.

21. Dorothy E. Cook and Eva Cotter Rahbek-Smith, *Educational Film Catalog* (New York: H. W. Wilson, 1937), 122.

22. "Birth of a Nation in Court Again," *Afro-American*, July 27, 1940, 13.

23. Dino Everette, February 10, 2010 (10:41 p.m.), comment on "What's missing from my 'Birth of a Nation' print?" *8mm Forum*, February 8, 2013, http://8mmforum.film-tech.com /cgi-bin/ubb/ultimatebb.cgi?ubb=get_topic;f=1;t=007902#000000.

24. "Film Group Announces New Program Series: Museum Library Compiles Film Series Four for National Showing," *Washington Post*, July 16, 1937, 13.

25. "Contacting the Circulating Film and Video Library," *MoMA*, 2016, https://www .moma.org/momaorg/shared/pdfs/docs/learn/pricelist_2018.pdf.

26. Stone Film Library, Advertisement in *Educational Screen*, February 1938, 60. See pages 246 and 259 of Stokes, *D. W. Griffith's* The Birth of a Nation, for a discussion of how the Stone version was protested by the NAACP in New York State and was the source of a lawsuit from Thomas Dixon against the Stone Film Library.

27. International Marketing Corp., Advertisement in *Home Movies*, June 1942, 242.

28. "McMurry Film Festival Selections Trace Growth, Changes of Country," *Abilene Reporter-News*, February 8, 1976, 24. Based on the description of the print to be screened, it is likely the festival projected the Thunderbird print that was released in the fall of 1975.

29. Theodore Huff to David Bradley, September 18, 1947, Series III. Correspondence, Box 95, Theodore Huff, 1947–1953 folder, Bradley mss., 1902–1997, Lilly Library, Indiana University.

30. Unknown company, Classified advertisement in *Popular Photography*, October 1948, 257; Unknown company, Classified advertisement in *Home Movies*, February 1949, 108.

31. Telephone interview with David Shepard, November 11, 2015.

32. "Old Time Movies with Sound," *Home Movies*, November 1954, 418 and 436.

33. William K. Everson to James Card, May 25, no year, Series I: Correspondence, Subseries A: Alphabetical, James Card folder, William K. Everson Collection, George Amberg Memorial Film Study Center, New York University.

34. "Actor John Griggs' 207 Vintage Print Nucleus of Yale Collection," *Variety*, April 10, 1968, 24.

35. Geoffrey Macnab, *Ingmar Bergman: The Life and Films of the Last Great European Director* (New York: I. B. Tauris, 2009), 116.

36. For a look at the other films Blackhawk was selling in addition to *The Birth of a Nation* at the time, see Blackhawk Films, Advertisement in *8mm Collector*, Spring 1966, 28.

37. James E. Ennis, "The 8 mm Feature Part 2: An Annotated Listing of 8 mm Silent Feature Films," *Classic Film Collector* (Winter 1973): 20.

38. For more on this lawsuit and the convoluted rights of the film, see Anthony Slide, *American Racist: The Life and Films of Thomas Dixon* (Lexington: University Press of Kentucky, 2004), 203–208; Stokes, *D. W. Griffith's* The Birth of a Nation, 262; and Bosley Crowther, "An Accounting Is Sought on *The Birth of a Nation*, *New York Times*, January 4, 1965, 35.

39. Thunderbird Films, Advertisement in *Classic Film Collector*, Fall 1975, x–5.

40. David Gill, "*The Birth of a Nation*: Orphan or Pariah?" *Griffithiana* 20, no. 60/61 (October 1997): 17, 19.

41. Thunderbird Films, Advertisement in *Film Collectors World*, September 1976, 26; Scott Vernon, "Pirates of the Film Kingdom," *Los Angeles Times*, April 23, 1976, E22.

42. *Blackhawk Film Digest: May 1979 Catalog*, May 1979, 48.

43. Barbara Klinger, "Cinema's Shadow: Reconsidering Non-theatrical Exhibition," in *Going to the Movies: Hollywood and the Social Experience of Cinema*, ed. Richard Maltby, Melvyn Stokes, and Robert C. Allen (Exeter, UK: University of Exeter Press, 2007), 276.

44. Klinger, "Cinema's Shadow," 281.

45. Universal 8, *1978 Super 8mm and 16mm Sound and 16mm Sound and Silent Catalogue*, Universal City Studios, 1977, 3, 9–10.

46. Myra Setliff, "Lubbock Man's Collection of Old Films Outstrips Those on Late, Late Shows," *Lubbock Avalanche-Journal*, January 11, 1972, 5.

47. George Markell, "'Rog' Gonda to Show Oldtime Films: Silent Movie Era Returning," *Salem News*, October 28, 1971, 10.

48. Samuel A. Peebles, "Films on 8 and 16," *Films in Review*, November 1976, 560.

49. "Silent Movie," *Los Angeles Times*, December 30, 1980, H9.

50. Philip K. Scheuer, "Silent Films Only: Horse and Buggy Movie House," *Los Angeles Times*, February 22, 1977, F1.

51. "Movies: Opening," *Los Angeles Times*, June 25, 1967, 5. The Laurel and Hardy short might have been *The Tree in the Test Tube*, which was produced in 1942 by the U.S. Department of Agriculture to promote the war effort. The film can be viewed on the National Archives YouTube channel at https://www.youtube.com/watch?v=vyY4W-ETC_Y.

52. Philip K. Scheuer, "All Is Not Quiet on the Silent Movie Theater Front," *Los Angeles Times*, April 10, 1966, B3.

53. Gladwin Hill, "Silent-Film Buff Shows His Wares: John Hampton of Hollywood Discusses Collection and Theatre He Operates," *New York Times*, November 21, 1960, 33.

54. "Museum of Films: Silent Films Glorified at Old-Time Theater," *Los Angeles Times*, November 28, 1960, 10.

55. Elihu Winer, "A Reminder of the Past in Present Day Hollywood," *New York Times*, October 24, 1978, X5.

56. For more information on the Museum of Modern Art's attempts to rehabilitate popular silent cinema as a high culture art form, see Haidee Wasson, *Museum Movies: The Museum of Modern Art and the Birth of Art Cinema* (Berkeley: University of California Press, 2005).

57. Winer, "A Reminder of the Past."

58. Ibid.

59. William K. Everson, *The Birth of a Nation*: Some Random Thoughts on Its Impact and Its Racial Attitudes, 1972, Series VIII: Unpublished Manuscripts, Subseries A: By William K. Everson, William K. Everson Collection, George Amberg Memorial Film Study Center, New York University, 1.

60. Ibid., 2.

61. Ibid. Melvyn Stokes expands on and critiques this line of defense of the film by Everson and other critics, including Richard Schickel, on pages 282 and 283 of *D. W. Griffith's The Birth of a Nation*.

62. Everson, *The Birth of a Nation*: Some Random Thoughts, 4.

63. Ibid.

64. Ibid., 5.

65. Patrick Stanbury, "*The Birth of a Nation*: Controversial Classic Gets a Definitive New Restoration," *Brenton Film*, February 17, 2016, http://www.brentonfilm.com/articles/the -birth-of-a-nation-controversial-classic-gets-a-definitive-new-restoration.

3

D. W. GRIFFITH'S *THE BIRTH OF A NATION*

Transnational and Historical Perspectives

Melvyn Stokes

O N February 8, 1915, Harry Aitken and D. W. Griffith founded the
Epoch Producing Corporation to handle the distribution of *The Birth
of a Nation*. The board of directors of the new company met in the middle
of March to decide how to distribute the film, which was already playing
to capacity audiences at the Liberty Theater in New York. Weighing the
alternatives of selling off the distribution rights in some areas and opt-
ing to "road-show" the film themselves, they worked out a compromise:
they would organize road shows to screen the film in major cities, potentially creaming off the most profitable sector of the market, and sell off
the distribution rights in areas such as California, some western states,
and New England outside Boston.[1] One or both of these strategies could
be applied to countries outside the United States. From the beginning,
Griffith and his collaborators were intent on capturing an international as
well as a national market for *The Birth of a Nation*. In neighboring Canada, Epoch adopted a strategy of selling off distribution rights. In July
1915, the company signed an agreement with the Central Canada Exhibition Association to show the film for a week (September 13–20) in the
capital, Ottawa.[2] On September 9, the company agreed to a ten-year deal
that would give exclusive rights to the Basil Corporation to exhibit the film
in "All the Provinces of Canada, and also Newfoundland, and Alaska."[3]

Shortly afterward, total income from Canada was already estimated to have reached $40,000.[4]

Reception in Canada

The reception of the film in Canada was heavily influenced by geographical propinquity to the United States. This had two main consequences in respect of *The Birth of a Nation*. First, many Canadians were already familiar, from coverage of US news in their own media or from US newspapers circulating across the border, with the protests against the movie in the United States. Second, there was already a sizable African community in Canada—a reflection of the fact that, before the Thirteenth Amendment in 1865, Canada had been the northernmost destination on the Underground Railroad for slaves escaping from the American South,[5] and of the post–Civil War "great migration" of African Americans from the rural South and Southwest northward in search of farming work or jobs in industrial cities.[6]

In 1915, however, African Canadians were under pressure for various reasons. They were poorer than their white compatriots and, for the most part, lived segregated lives. The migration of US blacks to Canada in the preceding decade and a half—although numerically quite small[7]—had prompted a range of measures, both official and unofficial, to prevent such immigration.[8] The outbreak of World War I in August 1914 underlined just how much discrimination there was against the black community: there was strong white resistance to the idea of blacks in the armed forces. J. R. B. Whitney, proprietor and editor of the Toronto black newspaper *The Canadian Observer*, launched a campaign to persuade Prime Minister Robert Borden to accept black enlistment in the army and militia.[9] It was against this background that *The Birth of a Nation* arrived in Canada; it must have appeared as yet another deliberate insult to African Canadians. One of them, having seen the movie in Ottawa, alerted J. R. B. Whitney and the readers of his paper to the impending arrival of the film in their city. The film's "object," the writer declared in a telegram of September 16, was "entirely [the] creation of race feeling and embitterment" and "the moral effect [of the film's screening] could engender nothing but race prejudice and hatred."[10]

When *The Birth of a Nation* opened at the Royal Alexander Theatre in Toronto on September 20, 1915, W. E. Cuthbert, the theater manager, endeavored to convince the local black community and other critics of the film that they had been misinformed about its true character. "I wish to state that about 500 feet of this film drama," he told the *Toronto Daily Star*, "is devoted to the present-day negroes, showing their school, industries, etc. and how it would be hard for the South to get along without them, and also showing them to be honorable and respected citizens."[11] It is difficult to believe that any version of *The Birth of a Nation* ever included anything like this. What seems to have happened is that the Basil Corporation, to dilute Canadian opposition to the film, had arranged to show the so-called Hampton Epilogue after *The Birth of a Nation*. This short film, titled *The New Era* and shot at the black Hampton Institute in Virginia, had already been shown with *The Birth of a Nation* in several cities in the United States. It foregrounded the social, economic, and educational progress made by African Americans since the Reconstruction era.[12]

Local protest against the screening of *The Birth of a Nation* in Canada seems to have been almost entirely black-led. On September 17, 1915, indeed, a story appeared in the *Toronto Daily Star* under the headline "Colored People Protest: Ask Province to Stop 'Birth of a Nation.'"[13] That same day, A. W. Hackley, the former secretary and now a presiding elder of the African Methodist Episcopal Church, announced that he planned to go to the provincial government to protest the film, insisting that it "engenders racial strife and that, in unmodified form, it is not good for any race to see."[14] Hackley was part of a delegation appointed by a mass meeting at the AME Church to lobby the provincial authorities to ban the film. The meeting had been opened by J. R. B. Whitney of *The Canadian Observer*, who had published an editorial condemning the film as "a deliberate and skilful bit of treachery . . . [that] teaches to hate, as well as despise."[15] Another member of the appointed delegation was William Peyton Hubbard. The son of slaves who had escaped Virginia to reach Canada by the Underground Railroad, Hubbard was the first black person to be elected to any public office in Canada, serving for many years on the Toronto Council and, from 1898 to 1908, on the city's powerful Board of Control.[16] The difficulty Hackley, Whitney, Hubbard, and their allies faced in calling for the film's suppression was that the Ontario Board of Censors had already passed it for public exhibition. Chief censor George E. Armstrong explained that the film portrayed "one period of history in the United States, with which period neither England nor Canada had any part." From the perspective of the two countries that were now at war with Germany, the censors had found that there were "no objectionable features from the national standpoint."[17] Despite the protests from the black community, *The Birth of a Nation* was apparently shown to sold-out audiences in Toronto. It returned to the city, observes Paul S. Moore, "for three more weeks at Christmas 1915, again in August 1916, and many times more in the future."[18]

Similar protests by African Canadians took place outside Toronto. In the prairie provinces to the west, racial issues were already salient as a consequence of immigration from the United States—particularly from Oklahoma, which, after it acquired statehood in 1907, proved deeply inhospitable to US blacks. In March 1911, for example, controversy erupted when an organized party of 194 black settlers from Oklahoma (and neighboring Arkansas and Texas) arrived in Winnipeg, Manitoba. Many African Americans, initially from Oklahoma, also moved to Calgary, Alberta, where they encountered so much discrimination that a Colored Protective Association was formed in 1910.[19] Both cities would later witness efforts by local African Canadians to ban *The Birth of a Nation*: blacks in Calgary protested the film,[20] and the arrival of *The Birth of a Nation* in Winnipeg prompted a public outcry "by delegations of colored citizens."[21]

Actions of this kind were not usually successful in preventing exhibition of the film in English-speaking Canada. In Halifax, Nova Scotia, however, according to James W. St. G. Walker, "with the compliance of white supporters, blacks were actually able to have the offensive film banned from city cinemas."[22] Given the recent history of blacks in Halifax (where they had inter alia been segregated in schools of their own and excluded from labor unions) and the fact that African Canadians in Nova Scotia generally had been unable to sustain "a high level of group solidarity and commitment to collective action," this was a considerable achievement.[23]

In French-speaking Québec, *The Birth of a Nation* experienced major difficulties with the local censorship system. The film was brought before the Office of Censorship in Montréal on September 17, 1915, in a version lasting about 180 minutes. This suggests that the Basil Corporation had already made ten minutes or so of cuts before submission. The film was approved on September 20, subject to certain cuts in specific reels:

Reel 2: White man hanging mulatto woman
Reel 9: Pursuit of girl by negro
Subtitle: "For her who had learned the stern lesson of Honor, we should not grieve that she found sweeter the opal gates of death."
Reel 11: Colored woman, immodestly dressed, drinking
White girl in the arms of a mulatto

It seems from this list that the entire so-called rape sequence—with Gus chasing Flora to her death—was required to be cut. But the official notification form was also accompanied by another, unsigned, sheet listing two additional cuts:

> Reel 4: Cut all scenes of white girl in mulatto office
> Subtitle: The town being given over to drunken negroes[24]

On September 23, four days before *The Birth of a Nation* was due to open at the Princess Theatre, the Montréal newspaper *La Presse* reported that: "An important group of black inhabitants of Montréal met together yesterday evening, at the Union Congregational Church, under the presidency of Dr. J. Arthur Thomas . . . to protest against the showing of . . . *The Birth of a Nation*. It appears that our black fellow-citizens have learned . . . that this drama . . . is of the kind to provoke public antagonism towards blacks. Those who were present at yesterday's meeting expressed the intention of doing everything they could to prevent these screenings."[25] That promise of "doing everything they could" to stop the film proved prophetic, perhaps, in light of what followed. On the morning of September 27, the day set for the film's first performance, the Princess Theatre was badly damaged by a fire. The previous evening, a black man had called on the theater manager and effectively threatened him if he did not withdraw the film. A police inquiry was launched, but it was impossible to prove that the fire had been caused by arson. *The Birth of a Nation* did open that day—but in the Arena Theatre, specially rented for the occasion. The film went on to become a popular success and returned to Montréal twice the following year. It was shown from May 1, 1916, at the Orpheum Theatre and from November 26, 1916, at the St. Denis. The publicity at the Théâtre St. Denis proudly proclaimed something new: that the film would be shown "with intertitles in French and in English, for the first time in the entire world."[26]

What the Canadian experience points to is that, as *The Birth of a Nation* began its career outside the United States, it would do so as a profoundly unstable text. The film could be edited at any point by distributors or exhibitors. Although it was rarely banned by national censors (France being the major national exception to this), local censors could and sometimes did insist on cuts being made in some parts of the movie. To make the film more comprehensible to non-English-speaking audiences, the intertitles had to be translated into other languages—a fruitful source of reinterpretation and repurposing. The length of the film—and thus its precise narrative—also seems to have differed profoundly from place to place. An American who had first seen the film in the United States wanted "to know why some of the best allegorical scenes" had been cut out when he saw it again in Australia, where, according to the film's manager, George Bowles, it ran for only two hours and forty-three minutes.[27]

The most dramatic example of cutting of this type appears to have been when *The Birth of a Nation* was first shown in Japan on April 25, 1924. The version screened seems to have been only 104 minutes long rather than the 193 minutes in the Kino Blu-Ray edition of 2011 or the 194 minutes in the British Film Institute's Centennial Blu-ray edition (released in November 2015). It was, in fact, less than the first part of the film in modern editions. It seems possible, indeed, that the version shown in Japan in 1924 (later known as the Kokumin creation) ended with Lincoln's assassination and the end of the Civil War, avoiding entirely both the Reconstruction period and the Ku Klux Klan.[28]

The Birth of a Nation in Britain

The Birth of a Nation was submitted to the British Board of Film Censors (BBFC), which passed it for universal viewing on August 5, 1915. James C. Robertson, the historian of the BBFC, notes that this award of a "U certificate without cuts to the antiblack *The Birth of a Nation* . . . is not easy to reconcile with the BBFC's new-found sensitivity to racialism within the British Empire as well as its aversion to excessive violence."[29] Since there are no records of the discussions at the BBFC for this period, we do not know whether there was any criticism of the film on the part of the censors. However, according to a report in *The Bioscope* on September 9, 1915, the distributors may have made some cuts to the film before it was first screened. Some of these cuts related to scenes of the Civil War, which were deemed too graphic for a nation itself currently at war, but also included the elision of "certain incidents dealing with the bestialities of the emancipated negroes" that it was thought might offend British spectators.[30] *The Birth of a Nation* opened on September 27, 1915, at the Scala Theatre on Charlotte Street. It was later also shown at the Theatre Royal, Drury Lane, in the heart of London's theatreland. It proved hugely popular with audiences for reasons—as Michael Hammond has argued—that may have had to do with the attempts of advertisers, exhibitors, and critics to reframe the film as a realistic description of modern warfare, as an expression of "Anglo-Celt" achievement contrasted with the threat of German "Huns," and as a symbol of how a nation could be regenerated after a war.[31]

There has traditionally been a general consensus among scholars that the film met no opposition in Britain. *The Crisis*, the journal of the National Association for the Advancement of Colored People (NAACP), even criticized what it described as the "complacent acceptance" of the film there.[32] Yet recent work by Brian Willan has challenged this view. Researching in the archives of the British Anti-Slavery and Aborigines' Protection Society (AS and APS), he discovered that Geo. S. Best, a private in the Army Service Corps and—Willan suggests—"probably of African American origin," wrote to the AS and APS, stating that he had taken part in a protest against the film "while a student in Boston" in the spring and insisting that it should not be screened in the United Kingdom. Best argued that Griffith's movie represented "a distortion (villainous in all its aspects) of the history of the American Civil War." Pointing out that "its avowed purpose is to stir up hatred of the Negro throughout the world," he insisted that it was "unthinkable" for the English people to "tolerate such a hydra-headed monster in their midst, especially at this time when Africans have assembled from all parts of the Empire to serve the mother country."[33] Best had simultaneously challenged the film's version of history, internationalized protests against it through his actions in Boston and Britain, and linked it to the issue of black solders fighting for Britain in World War I. Travers Buxton, secretary of the AS and APS, had not heard of the film before Best's letter but now wrote to G. A. Bedford, president of the BBFC, about it. "We feel," he declared, echoing Best's argument, "at this time especially, any exhibition which would tend to reflect on coloured races of the Empire who have proved themselves so loyal to the Mother Country is to be strongly deprecated."[34]

Best also contacted the NAACP in New York. "An attempt is being made," he informed W. E. B. Du Bois in a letter of September 4, 1915, "to produce 'The Birth of a Nation' in England. I have got the Anti-Slavery Society to take the matter up and also the Lord Mayor of London." Best, aware from his own experience of the campaign against the film conducted by the NAACP in Boston, also asked Du Bois to "forward as soon as possible any particulars you think would be of use to us."[35] It was almost certainly in response to Best's letter that May Childs Nerney, secretary of the NAACP, wrote to Travers Buxton on October 2, enclosing some pamphlets the NAACP had produced critiquing the film and asking Buxton to devote his "efforts to prevent the play which is at the same time a libel and a caricature of the Negro, from being produced in your country."[36] The AS and APS also heard from Nina Gomer Du Bois, Du Bois's wife, then living in London, about the movie, which she described as "disgusting and mean."[37] The organization set up a committee of four to decide what, if anything, to do about the film. The committee itself was divided over what to recommend, but one member, Georgiana Solomon, widow of a former prime minister of the Cape Colony and a dedicated suffragette, was so horrified by the film that she took direct action against it. She stood up from her seat at the Scala Theatre and denounced the movie, pointing out that "the news of it would spread to Africa, India and the Colonies. This was an insult to our glorious King's loyal Native subjects—everywhere." Solomon's speech was loudly supported by her friend and ally, Mrs. Cobden Unwin.[38]

Both Solomon and Unwin were close colleagues of black South African writer and political activist Sol T. Plaatje, who took direct action against the film in a somewhat different way. Sixteen years later, Plaatje recalled that: "Some of us asked the British Home Secretary why a foreign film . . . was permitted to libel the black race in England, at a time when black races by the thousands were dying in defence of England and the British empire. We were informed with regret that as the Film Censors had already licensed the play, the Government could do nothing."[39] In practice, according to Brian Willan, Plaatje was probably referring to a letter sent in late September 1915 to the Lord Chamberlain, describing the film as offensive and asking for it to be withdrawn. This letter, although subsequently lost, provoked considerable discussion among officials in the Colonial Office, who ultimately advised the Home Office that, although "the film might cause annoyance to American Negroes, . . . it does not appear to the Secretary of State that it could cause reasonable offence to negroes in other parts of the world." There, for the moment, the matter rested.[40]

The Birth of a Nation in France

The Birth of a Nation was advertised in France in September 1916 as a forthcoming attraction at the Casino de Paris.[41] But it appears to have fallen afoul of the new French national system of film censorship that had been introduced a few months earlier. After June 16, 1916, a Central Commission of Control vetted all films shown in France, awarding visas to those it approved for exhibition. By January 1917, 145 feature films had been refused visas because "their theme was judged immoral or contrary to the public interest." *The Birth of a Nation* was one of fourteen American movies denied a visa.⁴² Since the records relating to the granting or refusal of visas for this period do not exist, we can only guess at the reasons behind this decision. The censorship regulations banned films including "violent and dubious deeds," and *The Birth of a Nation* featured "scenes of looting and destruction, arson, one seduction (of Republican politician Austin Stoneman by his mulatto housekeeper), an assassination (Lincoln's), two (implied) rapes, at least three murders, and election rigging."⁴³ The regulations also banned movies that were likely "to influence in any manner whatever the 'Sacred Union'" of France at war. Some of the Civil War sequences in the film, particularly trench warfare at Petersburg, were of great brutality (in Britain, indeed, they had been singled out for praise by some reviewers because of the marked lack of graphic depictions in British films and newsreels of what fighting on the Western Front was really like).⁴⁴ There was, indeed, an antiwar tone to some scenes—and especially some intertitles—that French censors will certainly have noted. Above all, they must have been aware of the many black soldiers serving in the French army and worried about the consequences of the film's racism on these poilus. According to film historian Georges Sadoul, the French "censorship judged the projection of such a violently racist work inopportune whilst colonial soldiers were at the front."⁴⁵

It would take seven years for Griffith's *The Birth of a Nation* to be released in France. But when it was first screened to paying customers in Paris, it became something of a cause célèbre and—despite having received a visa from French censors—was promptly banned on the orders of the national government. The problem for the film's distributors was that Paris, in the summer of 1923, was fast becoming a major attraction for white American tourists. The tougher US immigration law of 1921 had inspired transatlantic steamship companies to turn former steerage accommodation into inexpensive "tourist third class," and the steeply falling franc also helped transform Paris into a major center of American tourism.⁴⁶ These new American tourists expected the French they met to adapt their behavior to meet the tourists' tastes, including speaking English.⁴⁷ More to the point here, many white tourists from the United States brought with them segregationist views. They refused to meet and socialize with black people in bars, nightclubs, restaurants, and cabarets. During the summer of 1923, many fights broke out as white Americans attempted to throw black Americans out of bars in Montmartre and Montparnasse.⁴⁸ It soon became clear, moreover, that the whites involved made no distinction between African

Americans and blacks from parts of the French colonial empire. On June 29, for example, Kojo Touvalou Houénou, a lawyer from Dahomey, was thrown out of Le Jockey, a bar in Montparnasse, at the request of its predominantly American clientele.[49]

France and Britain were both colonial powers with large overseas empires. But France—unlike Britain—had traditionally taken the view that the colonies could be integral parts of France and elected deputies to the National Assembly. As a consequence, by 1923, there were several black deputies. It was one of these deputies, Georges Boussenot from the Indian Ocean island of Réunion, who made the growing number of racial incidents between American tourists and black French residents into a major political issue. On July 24, 1923, he published an article titled "Appeal to Americans Visiting France" in the newspaper *Le Journal*. While thanking Americans for their help in the war, he reminded them of the excellent collaboration that had existed between white battalions and black French units, and warned that France recognized no difference between citizens based on the color of their skin.[50] Seven days later, Boussenot's advice became the public policy of the French government: the Ministry of Foreign Affairs, headed by Raymond Poincaré—who was also prime minister—announced that if "foreign tourists" continued to berate or demand the expulsion of "colored men originally from the French colonies," then "sanctions will be taken."[51] Three nights after this announcement, Kojo Touvalou Houénou was thrown out of El Garòn, a nightclub near Place Blanche in Montmartre at the request of a large group of white American tourists.[52] Houénou would later be a major figure in the "black Atlantic," being an important figure in protest movements in France, West Africa, and the United States (where he became a friend of Marcus Garvey).[53]

Houénou claimed to be a prince from Dahomey, the nephew of the last king before the country became a French colony. He had served as an auxiliary doctor in World War I, was wounded, and was later awarded French citizenship for his meritorious war service. More importantly here, he was also a lawyer, and he promptly sued the nightclub owner alleging grievous bodily harm.[54] Additionally, Houénou complained to Blaise Diagne, a Senegalese deputy who had been the first black man to hold government office in France. Diagne in turn wrote to Prime Minister Poincaré over what he termed "these regrettable incidents." Poincaré responded with an assurance that the government would treat severely the proprietors of hotels and bars that discriminated between blacks and whites.[55]

A few days later, two deputies—Joseph Barthélemy from Gers in southwest France and Gratien Candace, a black deputy from Guadeloupe—wrote to Poincaré threatening to table parliamentary questions over the rising tide of racial incidents.[56] Poincaré replied to both deputies assuring them he would "continue to follow this matter closely . . . French laws requiring equality will be strictly observed and . . . all those who break them, whether foreigners or French, will be punished as required."[57] *The Birth of a Nation* opened at the Marivaux Theatre in Paris on August 17, the same day Poincaré gave the deputies this assurance. Black deputies Boussenot and Candace each attended one of the opening performances and complained about the film (Boussenot described it as holding "an entire people up to ridicule and hatred").[58] After just four performances, the Paris prefect of police—prompted by the government (and ignoring the visa granted by the French censors)—banned the film as a threat to public order.[59] Several factors helped account for the suppression (which, in any case, would last only a few weeks).[60] These included traditional French ideals of equality going back to the 1789 Declaration of the Rights of Man, gratitude for the contribution of colonial troops in World War I (and the hope that they might offer a pool of manpower in future conflicts), growing hostility to white American tourists, the refusal of the US government to accept a link between the repayment of wartime American loans and continuing German reparations, and the fact that Poincaré and the other politicians involved were all aware of (and positioning themselves for) the general election due to take place in 1924.[61] At the same time, however, it seems certain that a key factor in the film's suppression was the position taken by influential black politicians in the National Assembly.

Road-Showing Abroad

In the early days of *The Birth of a Nation*'s exhibition in the United States and abroad, the key to much of the film's success was the organization of road shows. By the end of May 1915, three American companies were producing road shows and a fourth was in gestation. By the end of July, a fifth company had been organized, and by September, there were eight. By February 1916, twelve road shows were crisscrossing the United States.[62] Also by February 1916, three road shows had been organized abroad: in Australia, England, and South America. The fact that each was referred to in the accounts as "Company no. 1" pointed to the fact that further road shows were already planned in each of these venues.[63] At their peak, three road-show companies were touring Britain, three more in South America, and four in Australia and New Zealand. The manager of the South American road show, Guy Croswell Smith, first introduced it to Argentina, where it ran for more than two hundred performances at the Teatro de la Opera in Buenos Aires. He repeated this success in Chile, Peru, Bolivia, Uruguay, and Brazil.[64] Once the film had finished its initial run in London at the Scala Theatre and at Royal Theatre, Drury Lane, road-show companies managed by W. E. Burlock took the film out to British audiences in the provinces. Frustratingly, while the Epoch accounts tell us how profitable such companies were, they do not make it possible to trace precisely where and when the film was shown or the nature of its local reception. The same is true of the story of the film in Australia, though here we do have some evidence of whether it resonated with local audiences.

Australia

The Birth of a Nation had its Australian premiere at the Theatre Royal, Sydney, on Easter Saturday, April 22, 1916. The choice of location fit well with the road-show strategy. Sydney was the most populous city in Australia,[65] and the first advertisements emphasized that the film "will never be presented at any but the Highest Class Theatres, and the Prices will be those customarily charged in such places." The ads also reiterated the false claims invented by publicists Theodore Mitchell and J. R. McCarthy for the film's New York opening thirteen months earlier: that eighteen thousand people and three thousand horses had been involved in making the film, which had cost $500,000 (converted to its approximate Australian equivalent, 100,000 pounds sterling).[66] Other ads and planted publicity stories before the film opened emphasized that the film would "positively never be shown in the suburbs,"[67] that it had already been seen by a million people in New York in a record 802 performances,[68] that it had just been shown for charity at the Royal Theatre, Drury Lane, in London to a distinguished audience that included the Queen,[69] and that it would "be presented as a regular theatrical attraction, with an orchestra for the specially-composed incidental music."[70] The day after the film opened, an ad attempted to suggest that the highest price charged for admission (six shillings) was still much less than in London or New York. It also hailed *The Birth of a Nation* in large capital letters as "A Tremendous Argument for a White Australia."[71]

The so-called White Australia policy had its origins in the fact that Australian colonies had passed laws attempting to restrict immigration—first from China, later from Japan—from 1855 onward.[72] On January 1, 1901, Australia had become an independent nation within the British Empire when a federation of separate colonies joined to form a new Commonwealth of Australia. In 1901, one of the first pieces of legislation adopted by the new country was the Commonwealth Immigration Restriction Act, which formed the centerpiece of what became known as the White Australia policy. The legislation provided for entrance examinations only in European languages, effectively bringing an end to non-European immigration.[73] A supplementary law required the deportation by 1906 of all Kanakas, Pacific Islanders who had been brought to Australia as contracted plantation labor.[74]

Publicists for *The Birth of a Nation* seem to have believed that the racial aspects of the film could be used to promote its appeal in Australia. George Bowles, sent by the Epoch Producing Corporation to supervise *The Birth of a Nation*'s exhibition in Australia in collaboration with the local J. C. Williamson theater company, explained for the benefit of Australian audiences that the movie was based on Thomas Dixon Jr.'s novels and play, which "told the story of the American Civil War from the viewpoint of the defeated South, and it showed the horrors of the domination of the black man over the white which came when the slaves were freed and were given the franchise."[75] A few months later, indeed, a local newspaper in neighboring New Zealand commented that Griffith's film depicted "post-slavery days . . . of terror and tragedy, and if ever a national lesson were in a picture, it is contained in the film depicting the struggle between the white and black man in the Southern States of the Union. The production is an impressive statement upon Australia's national policy of race purity."[76]

In practice, however, few Australians seem to have made the connection between the movie and the White Australia policy, seeing the latter as directed primarily against Asians rather than blacks. One commentator noted rather vaguely that "our own weaknesses with the colored races has rather weakened our reverence for [Harriet Beecher Stowe's] Uncle Tom and his brethren," though he still perceived the "slave-owners of Dixie-land" before the Civil War as "brutal."[77] Another baldly stated that "the danger from the negro population is the underlying theme of the production. In Australia we are free of such problems, but there is still the lesson of what has been avoided. No doubt this will impress many minds."[78] There seems to have been no real attempt on the part of any Australian commentator to link the African Americans portrayed in *The Birth of a Nation* with the

Aboriginal population of Australia, variously estimated at between 80,000 and 150,000 in the second decade of the twentieth century.[79] Those tasked with publicizing *The Birth of a Nation* consequently seem to have realized very swiftly that there was little point in trying to link the film with the idea of a White Australia, and there was no further reference to this in subsequent advertisements for the film.

Where the film did connect was with the fact that Australia, like Britain and Canada, was involved in World War I. In common with British commentators of 1915, Australian reviewers saw the war scenes as unusually realistic. "What war is like—its grimness and cruelty, pathos and tragedy, horror and confusion—is shown with remarkable effectiveness," declared one critic. "Something quite new in the way of battle scenes is achieved in the tumultuous trench fighting."[80] Another praised "the spectacle of a startlingly realistic artillery duel, in which hundreds of guns and thousands of fighters are engaged."[81] Australian soldiers fought and died in the Gallipoli campaign, on the Western Front, and in places such as Egypt, Palestine, and Syria. "The tragedy of war," one critic of *The Birth of a Nation* reflected, "is brought home to observers in a way that, in Sydney at least, must find many responsive hearts."[82] Many Australians in 1916 still thought of themselves as British, and Griffith's film further encouraged for some a sense of racial pride. An early ad described the film's heroic Southerners as "proud and courageous Anglo-Americans" who "were of British breed."[83] When Colonel Cameron (Henry Walthall) holds up a "fiery cross," one writer commented, "this is where the spectators begin to realise that they are really watching the deeds of Britons. The Camerons . . . are a Scottish family . . . and it is the daring leadership of the eldest son . . . that rescues the whites from a black tyranny."[84]

Despite the hopes of the Epoch board and local manager, George Bowles, *The Birth of a Nation* was not hugely commercially successful in Australia. It was expensive to set up the road-show companies: the accounts show that Australian Company No. 1 had cost $9,301 up to February 29, 1916, and, in advance of the Easter opening in Sydney, had generated no income.[85] In September 1916, with three road-show companies established, total income stood at $13,427, and expenses—including Bowles's salary of $2,098—amounted to $13,426.[86] There also seems to have been significant resistance in Australia to paying inflated road-show prices: the top price for reserved seats in the Theatre Royal, Sydney was six shillings, equivalent to three-quarters of the two-dollar price tag in the United States. Even at this level, it seems to have become obvious during May that, while the cheaper seats were still selling well, there was far less demand for expensive ones. On May 6, 1916, the J. C. Williamson management announced that the run of *The Birth of a Nation* at the Theatre Royal had been extended and that the price of admission had been cut to between two shillings and sixpence and sixpence for evening performances and between two shillings and sixpence for matinees, an overall decrease of between a third and a half.[87]

In Melbourne, where *The Birth of a Nation* began its run (also at the Theatre Royal) on May 20, the top price of a seat was three shillings (half what it had been at the start in Sydney), with other seats at two shillings and one shilling.[88] Despite the usual barrage of publicity for the film,[89] and a successful opening night,[90] *The Birth of a Nation*'s season in Melbourne began under something of a shadow. A week before the premiere, Hoyt's Theatre in Melbourne started to advertise a movie titled *The Curse of a Nation*, to open on the same day as *The Birth of a Nation* and with seats at exactly half the price of those at the Theatre Royal. Brazenly, Hoyt's claimed that *The Curse of a Nation* had cost £200,000 to produce (twice what had been claimed for *The Birth of a Nation*) and that five thousand people had been involved in making it. In reality, *The Curse of a Nation* was a fifty-minute drama about miscegenation, based on a play by Edward Sheldon and earlier known as *The Nigger*. Renaming it and advertising it in this way was little more than an unscrupulous ploy by Hoyt's to profit from the publicity for *The Birth of a Nation* (the two films were advertised on the same page of the Melbourne *Argus*).[91] J. C. Williamson sued Hoyt's and asked for an injunction restraining the theater management from advertising or screening *The Curse of a Nation*, but these initiatives failed.[92] *The Curse of a Nation* ran for only a few days, but one consequence of its arrival was that ads for *The Birth of a Nation* were revised to include the statement that it was "the real thing in wonder picture. All others are imitations."[93]

The other problem in Melbourne was that the Theatre Royal was booked for a live play from June 3, so the management of J. C. Williamson arranged for *The Birth of a Nation* to move to the Auditorium Theatre from June 3 to June 9, and finally to the Town Hall until June 16.[94] This foreshadowed the film's move to shorter engagements of between one and four nights at lower prices (maximum two shillings and sixpence) in a range of smaller towns and cities.[95]

After leaving Sydney (where an ad claimed it had been seen by "over 140,000 people"[96]) and Melbourne, Australia's two largest cities, *The Birth of a Nation* seems to have been less successful. The three touring road-show companies reported to Epoch profits of $1,645 in October 1916 and $1,052 in November. In December, there was a loss of $191. By April 1917, with the three companies reduced to two, the monthly profit was $1,475.[97] One factor in putting off potential Australian spectators was that the film was advertised as "history revived and shown in the making."[98] Publicity emphasized the amount of research that had gone into its making.[99] But many Australians had little interest in American history or were unaware of the Reconstruction period depicted in the second half of the film. "The weakest part of the picture from an Australian standpoint," wrote one commentator, "is that it deals with a phase of American history about which the outside world knows little. . . . Australians know nothing of the events following the end of the civil war. As far as we are concerned, America was off the map from Lee's surrender until the arrival of the [American Great White] fleet in Sydney [Harbour on August 20, 1908]."[100]

A few film critics displayed an awareness that there were alternative views of the Ku Klux Klan to that expressed in the film. "Northern [American] writers," noted one, "say these clansmen were outlaws, Southern writers that they were the saviours of the Whites." "Now that we seek the simple story of the Ku Klux Klan," wrote another, "we find one-half of the authorities upholding them as Crusaders of the noblest type, and the other half discussing them contemptuously as larrikin push."[101] Apart from critics, a modern Australian commentator points out that ordinary spectators also at times displayed skepticism toward *The Birth of a Nation*'s construction of the Ku Klux Klan as heroes—something that expressed itself in queries to the advice columns of some newspapers. The same writer suggests two possible reasons for such popular querying of "the film's picture of race relations." The first was the continuing popularity in Australia of Harriet Beecher Stowe's antislavery novel *Uncle Tom's Cabin* (1852). The second was the fact that a film titled *In the Clutches of the Ku-Klux Klan*, offering a considerably more critical view of the organization, had already been shown there "less than two years previously." This 1913 production, made by the Gene Gauntier players in Florida, featured Gauntier herself as the daughter of a newspaper editor who has offended the Klan. The Klan captures and imprisons her, and a Klansman who falls in love with her is persecuted by other members of the secret order.[102]

Australia had no real movie censorship system operating when *The Birth of a Nation* arrived in 1916. This meant that, unlike in the United States,

Canada, and Britain, there was no possibility of critics of the film trying to put pressure on local or national censorship boards to suppress or amend it. Some Australian commentators reported in detail on the struggle to ban the film in the United States.[103] Yet in Australia, there do not appear to have been any protests at all. There seems no evidence that Aboriginals ever saw the film, let alone demonstrated against it. For most white Australians of 1916 and 1917, *The Birth of a Nation*'s endorsement of white supremacy was unexceptionable, even if they perceived such supremacy as something to be asserted primarily against Asians rather than blacks. Many had little interest in American history, and this, together, with the length of the film, the cost of going to see it in its road-show format, and perhaps some sense of disappointment that it did not live up to its advance publicity, probably accounted for its relative lack of financial success.[104]

Germany

Historian Leon F. Litwack claimed that *The Birth of a Nation* "scored particularly impressive triumphs in Germany and South Africa."[105] It appears, however, that the movie was not screened in either country until some years after its first release. In Germany, this was almost certainly a consequence of the international campaign launched against what would become known as the "Black Horror on the Rhine." Leading up to and during World War I, France recruited around 190,000 African soldiers. When the war ended, it used some of these troops in the French-occupied zone of the Rhineland. As Tina Campt points out, this "represented the first large-scale Black presence in Germany."[106] On March 20, 1920, in a letter to the periodical *Nation*, British left-winger Edmund D. Morel complained that the French had "thrust barbarians . . . with tremendous sexual instincts—into the heart of Europe."[107]

Two weeks later, in the *Daily Herald* newspaper, Morel published an article titled "Black Scourge in Europe: Sexual Horror Let Loose by France on Rhine."[108] Like Thomas Dixon Jr. in the United States (whose novels and play had provided the basis for the second half of *The Birth of a Nation*), Morel had developed an obsession with black male sexuality. But his insane imaginings became the basis for a broad transnational campaign that, of course, was seized upon by German nationalists as a weapon with which to undermine the Treaty of Versailles that had ended the war and specifically, Iris Wigger suggests, "to discredit France internationally, to put pressure on the French government and to get rid of the French colonial troops as soon as possible."[109]

Erika Kuhlman, in her book *Reconstructing Patriarchy after the Great War*, comments on what she saw as the profound similarities between Griffith's film and German tactics of the early 1920s. "The Rhineland horror campaign," she writes, "duplicated many of the themes of *Birth of a Nation*, such as the presumed inability of nonwhites to govern themselves (part of imperialism's paradigmatic civilized versus uncivilized supposition), the presumed natural desire on the part of black men for white women, and, of course, the myth of the black rapist. This extraordinarily popular movie . . . reminded Americans and Europeans of what could happen if white men lost control of their society."[110] Kuhlman adds that "the popularity of Griffith's epic film . . . helps explain the resonance of white supremacy in the 1910s and 1920s and the choice by the Rhineland Horror campaign to direct its propaganda across the Atlantic."[111] This suggestion that *The Birth of a Nation*, which had not yet been shown in Germany (the French authorities, indeed, had prevented it from being shown for obvious reasons in the occupied Rhineland[112]), nevertheless helped shape the Rhineland horror campaign of the early 1920s is a fascinating one.

The "Black Horror" campaign launched by the German government was international in scope and particularly focused on influencing American opinion. It tried to work through the network of German sympathizers in the United States, focusing particularly on German-language newspapers, the Steuben Society, and other organizations.[113] Considerable interaction took place between unofficial agencies of the German government, such as the Rhenish Women's League, and individuals in the United States.[114] Cultural products produced by the campaign often had an international circulation. These included novels, newspaper articles, songs, poems, cartoons, posters, medallions, and plays.[115] There was also at least one film, *Die schwarze Schmach* (*The Black Shame*), released in April 1921.

Die schwarze Schmach was shown in Munich, Stuttgart, Berlin, Dantzig, Nuremburg, Bremen, and Breslau.[116] Its makers, Carl Boese, John Freden, and Heinrich Diestler, were ambitious to have it shown in the United States, though, as far as is known, this never happened. The film's narrative was a remorseless account of the victimization of white German women by black French soldiers: the main female character in the story is kidnapped and locked up in a house of prostitution, and other women are raped. Some elements of the film parallel those of *The Birth of a Nation*. The major female character in *Die schwarze Schmach* is called Elsa; in *The Birth of a Nation*, she is Elsie. Both movies emphasize the supposedly insatiable desire of black men for white women. Both mythologize the idea of the black rapist. Both present a white-dominated society as the only means of preserving natural order. Both work narratively as films because they show white men defending white women from the lascivious attention of black soldiers. In *Die schwarze Schmach*, it is white French officers who do this; in *The Birth of a Nation*, of course, it is the white-robed Klansmen. Both films not only demonize blacks but also portray black bodies in strange, disorienting ways. Gus, in *The Birth of a Nation*, moves in some respects like an animal when he pursues Flora Cameron to her death. In the case of *Die schwarze Schmach*, suggests French scholar Jean-Yves Le Naour, the black French soldiers "seem not at all to belong to the human race: hidden behind great trees from which they appear suddenly like wildcats, they run with sideways steps, bandy-legged with shoulders dangling. On the face of it, they are large monkeys."[117]

If *Die schwarze Schmach* mimicked *The Birth of a Nation* in narrative and aesthetic terms, is it possible that Griffith's film even had direct influence on the German one? Since *The Birth of a Nation* had not been shown in Germany up to this point, the answer to this can only be found in the strong transatlantic links between members of the pro-German community in the United States and those living in Germany during and after the war. The evidence so far is suggestive rather than conclusive. One of the pioneers of the "black shame" campaign in the Rhineland was conservative American journalist and actor Ray Beveridge. Beveridge, a former employee of the German embassy in Washington, had spent much of the war living and writing in Germany. In February and March 1920, she gave a series of speeches in Hamburg and Munich attacking the presence of black troops in the Rhineland and warning of the threat posed by mulatto children "to the purity of the German race." She proposed that German men follow the example of white men in the American South and lynch blacks who insulted white women. In June, she spoke on the "black shame" at the University of Berlin and began a tour that would take her to twenty-five more German cities, finishing with a rally of fifty thousand people in Hamburg in the spring of 1921.[118] From where did Beveridge originally get her ideas—indeed, her obsessions? Belonging to a German American family (her grandfather was governor of Illinois in the 1870s), she began in 1915 to return to the United States as a propagandist for the German cause. She made speaking tours of the Midwest and Northeast, and, given the racial attitudes she would later espouse, it seems highly probable—but sadly there is no documented proof—that she saw *The Birth of a Nation* on one of these trips.[119]

South Africa

Equally frustrating in terms of the possible transnational effects of *The Birth of a Nation* is the making and career of *De Voortrekkers*, released in South Africa in 1916. Dealing with the movement of Boers, farmers of Dutch ancestry, away from the Cape Colony and British rule in the 1830s, *De Voortrekkers* fit well with the political conservatism of the period after the Act of Union of 1910, when white British and Afrikaans settlers reconciled at the expense of South Africa's black majority. As one contemporary critic observed, the movie "has probably done more to bring Dutchmen (i.e. Boers) and Englishmen together and to help each other to a better understanding of the other's point of view, than anything that has ever previously happened."[120]

De Voortrekkers shared many similarities with *The Birth of a Nation* that have already been explored by Jane Gaines, Edwin Hees, Jacqueline Maingard, and Peter Davis.[121] Both films deal with the foundation of a white "Edenic state," subsequently threatened by blacks, which is ultimately recovered. Both represent fair-minded white leaders destroyed by a "lethal alliance" between "generalized black iniquity and individual white villains."[122] Both show blacks made more threatening by alcohol. Both include "historical facsimiles." Both celebrate "the establishment of white supremacy by violence" and link the question of white supremacy with that of nationhood. Both end with the creation of new white families and "a clear religious sanction" for the reborn white nation. Both have "faithful souls": "good blacks, faithful servants who protect their masters and mistresses even against their own people."[123] The "sexual paranoia" of *The Birth of a Nation* might be lacking, but both it and *De Voortrekkers* "exploit black people as 'others' against which white identity is confirmed and celebrated." The two films, as Jane Gaines notes, have a similar lesson: "two white groups at ideological odds with each other [Boers and British in South Africa; Northerners and Southerners in the United States] must both claim commonality with one another in order to distinguish themselves from people of African descent."[124]

Was there a more direct relationship between the two films? Isadore W. Schlesinger of African Film Productions[125] brought Harold Shaw to South Africa specifically to direct *De Voortrekkers*, the first epic film to be shot there. Shaw had come from a remarkably similar background to D. W. Griffith: born two years after Griffith in Griffith's home state of Kentucky, he had also pursued for several years a career as an itinerant actor before moving into directing.[126] In the fall of 1915, Shaw was in Britain working for the company London Film Productions. It is very probable that he saw one of the London performances of *The Birth of a Nation*, but there is, once again, no direct evidence for this—or for Peter Davis's claim that *De Voortrekkers* was "probably inspired" by Griffith's movie.[127]

The Birth of a Nation was not shown in racially complex South Africa until 1931. Historians have offered differing explanations for this. Brian Willan suggests that the delay was a consequence of the campaign against the film in London in 1915. On October 13, Travers Buxton, secretary of the AS and APS, wrote to William P. Schreiner, the South African high commissioner in London, requesting him to use his influence to stop the film from being screened in South Africa. Schreiner replied on November 19, noting that he had watched the movie "and have taken certain unofficial steps which will, I hope, prevent the film from going to South Africa. . . . I think it would do harm there."[128] Three months later, Buxton declared to Mary White Ovington of the NAACP that he and his colleagues had thought "it well to call the attention of the authorities to the serious objections which existed to such a play being produced in South Africa and we have reason to believe that steps were taken which would effectively prevent its production in that country, where the question of colour is a very acute one."[129] John Trumpbour, by contrast, sees the long delay as a product of a political initiative: in 1923, the British government asked Will Hays, recently appointed head of Hollywood's Motion Picture Producers' Association, to block the exhibition of the film in South Africa. As usual in such cases, Hays explained that he had no legal grounds for doing so but gave assurances that the American producers would decline to distribute the film there.[130]

Whatever the reason or reasons for the delay, it took sixteen years before *The Birth of a Nation* was at last shown in South Africa. It was screened for four days at the Town Hall in Johannesburg in July 1931 and, two months later, at the Trocadero in Kimberley, Northern Cape Province, in the heart of Diamond Fields. Sol Plaatje, the black South African activist who had campaigned against the film in London in 1915 and in Boston,

Massachusetts, in 1921, published two articles vigorously condemning what he called "the cinematographic calamity."[131] Plaatje's opposition to the film had not diminished since 1915, but what had diminished sharply was the impact of *The Birth of a Nation*. Shown as a truncated version of the 1930 synchronized sound reissue—which did not include speech—it provoked mainly derision. The film, according to the reviewer in the Johannesburg *Star*, "portrayed the death of the old cinematography which used to delight our simple hearts many years ago." A critic in the *Rand Daily Mail* wrote that it was "odd at first to see the characters move their mouths while making no sound" and identified "moments in the picture when dramatic intensity according to up-to-date ideas falls short." A writer for the *Diamond Fields Advertiser* similarly noted that, "If proof was needed that the silent picture had served its turn, *The Birth of a Nation* . . . would be more than sufficient."[132] By 1931, a film that had once stirred passions though its racist depiction of American history, had itself come to be seen by many *as* history.

There were other reasons why the film may have had less impact. In 1931, having banned the film for "immorality and race prejudice" in both 1921 and 1924, the Bureau of Censorship in Montreal, Canada, finally agreed to approve the sound version, but insisted on the following cuts:

Eliminate
Reel 8—Negro servant tied up and shot for wrong voting
The passage of Bill providing (?) for the intermarriage of Blacks and whites
Reel 9—Negro chasing a white girl
Reel 10—Negroes shooting at white men
View of body on steps of Lieut. Governor's house
Reel 11—Ill treatment of Cameron (father) by negroes
The master (Cameron) in chains parraded [*sic*] before his former slaves
Negro struggling with Elsie
Reel 12—Girl tied to chair and gagged
Kidnapping of Elsie by negro

Most of the film's propaganda against miscegenation in particular seems to have been removed, and with it presumably much of the meaning it once had for earlier viewers.

Conclusion

There are still many things we do not know about the reception of *The Birth of a Nation* across the world. Digitalization of local newspapers is making it possible to fill in the story of local responses to the film. Yet language barriers still stand in the way. It is likely that the film was differently received and interpreted in many places according to the social and cultural context in which it was screened.

I do not believe there is any study of how the film was received in Latin America, where it was screened in many countries, including Brazil, the last country in the West to abolish slavery in 1888. I am also unaware of any analysis of the film's later career in Germany, although its message of white supremacy would have chimed well with Nazi racist propaganda. The film was apparently screened in Spain in October 1921, but the circumstances and reactions are currently unknown. We know that the Epoch Producing Corporation sold the rights to distribute the film across the whole of Scandinavia in May 1917 and that it was first shown in Denmark in March 1918, Sweden in September 1918, and Finland in April 1922, but we know nothing of the responses of audiences and critics.[133] "There is no evidence," states Brian Willan, "that *The Birth of a Nation* was ever shown in the Caribbean, or indeed in the [British] African colonies."[134] Was it ever shown in India? We simply do not know. Nor have we any knowledge, at least in English, of how it was received in Japan in 1924.

In 1903, W. E. B. Du Bois declared that "the problem of the Twentieth Century is the problem of the color-line."[135] Twelve years later, D. W. Griffith's *The Birth of a Nation* showed how a spectacular motion picture could recount a false version of the American Civil War era that justified continuing racial segregation in the United States. But Griffith's film was shown in many places outside the United States, and responses to it were heavily conditioned by local social, cultural, and political circumstances. In Australia, it was initially presented as a film supporting the White Australia policy of keeping out immigrants from Pacific nations. In France, by contrast, it was twice banned: during World War I for threatening the policy of recruiting soldiers from the colonies and in 1923 for seemingly providing support for the insistence of white American tourists on creating a color line in France. In South Africa and Germany, the film might have influenced the making of racist films with similar messages and narrative tropes. Among critics of the film, it encouraged the growth of the black Atlantic: activists such as Private Best in England and Sol Plaatje from South Africa, who resisted the film in both Britain and America (and, in Plaatje's case, also much later in South Africa). To these may be added Kojo Touvalou Houénou, who played a significant if inadvertent role in the French suppression of the film in 1923 and was later active in both the United States and West Africa. The international response to the movie over time was influenced by broader changes in cinematic art. The long delay before it was first shown in South Africa in 1931 meant that it was regarded as something of a museum piece from the era of the silents. At the same time, the tendency of some censors—as in Montreal in 1931—to require removal of the most racially charged passages before the movie could be screened meant that *The Birth of a Nation* had also lost much of its old capacity to shock.

MELVYN STOKES is Professor of Film History at University College London. He is author of *D. W. Griffith's* The Birth of a Nation: *A History of "The Most Controversial Motion Picture of All Time"* and *American History through Hollywood Film: From the Revolution to the 1960s.*

Notes

1. Melvyn Stokes, *D. W. Griffith's* The Birth of a Nation: *A History of "The Most Controversial Motion Picture of All Time"* (New York: Oxford University Press, 2007), 98, 118–119.

2. Agreement, Epoch Producing Corporation and Central Canada Exhibition Association, in *David W. Griffith Papers, 1897–1954*, microfilm ed. (Frederick, MD: University Publications of America, 1982), reel 2, frames 1246–1250. The agreement committed Epoch to supply an operator and a band leader as well as the film, in return for 70 percent of the gross receipts. Ibid., 1247.

3. Contract, Epoch Producing Corporation and the Basil Corporation, September 9, 1915, *D. W. Griffith Papers*, reel 2, frames 1258–1265, quotation from 1259.

4. Statement of Net Earnings, Epoch Producing Corporation, *D. W. Griffith Papers*, August 12 to September 10, 1915, reel 2, frame 1267.

5. See, for example, Adrienne Shadd, Afua Cooper, and Karolyn Smardz Frost, *The Underground Railroad: Next Stop Toronto!* (Toronto: Natural Heritage Books, 2009).

6. According to official records, approximately five thousand black migrants were admitted into Canada between the final decades of the nineteenth century and World War I. Sarah-Jane Mathieu, *North of the Color Line: Migration and Black Resistance in Canada, 1870–1955* (Chapel Hill, NC: Duke University Press, 2010), 13. They joined the 17,500 blacks (probably an underestimate) already living in Canada according to the census of 1901. Robin W. Winks, *The Blacks in Canada: A History* (Montreal: McGill-Queen's University Press/ New Haven, CT: Yale University Press, 1971), 291.

7. Dorothy W. Williams estimates that less than 1 percent of immigrants allowed into Canada from 1897 to 1920 "were of African descent." Williams, *The Road to Now: A History of Blacks in Montreal* (Montreal: Véhicule Press, 1997), 43.

8. James W. St. G. Walker, "African Canadians," in *Encyclopedia of Canada's Peoples*, ed. Paul R. Magocsi (Toronto: University of Toronto Press, 1999), 166; Howard Palmer and Tamara Palmer, "The Black Experience in Alberta," in *Peoples of Alberta: Portraits of Cultural Diversity*, ed. Howard Palmer and Tamara Palmer (Saskatoon, SK: Western Producer Prairie

Books, 1985), 365, 368, 370–372; Williams, *The Road to Now*, 40, 42. Sarah-Jane Mathieu notes that "[later] Canadians opposed to black migration persistently conjured up images of the black rapist, made popular in D. W. Griffith's internationally celebrated film *The Birth of a Nation*, when making the case for blocking the passage of blacks into Canada." Mathieu, *North of the Color Line*, 25.

9. Mathieu, *North of the Color Line*, 100, also see 100–108; James W. St. G. Walker, *A History of Blacks in Canada: A Study Guide for Teachers and Students* (Ottawa: Minister of State Multiculturalism, 1980), 95–96; Walker, "African Canadians," 165.

10. "'The Birth of a Nation' as Played in Ottawa, Ont.," *Canadian Observer*, September 18, 1915, 1.

11. Cited in Eric Veillette, "The Birth of a Nation: How Ugliness Changed Toronto's Movie-Going Landscape," first posted on Heritage Toronto, November 19, 2010, www .silenttoronto.com/?p=1365.

12. On *The New Era*, see Stokes, *D. W. Griffith's* The Birth of a Nation, 144–145, 224–225; and Allyson Nadia Field, *Uplift Cinema: The Emergence of African American Film and the Possibility of Black Modernity* (Durham, NC: Duke University Press, 2015), 161–181.

13. "Colored People Protest: Ask Province to Stop 'Birth of a Nation,'" *Toronto Daily Star*, September 17, 1915, 5. A paragraph in a fine article by Brian Willan ("'Cinematographic Calamity' or 'Soul-Stirring Appeal to Every Briton': *Birth of a Nation* in England and South Africa, 1915–1931," *Journal of South African Studies* 39, no. 3 [2013]: 624) was responsible for sparking my interest in *The Birth of a Nation*'s reception in Canada. I am happy to acknowledge this debt.

14. Cited in Veillette, "The Birth of a Nation."

15. "Dixon's Play a Scene of Skilful Treachery . . . Resolution Passed Denouncing Play," *Canadian Observer*, September 18, 1915, 1, 4; "Skilful Treachery" (Editorial), *Canadian Observer*, September 18, 1915, 4.

16. "Ex-Controller After Film: Mr Hubbard Denounces Play to Provincial Inspection Department," *Toronto Daily Star*, September 18, 1915, 5. On Hubbard, see Winks, *The Blacks in Canada*, 331, and Stephen L. Hubbard, *Against All Odds: The Story of William Peyton Hubbard, Black Leader and Municipal Reformer* (Toronto: Dundurn Press, 1987).

17. "'Birth of a Nation' Not Objectionable," *Toronto Daily Star*, September 15, 1915, 2; Veillette, "The Birth of a Nation."

18. Paul S. Moore, *Now Playing: Early Moviegoing and the Regulation of Fun* (Albany: State University of New York Press, 2008), 202.

19. Winks, *The Blacks in Canada*, 301–302; Mathieu, *North of the Color Line*, 22; Palmer and Palmer, "The Black Experience in Alberta," 369–370, 386–387; David Este and Wek Mamer Kuol, "African Canadians in Alberta: Connecting the Past with the Present," in *Multiple Lenses: Voices from the Diaspora Located in Canada*, ed. David Divine (Newcastle, UK: Cambridge Scholars, 2007), 32, 37.

20. Divine, *Multiple Lenses*, 6. Divine cites the *Calgary News-Telegram*, May 31, 1918.

21. Mathieu, *North of the Color Line*, 168. Mathieu cites the *Winnipeg Free Press*, November 20, 1920.

22. Walker, "African Canadians," 165.

23. Donald Clairmont and Fred Wein, "Blacks and Whites: The Nova Scotia Race Relations Experience," in *Banked Fires: The Ethnics of Nova Scotia*, ed. Douglas F. Campbell (Port Credit, ON: Scribblers' Press, 1978), 157–158, 162, quotation from 162.

24. Pierre Hébert, Yves Lever, and Kenneth Landry, *Dictionnaire de la censure au Québec: littérature et cinéma* (Québec: Éditions Fides, 2006), 83.

25. Ibid., 84 (my translation).

26. Ibid., 84–85. As a footnote to this story, *The Birth of a Nation* was reviewed again by the Montréal Office of Censorship, made up of new members and headed by Raoul de Roussy de Sales, on November 15, 1921; the office refused a visa for exhibition on the grounds of "immorality" and "race prejudice." On June 26, 1924, a "reconstructed" print was also rejected for the same reasons. But two days later, after an appeal, the visa was issued subject to further cuts: the removal in reel 10 of a shot of a "Negro shooting at a white man" and in reel 12 of "Elsie tied in chains + gagged/Lynch kidnapping Elsie." Ibid., 85.

27. "On the Screen and Off," *Graphic of Australia* (Melbourne), June 16, 1916, 10; "A Phenomenal Undertaking—The Making of 'Birth of a Nation,'" *Sunday Times* (Sydney), April 23, 1916, 4.

28. "The Birth of a Nation," *Allcinema Movie and DVD Database*, http://www.allcinema.net/prog/show_c.php?num_c=7799; "The Birth of a Nation (1915): Release Info," *IMDb*, http://www.imdb.com/title/tt0004972/releaseinfo. A DVD reissue of the Kokumin version has on its cover a shot of the Little Colonel (Henry Walthall) on horseback, leading Confederate soldiers off to war in 1861, instead of the much more common image used in advertising the film of a white-sheeted Klansman on a rearing horse waving a burning cross.

29. James C. Robertson, *The British Board of Film Censors: Film Censorship in Britain, 1896–1950* (London: Croom Helm, 1985), 11.

30. *The Bioscope*, September 9, 1915, 1114–1115.

31. Michael Hammond, "'A Soul-Stirring Appeal to Every Briton': The Reception of *The Birth of a Nation* in Britain (1915–1916)," in "Early Cinema," special issue, *Film History* 11, no. 3 (1999): 353, 355, 357–362, 364–366.

32. *The Crisis* 11, no. 4 (February 1916): 174–176.

33. Willan, "'Cinematographic Calamity,'" 628.

34. Travers Buxton to G. Bedford [of BBFC], September 14, 1915, quoted in Willan, "'Cinematographic Calamity,'" 629.

35. Geo. S. Best to W. E. B. Du Bois, September 4, 1915, National Association for the Advancement of Colored People Papers, Library of Congress (hereafter cited as NAACPP).

36. May Nerney to Travers Buxton, October 2, 1915, NAACPP. A week later, in a letter to novelist and former colonial administrator Sir Harry Johnston, Nerney explained that the two pamphlets were "Fighting a Vicious Film," produced during the Boston campaign in spring 1915, and a so-called English leaflet with an article by Professor [Albert Bushnell] Hart of Harvard on the inadequacies of the film's claim to represent "history." May Nerney to Sir Harry Johnston, October 9, 1915, NAACPP.

37. Willan, "'Cinematographic Calamity,'" 629.

38. Ibid., 629–631. Brian Willan points out that there may have been more direct demonstrations against the film than this, citing the London correspondent of the *Manchester Guardian* who remembered in 1923—at the time of the film's suppression in France—"that public protests were made against it during the exhibition in London because of the Ku Klux Klan scenes." Ibid., 631.

39. S. T. Plaatje, "An Inflammatory Bioscope Film," *Umteteli wa Bantu*, July 18, 1931, quoted in Willan, "'Cinematographic Calamity,'" 633.

40. Willan, "'Cinematographic Calamity,'" 633–634.

41. "Echos," *Ciné-Journal*, no. 370 (September 16, 1916): 7.

42. Jean Bancal, *La censure cinématographique* (Paris: Jose Conti, 1934), 94–97, 103–104. Also see Neville March Hunnings, *Film Censors and the Law* (London: George Allen and Unwin, 1967), 332–337; and Paul Léglise, *Histoire de la politique du cinéma Français*, vol. 1, *Le cinéma et la IIIe République* (Paris: L'Herminier, 1969), 32–33.

43. Melvyn Stokes, "Race, Politics, and Censorship: D. W. Griffith's *The Birth of a Nation* in France, 1916–1923," *Cinema Journal* 50, no. 1 (Fall 2010): 21–22, quotation from 22.

44. Melvyn Stokes, "Europeans Interpret the American South of the Civil War Era: How British and French Critics Received *The Birth of a Nation* (1915) and *Gone with the Wind* (1939)," in *The U.S. South and Europe: Transatlantic Relations in the Nineteenth and Twentieth Centuries*, ed. Cornelis A. van Minnen and Manfred Berg (Lexington: University Press of Kentucky, 2013), 185.

45. Georges Sadoul, *Histoire d'un art: Le cinéma des origines à nos jours* (Paris: Flammarion, 1949), 119.

46. Harvey Levenstein, *Seductive Journey: American Tourists in France from Jefferson to the Jazz Age* (Chicago: University of Chicago Press, 1998), 235–236. On the falling exchange rate of the franc to the dollar, see "Franc Falls to 17.29 a Dollar," *Chicago Tribune* (European ed.), August 2, 1923, 1; "Franc Falling Still in Paris," *New York Tribune* (European ed.), August 14, 1923, 1.

47. Levenstein, *Seductive Journey*, 246, 258, 262–263.

48. *Chicago Defender*, August 23, 1923, cited in Levenstein, *Seductive Journey*, 264.

49. Emile Derlin Zinsou and Luc Zouménou, *Kojo Tovalou Houénou, précurseur, 1897–1936: pannégrisme et modernité* (Paris: Maisonneuve and Larose, 2004), 132.

50. Georges Boussenot, "Appel aux Américains qui visitent la France," *Le Journal*, July 24, 1923, 4.

51. "Respect aux hommes de couleur," *Le Journal*, August 1, 1923, 1; "Des étrangers qui exagèrent," *Le Matin*, August 1, 1923, 1; "Les étrangers en France," *Le Temps*, August 2, 1923, 1; "No 'Color Line' in France Tourists Told," *Chicago Tribune* (European ed.), August 2, 1923, 3.

52. "A quoi sert le dernier avertissement sur le respect du aux Francais de couleur," *Le Journal*, August 7, 1923, 2; "Un noir vaut un blanc," *Le Petit Parisien*, August 8, 1923, 4; "Test Case to Be Brought in Paris after Montmartre 'Color-Line' Row," *New York Herald* (European ed.), August 8, 1923, 1; Zinsou and Zouménou, *Kojo Tovalou Houénou*, 132.

53. Zinsou and Zouménou, *Kojo Tovalou Houénou*, especially chaps. 8, 9, and 10; Melvyn Stokes, "Kojo Tovalou Houénou: An Assessment," in "Hommage to Michel Fabre," special issue, *Transatlantica* 2009, no. 1 (2009), https://transatlantica.revues.org/4271.

54. Zinsou and Zouménou, *Kojo Tovalou Houénou*, 39–40, 44, 57, 59, 65–66, 132; Stokes, "Race, Politics, and Censorship," 29, 31.

55. "Le prince Tovalou [*sic*] porte plainte contre le tenancier trop brutal," *Le Journal*, August 8, 1923, 2; "A quoi sert le dernier avertissement," 2; "Test Case," 1.

56. "Blancs et noirs: M. Barthélemy interpelle," *L'Ère Nouvelle*, August 11, 1923, 2; "Plans Interpellation on Drawing Color Line," *Chicago Tribune* (European ed.), August 10, 1923, 3; "Les français de couleur," *Le Temps*, August 12, 1923, 2; "Blancs et noirs," *L'Ère Nouvelle*, August 12, 1923, 1; "Les incidents entre Américains et gens de couleur," *Le Matin*, August 12, 1923, 2.

57. "Le français de couleur—un lettre de M. Poincaré," *Le Petit Parisien*, August 18, 1923, 2; "Les français de couleur," *La Lanterne*, August 19, 1923, 2.

58. Auguste Nardy, "Les incoherences d'Anastasie," *Le Courrier Cinématographique*, August 25, 1923, 7; "Une interdiction," *Ciné-Journal/Le Journal du Film*, no. 730 (New Series 28), August 24, 1923, 8; "Suit Threatened in Banned Movie," *New York Herald* (European ed.), August 22, 1923, 1. The text of Boussenot's letter to Maunoury was published in Jean Clair, "La politique et le cinéma—le film interdit," *L'Ère Nouvelle*, August 22, 1923, 2.

59. "Color-Line Discussion Has Sequel in Ban on 'The Birth of a Nation,'" *New York Herald* (European ed.), August 20, 1923, 1; "La préfecture de police interdit un film," *Le Petit*

Parisien, August 20, 1923, 3; "La représentation d'un film hostile aux noirs est interdit à Paris," *Le Journal*, August 20, 1923, 2; "Un film américain interdit," *Le Matin*, August 20, 1923, 1.

60. The ban was lifted in mid-September, and the film opened in Paris again in early October. Jean-Louis Croze, "Interdiction levée," *Comœdia*, September 17, 1923, 2; "Interdiction levée," *Le Cinéopse* 5, no. 50 (October 1923): 784.

61. Stokes, "Race, Politics, and Censorship," 34–38.

62. Balance Sheet, Epoch Producing Corporation, May 31, 1915, frames 1212–1213; Balance Sheet, Epoch, July 31, 1915, frame 1243; Statement of Net Earnings, Epoch, August 12 to September 10, 1915, frame 1267; Epoch Producing Corporation, Report and Accounts, February 29, 1916, frame 1520, all *D. W. Griffith Papers*.

63. Epoch Producing Corporation, Royalties Paid and Accrued, For the Period Ended February 29, 1916, *D. W. Griffith Papers*, frame 1541.

64. Kristin Thompson, *Exporting Entertainment: America in the World Film Market, 1907–1934* (London: British Film Institute, 1985), 79; João Villaverde, "'O Nascimento de uma Nação' marca o início do domíno de Hollywood sobre o cinema mundial," "Cultural Cinema," *Estadão* (Rio de Janeiro), March 29, 2015.

65. "Optus' response to the ACCC draft decision," Appendix C: Urban Growth, *Australian Competition & Consumer Commission*, January 7, 2009. https://www.accc.gov.au /system/files/Appendix%20C%20-%20Urban%20growth.pdf. Melbourne, the second most populous city (ibid.), was also second to screen *The Birth of a Nation*.

66. See, for example, advertisement in *The Sun* (Sydney), April 16, 1916, 7. On Mitchell and McCarthy, see Stokes, *D. W. Griffith's* The Birth of a Nation, 115–116.

67. Advertisement in *Sydney Morning Herald*, April 21, 1916, 2.

68. *Referee* (Sydney), April 12, 1916, 15; "On the Screen and Off," *Graphic of Australia* (Melbourne), April 20, 1916, 11.

69. "Royalty Sees Picture," *The Sun* (Sydney), April 17, 1916, 3.

70. "*The Birth of a Nation*," *The World's News* (Sydney), April 15, 1916, 5.

71. Advertisement in *The Sunday Times* (Sydney), April 23, 1916, 6.

72. Marjorie Barnard, *A History of Australia* (Sydney: Angus and Robertson, 1962), 446–450; Myra Willard, *History of the White Australia Policy to 1920* (London: Frank Cass, 1967), 20–118.

73. Barnard, *A History of Australia*, 466–467; Willard, *History of the White Australia Policy*, 119–121.

74. Barnard, *A History of Australia*, 468–469; Willard, *History of the White Australia Policy*, 182–185.

75. "A Phenomenal Undertaking—The Making of 'The Birth of a Nation,'" *The Sunday Times* (Sydney), April 23, 1916, 4.

76. "*The Birth of a Nation*," *Ashburton Guardian*, December 14, 1916, 2, National Library of New Zealand.

77. "The Moving Row of Magic Shadow Shapes," *The Sun* (Sydney), April 30, 1916, 19.

78. "Brilliant Premiere Accorded Big Film," *The Sunday Times* (Sydney), April 23, 1916, 10.

79. "Reports and Statistics," *Australian Institute of Health and Welfare*, http://www.aihw .gov.au/WorkArea/DownloadAsset.aspx?id=60129544179.

80. "Birth of a Nation—Battle Film at Royal," *The Sun* (Sydney), April 23, 1916, 2. On trench fighting, also see "The Playgoer," *Punch* (Melbourne), June 8, 1916, 41.

81. "The Birth of a Nation," *The Ballarat* (Australia) *Star*, June 12, 1916, 2.

82. "Brilliant Premiere Accorded Big Film," *Sunday Times* (Sydney), April 23, 1916, 10; cf. "£100,000 Production," *Punch* (Melbourne), May 18, 1916, 11.

83. "The Birth of a Nation," *Sydney Morning Herald*, April 11, 1916, 2.

84. "Scotland For Ever," *Sunday Times* (Sydney), April 30, 1916, 16; cf. "Historic and Informative," *The World's News* (Sydney), May 6, 1916, 5.

85. Epoch Production Corporation, Financial Statement up to February 29, 1916, *D. W. Griffith Papers*, reel 2, frame 1541. All numbers are rounded up or down to the closest dollar.

86. Epoch Production Corporation, Treasurer's Financial Statement for September, 1916, *D. W. Griffith Papers*, reel 2, frame 1682.

87. Advertisement in *The Sun* (Sydney), May 6, 1916, 2. The film would continue to be screened at these prices in Sydney until June 9, 1916. See advertisement in *Sydney Morning Herald*, June 5, 1916, 2.

88. Advertisement in *The Argus* (Melbourne), May 10, 1916, 16.

89. See, for example, advertisement in *The Argus* (Melbourne), May 12, 1916, 14; Advertisement in *The Age* (Melbourne), May 10, 1916, 16.

90. "The Theatre Royal was not large enough to accommodate the crowds which flocked to it on Saturday." "Gossip of the Theatres and Players," *Referee* (Sydney), May 24, 1916, 15; cf. "Wiliamson News," *Sunday Times* (Sydney), May 21, 1916, 6.

91. "The Curse of a Nation," advertisement in *The Age* (Melbourne), May 13, 1916, 16; *The Argus* (Melbourne), May 15, 1916, 14.

92. "The Birth of a Nation—Rival Picture Productions—Matter Before Supreme Court," *The Age* (Melbourne), May 20, 1916, 14; "What's in a Name?—Rival Picture Plays," *The Argus* (Melbourne), May 20, 1916, 21; "The Birth of a Nation—Rival Picture Productions—Injunction Refused," *The Age* (Melbourne), May 24, 1916, 12.

93. Advertisement in *Table Talk* (Melbourne), May 25, 1916, 26.

94. "The Playgoer," *Punch* (Melbourne), May 25, 1916, 40; Advertisement in *The Age* (Melbourne), May 27, 1916, 16; "Music and Drama," *The Argus* (Melbourne), June 12, 1916, 5.

95. Advertisement in *Newcastle* (Australia) *Morning Herald and Miners' Advocate*, June 12, 1916, 8; Garden Picture Palace, Advertisement in *Maitland* (Australia) *Daily Mercury*, June 12, 1916, 8; "The Birth of a Nation," *The Ballarat* (Australia) *Star*, June 12, 1916, 2; *Geelong* (Australia) *Advertiser*, June 15, 1916, 1.

96. Advertisement in *Sydney Morning Herald*, June 5, 1916, 2.

97. Statement of Net Earnings, Epoch Producing Corporation, October 1916, November 1916, December 1916, April 1917, *D. W. Griffith Papers*, reel 2, frames 1690, 1731, 1768, 1988.

98. "The Birth of a Nation," *Sunday Times* (Sydney), April 16, 1916, 19.

99. See, for example, Advertisement in *Sydney Morning Herald*, April 19, 1916, 2.

100. "The Moving Row," 19.

101. "Miscellaneous," *Sunday Times* (Sydney), May 21, 1916, 17; "The Moving Row," 19. "Larrikin push" was Australian slang for "hooligan gang."

102. "Brooksie's Silent Film Collection," May 30, 2014, http://brooksiescollection.tumblr.com/post/87247634902/a-1916-film-diary-birth-of-a-nation; "In the Clutches of the Klan," *Moving Picture World* 18 (1913): 50.

103. See, for example, "A Phenomenal Undertaking," *Sunday Times* (Sydney), April 23, 1916, 4.

104. See "Brooksie's Silent Film Collection," *brooksiescollection*, May 30, 2014. http://brooksiescollection.tumblr.com/post/87247634902/a-1916-film-diary-birth-of-a-nation.

105. Leon F. Litwack, "*The Birth of a Nation*," in *Past Imperfect: History According to the Movies*, ed. Marc C. Carnes, Ted Mico, John Miller-Monzon, and David Rubel (London: Cassell, 1996), 136.

106. Tina Campt, *Other Germans: Black Germans and the Politics of Race, Gender, and Memory in the Third Reich* (Ann Arbor: University of Michigan Press, 2004), 31–35, quotation from 35.

107. E. D. Morel, "The Employment of Black Troops in Europe," *The Nation* (London), March 27, 1920, 893.

108. E. D. Morel, "Black Scourge in Europe: Sexual Horror Let Loose by France on Rhine," *Daily Herald* (London), April 10, 1920.

109. Dick van Galen Last with Ralf Futselaar, *Black Shame: African Soldiers in Europe, 1914–1922*, trans. Marjolijn de Jager (London: Bloomsbury, 2015), 144–152, 156–159, 179–184, 188–200; Iris Wigger, "'Against the Laws of Civilization': Race, Gender and Nation in the International Racist Campaign against the 'Black Shame,'" in "Race and Ethnicity: In a Global Context," special issue, *Berkeley Journal of Sociology* 46 (2002): 114–115.

110. Erika Kuhlman, *Reconstructing Patriarchy after the First World War: Women, Gender, and Postwar Reconciliation between Nations* (New York: Palgrave Macmillan, 2008), 59.

111. Ibid.

112. "In France, the film was forbidden by the censorship. . . . It remained forbidden in the French-occupied zones of Germany, where the nationalists waged a lively campaign against the presence of Senegalese troops in the Rhine." Georges Sadoul, *Histoire Générale du Cinéma, Tome III: Le Cinéma devient un art (1909–1920)*, vol. 2, *La Première Guerre Mondiale* (Paris: Denoël, 1952), 17.

113. Keith L. Nelson, "The 'Black Horror on the Rhine': Race as a Factor in Post-World War 1 Diplomacy," *Journal of Modern History* 42, no. 4 (December 1970): 617, 620; Kuhlman, *Reconstructing Patriarchy*, 60–61.

114. The Rhenish Women's League had been founded in May 1920 inside the German Ministry of the Interior. Later that year, it distributed a pamphlet in English called *Colored Frenchmen on the Rhine: An Appeal of White Women to American Womanhood*. Julia Roos, "Nationalism, Racism and Propaganda in Early Weimar Germany: Contradictions in the Campaign against the 'Black Horror on the Rhine,'" *German History* 30, no. 1 (2012): 51–54; Kuhlman, *Reconstructing Patriarchy*, 54.

115. Wigger, "'Against the Laws of Civilization,'" 116–117, 122–123; Dick van Galen Last, "Black Shame," *History Today* (October 2006): 19.

116. Jean-Yves Le Naour, *La honte noire: l'Allemagne et les troupes colonials françaises, 1914–1945* (Paris: Hachette, 2004), 135. In August 1921, its exhibition permit was revoked by the censorship bureau on the orders of the German government, following strong French diplomatic pressure. Ibid., 136–137. Also on the film, see Julia Roos, "'Huns' and Other 'Barbarians': A Movie Ban and the Dilemmas of 1920s German Propaganda against French Colonial Troops," *Historical Reflections* 40, no. 1 (Spring 2014): 69–77.

117. Le Naour, *La honte noire*, 135.

118. Kuhlman, *Reconstructing Patriarchy*, 57–58; Peter Campbell, "'Black Horror on the Rhine': Idealism, Pacifism, and Racism in Feminism and the Left in the Aftermath of the First World War," *Histoire sociale/Social history* 47, no. 94 (June 2014): 474; Nelson, "The 'Black Horror on the Rhine,'" 615; Wigger, "'Against the Laws of Civilization,'" 120; Jared Poley, *Decolonization in Germany: Western Narratives of Colonial Loss and Foreign Occupation* (Oxford: Peter Lang, 2005), 188–205; Kuhlman, *Reconstructing Patriarchy*.

119. Campbell, "Black Horror on the Rhine," 474; Poley, *Decolonization in Germany*, 188.

120. *Stage and Cinema* (South Africa), September 1, 1917, quoted in Peter Davis, *In Darkest Hollywood: Exploring the Jungles of Cinema's South Africa* (Randburg, South Africa: Ravan Press, 1996), 129.

121. Jane M. Gaines, "Birthing Nations," in *Cinema and Nation*, ed. Mette Hjort and Scott Mackenzie (London: Routledge, 2000), 298–316; Edwin Hees, "The Birth of a Nation: Contextualizing *De Voortrekkers* (1916)," in *To Change Reels: Film and Film Culture in South Africa*, ed. Isabel Balseiro and Ntongela Masilela (Detroit: Wayne State University Press, 2003), 49–69; Jacqueline Maingard, *South African National Cinema* (London: Routledge, 2007), 16–34; Davis, *In Darkest Hollywood*, 128–135.

122. Hees, "The Birth of a Nation," 55–56.

123. Ibid., 57, 58, 62, 65; Maingard, *South African National Cinema*, 20; Davis, *In Darkest Hollywood*, 133.

124. Hees, "The Birth of a Nation," 59; Maingard, *South African National Cinema*, 20; Gaines, "Birthing Nations," 312. Gaines also points out that each film is associated "with a defeated group [Boers, Southern secessionists] whose history is glorified." Gaines, "Birthing Nations," 301.

125. Schlesinger, a businessman born in Eastern Europe in 1871, had emigrated to the United States in 1884. A decade later, he left for South Africa, where, according to James T. Campbell, he would become the principal founder of South African cinema. James T. Campbell, "The Americanization of South Africa," in *Race, Nation, and Empire in American History*, ed. James T. Campbell and Matthew Pratt (Chapel Hill: University of North Carolina Press, 2007), 140–142.

126. Maingard, *South African National Cinema*, 24. On Shaw, also see urbanora, "Harold Shaw and De Voortrekkers," *The Bioscope*, November 24, 2008, http://thebioscope.net/2008/11/24/harold-shaw-and-de-voortrekkers/.

127. Davis, *In Darkest Hollywood*, 128.

128. Brian Willan, "'Cinematographic Calamity,'" 636.

129. Travers Buxton to Mary White Ovington, February 18, 1916, NAACPP.

130. John Trumpbour, *Selling Hollywood to the World: U.S. and European Struggles for Mastery of the Global Film Industry, 1920–1950* (Cambridge: Cambridge University Press, 2002), 144.

131. Willan, "'Cinematographic Calamity,'" 637–638.

132. Ibid., 638.

133. Epoch Production Corporation, Financial Statement up to May 31, 1917, *D. W. Griffith Papers*, reel 3, frame 0070. For release dates, see www.imdb.com.

134. Willan, "'Cinematographic Calamity,'" 635.

135. W. E. B. Du Bois, *Dusk of Dawn* (Chicago: A. C. McClurg, 1903), 1.

4

DEFINING NATIONAL IDENTITY

The Birth of a Nation *from America to South Africa*

Peter Davis

SOUTH AFRICAN FILM HISTORIAN THELMA GUTSCHE WROTE IN the 1940s that *The Birth of a Nation*'s reputation in South Africa "approached that of a fetishism."[1] Although there must have been many other screenings, the first recorded screening of *The Birth of a Nation* in South Africa was in 1931; it took place at Johannesburg Town Hall, which suggests some kind of political intent. It was condemned by black intellectual Sol Plaatje, who asked whether the screening was "licensed to fan the embers of race hatred in South Africa."[2] Why would *The Birth of a Nation* strike such a chord in South Africa?

The Dutch filmmaker Joris Ivens wrote of Hollywood that it was "the world's greatest centre of propaganda."[3] That this propaganda was largely incidental does not make it any less influential. If we take as one aspect of *The Birth of a Nation* its assertion of white supremacy and black menace, we must not be surprised that this message, through the power of film, was snapped up and emulated in areas where it was deemed important to maintain such supremacy—and this was certainly the case in South Africa. Inextricably linked to these notions of white supremacy, but even more powerful, was the element of nationalism. Expressed in *The Birth of a Nation* as the welding together of North and South into one union, in South Africa the influence of Griffith's film can be felt in the rise of Afrikaner nationalism, the final fusion of the disparate factions of the people of mixed

Dutch, French, and German descent commonly called Boers (the Dutch word for "farmers") who ultimately would be known as Afrikaners, or what we might call "white Africans."

It is unfortunately common to human experience that nationhood is achieved through triumph over adversity, usually after much suffering, and frequently after massive bloodshed. This was certainly the case of the Afrikaner *volk*, who fought indigenous peoples and finally the British Empire in the attempt to carve out a living space in Africa. At the time of the dissemination of *The Birth of a Nation* in 1915–1916, Afrikaner unity had not been achieved; there is a strong case to be made that Griffith's film played an of-necessity indefinable role in winning that goal. An early one-reeler by Griffith, *The Zulu's Heart* (1908), shows an awareness in the director of the existence in South Africa of a parallel history with the United States. Primitive in every way, including Zulus played by whites in blackface, *The Zulu's Heart* depicts a white pioneer family traveling in a covered wagon and attacked by savages. The comparison with the American mythology of the winning of the West by hardy pioneers requisitely attacked by red Indians would have been immediately apparent to an American audience, just as myriad films about the American Wild West would already have been seen by audiences in South Africa.

To appreciate why *The Birth of a Nation* could have an influence in South Africa, it is important to understand South Africa's history; comparisons with America in the mid-nineteenth century should be obvious. Beginning with an overview of the social and political situation in South Africa in 1915–1916, it is necessary to consider three ethnic groups:

1. Indigenous Africans (Bantu) were the largest ethnic group by far, still mostly rural, but sending labor to the immensely profitable mines of South Africa. This was a workforce drawn from different indigenous groups, speaking different languages, often with ancient animosities, which made it difficult to achieve any kind of unity and hence bargaining power—which, of course, the white mine owners were adamantly opposed to. This labor force was migrant, often spending years away from the homeland, where they had left wives and children. It was a manual labor force that could never aspire to any kind of higher-level of employment, let alone participation in the South African political process.

2. Boers, also known as Afrikaners, had been in southern Africa almost as long as whites had been in the American South. In the early years of the twentieth century, they were still mostly small farmers, employing black labor. But with migration to the cities, they increasingly became overseers

and equipment operators, forming a level of labor above that of indigenous Africans on the mines. In numbers, the Boers were somewhat larger than the next white group.

3. People of British descent and recent British immigrants, often holding British passports, formed the upper echelon of society, the bureaucracy, and much of the middle class. Many had come as skilled workers from the mines of Britain, and from the colonies, where, in this caste system, they were higher than Boer or Bantu, though not of richer Afrikaners.

There were other ethnic groups, but they are less important for the purposes of this study. In one sense, the history of South Africa from the beginning of the twentieth century has involved the search for some kind of balance between these three groups—not (until the end of the century) of equality, but of pacification. These three ethnic groups had all, within the preceding eighty years, been in conflict: British troops against Africans; Boers against Africans; British against Boers. The battles of British against Africans were battles of conquest and subjugation, with the last such taking place in 1906. This was the last uprising before the turmoil that began in the 1950s.

Ironically, the relationship between Briton and Boer was exacerbated by the Boer–Bantu confrontation. The colony of Cape Town, with its long-established white settlement of a largely Afrikaner population, was taken over by the British at the end of the Napoleonic wars and became a vital staging area for British access to India. This seemed to work well until 1834, when slavery was abolished in British possessions. Boers saw this as a devastating blow to their farming economy. Unlike the situation of the American South, the Boers were not powerful enough to challenge the British by revolt, and in fact the urbanized part of the Afrikaans-speaking population was hardly affected. The solution of the farmers—those who depended on black labor—was to move northward out of Cape Province, seeking free land beyond British control. This migration of some twelve thousand Boers, beginning in 1835, is known as the Great Trek.

Unfortunately, the lands they moved into and settled, as with the experience of pioneers in the American West, were not "free." What followed was a low-level enduring warfare, in which the invaders regularly rustled cattle, and in their movement northward conducted slave raids on the local population, killing parents and seizing children to be raised as slaves. The skirmishes against the native population culminated in the 1838 Battle of Blood River. Presented by earlier white "histories" as the betrayal of an agreement on secession of some land by the Zulus, it should, of course, be rightfully seen as a response by the local populations to an alien and aggressive incursion. But however just the cause of the Zulus, it was not the decisive factor. Interpreted as a "miraculous" God-given victory, a covered-wagon convoy of 450 Voortrekkers defeated an attacking Zulu force of some fifteen thousand to twenty thousand warriors. Whether God had indeed given the Boers the canonry and musketry that were decisive is disputable, but what is not in dispute is that their overwhelming firepower ensured Boer supremacy in the areas they settled and where they established a number of "democratic" republics—the so-called democracy, of course, being limited to the Boers, who legalized slavery under the euphemism of "apprenticeship."

But these republics had the misfortune to be sitting on some of the world's most lucrative deposits of diamonds, gold, coal, and other minerals. Although situated in what was now Boer land, these mines were run by a gang of ruthless European entrepreneurs who managed to engineer the military intervention of a not-unwilling Britain to overthrow the Boer republics. On a smaller scale than the Northern conquest of the American South, the ensuing war was nevertheless just as clumsy and brutal, devastating for the Boer civilian population, whose farms were burned and whose women and children were held in concentration camps that were near death traps. This Anglo-Boer War, which ended in 1902 with British victory, managed to leave in its wake the stuff of heroic legend, which would be turned into an ongoing propaganda-as-history that would eventually lead to the creation of a united Afrikaner *volk*.

After the defeat of the Boers in 1902, their republics were absorbed as provinces into the British colony of South Africa, under a Pax Britannica that guaranteed a kind of peace in a highly stratified and segregated society, white from white as well as white from black. In 1910, South Africa was granted an independent status within the commonwealth. This status would lead to the gradual rise of Afrikaans political power, starting with the founding of the Nationalist Party in 1915, which sought and finally achieved unity among the various groups of Afrikaners. As a result, they assumed power through the voting box in 1948 and subsequently established the apartheid state of South Africa.

In 1916, South Africa was a society with an immensely rich overclass, elements of which, with the kind of hutzpah that is fired by the entrepreneurial spirit and backed by infusions of cash, in this white population of

Figure 4.1. I. W. Schlesinger, head of African Film Productions. *National Film Archive, Pretoria, South Africa.*

perhaps a little more than one million people, established a film industry. Prominent was the American-born I. W. Schlesinger, who in 1915 created African Film Productions and threw himself into filmmaking, of which he had no previous experience whatsoever (fig. 4.1). By the time of the making of the first of the two films under discussion, *De Voortrekkers*, South Africa had a film industry almost 100 percent white in all aspects except African actors and extras and low-level helpers, fed in the beginning by producers, directors, technicians, and actors drawn largely from Britain and the United States. Among the overseas talent Schlesinger imported was director Harold Shaw, another American, who may well have seen *The Birth of a Nation* before going to South Africa in 1916. It may be of some significance that he was from "an old Kentucky family." *De Voortrekkers* would be the most ambitious production hitherto undertaken in South Africa, and it would establish South Africa as a contender—albeit modest—on the world stage.

De Voortrekkers tells the story of the Great Trek up to the Battle of Blood River, as described earlier (fig. 4.2). Intended to celebrate the valor of the Boer invaders, the actual reenactment of the scenes portraying the Zulu warriors involved a massive irony. For the hundreds of extras involved in the staging of the Battle of Blood River—which was shot not at the actual site but just outside Johannesburg, center of the mining industry—African Film Productions approached what seemed to be the most convenient pool of young African men: those in the mines. The irony was that many of these young men were likely descendants of the actual Zulu *impis* (a group of Zulu warriors) from the last century. As a cautionary measure, the black extras were given spears that would bend, and not penetrate, when used.

The white miners who were acting the roles of the Boer pioneers held no love for the descendants of their former foes, who were also their subordinates on the mines. Some of the white miners allegedly took live ammunition with them into the circle of covered wagons, the laager, to withstand the Zulu onslaught. The result was a battle more lifelike than Shaw had intended:

> While the natives were charging the *laager*, the Europeans within had fired shots. Harold Shaw had shouted to them to stop firing and when they had failed to do so, he had run among the natives in an attempt to stop it . . . when (Police) Major Trew saw a native pull a white man off his horse and jab at him with his improvised assegai, he realized the danger of serious disturbance. So far from co-operating in the dispersal of the natives, the Europeans in *laager* fired at close range even when the natives were withdrawing. . . . The natives charged the *laager* furiously; but instead of recoiling and falling "dead", continued into the *laager* itself where blows with Europeans were exchanged. Mounted police under the command of Major Trew were forced to intervene and to prevent the natives from attacking the *laager* in earnest. In moving them away from the scene of the "battle", the police hustled the natives out of the *laager* and into the surrounding hills. Some escaped by swimming the river, and one was drowned.

Figure 4.2. *De Voortrekkers. Screen capture by author.*

Thus does Thelma Gutsche describe the chaotic situation.[4] With the resentments and desire for vengeance that had been aroused, it seems miraculous that more lives were not lost.

That the film was allowed to proceed to completion means that the authorities thought that there were higher issues at stake. To understand these issues, we have to look at the then contemporary context for this project—not at the implications of battles that had occurred some eighty years before in southern Africa but at battles that were taking place in the second decade of the twentieth century. The imperial power, Britain, was engaged in the most savage and devastating war in its history. This war spilled over into Africa and involved British invasion of Germany's African territories by South African troops. What was known as the South African Union Defence Force included Boers, many of whom had fought the British sixteen years earlier, and as early as 1914, the first year of the Great War, some of these plotted a rebellion to restore the lost republics. The rebellion was suppressed, but it showed the delicate nature of Boer–British relations at this desperate period of British rule in South Africa, with German forces just over the border in southwest Africa. What possible advantage could there be in making a film that praised the Boer as warrior?

Neil Parsons notes that the historian Gustav Preller had included anti-British material in his draft script but that this was firmly suppressed by director Shaw.[5] The government had full powers of censorship at all times and would not have allowed such scenes. To have stopped production on a film about a heroic episode of Boer history would certainly have had a dangerous backlash from the Boer population. Clearly the government must have seen some advantage in having a film that could be a sop to Boer feelings without arousing anti-British sentiment. In *De Voortrekkers*, the enemy is not a British army but a Zulu one. In the sense that the Zulus represent the black masses, there is an unstated subtext to the film that it is not the British who are the Boers' enemy but the blacks—the common enemy for both Brit and Boer in their claim on the land of South Africa. A reviewer in the South African publication *Stage and Cinema* understood this very well when he wrote, somewhat optimistically, in 1917: "[*De Voortrekkers*] has probably done more to bring [Afrikaners] and Englishmen together and to help each other to better understanding of the other's point of view, than anything that has ever previously happened . . . this great picture was produced, to form a lasting and glowing tribute to the heroism and self-sacrifice of the early Boers." And it was presumably in this portrayal of Boer "heroism and self-sacrifice" that the censors and the authorities, including those responsible for the war effort, saw opportunity. It was seen as potentially raising the martial spirit of young Boers, whose lives would otherwise be devoted to a humdrum existence on the farm or on the mines. This was the same spirit of adventure, the search for glory, that drew millions in Europe to volunteer for the terrible bloodbath that was World War I. The film was wildly successful, and young Afrikaners did volunteer by the thousands to defend the imperial power that had humiliated their people only a decade and a half earlier. At the time, the film was well received even by white audiences. A writer in *Stage and Cinema* wrote, on December 23, 1916, "I have seen *Birth of a Nation*, and *De Voortrekkers* is a greater film."[6]

Despite the subject, only one Afrikaner is recorded as having worked on the film. This was Preller, who is credited with the scenario. Preller's self-imposed mission in life was to participate in the creation of a united Afrikaner people. The great schism, which dated back at least to the time of the Great Trek, was the divide between those content to be ruled by Britain and those who sought independence. Preller's work, including his contribution to the film, would aid in ultimately achieving the aim of unification.

Both *De Voortrekkers* and *The Birth of a Nation* use sexual union in a church at the end of the film (in *De Voortrekkers*, a new baby; in *The Birth of a Nation*, the newly married couples) to symbolize and sanctify, in the first case, the creation of an Afrikaner nation and in the latter, a united America—both God-blessed and both, needless to say, without black participation.

A little over twenty years after the premiere of *De Voortrekkers* would come *Die Bou van 'n Nasie*—and the English title, *Building a Nation*, immediately invites comparison with *The Birth of a Nation* (fig. 4.3).[7] This film (now, of course, a sound film), also made by Schlesinger's studio, was far more ambitious than *De Voortrekkers* in that it sets out to depict not just one episode but the history of the Afrikaner people from their first arrival in South Africa at the beginning of the seventeenth century up to the establishment of a united South Africa in 1910, after the ending of the Anglo-Boer War in 1902. Its ambition was epic. Its agenda was actively propagandistic.

The title *The Birth of a Nation* is reasonably interpreted to mean the birth of a *united* states of America, where Northern whites and Southern whites have been reconciled but where blacks have been suppressed and have no political role. Similarly, *Building a Nation* purports to project a reconciliation between Afrikaner and Anglo, in which Afrikaners have

Figure 4.3. *Die Bou van 'n Nasie. Screen capture by author.*

finally achieved their rightful place. Again, blacks feature only as servants and enemies. Going back to the earliest years of white settlement, *Building a Nation* creates an idyllic portrayal of Boer South Africa very much like the South portrayed in *The Birth of a Nation*: a courtly society of genteel people living in an orderly earthly paradise. Differing from *De Voortrekkers*, where slavery is never mentioned, *Building a Nation* presents a somewhat labored discussion of that institution, which presents this specious argument from a slave owner: "[Slaves] depend on me as I depend on them." There is also this well-worn assertion: "These slaves were not unhappy. In the main, they were a cheerful and well-fed band of workers, devoted to their master, and their happy nature found expression in music and song." And to prove the latter, we are subjected to dance scenes exactly comparable to those in *The Birth of a Nation.*

African leaders are presented as tyrants with the unfortunate habit of spitting. The relationship of the Zulus with the white race is depicted as treachery and aggression. In a perversion of history, the prime motive behind the Great Trek is offered as unprovoked attack by savage Africans, not the British abolition of slavery. In the film, it is expressed as "the [British] government has failed [to give security]," so "[we must] free ourselves from the oppression of an unsympathetic government, and from the odium cast upon us by philanthropists"—the latter meaning the antislavery movement. Slavery is not mentioned in this apparently dispassionate argument, but one of the guiding principles is to "preserve proper relations between master and servant." For these reasons, the Boers set out to establish an "independent community with freedom, justice, and peace for all." Omitted is "providing it is white."

The making of *Building a Nation* was synchronized with a reenactment of the Great Trek around the centenary of that event, with ox wagons starting out from Cape Town to make the eight hundred-mile journey to the nation's capital, Pretoria. The appeal of the centenary of the Great Trek to "those Afrikaner hearts which do not yet beat together" was a clarion call for Afrikaner unity, and it was this aim that *Building a Nation* supported.[8] The film was the fruit of the new Afrikaans-language film industry, which dated from the early 1930s—that is, the commencement of the era of the talkies— and was itself conceived out of the Afrikaner nationalist movement.

Building a Nation includes the requisite triumph over adversity, after substantial letting of blood. In this longer history, this was the defeat of the Zulus at Blood River and other battles and, most provocatively, the war against British imperialism. Two versions of the film were made. The Afrikaans version premiered to a rapturous audience made up only of Afrikaners on May 29, 1939—too late for the December 16, 1938, centenary of the Blood River victory. (The earlier *De Voortrekkers* had been shown on that date.) The Afrikaans newspaper *Die Vaderland* celebrated the film's propaganda value, deeming it "a mighty factor in our nation-building."[9] The English-language version was not released for another six months. When it did, the South African *Sunday Times* baldly stated that it portrayed England as "the villain of the piece," and it enraged English-speaking audiences.[10] This was also the year, 1939, of the second great threat to British power of the twentieth century.

While there is a symbolic, and somewhat perfunctory, handshake between Brits and Boers at the depiction of the 1910 Act of Union, which gave South Africa independence, British South Africans felt that the British role in the building of white South Africa had been grossly neglected. Funding for the film had come from the government, and the English-language press was especially incensed that public money had gone into the making of a film that was blatantly propagandistic in tone. That the nationalistic aspirations of the film had been achieved was evidenced when Afrikaner audiences booed the on-screen Cecil Rhodes and British soldiers, both hated by Afrikaners. Just as in World War I, there were elements in Afrikaner society, many of them strongly influenced by Nazi Germany, ready to take advantage of Britain's peril by another rebellion that had to be suppressed. With the outbreak of war against Germany—South Africa once more siding with Britain—there were protests in Parliament against the film, and it was withdrawn from exhibition. Ten years later, after the war, the film would be reinstated, the Afrikaners' United Party would be voted into power, and it would dominate South African politics up to the end of apartheid. The structure of this new South Africa is foreshadowed in the final scene of *Building a Nation*: a white farmer guides the plow, his wife sows the seeds, a black leads the oxen. The "savage people" of the early text have been tamed to serve the whites, and there is nary an Anglo in sight.

So both films, I believe demonstrably, played an important role in South African politics. Whereas *Building a Nation* subtly tuned the lingering, and justified, resentment of the British, *De Voortrekkers* hides that adversarial relationship to dwell on the *swart gevaar*, fear of the blacks. In both films, blacks are the more substantial enemy. Yet by the time *De Voortrekkers* was made, and for the rest of the century, South Africa's indigenous population did not pose a real military threat. The overriding threat was economic. If blacks were ever to attain equal status in the workplace with whites, the Boers, with their long history as poor whites fully equal to that stratum of the American South, would be overwhelmed. This was the real terror behind the Afrikaner nationalist movement. Yet the economic element does not appear in *Building a Nation*; it would not have been a factor in the historical period of *De Voortrekkers*.

What all three films—*The Birth of a Nation, De Voortrekkers*, and *Building a Nation*—have in common is an expression of political power. The two ethnic groups—America's Southerners and South Africa's Boers—enjoy, then lose, power over another group. In the case of the Confederacy, it is slaves; in the case of the Boers, it is kaffirs, or black Africans. This lost hegemony was essential to their self-definition, their self-respect, and their economy. In all three films, they regain power by (in the American film) terrorizing freed slaves and, in the two South African films, by defeating African enemies. Historically, the struggle for power was much more complex—dare one say, less black and white; in all the films, the politics are simplified by scapegoating blacks. Although the vindictiveness toward the ex-slaves in *The Birth of a Nation* is quite absent from the South African films.

I began by mentioning Griffith's film *The Zulu's Heart*. The Zulu chief plays a dual role: first as an aggressor who leads the attack on the pioneer wagon; then, with a change of heart, he becomes the protector of the white woman he has widowed and of her child. Thus, succinctly, Griffith lays down the template for depictions of Africans and even African Americans for much of the rest of the century. In one Janus persona, he shows us the Savage Other and the opposite, the Faithful Servant—the Savage Other being those who attack whites and the Faithful Servant those who defend whites. (In *The Birth of a Nation*, the latter appears as "faithful souls.")

In both of the South African films, Africans are depicted as treacherous and killers of white women and children as well as being a military threat. However, in the South African films, significantly absent, perhaps surprisingly, is any overt, or even underlying, sexual threat. The notion of Africans as predators of white women plays a significant role in *The Birth of a Nation*. I offer this as a possible reason for the difference: in the two South African films, the threat to the settlers is overwhelmingly of being defeated in war by enemies of another race, whereas in *The Birth of a Nation*, the enemy is white, and in that sense presented as on a par with the Southerners. The black slaves cannot reasonably be offered as warrior enemies as the Zulus truly were. Instead, the sexual threat to the purity of the white race has to be manufactured as a fictional enemy more threatening than the real white Northerners—indeed, as a kind of subtle rationale for the war itself. And it is a rational that, in reality, would be used to justify the eternal shame of the lynch mob.

In the Union of South Africa in the first decades of the twentieth century there was no law against interracial marriage, although in the Afrikaner province of the Transvaal such marriages could not be solemnized.[11] Nationally, interracial marriages appeared to be below 1 percent. However, a law that made both intermarriage and sexual relationships criminal offenses was among the first to be passed by the apartheid Nationalist Party government after it came to power in 1949. In early American cinema, the threat of black rape of white women was an explosive subject not lightly invoked. Thomas Cripps mentions only one example—an unnamed film whose description in a catalog included, "the catching, taring [*sic*] and feathering and burning of a negro for the assault of a white woman."[12] Notably, the subject was so sensitive that the black villain—as in *The Birth of a Nation*—was portrayed by a white actor in blackface, creating a grotesque kind of protective barrier for the viewer's sensitivities.

The "good African," the faithful servant to whites, although a perennial figure in other South African films as well as featuring prominently in *The Birth of a Nation*, does not appear in *Building a Nation* other than in the final scene as a docile farmworker. It is hard to conjecture why. But such a character appears in *De Voortrekkers*, with surprising effect, because he comes to dominate much of the film, taking over from the white leads, who are largely cyphers.

In the earlier film, we are introduced to the Zulu warrior Sobuza (a nonhistorical character) when he is undergoing conversion to Christianity by missionaries who teach him that killing is wrong. Sobuza's first test comes when he disobeys the Zulu king Dingaan's order to kill the king's baby son, this being a habitual practice of the film's Zulu king. Sobuza is shamed and driven from the tribe. In his flight, he meets up with a missionary who advises him, somewhat oddly, to "Go South, to the White Man's country, where you may live without strife."

Sobuza follows this advice, is accepted by the Voortrekkers, and becomes a servant, but of a particular kind. He cooks for and looks after two young boys, work normally done by women (fig. 4.4). He has become emasculated, in effect, a nanny. However, enough of his warrior manhood is left for him to take on the task of tracking down Dingaan and slaying him in personal combat (this physical participation of the servant in what is effective assistance to the white masters appears also in *The Birth of a Nation*, as enacted by the "faithful souls").

So, curiously, once he appears on-screen, Sobuza becomes the central figure. His fidelity is absolute: he becomes the Faithful Servant who defeats the Savage Other. The final few scenes are remarkable. The Boers have built a church dedicated to the Covenant, carrying out their promise to God for preserving "their race and country" in the Battle of Blood River. Inside, they worship, seated in their pews. At the church porch is Sobuza, in

Figure 4.4. Sobuza with his white wards. *Screen capture by author.*

Western clothing, staring with ecstasy at the cross. This scene holds a terrible irony, obviously quite oblivious to the filmmakers. Although Sobuza
has devoted his life to serving whites, has fought for them and adopted
their religion, his skin prevents him from sitting beside them at service—
his greatest reward is to listen *outside* the white church. And this is surely
symbolic of the Afrikaners' positioning of blacks in their society: pacified,
servile, dutiful—above all, separate, and never approaching equality. It is a
defining image of apartheid.

PETER DAVIS is President of Villon Films. He is an award-winning
writer, producer, and director of more than seventy documentaries, and
author of *In Darkest Hollywood: Exploring the Jungles of Cinema's South
Africa.*

Notes

1. Thelma Gutsche, *The History and Social Significance of Motion Pictures in South
Africa, 1895–1940* (Cape Town: Howard Timmins, 1972), 314.

2. Edwin Hees, "*The Birth of a Nation*: Contextualizing *De Voortrekkers* (1916)," in *To Change Reels*, ed. Isabel Balseiro and Ntongela Masilela (Detroit: Wayne State University Press, 2003).

3. Joris Ivens, *The Camera and I* (New York: International, 1969).

4. Gutsche, *The History and Social Significance of Motion Pictures in South Africa*.

5. Neil Parsons, "Investigating the Origins of *The Rose of Rhodesia*, Part 1: African Film Productions," *Screening the Past*, July 23, 2009, www.screeningthepast.com/2015/01.

6. Jacqueline Maingard, *South African National Cinema* (London: Routledge, 2007).

7. The title *They Built a Nation* is the literal English translation of the film, but it is also common to see the film referred to as *Building a Nation*. This chapter privileges the latter translation because *Building a Nation* is the commonly accepted English denomination.

8. Words of Voortrekker leader Sarel Cilliers at the beginning of Great Trek, as quoted by Henning Klopper on the centenary celebrations.

9. Thelma Gutsche, "The History and Social Significance of Motion Pictures in South Africa, 1895–1940," (PhD diss., University of Cape Town, 1946), 348.

10. J. Langley Levy, editor of *The Sunday Times*, strongly criticized the film's anti-British stance in *The Sunday Times*, May 26, 1939.

11. Hermann Giliomee, *The Afrikaners: Biography of a People* (Charlottesville: University of Virginia Press, 2003).

12. Thomas Cripps, *Slow Fade to Black* (Oxford: Oxford University Press, 1993), 13.

5

COMMENT

Is The Birth of a Nation *a Western?*

Alex Lichtenstein

LET ME BEGIN WITH A STORY, PROVOKED BY Peter Davis's remarks about the interplay of Griffith's vision and that of white South African filmmakers. Today, if you travel through KwaZulu-Natal Province in South Africa, you can visit a historic site where the Battle of Blood River (known by the Zulu as *iMpi yaseNcome*) occurred on December 16, 1838. This isolated spot is located twenty kilometers down a dirt road in an impoverished—though stunningly beautiful—rural area. In fact, there are two adjacent historic sites here, narrowly separated by the Ncome River though widely separated in conceptualization and intention. One, established in 1999 by the ruling African National Congress's Department of Arts, Culture, Science and Technology, uses an elaborate museum display to recount the battle story from the point of view of African nationalism and, more particularly, Zulu nationalism. On the other side of the river, one finds a privately run older installation, the Bloedrivier Heritage Site, managed by the Stigting vir die Bloedrivier-Gelofteterrein (Foundation for the Site of the Blood River Vow).[1] On this latter site—first established in 1938 on the centenary of the battle—there sits a replica (built in 1971), of a round laager of wagons used by Boer pioneers (known as Voortrekkers) as a defensive rampart (fig. 5.1). In 1838, the story goes, the Voortrekkers had put their wagons in an interlocked circle to defend themselves against thousands of attacking Zulu warriors. This, of course, is the central event of Afrikaner nationalist mythology, dating right up to today.[2]

Figure 5.1. The recreated laager at the Blood River Heritage Site, KwaZulu-Natal, South Africa. *Used with permission from the Blood River Heritage Site.*

This incident, however, took on powerful significance in December 1938, when the centenary of the battle was celebrated by Afrikaners with a recreation of their Great Trek from the Western Cape into Natal and the Transvaal, where they had first directly encountered African peoples. Indeed, as Peter Davis notes, this commemoration proved the occasion for the 1938 release of a South African film, *Die Bou van 'N Nasie* (*They Built a Nation*).[3] That same year, the reenacted Great Trek culminated with the laying of a cornerstone of the Voortrekker Monument on a hill above South Africa's capital, Pretoria. On December 16, 1949, shortly after the electoral triumph of the Afrikaner nationalists, this monument was inaugurated with enormous fanfare, captured by, among others, Margaret Bourke-White for the pages of *Life* magazine (figs. 5.2a, 5.2b, and 5.2c).[4]

Visitors to the Bloedrivier Heritage Site today will find a small gift shop, run by a very pleasant Afrikaner family. If you ask, they will show you a forty-five-minute documentary film about the history of the Battle of Blood River. This film, it must be said, is narrated rather unapologetically from the Afrikaner point of view. The brave Voortrekkers are described

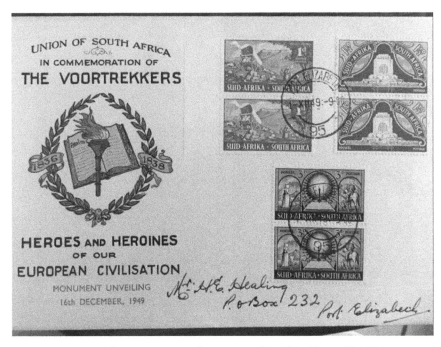

Figure 5.2a. A postcard commemorating the 1949 unveiling of the Voortrekker Monument. *Photograph by the author.*

Figure 5.2b. The Voortrekker Monument, commemorating the Great Trek.

Figure 5.2c. Photograph of the Voortrekker Monument by Margaret Bourke-White on December 16, 1949, the day of its inauguration. *Used with permission of Getty Images.*

as seeking to be "free from the stifling oppression and regulations of British rule," with no mention of the British Empire's abolition of slavery, to which they objected. Their antagonist, the "treacherous" Zulu king, Dingaan, murders the "unsuspecting" advance Voortrekker party led by Piet Retief (fig. 5.3).

Even the normally naïve British missionary, the film implies, chooses to flee Natal in the face of the stirred-up Zulu. What the Zulu warriors take to be wails of fear coming from within the circled wagons (the laager) of their enemies, the narrator assures, were instead the Voortrekkers bravely singing Christian hymns the night before the attack. The narration even gives some credence to the idea that the fortuitous natural defenses afforded by the laager's position in the valley may, in fact, have been divinely ordained. In more earthly terms, this historical propaganda film relies on three elements: standard documentary voice-over illustrated with photographs, documents, paintings, and battle maps; contemporary dramatic landscape shots of the recreated laager (at dawn, at night, in the fog) set to swelling music; and, most interestingly for our purposes, many intercut historical film clips (described in the credits as *rolprentinsetsels*, or "archive films"). The clips are from the 1938 government-produced film *They Built a Nation*,

Figure 5.3. Marble frieze inside the Voortrekker Monument depicting the slaughter of Voortrekker women and children by Dingaane's warriors after Dingaane's betrayal of Piet Retief in 1838. *Photograph by author.*

Figure 5.4. The "Vow of the Covenant," shortly before the battle of Blood River. Still from *Die Bou Van 'n Nasie* (1938), as used in the film *16 Desember 1838: Die Slag van Bloedrivier,* Voortrekker Monument Heritage Site, 2003.

Figure 5.5a. The Voortrekkers in their laager, fending off the Zulu attack, Blood River. Still from *Die Bou Van 'n Nasie* (1938), as used in the film *16 Desember 1838: Die Slag van Bloedrivier*, Voortrekker Monument Heritage Site, 2003.

Figure 5.5b. From *Die Bou Van 'n Nasie* (1938). The Voortrekkers in their laager at Blood River, awaiting the Zulus' attack. *Screen capture by author.*

a second South African dramatization of the Great Trek made in 1973 called *Die Voortrekkers*, and the 1986 South African Broadcasting Corporation television series *Shaka Zulu* (but not, oddly enough, from Harold Shaw's 1916 silent film *De Voortrekkers*).[5] The 1938 film, in particular, is drawn on heavily to dramatize key moments in Afrikaner history, such as the murder of Retief and the Afrikaner covenant sealed on the so-called Day of the Vow, and, of course, the battle itself, marked by the heroic and miraculous defense of the laager surrounded by Zulu warriors (figs. 5.4, 5.5a, and 5.5b).

The *Rand Daily Mail* applauded the fact that in the film, "both English and Dutch are depicted as willing and eager to cooperate"—a marked contrast to subsequent uses of the film in the service of Afrikaner nationalist propaganda. The similarity to Griffith's emphasis on a potential rapprochement of North and South at the expense of African Americans, then, is striking.[6] Given how the *rolprentinsetsels* footage is used in the Bloedrivier Heritage Site film, unsuspecting young viewers might be forgiven for imagining that this is actual footage of the event. Here, then, is a wonderful example of the repurposing of older films, in today's postapartheid South Africa, to memorialize and recreate through a kind of bricolage the Afrikaner nationalist mythology that retains its hold on a small minority of the population. The protean character of these films as cultural artifacts perfectly illustrates how the white nationalist mythology embodied in both *The Birth of a Nation* and *They Built a Nation* does not disappear. Instead, it is constantly repurposed, reenacted, and recreated. Both of these white nationalist films remain profoundly unstable as icons, despite our desire to think of them in stable terms.

A second, more provocative, point I want to make is to question the tendency to view these two films as mere documents of racism, and little else. They certainly are shot through with racist ideology, and thus are easily deployed in revanchist historical narratives; but as films, their narratives were fundamentally nationalist in character rather than just racialist. Because they were produced in the name of rebuilding white solidarity, we should interrogate them as products of certain kinds of nationalism and nationalist moments. Now, certainly, that nationalism needs to be understood as a racial nationalism. As Marilyn Lake and Henry Reynolds suggest in their fine work *Drawing the Global Colour Line*, *The Birth of a Nation* burst upon the cultural scene at the very moment when the global color line was being drawn in Australia, South Africa, and the United States, as all of these settler societies felt a strong need to reassert white nationalism in the face of the international "rising tide of color."[7] Yet such nationalism might be polyvalent. As Davis subtly suggests, in the South African case, in films such as *De Voortrekkers* (1916) and *They Built a Nation*, we need to consider how white nationalism operated on two planes. It was simultaneously white nationalism in the language of reconciliation between British and Boer after the South African War, and of Afrikaner nationalism in and of itself. That duality, of course, can also be applied to Griffith's film, which expressed both the triumphant pseudonationalism of the white South through the defeat of Reconstruction and yet was also very much about sectional reconciliation. Surely, this remains its fundamental contribution to a nationalist mythology in the United States, burying the hatchet to reunify divided North and South once and for all by denigrating Reconstruction, its traitorous white enablers, and, most of all, its black beneficiaries and agents.

If these films both draw on narratives of renewed white supremacy and national reconciliation, we can simultaneously read *The Birth of a Nation* as a spectacular war film, shot through with battle scenes, not least because one could easily apply the same analysis to *They Built a Nation*. Certainly the latter is used that way by the sponsors of heritage at Bloedrivier, who cannibalize its battle scenes with abandon. A similar collection and recycling—dare I say curation—of images drawn from *The Birth of a Nation* as a war film seems to have occurred at crucial historical junctures within the United States. The film in its entirety may have been retrofitted as a nationalist trope, or as a "canonized history of film art," but, as Andy Uhrich suggests in his essay in this volume, the manner in which collectors clipped up, repackaged, and resold *The Birth of a Nation* proved significant as well. In 1942, it was Griffith's battle scenes that seemed most worthy of reanimation. That was a moment when everyone on the US home front was sitting in a movie theater watching battle scenes of what was happening in Europe or in the Pacific, in the name of promoting national unity against "slavery," as the world of the Axis powers was termed in Frank Capra's World War II film series *Why We Fight*. American moviegoers were accustomed, in 1942, to cinematic battle sequences filled with scenes of spectacularization. In 1953, of course, valorization of Griffith's film took on—or reclaimed—a different, more sinister meaning, as it came to represent a means disguising a certain racial-nationalist narrative in the guise of film heritage. This, of course, occurred on the eve of the moment when the Confederate battle flag reappeared over Southern state capitals, the "Third Klan" began to ride against civil rights workers, and many white Southerners sought to fend off what they saw as the threat of a second Reconstruction.[8]

Yet we need to be cautious, and not condescend to the past. It is easy enough in our enlightened and allegedly postracial era to wonder how people watching at the time could possibly have missed the obvious racism of Griffith's vision. But we should recall that in 1953, Griffith's interpretation of Reconstruction that *The Birth of a Nation* had culturally crystallized for the nation in 1915, remained the dominant, mainstream understanding in North and South alike. As historian of Civil War memory David Blight notes, "by using powerful imagery . . . [*The Birth of a Nation*] etched a story of Reconstruction that has lasted long in America's historical consciousness." And although the National Association for the Advancement of Colored People protested the film in 1915, Griffith's view of Reconstruction would have hardly been at odds with the view promulgated by Booker T. Washington at the time, notwithstanding his own occasional objections to the film (although, as Blight points out, "Washington supported Griffith's right to show the film").[9] In *Up from Slavery* (1901), Washington had declared that during Reconstruction, "the ignorance of my race was being used as a tool with which to help white men into office, and that there was an element in the North which wanted to punish the Southern white men by forcing the Negro into positions over the heads of the Southern whites." A better synopsis of the historical narrative dramatized in Griffith's film is hard to find. Four decades later, it didn't take a stretch of imagination in either region for white audiences to agree that it was the carpetbaggers and the incompetent black voters they had manipulated that had made Reconstruction a terrible mistake. Griffith effectively played to white Americans' preconceptions, which historians in the decades between 1915 and the rebirth of the civil rights movement during the 1950s had done very little to challenge or displace. With the major exception of W. E. B. Du Bois's 1935 classic (though largely ignored) work *Black Reconstruction*, it was only in the wake of the civil rights movement and the historiographic revolutions that accompanied it that American historians rewrote the popular understanding of Reconstruction—which it seems even Hillary Clinton still clings to.[10]

A narrative of racial nationalism; a sign of reconciliation; a war film; a collection of ready-to-hand images attractive to those rummaging in the attic of heritage to defend or reclaim a lost world of white pride—when placed side by side, *The Birth of a Nation* and *They Built a Nation* conjure these political imaginaries. Yet we can also rethink their place within a different film narrative convention that is peculiar to both nations, even if in quite distinctive ways. There is a long, if now neglected, tradition of comparative US and South African history that takes the "frontier" as its basic analytical template. In both cases, despite many differences, for example, although both Native Americans and Africans welcomed European visitors at first, "it was not long before it dawned on the indigenes that they were up against a completely new type of person whose impact was more fundamentally devastating than anything they had previously experienced," write Howard Lamar and Leonard Thompson.[11] Over the past several decades, however, a historiography more oriented to twentieth-century developments in both countries—including capitalist development, national integration, and modern black nationalism—has swept aside that earlier framework. Returning to these films as sources, however, reminds us that the modern white racist imagination at least remained imprinted with moving images that posed the taming of "savagery" by the spread of white "civilization" as central to defining national mythologies about frontier expansion. In the South African case, these two processes occurred in tandem, as the Voortrekkers' wagon trains penetrating the interior of southern Africa entailed the eventual destruction of diverse indigenous societies that, in twentieth-century South Africa, became collectively subordinated as black to the white nationalist project. In the United States, the crushing of Native American resistance to the spread of whiteness and the perpetuation of white supremacy rooted in African American slavery and then the reassertion of post–Civil War Jim Crow are understood as distinctive (if perhaps related) processes, in both time and, especially, geography. They tend to draw on different tropes (the wagon train and the noble savage, the genteel plantation and the "happy negro," for example), and we have become accustomed to experiencing these narratives visually within distinctive genres of film. Yet when we place Griffith's work in dialogue with South Africa, we can discover some peculiar affinities.

This is especially the case if we return to the film that effectively bridges South African and American frontier narratives, Griffith's 1908 short *The Zulu's Heart*.[12] We often ask the wrong questions when we try to compare South African "race" films with *The Birth of a Nation*; we might even be asking the wrong genre question when we look at *The Birth of a Nation* as a war film, as interesting as that exercise may be. Consider Griffith's "masterpiece" for a moment through the lens of a different transcultural narrative convention, the Western. *The Zulu's Heart*, shot in New Jersey,

Figure 5.6. Still from Griffith's film *The Zulu's Heart* (1908). *Screen capture by author.*

allegedly set in nineteenth-century Natal to dramatize the encounter of a (lone) Voortrekker family with a Zulu chief, unquestionably was a Western, not a coherent or realistic narrative about the experience of whites in southern Africa. When Griffith shot this film, seven years before the release of *The Birth of a Nation*, he was imagining (or inventing) the Western, the (just vanished) North American frontier, and Native Americans in the West as the Other, not African Americans in the South. Even while casting his narrative in the guise of innocent white settlers in conflict with indigenous Africans on the southern African frontier, Griffith was obviously drawing on American frontier captivity narratives. The Zulu king who gallantly rescues the Boer mother and child from his savage comrades should be understood as a stand-in for a Native American, not an African American "savage." Similarly, when the American filmmaker Harold Shaw premiered his South African–made 1916 epic about the "birth" of that nation, *De Voortrekkers*, the *Rand Daily Mail* swooned over "the loyalty to the trekkers of a simple [Zulu] savage."[13] So while we surely can regard *The Birth of a Nation* as a pure expression of white nationalism, or even as a spectacular war film, we might also consider it from this different angle. Indeed, I would argue that when the war film meets the racial nationalist film in a settler society—whether it be Australia, South Africa, or the United States—it comes clothed in the narrative conventions of the Western (fig. 5.6).

ALEX LICHTENSTEIN is Professor of History at Indiana University. He is author of *Margaret Bourke-White and the Dawn of Apartheid.*

Notes

1. For an analysis of these competing heritage sites, see Nsizwa Dlamini, "The Battle of Ncome Project: State Memorialism, Discomforting Spaces," *Southern African Humanities* 13 (December 2001):125–138; and Paula Girshick, "Ncome Museum/Monument: From Reconciliation to Resistance," *Museum Anthropology* 27(1–2): 25–36.

2. Leonard P. Thompson, *The Political Mythology of Apartheid* (New Haven, CT: Yale University Press, 1985), 144–184.

3. See Peter Davis, *In Darkest Hollywood: Exploring the Jungles of Cinema's South Africa* (Johannesburg: Ravan Press, 1996), 147–149. The title *They Built a Nation* is the literal English translation of the film, but it is also common to see the film referred to as *Building a Nation*.

4. Alex Lichtenstein and Rick Halpern, *Margaret Bourke-White and the Dawn of Apartheid* (Bloomington: Indiana University Press, 2016).

5. On *Shaka Zulu*, see Davis, *In Darkest Hollywood*, 167–182.

6. *Rand Daily Mail*, December 20, 1938, 23; Nina Silber, "Reunion and Reconciliation, Reviewed and Reconsidered," *Journal of American History* 103 (June 2016): 59–83.

7. Marilyn Lake and Henry Reynolds, *Drawing the Global Colour Line: White Men's Countries and the International Challenge of Racial Equality* (Cambridge: Cambridge University Press, 2009); Lothrop Stoddard, *The Rising Tide of Color against White World-Supremacy* (New York: Scribner, 1920).

8. David Goldfield, *Still Fighting the Civil War: The American South and Southern History* (Baton Rouge: Louisiana State University Press, 2013), 311–312.

9. David Blight, *Race and Reunion: The Civil War in American Memory* (Cambridge, MA: Harvard University Press, 2001), 395–396.

10. Booker T. Washington, *Up from Slavery: An Autobiography* (New York: Doubleday, 1901), 84; W. E. B. Du Bois, *Black Reconstruction: An Essay Toward a History of the Part Which Black Folk Played in America, 1860–1880* (New York: Russel & Russel, 1935). The most important "revisionist" account of Reconstruction is Eric Foner, *Reconstruction: America's Unfinished Revolution, 1863–1877* (New York: Harper & Row, 1988); Ta-Nehisi Coates, "Hillary Clinton Goes Back to the Dunning School," *The Atlantic* (online), January 26, 2016.

11. Howard Lamar and Leonard Thompson, eds., *The Frontier in History: North America and Southern Africa Compared* (New Haven, CT: Yale University Press, 1981), 18; George Frederickson, *White Supremacy: A Comparative Study in American and South African History* (New York: Oxford University Press, 1981), chap. 1.

12. Davis, *In Darkest Hollywood*, 8–9, 124–125.

13. *Rand Daily Mail*, December 27, 1916, 7.

PART II

REPRESENTATIONAL AND
RHETORICAL STRATEGIES

By Adele Stephenson.

6

SERIAL MELODRAMAS OF
BLACK AND WHITE

The Birth of a Nation *and*
Within Our Gates

Linda Williams

D URING THE STIMULATING DISCUSSION THAT INSPIRED THIS BOOK at
the 2015 symposium about *The Birth of a Nation* (1915), someone asked
whether there was a "grand narrative about race." I think that there is such
a thing, but it is not one single narrative—it is several. Of course, *The Birth
of a Nation* is a huge part of this narrative, but we misunderstand it if we
think it is the beginning. We misunderstand it also if we think it is pure
and simple racism, for racism is neither pure nor simple. Most importantly, we—black, white, and all others who find themselves hailed as racial
subjects—need to understand how each new part of the narrative is in dialogue with its past parts. The story both accretes and repeats over time. I
tend to think of it as a kind of serial argument that begins with a thoroughly
maternal expression of pity for the wrongful suffering of black lives and is
answered by an equally thorough patriarchal rejection of such sympathy.
To put it simply and in a way that suggests how stuck the United States is
in this melodrama's repetitive forms, it is an argument that begins by stating that, at the time of its first iteration, the word *American* did not include
slaves and that Americans should pity the suffering of helpless slaves at the
whims of evil white masters.

This was the first installment in the serial melodrama of black and
white. It was written by a white mother of seven who saw in the sufferings

of slaves something like the suffering of her own sick or dying children. It is the melodrama of *Uncle Tom's Cabin*. The climax of this suffering was the beating death of Uncle Tom himself, the slave who in the future would forever be hated by blacks for staying faithful to his "good" master, but who we should not forget was also at one time revered by whites and blacks for defying his evil master by saying that his soul belonged to God. This initial argument for the humanity of suffering slaves was answered, dialectically, in American popular culture by its reversal: the portrayal of the suffering of whites at the hand of blacks. In a nutshell, this is the original argument. It begins with a claim that black lives matter. It is refuted by *The Birth of a Nation*, which says black lives do not. It has been going on, in one form or another, since 1852.

The argument plays out in popular culture over the time of US history since before the Civil War, and, sadly, it continues to the present. At first it is an argument between whites about blacks: Are they saintly sufferers, or are they evil, rapacious villains? The terms of the argument were set by its first, incendiary claim that blacks are human—not necessarily deserving of rights but human nevertheless. But over time, black voices have joined in to demand rights. In this chapter, I will isolate the first moment in popular film culture when an African American voice had its say. It can only have its say, I argue, within the terms of the argument already established: effectively the issue of whether, or how much, as I have already suggested, black lives matter. That this is *still* the argument attests to a long history of black enslavement, lynching, disenfranchisement, and inadequate civil rights. Although it might seem like progress to observe the newfound ability of whites to perceive injustice to blacks in the form of lethal policing, it may also seem like the deepest rut imaginable: This rut—what I have elsewhere called the "melodrama of black and white"—still determines the basic terms of this argument.[1] It also shows the extent to which this archaic melodrama of racial good and evil still forms the framework for our national dilemma of race.

By *melodrama*, I mean, most simply, rhetorical-dramatic forms that strive to move audiences to pity the sufferings of the innocent. And in the strange alchemy of the melodramatic form, the more one suffers, the more one seems to acquire virtue. Contrary to received opinion, melodrama is not an archaic, badly acted excess of emotion. That is yesterday's melodrama. Today's melodrama, the one that galvanizes people to love a victim or to hate a villain, is playing out at this moment in the deaths of Michael

Brown, Trayvon Martin, Freddie Gray, Eric Garner, Tamir Rice, Laquan McDonald, and others.

Gradually over time, the story changes: It is not just white people making the arguments. Black voices enter in, but what can be said in mainstream popular infotainment viewed by large numbers is determined by what has already been said. In this chapter, I examine the first two moves in this melodrama—to show how *Uncle Tom's Cabin* was answered by *The Birth of a Nation*. Then I ask, through a look at Oscar Micheaux's *Within Our Gates* (1919), how these two originally white-authored melodramas were answered by a black filmmaker.

Before *Uncle Tom's Cabin*, the minstrel figure of fun was the dominant black stereotype. Except for an occasional Stephen Foster sad home song, the minstrel was not a figure to show much suffering. But when the minstrel home songs were appropriated by stage versions of *Uncle Tom's Cabin*, the very question of what was the proper home for former slaves became a loaded one. Could the American home, the slave cabin, or the former slave cabin ever become the good home of melodrama?

The (Serial) Melodrama of Black and White

If Uncle Tom was the original black stereotype that black political consciousness resisted, he was also part of a much larger cycle of stereotypes originally forged in the white imagination. Eric Lott has shown that the original spirit of blackface minstrelsy—the imitation of what whites have stereotyped as black vernacular culture, especially black forms of song and dance—is at the very origin of American mass culture.[2] Given the abundant evidence of this contradictory "love and theft" of black culture by whites, it may not be surprising that the claim that black lives matter has had to operate in the face of a whole repertoire of demeaning stereotypes, which either implicitly or overtly argue that they do not.

However, as our contemporary real-life news reports return repeatedly to ever-new versions of the moral power of the Tom beating scenario, the elimination of stereotypes may not be the solution to the denigration of black lives. For the Tom story was the first influential claim in American mass culture that black lives *do* matter; only later was Tom's stereotype despised. The answer to stereotypes has never been truer, more "authentic" depictions, free of stereotypes, but anti-stereotypes that are, of course, stereotypes themselves.

Tom himself grew out of the combination of two conflicting stereotypes of the white supremacist imagination: an older strain of minstrelsy, which, in addition to the burlesque antics of "minstrel fun," cultivated the tradition of sad "home songs" in which otherwise happy-go-lucky slaves would long for a lost home figured as the "old plantation." This plantation home was always a troubled site of virtue, but upon it Harriet Beecher Stowe erected the narrative of *Uncle Tom's Cabin* about one slave (Tom), who stays loyal to his master, and another (Eliza), who flees north to Canada and freedom. If the stereotype of the Uncle Tom was what seemed to need overthrowing by the black racial imaginary in the 1950s and 1960s, the stereotype of the Uncle Tom in its own day was what melodramatically demonstrated the humanity of slaves in the first place.

I begin with the assumption that there is little use in isolating one particular stereotype—for either approbation or denigration—without considering the full context of its serial evolution. By *serial evolution*, I mean the way one kind of stereotype emerges connected to a particular narrative—say, the black man as the quintessential Christian martyr—and then gets reversed in a new kind of melodrama in which black and white, good and evil invert. This is what *The Birth of a Nation* did. It turned the black victims into villains and the white villains into racially beset white men desperate to protect "their" women from a paranoid vision of black threat. Serials repeat, but repetition is never exactly the same. The melodrama of black and white is remarkably repetitive even as its moral valences careen from good to evil in radical reversals.

In *Playing the Race Card* (2001), I traced some of the more important aspects of the melodrama of black and white across American culture from Uncle Tom to O. J. Simpson, from novel to theater to film and television through the popular consumption of race trials such as the police beating of Rodney King and the O. J. Simpson murder trial.[3] "Melodrama of black and white" is the phrase I used to describe the reversals of stereotype from victim to villain that have taken place throughout American history. D. W. Griffith's racist masterpiece is the key moment when the original Tom melodrama turned into a serial through the insidious process of reversal that has made this ongoing story the longest-playing melodrama in US history.

Thomas Dixon was a Southern white supremacist who consciously reversed the moral poles of the Tom stereotype of black humanity of the antebellum era. Through the lens of the white supremacist view of

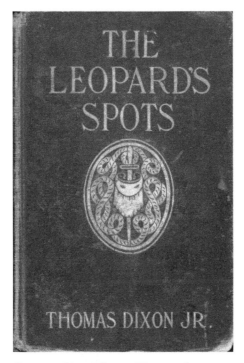

Figure 6.1. Dixon's first anti-Tom novel.

Reconstruction, he reversed the moral and racial valence of the Tom stereo-type while keeping the black/white antimony of racial melodrama intact. His first novel, *The Leopard's Spots* (1903) begins what has been called his Reconstruction trilogy, but which might also be called, after Leslie Fiedler's (1979) still-useful term, his anti-Tom trilogy (fig. 6.1). In part, it is a sequel to *Uncle Tom's Cabin*, showing the disastrous results of the freeing of slaves in the South. It chronicles the further adventures of Simon Legree, the origi-nal villain of *Uncle Tom's Cabin*, and the mulatto couple George and Eliza and their son, Harry, the original victims. When a grown-up post–Civil War Harry seeks to marry into a white New England family, the racism of would-be liberals is exposed as they "naturally" reject miscegenation. Such was the origin of what would become, in Griffith, Silas Lynch's proposal to marry Elsie Stoneman. Dixon's second novel, *The Clansman: A Historical Romance of the Ku Klux Klan* (1905), is less explicitly aimed at showing the disastrous outcome of Stowe's story (fig. 6.2). Here, Dixon hones the mate-rial of the previous novel into a more focused melodrama of action that became the stage play *The Clansman* and the basis for Griffith's film.

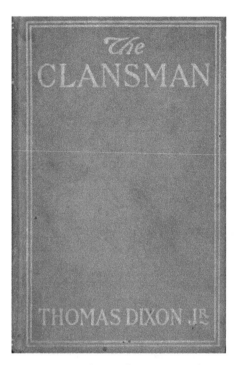

Figure 6.2. Dixon's second anti-Tom novel,
which became a play of the same name, on
which *The Birth of a Nation* is based.

Dixon's novels and plays were mostly popular in the South. They did
not succeed in generating a new national racial antipathy toward blacks.
But Griffith's film based on Dixon's first two novels did. And this new racial
feeling, this new turn of the screw in the ongoing serial melodrama of black
and white, was inextricably linked to the new power and epic sweep of the
medium of cinema. Griffith thus succeeded in creating the white supremacist classic of which Dixon had only dreamed. And the reason for this, paradoxically, is that, unlike Dixon's work, *The Birth of a Nation* did not seem to
be the antagonist of Stowe's Tom melodrama but rather its inheritor.

The probably apocryphal story of Thomas Dixon renaming Griffith's
film from his own title, *The Clansman*, to *The Birth of a Nation*, upon seeing
its New York preview, nevertheless suggests his recognition that Griffith's
film, unlike his own works, had broken through to speak to a national, not
just a sectional, audience (fig. 6.3). Though Dixon promulgated the idea of
national rebirth forged through the hatred and expulsion of racial scape-
goats, it was Griffith's film that actually achieved this new national feeling

Figure 6.3. Poster advertising *The Birth of a Nation*.

by seeming to be democratic and fair. This, I think, is the real trick of each new incarnation of the Tom/anti-Tom material—it not only reverses but injects each new serial instance with new qualities borrowed from previous instantiations.

Here we encounter the nature of a mass media seriality that seeks not originality but repetition, though always repetition with a difference. Dixon recycled characters from *Uncle Tom's Cabin* to exploit their popularity but also to *détourné* the original political impact of interracial amity into interracial hatred. He was also exploiting the popularity of the melodramatic family saga, only this time making whites the central characters in a later era of Reconstruction. Essentially, Dixon tried to repeat *Uncle Tom's Cabin* with its feelings of interracial amity inverted to race hatred. To the usual serial dialectic of repetitive schema and innovation, he added the negative dialectic of a (good, Christian) Tom turned into his evil, bestial opposite.

Try as he might, however, Dixon failed to galvanize national racial feelings. One reason for this failure lies in the fact that Dixon's starting point had been a vehement opposition to the sympathetic racial sentiments of

Figure 6.4. "The bringing of the African to America planted the first seed of disunion." *Screen capture by author.*

Uncle Tom's Cabin, which had especially moved Northern readers to weep for the sufferings of Uncle Tom at the hands of his cruel white masters. Griffith's starting point, in contrast, was to incorporate *both* Stowe's antebellum story *and* Dixon's story of Reconstruction, thus not seeming to overtly spread hatred of blacks. This was his terrible genius.

Dixon himself had refused to tell "the story of slavery," not wanting to become an apologist for an institution that, in his eyes, had so disastrously brought the villainous "black seed" to American shores. Griffith might seem to follow Dixon's sentiment toward slavery when, at the beginning of his film, an intertitle informs viewers that "The bringing of the African to America planted the first seed of disunion"—thus blaming disunion on both the Africans and on the slave traders that brought them (fig. 6.4). However, Griffith's willingness to present a happy plantation version of the story of slavery in the first half of his film (the part that most critics have praised) borrows much from the beginning of Stowe's narrative of good masters and happy slaves—the part before Tom is "sold down river"—and enables Griffith to repurpose much of the "romantic racialism" of the Tom

Figure 6.5. Griffith's "faithful souls" helping their masters escape a black uprising. *Screen capture by author.*

story. In this way, Griffith does not fully invert the Tom story but instead adapts elements of its apparent democratic inclusion.

For example, the presence of the "faithful souls," Mammy and Jake, in Griffith's story, modeled on Tom and Chloe in *Uncle Tom's Cabin*, offers Tom-like elements of racial sympathy toward the "good," "faithful souls" that allowed *The Birth of a Nation* to become an agent of national (white supremacist) reunion under seemingly democratic, but actually exclusionary, auspices (fig. 6.5). It did this by offering whites in the North and South what *felt* like a fitting conclusion and answer to the sectional disunions originally sparked by Stowe's version of the melodrama of black and white.

In *The Birth of a Nation*, the extreme pathos of the defeat of the South, which Dixon did not represent, resonates powerfully against the extreme action of the climax, in which the Klan rescues first Elsie, who is caught in the clutches of the mulatto Silas Lynch (fig. 6.6), and then an entire interracial group (fig. 6.7) surrounded in the cabin and fighting off "black hordes." In these two action climaxes, Griffith, unlike Dixon, sets up two sites in need of rescue. The second of these is something Dixon could not

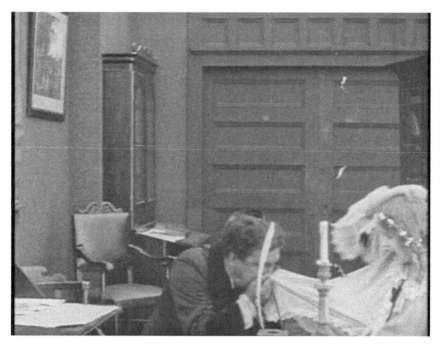

Figure 6.6. Elsie caught in the clutches of the mulatto Silas Lynch. *Screen capture by author.*

have countenanced. Michael Rogin has argued that this rescue of the family from the cabin is not just from any cabin, but from a "Lincoln log cabin," whose refuge ironically democratizes and merges, as the film's most egregious intertitle puts it, "former enemies of North and South . . . reunited again in common defense of their Aryan birthright."[4] But what Rogin did not note and what is visually apparent but not spoken in the intertitle is that former master and slaves are also united not in defense of an Aryan birthright but in defense of the cabin. This cabin wraps the former slave owners in the mantle of humble beginnings associated with the likes of Lincoln. Although it is technically the Southern "former master," Doctor Cameron, who is rescued from the cabin and who rubs elbows with the humble Union veterans frying bacon over their hearth, he is here disassociated from the once-grand Cameron Hall plantation and the institution of slavery.[5] Griffith, unlike Dixon, thus makes his audience feel Stowe-like emotions of democratic inclusion and brotherhood even while rooting for the "common" defense of their "Aryan birthright."

But perhaps the real reason Griffith can get away with such contradictory gestures of white supremacy and democracy is that the icon of the

Figure 6.7. "Former enemies of North and South in common defense of their Aryan birthright." Notice how former slaves are enlisted in defense of a "birthright" that is not theirs. *Screen capture by author.*

cabin goes well beyond the democratic associations with Abraham Lincoln (fig. 6.8). I have argued that nostalgia for a democratic and humble "home space of innocence" central to the felt virtue of so much melodrama, and so central to Stowe's melodrama, was located in the icon of Tom's cabin—the integrated place where Master George Shelby Jr. once taught Tom how to read, where Mrs. Shelby came to weep with Tom and Chloe, and about which the songs "Old Folks at Home" and "My Old Kentucky Home" are performed in many Tom plays.[6] This cabin seems to function out of proportion to its actual importance as a locale in Stowe's novel and in the many "Tom Shows" that paraded model cabins through towns to attract audiences. It hovers over all Tom's longing for his always problematic good, lost Kentucky home. As the American locus classicus of honest and humble beginnings, the cabin in Griffith's film now becomes as important a place of virtue for the former masters as it once had been for the Tom slave.

By "integrating" the cabin with the Tom figures of Mammy and Jake and with the humble Northern Union veterans, Phil Stoneman, son of the

Figure 6.8. The Lincoln (and the Tom) cabin surrounded. *Screen capture by author.*

radical Republican, as well as with the former members of the slavocracy, Griffith repurposed the previously dominant version of the melodrama of black and white and its "home space of innocence" to representative members of the whole nation. In a move of apparent democratic inclusion, Mammy and Jake willingly roll up their sleeves to join the whites to fight off the black marauders. When the group runs out of ammunition, Mammy clubs intruding black heads. Henceforth, all future film Mammies, such as the one in *Gone with the Wind* (dir. Victor Fleming, 1939), would devote themselves fiercely to the well-being of their white masters as if slavery had never ended. Thus, while Griffith freely includes Mammy and Jake as part of the good folks in need of rescue by the Klan, this very inclusion enables our not quite noting her later exclusion from the reborn nation.

Dixon had been consistent in his exclusion of blacks from any nostalgic image of the past or any happy ending pointing to the future. Griffith, however, freely borrowed the nostalgic musical associations with black culture that Dixon had so vehemently eschewed. Dixon even had Elsie give up the banjo and all "vulgar" Negro associations. With the *melos* of this older Tom melodrama insinuating the racial feelings of minstrelsy, Griffith's eventual

Figure 6.9. Dark frames "flushed out" into light. *Screen capture by author.*

exclusion of blacks thus seems less a calculated policy of contemporary Jim Crow politics than a "natural" love of black culture consistent with the dominant culture of minstrelsy. It also seemed an equally "natural" exclusion of blackness when it does not behave so lovably. In the rescues carried out in the last third of the film, black men are quite literally wiped from the screen by what poet Vachel Lindsay once tellingly called a white "Anglo-Saxon Niagara."[7] Indeed, the ride of the Klan is repeatedly figured as a flushing out of black chaos and violence as dark frames are suddenly flooded with white (fig. 6.9). A culminating shot effectively "parades" the racial cleansing that the multiple rescues have accomplished as the "Parade of the Clansmen" (fig. 6.10). Not surprisingly, neither Mammy nor Jake—nor any other "faithful souls"—are anywhere to be seen.

Moreover, whereas Dixon gives secondhand accounts of sexual attacks by black men on white women, even in his play *The Clansman*, Griffith much more luridly enacts them, even if censors forced him to change Gus's overture to the little sister to a proposal of marriage (fig. 6.11). In the attack on Elsie Stoneman, Lynch's handling of Elsie in lascivious ways that Dixon never dared portray is not only more lurid, but it seems as if the ride of the

Figure 6.10. The "Parade of the Clansmen" with no black faces. *Screen capture by author.*

Figure 6.11. Gus proposes marriage to the little sister. *Screen capture by author.*

Klan is activated by this miscegenous sexual assault on a white woman. And in the cabin itself, that rape of the white women is the real threat is made clear by the way the white men prepare to kill the women lest they meet the "fate worse than death."

It is thus in Griffith's film that we first discover how a bad-faith white version of the melodrama of black and white came to believe in its own melodramatic virtue by appropriating the mantle of the good, humble cabin. By 1915, with *The Birth of a Nation*, three variations of a new, anti-Tom, stereotype had emerged—all of which sexualized warnings of the dangers of a racial amalgamation that had already been accomplished through the exercise of the droit de seigneur of former masters: Silas Lynch, the mulatto who lusts after Elsie Stoneman; Lydia Brown, the mulatta who holds sexual sway over Austin Stoneman; and Gus, the renegade Union soldier who lusts after the "little Sister." All three refuted the humanity of the Christian slave.

The moral binaries of the melodramatic form proved their power in a new medium that seemed more modern and "realistic" than the older media of, first, novels and then plays. Cinema consolidated the very modernity of melodrama, making it relevant to a new age of national, not just sectional, union. With Griffith's "answer" to *Uncle Tom's Cabin*, a singularly popular melodrama of black and white became a serial phenomenon, asserting diametrically opposed forms of racial injury. Henceforth, in life or in fiction, no form of injury could seem innocent of racial motivation if blacks and whites were involved.

Black Reactions to *The Birth of a Nation*

The melodrama of black and white continued full speed ahead in mainstream American culture. Having leaped from novel and stage to silent film to sound film to television and, most importantly, into a twenty-four-hour news cycle and an internet-driven new media often fueled by citizen cell phones, it reaches into our contemporary moment. In this moment, it might seem that something like the perception of Tom suffering holds sway but perhaps only until the next O. J. Simpson comes along.

And finally, of course, blacks themselves would begin to enter into the discourse of this American melodrama of black and white, though in ways that were often predetermined by the fact that they were not in on it at the beginning. By definition, these were reactions that came from outside the mainstream. Melvyn Stokes has shown that, by far, the most prevalent reaction among blacks to *The Birth of a Nation* was that of the National

Association for the Advancement of Colored People, in which whites and blacks worked together tirelessly either to ban or at least cut some of the more egregious scenes from the film. Epic court battles ensued from city to city, with little success early in the film's run and more success after World War I, when the argument could be made that the film harmed the war effort and incited race hatred at a time when the nation needed unity.[8] The coincidence of the Supreme Court *Mutual* decision (in *Mutual Film Corp. v. Industrial Commission of Ohio*), which declared film not to be a form of speech and thus not entitled to protection, three days after the first Washington screening of the film meant that all film was vulnerable to censorship, not just Griffith's. The NAACP treated each minor censorship of the film as a victory, but it is important to recognize that the arguments for censorship were the same arguments that would later be deployed against black films that tried to answer Griffith.

Another reaction to the film, and one that I find especially eloquent, testifies to the extreme anger and frustration felt by black audiences who saw the film. In Kevin Brownlow and Brendon Gill's 1993 documentary *D. W. Griffith: Father of Film*, William Walker, now an elderly black man who saw the film in a colored theater in 1916, recalls, "Some people were crying. You could hear people saying God . . . You had the worse feeling in the world. You just felt like you were not counted. You were out of existence."[9] Walker does not explain how the film accomplished his sense of eradication, of being "out of existence," but I would submit that it had much to do with the way the film itself makes black people just disappear, as described above. Indeed, Walker's frustration is palpable as he extends the logic of his own violent sense of having been rendered invisible onto a now thoroughly white supremacist world: "I just felt like . . . I wished somebody could not see me so I could kill them. I just felt like killing all the white people in the world." Perhaps because he realized how much the race hatred of the film had already made his humanity invisible, Walker wished to use it as an advantage to return the violence he had experienced. Walker was caught up in the melodrama of black and white in a way that only allowed him the alternative of becoming the anti-Tom himself—the "black image in the white mind," as George Frederickson once put it.[10]

But William Walker's impotent despair at being counted out of existence and his desire to kill white people may have been something more than the anti-anti-Tom move that perpetuates the cycle of violence. It reacts not only to violence against blacks—Brownlow and Gill's film shows the depositing of Gus's lifeless body on the steps of the statehouse by the Klan as Walker speaks—but also to the powerful cinematic rhetoric that makes *this* interracial violence seem so natural and necessary. For what was also being counted out of existence was the future of African American representation in any but the roles of "faithful souls" for the next fifty years of mainstream film. Black autonomy and will, black sexuality in anything but its most threatening forms, black families, miscegenation itself—all these topics that are so central to black lives *were* being "counted out of existence" in American life and mainstream cinema. By the time the production code was in force, these topics, which Griffith had broached in the most negative, anti-Tom ways, would be taboo to both black and white filmmakers. Perhaps Walker's deepest despair lay in an understanding of how the Tom scenario had been hijacked to create a bogus feeling of interracial amity only for those former slaves who were no longer "uppity" and did not seek to vote.

Within Our Gates, Oscar Micheaux's 1919 filmic response to *The Birth of a Nation*, is the one film that best answers William Walker's despair (fig. 6.12). It has, deservedly, received a great deal of scrutiny from film scholars, especially in Jane Gaines's *Fire and Desire: Mixed Race Movies in the Silent Era* and, more recently, in Cedric Robinson's *Forgeries of Memory and Meaning: Blacks and the Regimes of Race in American Theater and Film before World War II*.[11] I will not try here to fathom the great mystery and challenge of Micheaux's fascinating body of work, or even the full importance of this one film. But I would like to place *Within Our Gates* in the context of the American melodrama of black and white that I have been describing. For what is important about Micheaux is how he navigates, without ever being able to negate, the dominant features of this serial melodrama. I thus argue, contra Cedric Robinson, that in this film, Micheaux does not disdain, subvert, or shatter the form of melodrama—all terms used by Robinson—but constructs his own melodrama of black and white in a fashion that might have assured a William Walker—had he been fortunate enough to see the film—that he was not "counted out of existence" and need not have recourse to a suicidal race war.

This is not to say that Micheaux's film had any immediate influence in the ongoing evolution of this serial melodrama. Though it is the "black answer" to *The Birth of a Nation* in its time, it was seen by very few and soon disappeared for over half a century. There is thus no sense in which this work—which was censored in its day for some of the same reasons that *The Birth of a Nation* was censored, and, most importantly, for its treatment of miscegenation—could be said to have influenced national audiences. It may not even have influenced many black audiences for, as Jane Gaines notes,

Figure 6.12. Low-budget poster for "Within Our Gates."

some of those black audiences joined with whites in protesting its incendiary depiction of the lynching of blacks. But at the same time, the film's very existence attests to the creative power of a black sensibility that was acutely aware of the Scylla of the Tom route of sympathy for beset blacks and the anti-Tom Charybdis of violent race war.

Consider Oscar Micheaux's narrative options in the wake of *The Birth of a Nation*: If Micheaux had simply been able to invert the moral and racial polarities of Griffith's film, much as Griffith and Dixon had done to the Tom story, and if all other things had been equal, Micheaux might have told a story of an innocent black woman sexually threatened by a white man and, following the rescue model of *The Birth of a Nation*, depicted black heroes riding, running, or driving to her rescue and thus punishing the lascivious white aggressor. This would have been an immensely satisfying outcome for a William Walker. And if the story, like *The Birth of a Nation*, had been set in the era of slavery and then Reconstruction, it would have given him the added opportunity for revenge. It would also have set the historical record straight as to who was responsible for the very creation of the mulatto villains so prominent in *The Birth of a Nation*. But, of course, all other things were not equal; Micheaux could not tell such a story unless he created an outright fantasy, as in 1970s blaxploitation, or the contemporary counterfactuals of Quentin Tarantino, as in *Django Unchained* (2012). Historically, black heroes would have been singularly unable to rescue black women from the lust of white masters and overseers—not during slavery, not during Reconstruction, and not in the so-called Progressive Era of Griffith's film. To simply reverse the Griffith/Dixon anti-Tom inversion of the Tom narrative was not an option.

The option that Micheaux did follow was to revert to selective aspects of the Tom story, repurposed and updated to counter *The Birth of a Nation*. For example, he depicted the suffering of a whole black family and the female heroine modeled on Eliza, who, unlike Tom, escaped to freedom and self-improvement. An ad for *Within Our Gates*, undoubtedly written by Micheaux since he did all his own promotion, called it the "Most sensational Story on the Race Question Since Uncle Tom's Cabin," indicating a tacit awareness of the more recent "sensation" of *The Birth of a Nation* and indirectly promising to return to the Tom model of the melodrama offering sympathy for black suffering. At the same time, however, Micheaux, like Dixon, adjusts his story to a later time—in this case, the late Progressive Era—which allows him to engage with at least one of the pressing issues of concern to Americans in this period. For though African Americans, most of whom had no vote, were generally excluded from many of the reform issues of this period—including women's suffrage, election reform, government reform, and philanthropy—Micheaux joins the spirit of the age by focusing his reform narrative on the one issue that did allow his updated Tom family to participate in the reformist spirit of the time: the pressing need for Negro education. Through this route, Micheaux shows how his race can also engage in the contemporary Progressive issues of the time. Thus, in the best tradition of the melodrama of black and white, *Within Our Gates*, like both the many stage and film versions of *Uncle Tom* and the unprecedentedly popular singular *The Birth of a Nation*, offers a crusade for the cause of black uplift, updates Stowe with more active black heroes, and answers Dixon and Griffith but with a sensational topper.

The story is this: Sylvia Landry is a light-skinned Negro woman living with her cousin, Alma, in a middle-class home in Boston after working as a schoolteacher in the South. Sylvia attracts suitors—one of whom, Larry, is a shifty relative of Alma and a thief. Sylvia awaits the arrival of the man to whom she is engaged, the hardworking and respectable Conrad. When Conrad returns from work in Brazil, he finds Sylvia in a compromisingly intimate meeting with an older white man. Insanely jealous, he begins to strangle Sylvia and then abruptly leaves. No explanation is forthcoming.

Sylvia returns to the South to teach. When the school lacks funds, she travels north to Boston again to seek help from philanthropists. While there, she is robbed but rescued by a black doctor (Dr. Vivian), who, like every other man in the film, is soon enamored of her. While resting on a park bench, Sylvia sees a white child in the trajectory of a speeding car. She saves the child but is hit herself. A stay in a hospital allows her to get to know the elderly woman philanthropist whose car hit her and to explain her need to fund her school. The philanthropist, Mrs. Elena Warwick, consults with an equally wealthy Southern woman to determine how to best help the school. The Southern woman opines that money for Negro education would be wasted and that she would be much better off giving just $100 to Old Ned the Preacher. A vignette shows us Old Ned—Micheaux's first, but not last, portrait of a hypocritical black preacher—exhorting his Southern congregation to worry about heaven rather than education and weaseling money from them during the collection. This vignette further shows Ned toadying up to his presumed white "friends," who only laugh at him and kick him in the behind. In an extraordinary moment that cannot strictly belong to this Southern woman's portrait of Ned, we see him drop the minstrel mask to reflect on the race betrayal that has led him to such a humiliating pass. In this vignette, Micheaux shows that the Tom stereotype of the white man's friend has now taken on a modern, race-betraying sense of the word.

As Mrs. Warwick weighs the prejudiced advice of her Southern friend against Sylvia's appeals, fast cuts build suspense as various scenes from the past are repeated: Dr. Vivian recalls past tender moments with Sylvia and pines for her, the Southern woman repeats her racist diatribe, Mrs. Warwick considers her choice. At this point, the climax of the film appears to be the decision of the white philanthropist, who finally decides to give not $5,000 but $50,000 to the Southern school. Mission accomplished, Sylvia returns south to the school, leaving Dr. Vivian bereft.

At the point of this weakly happy end to a narrative of uplift, Micheaux ties up a loose end of the story: the mystery of Sylvia's past and that compromising, intimate encounter with the white man that drove her fiancé away. Micheaux brings back a minor character—Larry, the thief—who has coincidentally taken his stolen goods to the South and hidden out near Sylvia's school, where he threatens to reveal some scandalous fact (or lie) about her past if she does not collude with him. In a move that is typical of many Micheaux's films that depict restless migrations from South to North and back again, Sylvia leaves the school and returns to the North again. In a coincidence typical of melodrama of this era, Larry's further criminal adventures in Boston lead him back to Sylvia's cousin, Alma, where he is fatally shot in a robbery and Dr. Vivian is called to tend to him. A repentant Alma, Sylvia's jealous cousin, then explains to Dr. Vivian who that white man was. An intertitle introduces this section as "Sylvia's Story."

A flashback that occupies the last twenty minutes of the film allows Micheaux to counter the racist Southern woman's story of black ignorance and explain Sylvia's deeper reasons for her relentless crusade in the cause of black education and delivers his pointed, sensational rebuttal to Griffith and Dixon. It is a story of Sylvia's family set in the past but after the time of the events recounted in both the Tom story and Dixon's and Griffith's anti-Tom. It is a Tom melodrama of black suffering at the hands of whites but emphasizing the female self-reliance of the Eliza part of that story—the mulatta who must fend for herself.

The flashback begins in a sharecroppers' cabin at the moment that the "father" of the family, Jasper Landry, is about to pay his debt to the white landowner. He is able to pay an accurate sum because now his adopted daughter, Sylvia, is educated and can keep his books so Landry will no longer be swindled. Nevertheless, Gridlestone, the landowner, does try to swindle Landry, and a struggle ensues. Efram, a nosy black servant of Gridlestone—another toadying race betrayer—sees this struggle between Landry and Gridlestone but misses the moment when a white sharecropper who has also been swindled shoots Gridlestone through the window of his decayed mansion. Efram assumes Landry has committed the crime and informs the community of poor white sharecroppers, who then search for the Landry family to lynch them (fig. 6.13).

What follows is Micheaux's great sensation scene: the lynching of the Landry family cross-cut with a sexual attack on Sylvia by the brother of the murdered landowner.[12] Like *Uncle Tom's Cabin* and unlike *The Birth of a Nation*, there will only be one rescue in the nick of time. The black family—father, mother, and son Emil (who alone escapes)—informed on by Efram, are captured, beaten, lynched, and burned, giving Micheaux the opportunity to show a truer side of lynching than the Klan's highly

Figure 6.13. Efram accuses Landry of murdering Gridlestone. *Screen capture by author.*

ritualized ceremony around the punishment of Gus. Without close-ups or grisly details, yet not avoiding the facts, Micheaux exposes the brutality and violence of the bloodthirsty white mob, composed of poor white men, women, and children, as the poor white resentment it is. Neither too particular about why or whom it lynches, this mob does nothing to ascertain the guilt of Sylvia's father, simply taking Efram's gossip for truth, and, when the Landrys first prove hard to find, they seize Efram himself as a handy "boy" to string up in the interim. Like the story of Old Ned, Micheaux again elaborates on the fate of the race betrayer (fig. 6.14).

As Jane Gaines notes, the film cuts from the attack on Sylvia five times to different stages of the lynching, including the fire that consumes the bodies of the victims.[13] If ever a black woman needed rescue, this scene (melo)dramatizes that need, though also the tenacity of Sylvia's defense. But when Gridlestone pulls away her bodice to expose her chest, he suddenly recognizes a scar that identifies Sylvia as his own daughter (fig. 6.15). Horrified, Gridlestone ceases his attack and the film abruptly cuts back to Alma, who has been telling this story to Dr. Vivian. We now understand with whom Sylvia had had her mysterious liaison—not a white-haired lover but her own father who was almost her rapist. Although Micheaux is careful to tell us in an intertitle that Sylvia was his "legitimate daughter from marriage to a woman of her race—who was later adopted by the Landrys," one can only wonder how legitimate a Southern white man's marriage to

Figure 6.14. Efram imagines his fate, which Micheaux does not depict except to show him pursued by the white lynch crowd. It is clear, however, that this is Efram's fate. *Screen capture by author.*

Figure 6.15. Gridlestone discovers his own daughter is the woman he is about to rape. *Screen capture by author.*

a black woman ever could have been in this period. Indeed, the film may insist on Sylvia's legitimacy a little too much. As Jane Gaines puts it, "The scene is symbolically charged as a reenactment of the White patriarch's ravishment of Black womanhood, reminding viewers of all the clandestine, forced sexual acts that produced the mulatto population of the American South."[14] In other words, the coincidence of this highly charged recognition scene with the lynching of Sylvia's adopted family forces the white patriarch to face, if not his past crime, at least his present one.

Sylvia is thus rescued, to some degree, by her putative respectability as Gridlestone's daughter: to rape her would be incest, and it would further sully both her and his "legitimacy." Sylvia's rescue in the nick of time by her white father's conscience is yet another aspect of Micheaux's redeployment of the Tom story. Like *Uncle Tom*'s Eliza, Sylvia must fend for herself in a masculine and white supremacist world that threatens her on all sides. Where Eliza, the escaped mulatta slave was threatened with recapture and separation from her child, Sylvia faces the lynching of her adopted family, rape by her own father, strangulation by a jealous fiancé, and extortion by Larry, the thief. Such is still the "helpless and unfriended" situation of the mulatta. Both Eliza and Sylvia are vulnerable beauties. But unlike the white heroines of Dixon's and Griffith's racial melodramas, they are strong and defiant; they do not throw themselves off cliffs to avoid fates worse than death, nor are they prone to fainting. And although Cedric Robinson argues that the attack on Sylvia echoes that of Lynch on Elsie in *The Birth of a Nation*, it is only in the fact of the attack and the white gown worn by both women, not in its form of enactment, for Sylvia's struggle is long and hard. In the end, however, Sylvia, like Eliza (and like Elsie in *The Birth of a Nation*) can only be rescued by white men—the good abolitionist Quaker who pulls Eliza out of the Ohio River and the less-good but conscience-stricken white father who suddenly recognizes the vulnerable condition of the mulatta daughter whom he himself created.

However, as the film's ending shows, the final union of Sylvia and Dr. Vivian, like the reunion of George and Eliza in *Uncle Tom's Cabin*, cannot solve the ultimate problem of white hegemony. These unions cannot provide a happy ending the way the double union of Camerons and Stonemans does at the end of *The Birth of a Nation*. Nor, to his credit, does Micheaux pretend that it does. Instead, and quite appropriately for the basic serial argument that the American melodrama of black and white is, we discover the couple in the midst of an argument. Sylvia is depressed, where an ordinary white heroine would be happy. The prospects for the future of the race worry her. Dr. Vivian tries to reassure her, but it is clear that their union, which does not even permit itself the triumph of romantic love, cannot conquer all. Race hatred endures. Dr. Vivian asks Sylvia to forget the distant past and to think of more recent instances of black heroism in the Spanish-American War and the recent "Great War." Finally, and even more ambivalently, he resorts to the claim that what sets African Americans apart from others who are also less-than-welcome in the United States is that, "We are not immigrants." This is indeed not a happy ending.

Cedric Robinson argues that with this ending Micheaux returns to the hackneyed melodrama of the rest of the film, and that only in the lynching episode has he managed to subvert the typical melodrama of Griffith's or even his own film. "Neither Griffith's end or Micheaux's can trump the enduring impact of the images of violence and hatred which preceded them. Bourgeois couplings are 'fake' resolutions, an escapist fantasy lacking even the imaginative power to will away the horrific sights and sounds emanating from a society engaged in racial conflict."[15]

I understand Robinson's desire to see Micheaux as having escaped the constraints of melodrama. Melodrama can only offer imperfect solutions to the problems of racial injustice. The putative moral empowerment it offers is only that of the injured person or race. As we have seen, the melodrama of black and white is as perfectly capable of depicting whites as suffering injury from blacks as it is the reverse. And what could be more melodramatic than this recognition by a white father of his black daughter through the scar that symbolizes all the racial injury suffered by her race? Robinson wants to see the lynching-rape sequence as anything but melodrama—"an extended jazz improvisation . . . effectively subverting and trivializing the melodrama," revealing that "the principal forces acting on our characters are not love, or romance, or jealousy or even coincidence" but a "racial conspiracy enforced by spontaneous acts of violence." But the "jazz improvisation" Micheaux offers—a quality that belongs more to the casual style of his storytelling throughout than to this sequence— is founded on the hand of black and white melodrama he has already been dealt. He cannot break free from the melodrama of racial injury.

Robinson argues that Micheaux unconvincingly imitates Griffith's happy ending in the form of "bourgeois coupling." I argue instead that Micheaux had no alternative but to answer Dixon and Griffith (who were themselves answering Stowe) within the framework of the racially motivated injuries of the melodrama of black and white. What is new in Micheaux is the yoking of a new melodrama of racial uplift to the old melodrama of racial injury and his willingness to show that injury in an almost incestuous context. Crucial to the theme of racial uplift is the idea that Dr. Vivian and Sylvia remain firmly implanted in the only home they have ever known, whether North or South. Unlike George and Eliza at the end of

Uncle Tom's Cabin (the novel), who, when they finally reach Canada, then seek a "Freedom in Africa"—an Africa that has never been their home—return to Africa is decidedly not their future. It is precisely Micheaux's commitment to uplift as a proud American native, and not as a fugitive or immigrant that is key to his new iteration of the Tom story in response to Griffith. Micheaux's melodrama makes its claim for the "home" that Tom himself never actually owned.

Oscar Micheaux's audacious solution was thus to presume that the bogus home once indicated by the ur-sentimental racial melodrama of *Uncle Tom's Cabin*, was, in fact, the true home of African Americans, who were not immigrants but, in the experience of most blacks living at his time, born in the United States. That this statement promotes blacks at the expense of more recent immigrants—Irish and Italians especially—is a form of nativism that seems inherent to the American melodrama of black and white, which seeks a virtue linked to a home(land).

To work within the melodramatic mode is thus not to sell out to white, bourgeois hegemony. It is to work with the plausible narrative means available at a given time. Melodrama is the form by which the powerless gain a certain, and entirely provisional, righteousness; and it is not unusual for that righteousness to even become self-righteousness on either side of the racial divide. But as a form prone to serial repetition, new iterations of its basic scenario of suffering can enable new forms of action. This essay attempts to understand how a Tom-victim can be inverted into an anti-Tom villain and how one African American director tried to reclaim the Tom-function of racial injury.

We might think of it this way: If William Walker had seen Micheaux's film, he might not have wished to become invisible in order to "kill all the white people in the world." If race war is the alternative, then it is not surprising that melodramas of racial injury have held such pride of place. But it is also not surprising that melodramas of racial injury can never be resolved; they can only perpetrate further melodramas of racial injury. Oscar Micheaux's may represent one of the more ingenious responses, but, as we know, the story continues.

LINDA WILLIAMS is Professor Emeritus of Film and Media and Rhetoric at the University of California, Berkeley. She is author of *Playing the Race Card: Melodramas of Black and White from Uncle Tom to O. J. Simpson* and *Screening Sex*.

Notes

1. In *Playing the Race Card*, I recount the high points of this melodrama from *Uncle Tom's Cabin* through *The Birth of a Nation*, *The Jazz Singer*, and *Gone with the Wind*, to television in the form of the miniseries *Roots*, television news, and the mediated trials of the police in the Rodney King beating and the trial of O. J. Simpson. Linda Williams, *Playing the Race Card: Melodramas of Black and White from Uncle Tom to O.J. Simpson* (Princeton, NJ: Princeton University Press, 2001).

2. Eric Lott, *Love and Theft: Blackface Minstrelsy and the American Working Class* (New York: Oxford University Press, 1993).

3. Williams, *Playing the Race Card*.

4. Michael Rogin, "'The Sword Became a Flashing Vision': D. W. Griffith's *The Birth of a Nation*," in "American Culture Between the Civil War and World War I," special issue, *Representations* 9 (Winter 1985): 179.

5. Griffith could easily have had the doctor take refuge in his own home. In fact, during the first half of the film, he had done just that when he showed the Cameron parents and daughters besieged in the house while "black guerilla" troops raided the town.

6. Williams, *Playing the Race Card*, 2001.

7. Vachel Lindsay, *The Art of the Moving Picture* (New York: Macmillan, 1916), 47.

8. Melvyn Stokes, *D. W. Griffith's* The Birth of a Nation: *A History of "the Most Controversial Motion Picture of All Time"* (Oxford: Oxford University Press, 2007), 229–231.

9. *D. W. Griffith: Father of Film*, directed by Kevin Brownlow and David Gill (New York: Kino Lorber, 1993), DVD.

10. George Fredrickson, *The Black Image in the White Mind: The Debate on Afro-American Character and Destiny* (Middletown, CT: Wesleyan University Press, 1987).

11. Jane Gaines, *Fire and Desire: Mixed-Race Movies in the Silent Era* (Chicago: University of Chicago Press, 2001); Cedric Robinson, *Forgeries of Memory and Meaning: Blacks and the Regimes of Race in American Theater and Film before World War II* (Chapel Hill: University of North Carolina Press, 2007).

12. As Jane Gaines notes, Micheaux's great stroke of genius is to cross-cut the lynching of the Landry family with the simultaneous sexual attack on Sylvia by Arnold Gridlestone, the brother of the murdered landowner. Gaines, "Fire and Desire: Race, Melodrama and Oscar Micheaux," in *Black American Cinema*, ed. Manthia Diawara (New York: Routledge, 1992), 56.

13. Gaines, *Fire and Desire*, 57.

14. Gaines, "Fire and Desire," 49–70, 56–57.

15. Robinson, *Forgeries of Memory and Meaning*, 260–261.

7

THE RHETORIC OF HISTORICAL REPRESENTATION IN GRIFFITH'S *THE BIRTH OF A NATION*

Lawrence Howe

Along with his many advances in cinematic narrative, D. W. Griffith deserves credit for consistency in the face of pointed criticism about his film's use of history. Right up to the last year of his life, thirty-two years after the release of *The Birth of a Nation*, he maintained a defensive posture: "In filming *The Birth of a Nation*, I gave to my best knowledge the proven facts, and presented the known truth, about the Reconstruction period in the American South. These facts are based on an overwhelming compilation of authentic evidence and testimony. My *picturisation* of history as it happens requires, therefore, no apology, no defence, no 'explanations.'"[1]

In emphasizing his use of "proven facts" and his "compilation of authentic evidence and testimony," Griffith downplays another important fact: his film is primarily a melodrama of two families from opposites sides of the regional divide before, during, and after the Civil War. Although the Civil War and Reconstruction are undeniable historical facts, Griffith's representation of them is drawn from the tradition of the Southern romance, largely influenced by Walter Scott's *Waverly* novels and the plantation myth that many Southerners nostalgically embraced after their defeat in the Civil War. Indeed, *The Birth of a Nation* is a reiteration of a very ambitious fiction. Thomas Dixon, a fellow Southerner, adapted his two novels *The Leopard's Spots* and *The Clansman* into a theatrical drama, and Griffith adapted this stage work into the vexed landmark of American cinema. Following

Dixon's lead, Griffith originally titled his film *The Clansman*, which he altered to square up with the Dunning interpretation of the United States as a nation born not out of the American Revolution but from the crucible of the American Civil War. Thus, despite Griffith's insistence that he constructed a sound historical account, the film promotes a Southern mythology that extols the virtue of white resistance to black oppression. In casting blacks as primitive and morally deficient Others, the film shares the pernicious ideology of its source material. This troubling content complicates any discussion about the merits of its cinematic narrative technique.

Still, despite the film's basis in melodrama, Griffith's claim that his film is a "picturisation" of history is understandable, for he assiduously worked plenty of history into it. Indeed, the emphasis that he repeatedly placed on the film's historicism is, I contend, an important tactic in an overarching rhetorical strategy. Griffith and Dixon, in tandem, sought to imbue the film with the authority of history both diegetically and extradiegetically to bolster the film's argument about white supremacy. The collaboration between filmmaker and novelist serves to call attention to an intellectual debate about history's synthesis of science and art that, as Hayden White has suggested, polarized intellectuals at the end of the nineteenth century.[2] In taking up this question, White emphasizes that the historian frames content within recognizable narrative forms with specific structures of "emplotment" that condition its representation of history as either epic, romance, comedy, tragedy, or satire. Concluding, he writes, "We may say, then, that in history—as in all of the human sciences—every interpretation has ideological implications."[3] Thus Dixon's romance of white Southerners to re-ascendancy is a ready form for Griffith to adapt to a historical cinematic narrative rife with ideological interpretation.

In 1915, the cinematic approach to history was arguably naïve, as Griffith's statements suggest. And cinema's tendencies to focus on identifiable protagonists and antagonists and to oversimplify complex events, their causes, and consequences drew criticism from historians throughout the twentieth century. In recent decades, however, several historians have reconsidered the potential virtues of film as a medium of historical representation, leaving the field in another round of debate. Robert Rosenstone, one of the most vocal proponents of history on film, cites the oppositional views of philosopher Ian Jarvie and historian R. J. Raack as exemplary of the divide. Jarvie criticizes film as discursively weak due to its "poor information load," resulting in "a descriptive narrative" that lacks the kind of polemical complexity that he sees as the arena of serious historical practice. In contrast, Raack sees film as a remedy to the linearity and narrow focus of "traditional written history," citing film's "ability to juxtapose images and sounds, . . . its quick cuts to new sequences, dissolves, fades, speed-ups [and] slow motion" as necessary techniques for rendering the lived experience of history.[4] Rosenstone grants that Raack's position is an unorthodox one, but he also finds merit in the idea that cinema's command over time and space enables it to provide insight into other eras and places. And he questions Jarvie's criticism that cinema lacks information, noting that the kind of information may be different from what historians have traditionally valued; but from his own experience of working on a feature film and a documentary drawn from his scholarship, he has come to see cinematic data as quite rich in what it illuminates to the viewer. Following Rosenstone, Alison Landsberg argues that film can foster "affective engagement" that has the "capacity to bring the past literally into view, to make it feel real, to flesh it out." But she hastens to note that, "in some cases it offers the illusory promise that the viewer can slip back into the past and 'know what it was like' by means of a simplistic, facile identification with an onscreen character"—precisely the point on which many historians have often rested their critique.[5] The distinction, for Landsberg, lies in the filmmaker's sense of responsibility to evoke "an embodied and powerful mode of engagement that might be conducive to the acquisition of historical knowledge."[6]

Griffith's responsibility is precisely the focus of my argument. The degree to which the filmmaker and novelist contrived to couch the film's racist polemics as historically objective has received considerable critical attention. But these examinations have stopped short of a full analysis of how the film's historical representations serve a rhetorical design. In this essay, I aim to move the critical debate in that direction. The point that I will make about the film's historicism is a fairly simple one, but a crucial one nonetheless: Griffith's multiple forms of historical representation are scaffolded in order to persuade his audience of the film's reliability and historical authority. Among these various forms of representation, the scene of Lincoln's assassination is both central to the film's diegesis and key to its rhetorical design. In particular, Griffith's exploitation of his audience's position as spectators during this pivotal scene was a rhetorically shrewd, though ultimately deceptive, manipulation of the viewer's perspective.

Griffith's claim that he relied on "proven facts" and "authentic evidence and testimony" suggests that he sees history as a set of uncomplicated givens, with little or no regard for the contingency of interpretation, the importance of context, and the inevitable ideological bias of any narrative framework that contains historical "facts." James Snead argues that Griffith's use of history was "not casual," but rather "a self-conscious aim of *The Birth of a Nation* to write history with cinema, particularly with its so-called 'historical facsimiles,' which are both obtrusive and dilatory to the plot, but which are crucial to ideological, rather than narrative, aims."[7]

I will address the historical facsimiles at greater length later in this chapter, agreeing with Snead that they are crucial. However, I argue that their importance is not only ideological but also rhetorical, which, as Mikhail Bakhtin argues, is a fundamental condition of prose narrative in the form of the novel.[8] Indeed, White, in noting the commonplace that "*all* historical accounts are 'artistic' in some way," goes further to contend "that the artistic component in historical discourse can be disclosed by an analysis that is specifically *rhetorical* in nature, . . . [deploying] a 'code' by which the reader is invited to assume a certain attitude toward the facts and the interpretation of them" (emphasis in original).[9] To achieve his historicist strategy, Griffith deployed various tactics that registered the film as a reflection of what he took to be historical fact; however, that historical narrative is framed in the terms of a rhetorical code.

According to Michael Rogin, "Griffith, claiming historical documentary status for his own fiction, made film the ultimate authority. Fully realizing film's power to seize the audience, Griffith replaces history with the illusionistic, realistic, self-enclosed, cinematic epic."[10] Although I agree with much of what Rogin contends, I argue that the filmmaker did not replace history as much as he constructed a version of history, selecting and framing historical elements in order to transmit identifiable signals to the audience. And his intended audience also accepted Griffith's account of history and even approved of his deliberate blending of history with melodrama. As with all films that are considered historical, "audiences recognize the existence of a system of knowledge that is already clearly defined—historical knowledge, from which film-makers take their materials," drawing on a common heritage that functions as "'historical capital,' and it is enough to select a few details from this for the audience to know that it is watching an historical film."[11] It is the structure of the historical gestures in *The Birth of a Nation* and their effect on the audience on which my analysis will focus.

A Divided Nation Finds a Common Audience

In emphasizing the film's designed effect on the spectator, it is important to note that, for Griffith, the audience was composed of exclusively white spectators from the North and South. The explicit purpose of Griffith's narrative is to reunite the divided nation by showing how white families on both sides of the regional divide, represented by the Stonemans and Camerons, shared the toll of the Civil War. Both families lose sons in the Civil War; moreover, Tod Stoneman (Robert Harron) and Duke Cameron (Maxfield Stanley)—antebellum "chums" now cast as Union and Confederate enemies—die in a quasi-erotic fraternal embrace that immortalizes their earlier affinity for each other. The compassionate heroism of Confederate Colonel Ben Cameron (Henry B. Walthall), in providing comfort for a fallen Union soldier, projects his honorable character, suggesting the South's worthiness of the North's respect.

In focusing the second half of the narrative on the consequences of Southern defeat, the film implies the racial identity of its intended audience, emphasizing that whites of both regions had a mutual stake in restoring the racial order that Griffith posits as natural. The occupation of the South by Northern troops exposes the daughters of both families to the dangers of black male sexuality. In her study of spectatorship in early cinema, Miriam Hansen notes that, despite the efforts of early filmmakers such as Griffith and other promoters of the industry to endorse film as a universal language, it was not the democratically diverse art form they imagined. Applying theories of the public sphere, Hansen argues that the cinema's influential imagery produced an alternative public sphere that minimized class and ethnic diversity: "The invocation of the universal-language myth came to mask the institution's suppression of working-class behavior and experience. . . . By taking class out of the working class and ethnic difference out of the immigrant, the universal-language metaphor in effect became a code word for broadening the mass-cultural base of motion pictures in accordance with middle-class values and sensibilities."[12]

Furthermore, *The Birth of a Nation* did not simply promote narrow class-based values; rather, it stressed the virtues of a white-centric society. Although this had long been a constituent of the Southern ethos, the film's release occurred in the midst of the first wave of the "great migration," marking the arrival of many African Americans to Northern industrial cities. This demographic shift stirred anxieties of working-class whites about competition for jobs and of middle-class white homeowners fearful of a loss of property value from integrated neighborhoods. So the message of Griffith's film about white virtue and privilege found a receptive audience among white spectators across the nation.

The film's postbellum narrative traffics in denigrating African American stereotypes as justification for the rise of white vigilantism to restore the ostensible order that Reconstruction violated. Needless to say, black spectators have no opportunity to identify with a narrative that unilaterally casts black characters in roles of moral degradation. In a close reading of the famous sequence in which Gus pursues Flora, Manthia Diawara highlights the dilemma for black spectatorship of *The Birth of a Nation*: "At issue is . . . the contradiction between the rhetorical force of the story—the dominant reading compels the black spectator to identify with the racist inscription of the black character—and the resistance, on the part of Afro-American spectators, to this version of US history, on account of its Manichean dualism."[13] Indeed, William Walker, a black spectator interviewed in Kevin Brownlow and David Gill's 1992 documentary, *D. W. Griffith: Father of Film*, reported feeling erased from the national narrative upon viewing the film in 1916 in a black theater: "Some people were crying. . . . You had the worst feeling in the world. You just felt like you were not counted. You were out of existence."[14] Walker's subsequent desire suggests the potential consequences of the film, about which civil rights leaders had warned: "I wished somebody would not see me so I could kill them. I just felt like killing all the white people in the world." Although Walker's admission approaches the rage that Richard Wright would fictionally embody in Bigger Thomas, the notorious protagonist—and movie spectator—in *Native Son*, the violence that took place with the release of *The Birth of a Nation* was perpetrated by whites against blacks. Civil rights leaders warned about the likelihood of the film promoting violence. The accuracy of their foresight can be measured in the resurgence of the Ku Klux Klan. After lying dormant since the passage of three Enforcement Acts, which criminalized vigilante intimidation practices in the early 1870s, the organization rose again in the wake of Griffith's film, its recruitment increasing steadily from 1915 and peaking in the mid-1920s.

Griffith may not have foreseen these consequences, but he did forge the film's historical authority consistent with a racial ideology. At strategic intervals, the film constructs a series of historical gestures that project the racist melodrama as an authentic continuation of the historical representation. By capitalizing on the white audience's sentiments and, especially, their position as spectators, Griffith's historical representations are central to a rhetorical design that seeks to leverage the audience's trust in the narrative's biases. Once the film elicits that trust in its historical authority, it induces the audience to give credence to the full arc of the film's narrative— the mythology as well as the history.

Framing Historicist Rhetoric

The historical gestures Griffith deployed in *The Birth of a Nation* are varied and sequential, designed to project authority. The film begins with extradiegetic historical references, laying the groundwork for its bona fides. Providing the backstory of slavery, an early intertitle declares that "The bringing of the African to America planted the first seed of disunion." Despite eliding agency for the planting of this seed, the ensuing scene shows a figure in Puritan dress overseeing the importation of slaves, suggesting that New Englanders were primarily responsible. This is followed immediately with a reference to abolitionists—more meddlers from New England—who demanded the end of slavery. The narrative conveys no concern for the slaves, treating them as objects that the North has exploited.

The opening of the film's second half parallels these polemics in its commentary on Reconstruction. A series of three intertitles introduce quotations from Woodrow Wilson's magisterial *A History of the American People* to buttress the film's historical validity. This historical commentary frames Reconstruction as the scheme of "adventurers" who "*swarmed* out of the North, as much enemies of the one race as the other, to *cozen, beguile,* and *use* the negroes" (emphasis added). The series of carefully selected verbs portray the Northerners as unscrupulous, and their deceptive practices were abetted by "congressional leaders" to effect "a veritable overthrow of the civilization in the South . . . in their determination '*to put the white South under the heel of the black South*'" (emphasis in the original). From this cause, the excerpts from Wilson's narrative history conclude, "The white men were roused by a mere instinct of self-preservation . . . until at last there had sprung into existence a great Ku Klux Klan, a veritable empire of the South, to protect the Southern country." The language of Wilson's account of the Klan is telling: in the face of hordes of deceitful invaders, white Southern men were naturally "roused" by "instinct." Indeed, the Klan seems to emerge on its own unbidden, albeit fortunately to right the corruption visited on the historian's beloved South.

Wilson's framing of both sides in coded language makes clear that the practice of history is an interpretive field, and the historian's bias prompts him to read the record with compassion for his region and contempt for the cynical motivations of the Reconstructionists. But even allowing for regional bias, the praise of the Klan as "great" and a "veritable empire of the South" strikes a discordant note today, given what we know of the hateful terrorism Klansmen inflicted. Still, for Griffith, the president's words are important validation because they square with the representations that his adaptation of Dixon's narrative converts into vivid "picturisations."

Indeed, Wilson's authority lends credibility to the film's case because he was not only the president of the United States at the time the film was released but also the first president to hold academic credentials. He held a PhD in history from Johns Hopkins University and had been on the history faculty at Bryn Mawr, Wesleyan, and finally Princeton, where he was also appointed university president. Thus, the inclusion of his words is an attempt to validate the film's cinematic spectacle by attaching to it Wilson's authority as de facto "historian-in-chief." Prior to the release of the film, Griffith and Dixon also externally parlayed Wilson's credentials to reinforce its historical status. Having known Wilson at Johns Hopkins, Dixon proposed an advance screening of the film for the president and members of his cabinet. Wilson agreed, granting the film the distinction of being among the first, if not the first, to have been shown in the White House. Dixon and Griffith took this occasion a step further by promoting the film with an unauthorized endorsement from Wilson. Although the film's heroic depictions of the Ku Klux Klan's terrorism match Wilson's praise of the Klan, there is no corroboration that Wilson ever famously announced that *The Birth of a Nation* "is like writing history with lightning, and my only regret is that it is all so terribly true."[15] Indeed, the controversy over the film was such a political liability for Wilson that he instructed J. P. Tumulty, his private secretary, to issue a statement "that he had at no time approved the film," and in 1918 he deemed the film an "unfortunate production."[16] But the frequency with which the approbation of the film as "writing history with lightning" has been assigned to Wilson indicates the effectiveness of the strategy that Dixon and Griffith had devised.

Still, as peripherally useful as the Wilson quotations within the film and his apocryphal endorsement are, they are also entirely uncinematic and supplementary to the film's designed effect. The "picturisation of history" begins to emerge in the historical dramatizations, and these take three different forms. The first includes Civil War battle scenes, representations of historic events such as Sherman's burning of Atlanta, and the siege of Petersburg. None of this was entirely new for Griffith. He had honed his representation of the spectacle of Civil War battles in short films prior to *The Birth of a Nation*. We know of twenty-seven short films that included Civil War battle scenes made in the United States from the onset of Griffith's directing career in 1908 to the release of his epic film in 1915. Of those, twelve were written, produced, and directed by Griffith and included many of the actors and crew who collaborated on *the Birth of a Nation*—especially the cinematographer G. W. "Billy" Bitzer, with whom Griffith had pioneered his innovative visual narrative techniques. Griffith cast Henry Walthall in the leading role of Confederate soldier in three of those early films. Thus, the filmmaker and his company had considerable experience in filming and editing the drama of Civil War combat. Although Civil War films make up only a small percentage of early films, the topic fascinated audiences. But none, not even Thomas Ince's fifty-minute film *The Battle of Gettysburg* (1913), compares to the epic sweep of *The Birth of a Nation*, which explicitly linked the war to the upheaval of Reconstruction and the consequent rise of the Ku Klux Klan. The Civil War scenes in *The Birth of a Nation* have impressive dramatic value, diegetically integrated with the primary plot of the central characters. However, the film's military engagements are imagined representations, drawing on conventions of Griffith's early filmmaking rather than on fidelity to the specifics of history. The battle scenes subordinate history to the nostalgic melodrama centering primarily on the Cameron family, making an emotional appeal about the honor and tragedy of war.

The second form of historical representation consists of tableaux of momentous national events, such as Lincoln signing the order to muster Union troops and Lee surrendering to Grant at Appomattox. Each of these scenes is introduced by an intertitle verifying it as "an historical facsimile" with a citation to a source text. As with the quotations from Wilson's magisterial *A History of the American People*, the sources for the tableaux bolster the film's historical authority. The scene of Lincoln signing the order to raise Union troops in his "Executive Office on that occasion, after Nicholas and Hay in *Lincoln, A History*," cites a highly regarded source, given that the authors were Lincoln's private secretaries. But, as Pierre Sorlin points out, their ten-volume work does not describe or depict the setting that Griffith screens for his audience. The historiographical source functions

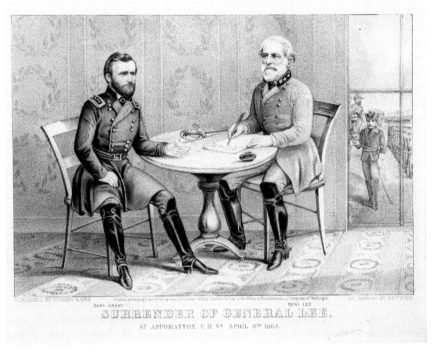

Figure 7.1. "Surrender of General Lee—at Appomattox, C.H. Va. April 9th 1865." *Currier and Ives, Library of Congress Prints and Photographs Division.*

more as credence than reference. Spectators would not be inclined to seek out sources in order to be persuaded of the reliability of the scenes, because what they saw on the screen had been disseminated in mass-produced prints such as those sold for framing by Currier and Ives or reprinted in school texts (see figs. 7.1 and 7.2), making them highly familiar to the film audience. Other mass-produced images, such as Lincoln's signing of the Emancipation Proclamation, are quite similar to Griffith's screening of his proclamation mustering volunteer troops for the Union army, and thus similarly convey the historical reliability of the cinematic image.

Griffith's screening of these representations amounts to the first form of "cine-memory" as Michael T. Martin and David Wall define it: "Class 1 *cine-memory* serves to affirm received assumptions and discourses about the past. It confirms the ideological certainties of the implied viewer, valorizes the beliefs, and conforms to the expectations of the audience. In doing so it functions to portray the hegemonic order as a consequence of nature rather than culture. Yet, the past it represents hides ideological assumptions and

Figure 7.2. "The room in the McLean House, at Appomattox C.H., in which Gen. Lee surrendered to Gen. Grant," no date. *Library of Congress Prints and Photographs Collection.*

values that normalize the 'reality' it claims to express. Events appear fixed in time, discrete, simplistically framed, and analytically wanting."[17] Hence, "class 1 cine-memory" visually reinforces a previous impression from experience or cultural document, which matches Griffith's ostensible purpose in the film. By themselves, however, the tableaux render historical validity at the expense of cinematic drama. The nearly static images of highly recognizable historic figures signing documents, as well as their function as cine-memories that reaffirm viewers' recollections of images in galleries and books, underscores the lack of cinematic quality in the tableaux.

The Lincoln Assassination as Common Historical Capital

Griffith warrants the Lincoln assassination scene as another "historical facsimile"; however, the historicism of this representation is notably different from the tableaux by being diegetically integrated within the film's narrative. Thus, in its synthesis of the diegetic content of the Civil War battles and the extradiegetic content of the historical tableaux, the

Lincoln assassination is a third form of historical representation that exerts a more complex and more vivid rhetorical leverage. Given its function, it seems rather surprising that critics have rarely commented on the assassination scene; only one, Mark Charney, grants it the central importance that I ascribe to it. If critics give the assassination any notice, most simply do so in passing, perhaps because, as Paul McEwan notes, "the outcome of the scene is preordained. The fact that the audience obviously knows what will happen means that rather than true suspense we have a sense of foreboding."[18] Critics have focused, instead, on the melodramatic consequences of Reconstruction that proceed from the abrupt ending of Lincoln's presidency. Rogin suggests as much, noting that "The death of Griffith's Lincoln sets the white-sheeted knights of Christ in motion."[19] His direct linkage acknowledges the central narrative purpose of the scene. According to Charney, the assassination scene serves Griffith's larger purpose to highlight the documentary function of narrative cinema. However, he criticizes Griffith's representation as "inevitably founded in *theater* not 'facts'" (emphasis added).[20] Noting its "play-within-a-play" structure, Charney argues that the scene creates an "artificial distinction between what is real or 'true'—Lincoln's assassination—and what is representation or false— *Our American Cousin.*"[21] Contrary to presenting an objective representation of history, Charney claims, Griffith's innovative techniques "emphasize the subjective development of character and plot through selective vision, and he never sacrifices the *histrionic potential of a scene* to faithful realism, despite his earnest insistence that his object is the 'truth'" (emphasis added).[22] Given that Griffith had aspired to be a playwright before finding his way into the cinema, and that his film is an adaptation of Dixon's theatrical play, we should hardly be surprised to find theatrical elements in the film. But while Charney's analysis effectively unites form with ideology, I disagree with his critique of Griffith's privileging of histrionics over "faithful realism." To the contrary, Griffith conflates the two, paying meticulous attention to detail in his cinematic staging of the historic tragedy. This signals his fidelity to realism, while also maximizing the dramatic effect of the scene. Moreover, Griffith is not deploying realism for its own sake, but as a further investment in the rhetorical force of his film's historical authority.

As has been often noted, the events of the film still had a hold on the national consciousness at the time of the film's release. In *Life on the Mississippi* (1883), Mark Twain observed, "in the North one hears the war mentioned . . . once a month; sometimes as often as once a week." And in the

South, "[t]he war is the great chief topic of conversation. The interest in it is vivid and constant. . . . the war is what A.D. is elsewhere: they date from it."[23] The Civil War, admittedly, commanded less attention thirty years after Twain's visit to the South, but the release of *The Birth of a Nation* was timed to the fiftieth anniversary of the end of the Civil War, renewing the remembrance of the war and its aftermath. At the New York premiere of the film, theater attendants wore uniforms of the Union and Confederacy, while women ushers were dressed in period costume, theatrical flourishes that reinforced the film's historical references, nostalgically embodying them for the audience.[24]

If the Civil War had emotional power, Lincoln's assassination would have an even more galvanizing charge because it was a highly specific and personalized event. Unlike the war's diffusely scattered and protracted experiences, the who, what, why, when, where, and how of the Lincoln assassination are extremely concrete details—especially the where. Griffith's decision to dramatize the scene, rather than allude to it, as Steven Spielberg did in *Lincoln* (2012), capitalizes on the importance of the Lincoln assassination as a national event that generated an outpouring of mourning. Griffith's return to the event as the closing scene of his first talking picture, *Lincoln* (1930), suggests its cultural staying power and its continued interest to the filmmaker. Martha Hodes's recent study of the responses to this singular tragedy highlights the universal shock that many Americans experienced. Many were in disbelief, finding the murder of the president as an unfathomable turn of events, hard on the heels of the Union victory.[25] Numerous newspaper accounts, the only mass media of the day, reinforced the reality of what had occurred. Hodes also points out that, for those at Ford's theater that night, the trauma was almost unrecoverable.[26] Given the assassination's political and cultural impact, and the national mourning that swept the nation, it seems impossible to overstate the power of the assassination scene for the spectators of *The Birth of a Nation*. The New York premiere was only five weeks before the fiftieth anniversary of the assassination. And newspaper coverage of the anniversary included many eyewitness accounts including from some of the living cast members of the 1865 production of *Our American Cousin*, thus insuring the cultural significance of the film's representation.

Griffith strives for a documentary effect from the outset of the scene, specifically announcing "the fated night of April 14, 1865" in an intertitle. The late arrival of the presidential party to the theater is similarly noted, and the moment just prior to the assassination is time-stamped and cross-referenced to the act and scene of the play. While these temporal details may prompt derision, as intrusions—explicit gestures meant to inform the audience, "you are watching the absolute truth . . . seeing is believing"—the attention to detail in this central scene, unmatched elsewhere in the film, suggests the heightened importance of historical precision.[27] As with the tableaux, an intertitle noting Ford's theater as "an historical facsimile" introduces the scene, again citing Nicolay and Hay's ten-volume Lincoln biography for authority. Like the tableaux, the image of the stage at Ford's theater and the presidential box where Lincoln was slain would have been familiar to the audience from countless reports and illustrations of the historic tragedy. Mass media in the late nineteenth and early twentieth centuries were no match for the image saturation to which we have become accustomed. The prevalence of media images of events, such as the Kennedy motorcade in Dallas in 1963 or the falling twin towers of the World Trade Center in 2001, give rise to the phenomenon that Baudrillard terms hyperreality. Visually mediated memory was only getting underway with the medium that Griffith was pioneering. Still, what spectators had seen, heard, or read about the events at Ford's theater had prepared them for the spectacle of Griffith's representation, visually confirming their cultural impression of history. The film's marketing campaign reflects the ways in which these images would register with the public. In addition to the movie posters bearing images of mounted and robed Ku Klux Klansmen, others featured the scene of John Wilkes Booth jumping from the presidential box to the stage after firing the fatal shot, graphically capitalizing on the drama of the assassination and recalling images in the popular press (see figs. 7.3 and 7.4).

In contrast to the historical tableaux, which struck objective postures, the Lincoln assassination scene not only is diegetically integrated within the narrative but also presents multiple point-of-view shots from the vantage point of Phil Stoneman (Elmer Clifton) and his sister Elsie (Lillian Gish), who attend the performance. Miriam Hansen notes that the iris shot of Booth enables the spectator to share Elsie's view of the matinee idol and soon-to-be assassin through her opera glasses, highlighting this moment as "narrationally significant" for the subjective identification that it affords the spectator.[28]

Elsewhere, Hansen comments on the ability of classical cinema narration to expand "the possibilities of placing, or 'positioning,' the spectator in

Figure 7.3. "Assassination of President Lincoln—the murderer leaping upon
the stage, and catching his spur in the flag which hung before the president's
box." *Frank Leslie's Illustrated Newspaper*, 20 (May 6, 1865), 98 (cover).

relation to the represented events, in both the figurative and literal sense of
'position.'"[29] Although Hansen does not address it, the Lincoln assassination exemplifies this phenomenon. The composition of the scene grants the
spectator both a subjective identification with the Stonemans and a quasi-
omniscient perspective, intercutting their observations with details not visible to them or to other patrons at Ford's theater on the fateful night. In a
scene that runs slightly longer than five minutes, Griffith's editing assembles

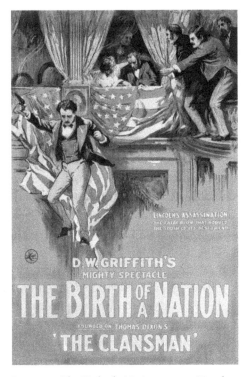

Figure 7.4. *The Birth of a Nation* poster—Lincoln assassination. Distributed by Epoch Film Co. 1915. *Courtesy Wikimedia Commons.*

fifty-five shots that move smoothly from the Stonemans taking their seats in Ford's Theatre, through the performance of the light comedy on the stage and the Stonemans' differing responses, to their enthusiastic applause when Lincoln (Joseph Henabery) and his entourage make their celebrated arrival, and to Elsie's blushing observation of Booth (Raoul Walsh) on the balcony beside the presidential box. But the constructed sequence also reveals Lincoln's bodyguard leaving his post to watch the performance onstage and Booth's furtive access to the back corridor just vacated by Lincoln's negligent bodyguard. We watch with dreaded anticipation as Booth, lurking outside the presidential box, takes his derringer from concealment within his coat. In other words, the film allows the viewer a privileged and informed line of sight, quite different from the vantage points of Phil and Elsie and the audience at Ford's Theatre, who observe only what they can see from their theater seats. The film spectator's privileged view amplifies not only the drama of the scene but also the persuasive power of the film's historicism.

Most importantly, the scene leverages one additional element, a by-product of an often overlooked historical fact, giving it distinctive power over the spectator and heightened meaning to Hansen's observations about cinema's positioning of the spectator. Namely, Lincoln was assassinated in a theater. By grim coincidence, the film's spectator watches the cinematic representation of that historic event while also seated in a theater that is similar in nearly every way to the one on-screen, except that the screen has replaced the proscenium stage. Griffith exploits the coincidence, creating a moment of reflexivity of the film's consumption that postulates the illusion of subjective experience for the spectator. In effect, the film's audience is imaginatively converted from a cinematic spectator into a witness to history, experiencing what Alison Landsberg calls a "prosthetic memory," a "personally felt public memor[y] that result[s] from the experience of a mediated representation of the past."[30]

The 1915 spectator's experience would be equivalent to a contemporary viewer watching Paul Greengrass's *United 93* (2006) while onboard a transcontinental flight. According to Airlines for America, the industry trade organization, the airlines have taken it on themselves to exclude from in-flight entertainment programs even a fictional airplane disaster film—let alone a docudrama about the 9/11 tragic flight. Most recently, American Airlines, which was involved in the making of *Sully* (dir. Clint Eastwood, 2016), acknowledged that, despite its pride in the actions of the crew of Flight 1549, it would not screen the film as in-flight entertainment. American Airlines spokesperson Michelle Mohr represented the company's logic: "It could be upsetting to someone flying with us or someone looking over and seeing those images, so we decided not to provide it."[31] By ruling out airplane dramas as in-flight entertainment, the airlines implicitly acknowledge that the spectator's position can be determined by more than gender, class, or race.

Griffith understood this and took advantage of the cinema spectator's position in a theater to amplify the narrative effect of the Lincoln assassination scene, just as Buster Keaton did in *Sherlock Jr.* (1924) and Quentin Tarantino did in the climax of *Inglourious Basterds* (2009). The critical difference with *The Birth of a Nation*'s pivotal scene is that Griffith's audience was prepared to feel the emotional weight and grasp the historical meaning of Lincoln's assassination, affirming the film's historical authority. Part of that preparation came through images and accounts to which the audience had been repeatedly exposed, and Griffith's film strategically reinforces that content to drive home his film's rhetorical design. The cinematic image of this infamous event brought the past into the spectator's present point of view. For perhaps the first time in modern history, a cinematic representation of a historic event blurred the line between mediation and immediacy.

Arriving halfway through the film, this powerful cinematic moment is not the effect but rather the final catalyst of the film's rhetorical purpose. The effect is explicitly announced about twenty minutes later in the scene titled "Riot in the Master's Hall." The intertitle warranting that the set is another "historical facsimile" from a newspaper photograph in 1870 leads the spectator to believe that what follows has been photographically documented. However, the scene employs the visual magic of a dissolve in which the empty legislative chamber, from the cited 1870 photograph, is gradually populated with its "negro majority" newly elected in 1871. Thus, it is not the documentary photograph but Griffith's camera that places the spectator in the midst of unruly and uncouth black legislators who make a mockery of decorum and policy. Metaphorically drunk on newly acquired power, if not literally drunk on alcohol sipped from hidden flasks, the raucous assembly passes a series of orders that extend the social power of black citizens. This meeting culminates in a law that permits racial intermarriage, received with exultation by black members on the floor of the chamber who then turn their menacing gaze at Southern white women in the gallery. The mix of shots that Griffith assembles in this episode situates the viewer in various positions in the legislative chamber, granting multiple proximities to the unqualified members on the floor of the assembly as well as with the white visitors in the gallery, who flee the lurid looks of the black men now in power.

Taken together, all of Griffith's historical gestures function as a visual syllogism, concatenating a logical deduction about the ostensible perversity of the Reconstruction South. The quotations from Wilson and the historical tableaux extradiegetically lay the foundation of the film's claim of authority, magnified by the authenticity and reflexive immediacy of the representation of Lincoln's assassination functioning as a mediating rhetorical warrant for the denigrating portrayal of the South Carolina legislature and, by extension, all African Americans. Where Griffith's representations of history vivify images already embedded in public memory, his scandalous portrayal of the "Riot in the Master's Hall" affirms white anxieties about the racial Other, especially magnifying the fear of sexual violation. In short, *The Birth of a Nation* leverages the reliability of the historical representations as ideological collateral that justifies extending the same credit to its racist propaganda.

The Rhetorical Payoff

Having piqued anxieties of race and sex, the film increases those tensions in the infamous scene in which Gus (Walter Long), a black Union soldier, approaches Flora Cameron (Mae Marsh). Even though Griffith has toned down the confrontation from Dixon's novel—in which a mother and daughter are raped by Gus and subsequently kill themselves rather than live with the shame of their defilement—by reframing the encounter as Gus's marriage proposal to Flora, both she and the audience have been primed to read his intentions as salacious defilement. It is, after all, Flora's horror at Gus's proposal, not his lust, that precipitates the suspenseful chase. But Griffith's film does not require the overt depiction of Gus as a violent sexual beast; Flora's vulnerability is perfectly understandable to the white audience. Her death, though a tragedy that must be avenged, is a lucky escape from the fate of Gus's proposal. The abduction of Elsie by Silas Lynch (George Siegmann) reinforces the message by relying explicitly on white fear of the black man's rapacity. Lynch's predatory claim on the daughter of his political benefactor is both an unmistakable gesture of Griffith's poetic justice for Austin Stoneman's (Ralph Lewis) misguided leadership of radical Reconstruction and a sign of the fragility of the angelic Elsie in a society that has lost its sense of order.

The film's climactic rescue scenes, triggered by multiple instances of white families besieged by rampaging black Union troops, track a rhetorical trajectory that inevitably leads to the erroneous conclusion that the Ku Klux Klan is the corrective justice to the abomination of radical Reconstruction. Through these dramatically suspenseful sequences, the film dispenses with claims to historical authority. Instead, these melodramatic tropes of damsels in distress are tacitly framed as objective fact on the earlier warrant of the film's historical authenticity. In one sense, the film's frenzy of anxiety is ironic, because it not only diverges from the explicitly brutal content of Griffith's source text but also draws from stereotypical fear of black male lust. Even the enlightened Thomas Jefferson iterated that fear in *Notes on the State of Virginia*, when he analogized the black man's desire for white women to the "preference of the Oranootan for the black women over those of his own species."[32] Given what we now know about Jefferson's long, and fruitful, relationship with Sally Hemmings, a slave of his late wife, his odd bestial analogy seems more like a projection of his own desire onto black men. The practice of white slave owners expanding their stock of slave property through rape was common enough to be condemned by the genteel Southern diarist Mary Chesnutt, suggesting white male desire as the source of the taboo against interracial sexuality as well as the motivation for the Klan's vigilante terror in the guise of justice.

In the film's climax, the promise of the Klan's protection is fulfilled in two rescues of vulnerable damsels: Elsie Stoneman, abducted by the mulatto carpetbagger Lynch, and Margaret Cameron (Miriam Cooper), under siege by hordes of black soldiers. In parallel scenes, Dr. Cameron (Spottiswoode Aiken) and a Union veteran are poised to kill their daughters to prevent them from falling victim to the black soldiers' lust. These gestures appropriate the maternal sacrifice of Margaret Garner—the historical inspiration for Toni Morrison's novel *Beloved*—a slave mother who killed her daughter to save her from slavery. The maximum cathartic effect of this climax is achieved through Griffith's decision to include multiple rescues. As he acknowledged in his autobiography, Griffith envisioned his film as a move beyond the melodramatic formula of rescuing a damsel in distress: "We had all sorts of runs-to-the-rescue in pictures and horse operas. . . . Now I could see a chance to do this ride-to-the-rescue on a grand scale. Instead of saving one little Nell of the Plains, this ride would be to save a nation."[33] Griffith's account of the narrative opportunity undercuts his insistence on the film's historical reliability. Indeed, it suggests itself as evidence of Baudrillard's claim that "history is our lost referential, that is to say our myth. It is by virtue of this fact that it takes the place of myths on the screen."[34]

Melodrama was Griffith's stock-in-trade, and in making a film that expanded his narrative reach to the fullest, he ensures that the Klansmen arrive in the nick of time to thwart sexual violation, both saving the nation and realizing the film's emotional potential and its rhetorical objective. In the anticlimax, the surviving sons and daughters of the Cameron and Stoneman families unite as couples that will extend the specious common virtue of white supremacy for future generations. Most importantly, this closure effects Griffith's and Dixon's ideological vision by carefully guiding the audience to understand the narrative consequences as an inevitable process of the film's historicism.

In this conclusion—indeed, in the last four reels of the film—Griffith no longer has need of the historicism that set up the argument. Contrary to Wilson's apocryphal claim, the film is not writing history with lightning but reigniting myth with cinematic images of flaming torches. Baudrillard writes: "In the 'real' as in cinema, there was history but there isn't any anymore. Today, the history that is 'given back' to us (precisely because it was taken from us) has not more of a relation to a 'historical real' than neofiguration in painting does to the classical figuration of the real."[35] Baudrillard's sense of loss stems from the multiplication of media images of a later era. But in light of Griffith's use of history, Baudrillard's embrace of an earlier time, when, he suggests, history was available in film without ulterior rhetorical motives, looks more like a false nostalgia. *The Birth of a Nation* gives us a reason to question whether the "real" was ever present in cinematic representations of history.

Coda: Beyond Griffith's Racial Epic

We often hear the recurrent refrain that, although the United States still has a long way to go, the nation has made great progress in remediating the racism that is central to the narrative of *The Birth of a Nation*. This is not to say that history is no longer wrought to serve rhetorical purposes, cinematically or otherwise. Director Alan Parker faced criticism for his portrayal of white FBI officers as the heroes of Freedom Summer in *Mississippi Burning* (1988). That a film whose narrative was decidedly critical of racist backlash against the civil rights movement should get an important part of its story wrong suggests the difficulty of treating history cinematically. *Glory* (dir. Edward Zwick, 1989) was also questioned for granting the central point of view to Robert Gould Shaw (Matthew Broderick), the white officer in command of the Massachusetts Fifty-Fourth Regiment rather than to the black soldiers whose experience might have been the center of the narrative. Even *Argo* (dir. Ben Affleck, 2012), a historical film lacking conventional racial dynamics, has been criticized for several misrepresentations, especially minimizing the role of the Canadian embassy staff in the escape of the American hostages from Iran in 1980. On the positive side, Ava DuVernay's *Selma* (2014) has been praised for avoiding hagiography of Martin Luther King Jr. and presenting a more evenhanded account of the political challenges of the landmark Selma-to-Montgomery voting rights march of 1965.

More recently, Nate Parker's *The Birth of a Nation* (2016), a Sundance Vanguard Award winner, has garnered much critical praise for its account of the Nat Turner Rebellion. Parker's film is historical both in its depiction of the 1831 slave revolt and historic in its potential to disrupt the Hollywood pattern of minimizing black-centric films. Indeed, Parker expressed his hope that the many distribution offers that his film attracted and the record-breaking deal that he accepted may strike a blow against white supremacy in the film industry.

Yet, as if Styron's 1967 Pulitzer Prize–winning novel, *The Confessions of Nat Turner*, had not sparked enough controversy, Parker's film has become embroiled in, if not eclipsed by, a troubling episode from the filmmaker's past. Although Parker was acquitted of sexual assault charges as a Penn State student in 1999, it has since come to light that the accuser later committed suicide. As a result, press conferences for the film's release veered away from questions about the film and its historical content to interrogate Parker's role in the campus event years earlier, the charges, the trial, and the subsequent death of his accuser. The scandal strikes a dark note that ironically resonates with Parker's decision to adopt—in fact, to reinscribe—the title of the most notorious film about race. But rather than challenging the racism of the earlier film, Parker's film has been overshadowed by the publicity of his past, showing that the effects of Griffith's historicism have rippled out to affect the present. What has remained obscured in the media glare is how the personal history of a contemporary black filmmaker has been reframed in the very terms that Griffith exploited: race, sex, and suicide. Although it would be far-fetched to imagine that the coincidence of factors in Griffith's film and the media concern about Parker's past was ideological payback, as Griffith's retribution for Parker's attempt to project a historical counternarrative repurposing the 1915 title, the unfolding treatment of Parker's film indicates that, at the very least, the ideological vestiges of the first *The Birth of a Nation* are difficult to shake. The United States may have achieved a degree of racial progress, but the residue of a 1915 "picturisation of history" lingers.

LAWRENCE HOWE is Professor of English and Film Studies at Roosevelt University. He is author of *Mark Twain and the Novel: The Double-Cross of Authority*, and editor with James Caron and Ben Click of *Refocusing Chaplin: A Screen Icon through Critical Lenses*.

Notes

1. Quoted in Robert Lang, "*The Birth of a Nation*: History, Ideology, Narrative Form," in *The Birth of a Nation, D. W. Griffith, Director*, ed. Robert Lang (New Brunswick, NJ: Rutgers University Press, 1994), 3.

2. See Hayden White, "The Burden of History," in *Tropics of Discourse: Essays in Cultural Criticism* (Baltimore: Johns Hopkins University Press, 1978), 27–50.

3. Hayden White, "Interpretation in History," in White, *Tropics of Discourse*, 61–62.

4. Robert A. Rosenstone, "History in Images/History in Words: Reflection on the Possibility of Really Putting History onto Film," *American Historical Review* 93 no. 5 (1988): 1176.

5. Alison Landsberg, *Engaging the Past: Mass Culture and the Production of Historical Knowledge* (New York: Columbia University Press, 2015), 29.

6. Ibid., 16.

7. James Snead, *White Screens/Black Images: Hollywood from the Dark Side* (London: Routledge, 1994), 41.

8. M. M. Bakhtin, "Discourse in the Novel," in *The Dialogic Imagination: Four Essays*, ed. Michael Holquist, trans. Caryl Emerson and Michael Holquist (Austin: University of Texas Press, 1983), 267–270.

9. Hayden White, "Historicism, History, and the Imagination," in White, *Tropics of Discourse*, 107.

10. Michael Rogin, *Blackface, White Noise* (Berkeley: University of California Press, 1996), 77.

11. Pierre Sorlin, *The Film in History* (Totowa, NJ: Barnes and Noble, 1980), 20.

12. Miriam Hansen, *Babel and Babylon: Film Spectatorship in the American Silent Film* (Cambridge, MA: Harvard University Press, 1991), 78.

13. Manthia Diawara, "Black Spectatorship: Problems of Identification and Resistance," in *Film Theory and Criticism*, 7th ed., ed. Leo Braudy and Marshall Cohen (New York: Oxford University Press, 2009), 769.

14. Linda Williams, *Playing the Race Card: Melodramas of Black and White from Uncle Tom to O. J. Simpson* (Princeton, NJ: Princeton University Press, 2001), 128.

15. Michael Rogin, "'The Sword Becomes a Flashing Vision': D. W. Griffith's *The Birth of a Nation*," in Lang, The Birth of a Nation, *D. W. Griffith, Director*, 251.

16. Arthur S. Link, *Wilson: The New Freedom* (Princeton, NJ: Princeton University Press, 1956), 253–254.

17. Michael T. Martin and David C. Wall, "The Politics of *Cine-Memory*: Signifying Slavery in the History Film," in *A Companion to the Historical Film*, ed. Robert A. Rosenstone and Constantin Parvulescu (Malden, MA: Wiley-Blackwell, 2016), 448–449.

18. Paul McEwan, *The Birth of a Nation* (London: BFI/Palgrave, 2015), 42.

19. Rogin, *Blackface, White Noise*, 76.

20. Charney, "'Picturizing' History: The Assassination of Lincoln in D. W. Griffith's *The Birth of a Nation*," *South Carolina Review* 22, no. 2 (Spring 1990): 58.

21. Ibid., 62.

22. Ibid., 58.

23. Mark Twain, *Life on the Mississippi* (New York: Oxford University Press, 1996), 454.

24. Arthur Lenning, "Myth and Fact: The Reception of *The Birth of a Nation*, Film History 16, no. 2 (2004): 123.

25. Martha Hodes, *Mourning Lincoln* (New Haven, CT: Yale University Press, 2015), 56.

26. Ibid., 48–49.

27. Snead, *White Screens/Black Images*, 41.

28. Hansen, *Babel and Babylon*, 150.

29. Ibid., 80.

30. Alison Landsberg, *Prosthetic Memory: The Transformation of American Remembrance in the Age of Mass Culture* (New York: Columbia University Press, 2004), 3.

31. Mia Galuppo, "American Airlines Assisted *Sully*, but Won't Show the Movie on Its Planes," *Hollywood Reporter*, September 9, 2016.

32. Thomas Jefferson, *Notes on the State of Virginia*, in *Thomas Jefferson: Writings*, ed. Merrill D. Peterson (New York: Library of America, 1984), 265.

33. D. W. Griffith, *The Man Who Invented Hollywood: The Autobiography of D. W. Griffith*, ed. Thomas Hart (Louisville, KY: Touchstone, 1972), 88–89.

34. Jean Baudrillard, "History: A Retro Scenario," in *Simulacra and Simulations*, trans. Sheila Faria Glaser (Ann Arbor: University of Michigan Press, 1994), 43.

35. Baudrillard, "History: A Retro Scenario," 45.

PART III

CINEMATIC ITERATIONS
IN THE PRESENT

By Adele Stephenson.

8

SOMETHING ELSE BESIDES
A WESTERN

Django Unchained's *Generic Miscegenations*

Paula Massood

Early in Quentin Tarantino's *Django Unchained* (2012), a group of torch-wielding Klansmen surround a wagon with the intention of punishing its owner, Dr. King Schultz, for his earlier "indiscretion" of killing three fugitives to collect the bounty on their heads. As Schultz had indicated in the scene preceding the Klan confrontation, both he and his assistant, Django Freemon, were within their legal rights to take the men "dead or alive" (they chose the former). The problem for the threesome's employer (Big Daddy) and his Klan compatriots is that the pair includes Django, the black man responsible for the deaths of two of the three white fugitives. Earlier in the film, Django had joined forces with Schultz in order to earn enough money to buy his wife's freedom. For Django, an escaped slave, the operation comes with an added appeal: shooting white people. As the Klan's ride suggests, this latter perk is not without its perils, at least if one is a black man in the antebellum South.

The Klan's attack occurs about forty minutes into *Django Unchained* in what is generally identified as the film's "Western" section. However, the violence—both actual, in the killing of the three white men, and implied, in the presence of the Klan—takes place on an extensive cotton plantation in Tennessee, a setting more befitting the film's later "Southern" section.[1] Much of the film's earlier portions resemble a Western film and include many of the markers of the genre: men on horseback, wide-open land-scapes, and frontier justice. The Klan's existence in this early scene never-theless suggests that *Django Unchained* as a whole may be something other, or something more, than a Western. What this something might be, how-ever, has yet to be fully considered. Taking the lead from Tarantino, for example, most critical analysis of the film has focused on its connections to the Western, the spaghetti Western, the African American Western, or Western variations of the blaxploitation film.[2] The film, after all, references Italian spaghetti Westerns from the 1960s, especially Sergio Corbucci's *Django* (1966), which serves as *Django Unchained*'s inspiration. Corbucci's original, featuring Franco Nero (who makes a cameo in Tarantino's film), is a violent variant of the spaghetti Western that focuses on a loner seeking revenge on the man who murdered his wife. Likewise, *Django Unchained* is a hyper- (some would say meta-) violent revenge story, but its location shifts over the course of the narrative from the West to the South, and because of this movement, the film becomes something different.

The film's border crossing thus extends beyond its settings to its generic referents—a fact suggested by Tarantino himself, who referred to *Django Unchained* as not really "a Western proper. It's a southern. I'm playing Western stories in the genre, but with a southern backdrop." For the direc-tor, the film was a "new, virgin-snow kind of genre"[3] that had never been seen before. Tarantino is obviously exaggerating: generic hybridity is not the same as creating a new genre. Moreover, the director did not invent the art of playing with cinematic form. Discussions of the film, however, repeat-edly return to the issue of genre, particularly focusing on the intersections of genre film and the form's ability to accurately depict history. The criti-cal emphasis on history has been less concerned with its Western elements and more focused on the film's slave narrative. Johannes Fehrle suggests, for example, that "many debates about [the film] circle around questions about the adequacy of Tarantino's chosen genre for the representation of slavery."[4] Yarimar Bonilla, likewise, has observed that many have "won-dered" whether certain genres are "inherently inadequate for capturing the experience of enslavement."[5] And Terri Francis argues that, although the film "looks like it could be a historical movie about slavery," such a possi-bility is "undermined" by the text's self-conscious reliance on the Western and the spaghetti Western.[6] While each of these studies offers a compelling analysis of the film, I aim to expand the discussion beyond questions of its generic adequacy to represent slavery in order to examine the ways in which *Django Unchained* draws from a number of classic American story types, including the plantation genre, the melodrama, the action film, and the comedy.[7] The result is a somewhat schizophrenic film that is simultaneously deadly serious and playfully parodic about how it represents racially motivated violence.

Although Tarantino may believe that the Southern, his "virgin" genre, was his brainchild, variations on this cinematic type stretch back to the beginnings of American film in what has been called the "plantation genre." According to Ed Guerrero, the plantation genre refers to films that depict slaves and slavery and make manifest the "cinematic devaluation of African Americans." Guerrero charts three different stages of the genre, starting with *The Birth of Nation* (1915) and ending in the 1970s with "a sharp reversal of perspective . . . in films such as *Mandingo* (1975)," a title that has been linked repeatedly to *Django Unchained*, particularly because of the latter's use of blaxploitation tropes.[8] Even though his consideration of the genre ends with the blaxploitation era, Guerrero argues that "fragments of the [slavery] motif still resonate in sedimented themes, metaphors, and icons in the content of many contemporary films," regardless of whether they are set on plantations.[9] The history of the plantation genre predates *The Birth of a Nation*—the various adaptations of *Uncle Tom's Cabin* provide earlier examples—but there is no doubt that Griffith's film, itself pulling from multiple genres, codified cinematic representations of race in American cinema for decades to come. Part melodrama, part action film, and part "romantic representation of the Old South," the film's images of racial and sexual violence have resonated over time and in a variety of films, including *Django Unchained*.[10] In fact, I believe that *The Birth of a Nation* functions as one of the repressed presences in Tarantino's film.

Returning to the Klan scene from *Django Unchained*, it is difficult not to be reminded of the last third of *The Birth of a Nation*, which infamously features an extended ride of the organization presented in heroic terms through powerful cinematography and editing that links together different spaces and plot points. *Django Unchained* introduces the Klan early in the film through similar devices: The group appears aurally; sounds of galloping horses accompany a black screen before a band of hooded riders becomes visible in the frame. At their appearance, Verdi's *Requiem* swells on the soundtrack, providing a chorus to the visuals of men and beasts in motion. The scene then cuts to a black screen, with the Verdi still audible, before the riders appear again on the crest of a hill in a long shot. As they descend the hill and approach the wagon, the pace of the editing increases and the cinematography shifts from long to medium shots. The overall effect is to present the Klan as an overwhelming and terrifying force in an abbreviated form of, though in a similar manner to, its appearance in *The Birth of a Nation*.

In Griffith's film, the Klan's first appearance occurs approximately 140 minutes into a narrative lasting over three hours and spanning the nation's antebellum, Civil War, and Reconstruction periods. While in nascent form early in the film's Reconstruction section, the Klan springs into action as a response to Flora Cameron's death following her near-rape by Gus, a black ex-Union soldier affiliated with the carpetbaggers who have descended on once-idyllic Piedmont, South Carolina. Eventually the Klan, in a filmic climax lasting almost twenty minutes and cutting across three distinct settings, saves Elsie Stoneman from a forced marriage to the mulatto Silas Lynch, rescues members of the Cameron and Stoneman families from black ex-soldiers bent on revenge for past injustices, and liberates the town from a gang of marauding African Americans.

Much has been written of the technical virtuosity of these scenes, especially the ways in which Griffith utilized editing and shot structure to build suspense, communicate action, and create an overall sensory experience for spectators, transforming them from passive audience members to engaged participants in a kinesthetic event. The film's successful combination of spectacle and melodrama can be linked to the action film—a genre that, in its earliest iterations, "regularly stake[d] out obvious moral oppositions between heroes and villains . . . trade[d] in culturally disreputable but thoroughly popular sensational material, and . . . feature[d] the suspenseful races depicted through parallel editing."[11] *The Birth of a Nation* not only advanced narrative and cinematic form; it also contributed to the transformation of the plantation genre, a story type usually associated with melodrama (again, *Uncle Tom's Cabin*), into an action film. Likewise, *Django Unchained* combines historical fiction, spectacle, and melodrama (particularly in Django's quest to be reunited with his wife, Hildi) in what is as much an action film as it is a plantation film or a Western. Could it be, then, that its generic similarities with *The Birth of a Nation* create certain expectations for its treatment of slavery?

In an interview with Henry Louis Gates Jr., Tarantino does not dispute the scholar's claim that he "deconstructed *The Birth of a Nation*" in *Django Unchained*, yet neither does he identify any direct references to Griffith's

Figure 8.1. Still from the Klan ride. *Screen capture by author.*

film. In fact, Tarantino argues that the Klan is not even the "Klan yet" in the film (he calls them "Regulators").[12] It is difficult, however, not to see the film's treatment of the hooded mob and its racially motivated violent acts without being reminded of the group's actions in *The Birth of a Nation*, and a comparison of the Klan's ride in each of the films supports such an analysis. In *Django Unchained*, for example, the Klan's ride occurs at night. The riders first appear on a hilltop, before approaching and encircling Schultz's wagon, which is positioned below them at the bottom of the hill. The group appears in a long shot, as an illuminated line of moving bodies positioned in the top third of the frame. The sky behind them is black, and the landscape is likewise shadowed, thus focusing spectators' eyes on the illuminated men and beasts positioned near the top of the frame. As they ride over the crest of the hill, they move to the left, yet the proportions of the shot privilege the right side of the frame (fig. 8.1).

The composition of the shot in Tarantino's film closely matches that of a similar shot from Griffith's film as the Klan members are gathering before their ride. In *The Birth of a Nation*, as in *Django Unchained*, the band of riders appears in a long shot in the upper third of the frame, the image taken from a low angle. The riders are backlit as they move over the crest of a hill that is itself shadowed in black. The sky, at least in most prints, appears to have been tinted red (and thus is brighter than the dark figures on the hill), adding to the excitement and foreboding of the scene by having the riders stand out against both the background and the foreground. The riders move to the right, and the proportions of the shot favor the right side of the frame. Even with almost a century's technological differences between the films—including color stock, sound, and digital editing—the two shots share a surprising number of visual tropes: the Klan is presented as a powerful, frightening, and anonymous force that starts out small on-screen and becomes larger over the course of the scene.[13]

Another, less direct example of the connections between the two films can be found in the cinematic presentation of the culmination of the Klan's ride. In *Django Unchained*, once the band moves over the hill, the pace of the editing increases and the composition shifts from long shots of the multiple riders to medium shots of individuals. The Verdi accompaniment continues through this section of the scene, which lasts five minutes. The overall effect is to present the riders as a dangerous force as they surround the wagon. At first glance, the scene from *The Birth of a Nation* appears to be dissimilar. The Klan's ride, for example, is much longer in duration, lasting over twenty minutes. It also intercuts different spaces, cutting from exteriors to the interiors of a house in Piedmont and an isolated cabin, locations where marauding black people surround members of the innocent white Stoneman and Cameron families. Yet similarities exist between the two, particularly in the increased pace of the editing and the variations of compositions—from long to medium shots—used during the ride. As in *Django Unchained*, the overall effect of the Klan ride in *The Birth of a Nation* is to present the band of outlaws as an intimidating and invincible force.

Although these similarities are noteworthy in that they suggest that *The Birth of a Nation* was a significant influence on *Django Unchained*, the differences between the scenes are even more telling for what they say about the function of genre in each film. As *The Birth of a Nation* clearly suggests, the Klan's function is to reinsert order into a region torn apart by war and bruised by the indignities of Reconstruction, offering, argues Amy Louise Wood in a slightly different context, "visual authenticity to [white supremacist] rhetoric."[14] Griffith's heroic presentation of the Klan not only provides a satisfying resolution to narrative conflict as each of the film's protagonists is rescued by the riders, but the film also symbolically suggests a reunification of the nation through paternalistic and heteronormative tropes of white masculinity and womanhood. *The Birth of a Nation*'s not-so-repressed sexual obsession was, in Griffith's own words, "to prevent the mixing of white and Negro blood through intermarriage."[15] Moreover, the film's kinetic combination of melodramatic narrative and form made it an entertaining and powerful political tool in the organization's recruitment efforts during the 1920s.

Tarantino's version of the Klan's ride, on the other hand, appears early in *Django Unchained*, and the group's narrative function is less clearly delineated than it is in Griffith's film. Once the riders surround the wagon, the scene cuts to a discussion between Big Daddy, the plantation owner and employer of the dead fugitives, and members of the gathered mob. After the rapid editing of the earlier action shots, this sequence is cut in a classic shot-reverse-shot pattern, the switch in pace both within and across shots suggesting a change in tone even before the dialogue begins. Big Daddy initiates his speech by warning the riders to avoid shooting either Schultz or Django. Such a fate, according to the plantation owner, is too good for the pair. Instead, he has other plans for the men: "We're gonna whup that nigger lover to death. And I'm going to personally strip and clip that gaboon myself." Unlike the previous shots of the Klan's ride, where the group's menace is suggested through visuals and sound, this moment directly references the organization's history of terrorist acts—including flogging, mutilation, and lynching—against African Americans and their supporters. Schultz, already marked as an outsider by virtue of his clothing and his accent, is considered to be a traitor to his race, an irony given his German nationality. And Django is guilty of two even more outrageous crimes: acting like a free man rather than a slave and killing two white men. At this point in the narrative, the Klan's words align well with the group's impressive introduction to the scene.

Big Daddy's plan to lynch the partners also connects *Django Unchained* to the Western and the plantation genres (the latter of which, as mentioned, has one of its canonical models in *The Birth of a Nation*), both of which have historical links to representations of mob violence. According to Wood, for example, cinematic scenes of lynching can be traced back to the earliest American films, starting with the Edison Company's *Lynching Scene* from 1895. During this early period, lynching contents tended to fall into one of two geographical categories: those set on the Western frontier or those set in the South and featuring "southern-style vigilantism."[16] As Wood argues, early Western films were less racially marked than their Southern counterparts, and films like *Cowboy Justice*, an early Western from 1903, tended to project "images of mobs punishing crime and establishing moral justice with speed and precision, providing a thrill for audiences fearing crime in modern life and frustrated by the slow wheels of judicial bureaucracy."[17] Victims were often murderers or horse thieves, and their punishments were frequently wrought in territories with little legal representation.

Whereas this strain of vigilante justice runs throughout the early Western, later films in the genre began to present lynching as a sign of the frontier's lawlessness and lack of civility. Such violent behavior becomes a problem to be eradicated, and this is most often accomplished with the help of a lone hero who rides into town and aids in restoring order (in lieu of an effective sheriff or marshal).[18] In the Western's moral universe, therefore, lynching becomes an avoidable wrong that needs to be made right, especially when it is not specifically connected to race discourses (as it was in southern films). One of the earliest versions of this sort of frontier justice, for example, appeared in Owen Wister's 1902 *The Virginian*, a novel that tells the story of a man who reluctantly takes part in the lynching of a cattle thief (one of his friends), an act that haunts him through the remainder of the story. The novel was adapted for the screen multiple times, including two silent versions (dir. Cecile B. DeMille, 1914, and dir. Tom Forman, 1923), two sound versions (dir. Victor Fleming, 1929, and dir. William A. Wellman, 1946), a made-for-television version (dir. Bill Pullman, 2000), and a long-running television series that aired on NBC for nine years (1962–1971). Likewise, *The Ox-Bow Incident* (dir. William A. Wellman, 1943) tells the story of two drifters who help a posse identify a group of cattle rustlers who are accused of murdering a local rancher. Once the outlaws are located, they are lynched by the posse.[19] Only after the men are murdered does the posse learn that they killed the wrong people. In these examples, lynching is a response to a clearly defined criminal act: cattle rustling and murder. Even so, it is not without its problems, as the protagonists involved in the violence are roundly haunted by their actions. Although the remorse felt by the Western hero conforms to the character traits of the genre, it also suggests that the Western had rapidly altered its outright endorsement of lynching.

In the plantation genre, on the other hand, lynching plays a different and far more symbolic role in the narrative, lending "visual authenticity to pro-lynching narratives and political rhetoric which typically characterized

Figure 8.2. Gus surrounded by the Klan. *Screen capture by author.*

the African American victims of lynching as drunken, unmanageable, and depraved, and white mobs as a united front of honorable, solid citizens."[20] In *The Birth of a Nation*, for example, Gus's mutilation and murder is one of the Klan's first actions, which aids the group's transformation from a disparate mob of unhappy former Confederates to an organized force intent on protecting Southern property (here in the form of white womanhood). Until its kidnapping and murder of Gus, the organization is seen only through symbolic objects: the robes and hoods sewn and secreted away by the Cameron women. In the film's initial version, Gus's lynching was shown in full, but as a result of protests and threats of censorship, the film's more explicit footage was cut.[21] Instead, we see Gus first hiding from the mob and eventually being found and dragged away by Klan members (fig. 8.2). When audiences last see Gus alive, he appears in a medium shot with hooded Klan members surrounding him on three sides and more on horseback in the background. It is clear from Gus's frightened facial expressions (and the red tinting of most prints) that he knows his fate. Later in the narrative, Gus reappears when his dead body is deposited on the steps of the

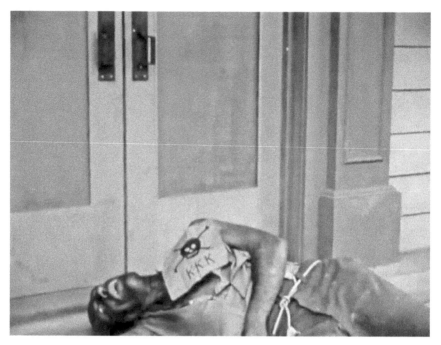

Figure 8.3. Gus's lifeless body. *Screen capture by author.*

Stoneman's house. In this shot, his body appears in a medium close-up, lying prone with eyes and mouth open. Attached to his body is a sheet of paper bearing the image of a skull and crossbones, and a "KKK" inscription (fig. 8.3). Despite the fact that Gus's death occurs offscreen, this portion of *The Birth of a Nation* clearly links racial violence to the maintenance of borders, most immediately as they pertain to sex and the threat of miscegenation and more symbolically as they apply to African Americans knowing their social, political, and economic place in American society. In Griffith's version of the plantation genre, therefore, lynching is presented as the right and righteous response to uncivilized behavior, one that restores "social and moral order."[22]

From *The Birth of a Nation* onward, explicit footage of lynching was, if not banned outright, then off-limits in American film. This situation did not change until the late 1960s, when the Motion Picture Production Code was replaced with the Motion Picture Association of America film rating system, thus enabling US films to include previously prohibited content.[23] One of the first post-Code examples of lynching in the plantation genre appeared in *Mandingo* (dir. Richard Fleischer, 1975), a film that, like *Django*

Unchained, borrows from and revises a number of genres, including the action film and the plantation genre. As Guerrero suggests, by the 1970s, Hollywood's "plantation myth" began to "collapse and reverse its ideological direction." *Mandingo* contains several "ideological reversals" in, for example, the presentation of relationships between the master and slave, themes of miscegenation, and the representation of racial violence, particularly lynching. These reversals, according to Guerrero, "echo with other insurgent voices and influences [and] mediate the militant thinking, language, and aspirations of the Black Power movement of the time."[24] In one scene of the film, for example, a runaway slave is lynched, but not before he makes a speech indicting those in the mob (black and white) for their involvement in chattel slavery:

CICERO, TO THE SLAVE WHO HELPED CATCH HIM: "You killed me.... Niggas like you just prove what the peckerwoods say. We're just beasts. Willing to do anything. Kill each other. No mind. No feeling.... Leastwise I ain't gonna die like you gonna die. Like a slave!"

CICERO, TO THE ASSEMBLED CROWD: "You peckerwoods was oppressed in your own land. We was free! And you brought us here. In chains. But now we here. And you just better know this is just as much our land as it is your'n. And, after you hang me, kiss my ass."

Such content not only revises *The Birth of a Nation*'s and other films' representations of lynching by providing its victim with a voice but also asks audience members to consider slavery's myriad mental and physical crimes. In *Mandingo*'s rendering of Cicero's end, lynching is just one act in a long chain of racially motivated violence.

Django Unchained also reinterprets the social and cinematic history of racial violence, but its tone differs from both *The Birth of a Nation* and *Mandingo*.[25] As mentioned, the Klan raid suggests the film's first threat of lynching and castration. Once Big Daddy addresses the mob about his intentions to "strip and clip" Django, the group dons their hoods and prepares to attack the pair. Before they can begin, however, Big Daddy mutters, referring to his hood, "I can't see fucking shit out of this thing." His words begin an extended discussion among the riders about the impracticality of the Klan's hoods for successfully accomplishing their goals. After a period of humorous complaining and finger-pointing, which ends with one member angrily riding off because of insults directed toward his wife, the group decides to continue with the raid while wearing the hoods. As they surround the wagon, believing that their victims are inside, Schultz (who has been hiding in the hills with Django) sets off explosives, killing and maiming most of the riders. Afterward, Django shoots Big Daddy as the plantation owner tries to escape, adding another white man to his roster of victims. With this obstacle eliminated, the pair continue on their journey. As mentioned, the Klan scene occurs early in the film, and its purpose is to establish the character traits of each protagonist: Schultz is cunning and experienced with explosives, and Django is a skilled and patient marksman. The specter of lynching is raised—and in this way Tarantino relies on spectators' familiarity with this aspect of American history—but it remains a threat that isn't acted on at this point in the narrative. Still, the Klan's presence suggests the ways in which Django's audacity in killing white men must be met by humiliation and mutilation, just like Gus's desire for Flora was met with castration and death in *The Birth of a Nation* and Cicero's desire for freedom was met with a noose in *Mandingo*. The difference is that Django survives—a fact I will return to momentarily.

Another example of the *Django Unchained*'s lynching discourse occurs near the conclusion, after Django surrenders during a gun battle at the Candie Land plantation, where he and Schultz have gone to rescue Django's wife, Hildi. Once Django is captured, he again faces the threat of lynching and castration as punishment for killing more white men (and for not knowing his place in Southern society). The scene opens with an overhead medium shot of Django's nude body, with his legs and genitals exposed. He has been strung up with a rope and is hanging by his ankles from the rafters of a horse barn. The only sound accompanying the image is the creaking of the ropes holding his hanging body as it sways back and forth.[26] The film cuts to a medium close-up, and the camera tilts downward and tracks around Django's head, in the process revealing his scarred back and manacled face, his body acting as a palimpsest for the experiences of the enslaved.[27] One of the plantation's overseers then enters the room and prepares to castrate Django with a red-hot knife, thus fulfilling Big Daddy's desire to "strip and clip [the] gaboon." Django's crime, according to his torturer, is being a "black man paid to kill white men." The scene lasts a mere two minutes, but during that time, Django's defenseless body is humiliated, threatened, and tortured. Here, like the earlier moments with the Klan, the danger of lynching and castration remains nothing more than a threat: at the last moment, Django's life is spared so that he can be sold to a mining company, yet the camera lingers over Django's nude body, hanging helpless in the barn.

To understand the effect of this moment, it seems important to return to the film's handling of the earlier scene with the Klan. While the riders' demise may provide a satisfying resolution to a plot point, the scene, like the later near-castration scene, troubles the parameters of the plantation genre, but not in the ways that Tarantino may have intended. The director's films have often presented people in positions of power alternately as threats or fools, and this strategy has often contributed a political, if not necessarily satirical, component to a film's humor, whether concerning Nazis in *Inglourious Basterds* (2009) or drug dealers in *Pulp Fiction* (1994). There's no doubt that this was the intention with the Klan ride in *Django Unchained*, which was shot and structured to present the mob as a formidable and frightening force, only to reveal that it consists of clueless nincompoops lacking any real plan. Such a strategy can deflate the group's importance by offering, in Gates's words, "an opposite extreme of *The Birth of a Nation*."[28] Tarantino's mob is not only ineffectual at restoring order but also suffers the consequences (violence and death) of its members' shortcomings, whereas Griffith's riders are the narrative's heroes. But generic volte-faces and cinematic self-referentiality do not necessarily equate with political critique or cohesive filmmaking, and in the same interview with Gates, Tarantino stresses the film's adherence to the conventions of the spaghetti Western, the Western, and the comedy—the latter of which functions, according to the director, "to bring [audiences] back from the horrific."[29] It comes as no surprise, therefore, that the Klansmen are the victims of Schultz's ruse; the once threatening mob is reduced to Wile E. Coyote-like victims of their own stupidity. Once a threat, the Klan and its racist intentions are left behind in the narrative.

Django Unchained's humorous treatment of the Klan may offer some release in a film overflowing with racial violence (or its potential), but it sits uncomfortably next to quotations from Griffith's film and the plantation genre (and the related lynching film) as a whole. It also sits uncomfortably near other scenes, including Django's near-castration. The later scene of Django's humiliation is not played for comedy, despite the fact that it occurs after a hyperviolent shoot-out that takes on laughably comic proportions: blood spatters, bodies fly through the air, and walls are riddled with hundreds of bullet holes. Once Django is captured, the self-consciously comic tone shifts, and spectators are asked to participate in the graphic spectacle of his mental and physical violation—hung and tied by his feet, he is defenseless against a man kicking him in the face and grabbing his testicles.

The imagery used in the scene—particularly near its conclusion, when we see Django hanging in profile in a medium long shot—visually references more than a century of lynching photographs and lynching films. In this moment, *Django Unchained* steps away from its hyperreferential generic play to acknowledge a national legacy of racism and violence that continues in the present in ongoing acts of police brutality and the rise of white nationalist groups.[30] But, as with the earlier Klan scene, which starts as an analysis of the history it conjures, this moment raises the topic only to push it aside with a happy ending that sees Django and Hildi ride off into the distance.

While *Django Unchained*'s unbridled borrowings from a wide swath of genres—the Western, the African American Western, blaxploitation, the southern, the plantation film, the action film, and even the comedy—provide a rich and appealing mix of references for the director's fans, it has led to confusion regarding its narrative treatment and visual rendering of slavery. In my opinion, it is a mistaken, and losing, enterprise to question whether the film's genre adequately captures the historical realities of slavery, especially when such subject matter has its roots firmly entrenched in melodrama. Tarantino's film may be melodramatic at times, but it draws from multiple genres, resulting in shifting tones over the course of the narrative. In the end, *Django Unchained*'s generic polyphony provides little guidance for spectators reading the text's various references, and it points to the implications of a mere surface retelling of the nation's and film's racial past. It is not so much a "new, virgin-snow kind of genre," as suggested by its creator, as it is a generic mash up that lacks a cohesive identity or message. So, to assume that it will adequately represent slavery, or the Western, or any other genre, is ultimately an incorrect approach to a film that offers a little of everything, at least on its surface.

PAULA MASSOOD is Professor of Film Studies at Brooklyn College, City University of New York. She is author of *Black City Cinema: African American Urban Experiences in Film* and *Making a Promised Land: Harlem in Twentieth-Century Photography and Film.*

Notes

1. Tennessee became a state in 1796 and adopted the slave code from North Carolina, which had previously administered the region. The state formalized its own slave laws in 1857, the year before *Django Unchained* is set. (And the film not-so-subtly stresses the links

between racial violence and the plantation economy through its inclusion of shots of blood-spattered cotton plants following the death of the third fugitive.)

2. A brief sampling of discussions of genre and the film include Johannes Fehrle, "'And I Would Call It A Southern': Renewing/Obscuring the Blaxploitation Western," *Safundi: The Journal of South African and American Studies* 16, no. 3 (2015): 291–306; Michael K. Johnson, "The D Is Silent: *Django Unchained* and the African American West," *Safundi: The Journal of South African and American Studies* 16 no. 3 (2015): 256–266; and Terri Francis, "Looking Sharp: Performance, Genres and Questioning History in *Django Unchained*," *Transition* 112 (2013): 32–45.

3. Charles McGrath, "Quentin's World." Interview with Quentin Tarantino. *New York Times*, December 19, 2012, http://www.nytimes.com/2012/12/23/movies/how -quentin-tarantino-concocted-a-genre-of-his-own.html.

4. Fehrle, "'And I Would Call It A Southern,'" 291.

5. Yarimar Bonilla, "History Unchained," *Transition* 112 (2013): 69.

6. Francis, "Looking Sharp," 44.

7. The film also pulls from the buddy film and the road film, but these genres have a less influential presence in the narrative.

8. Ed Guerrero, *Framing Blackness: The African American Image in Film* (Philadelphia: Temple University Press, 1992), 10.

9. Ibid., 40.

10. Daniel Bernardi, "Integrating Race into the Narrator System," in *Film Analysis: A Norton Reader*, ed. Jeffrey Geiger and R. L. Rutskyu (New York: W. W. Norton, 2013), 84. A recent example of *The Birth of a Nation*'s ongoing influence can be found in Nate Parker's *The Birth of a Nation* (2016), a film based on the biography of Nate Turner. Here Parker makes ironic reference to Griffith's film by reinterpreting the earlier film's fear of African American violence.

11. Scott Higgins, "Suspenseful Situations: Melodramatic Narrative and the Contemporary Action Film," *Cinema Journal* 47, no. 2 (Winter 2008): 78.

12. Henry Louis Gates Jr., "An Unfathomable Place: An Interview with Quentin Tarantino," *Transition* 112 (2013): 52. The term *regulators* refers to different sorts of pre-Klan police groups. According to Daniel R. Weinfeld, regulators refer to different groups that used a "variety of names." "The goal of all these groups," argues Weinfeld, "was to re-impose the dominance of white southerners in states where blacks, beginning to assert their civil rights had voted Republican administrations into power." Weinfeld, *The Jackson County War: Reconstruction and Resistance in Post–Civil War Florida* (Tuscaloosa: University of Alabama Press, 2012), 65. Groups of regulators existed before the Klan, which was not fully established until 1866, but they were similar in terms of intent and tactics.

13. Spike Lee has also wrestled with the cinematic and political resonances of *The Birth of a Nation*, particularly its depiction of the Ku Klux Klan. *Malcolm X* (1992), for example, includes a moment from Malcolm's childhood when his family's Michigan house was surrounded by torch-wielding and hooded white supremacists (made to look like Klan members) unhappy with his father's outspoken political beliefs. Although it only loosely echoes Griffith's film in style (it is a very short scene, and the participants are not on horseback), it's thematically connected to the earlier film. Moreover, it suggests that organized racial violence was not confined to the South or the West.

14. Amy Louise Wood, "The 'Vicarious Play' of Lynching Melodramas: Cinema and Mob Violence in the United States, 1895–1905," in *Violence and Visibility in Modern History*, ed. Jürgen Martschukat and Silvan Niedermeier (New York: Palgrave Macmillan, 2013), 120.

15. Robert Lang, The Birth of a Nation: *D. W. Griffith, Director* (New Brunswick, NJ: Rutgers University Press, 1994), 17.

16. Wood, "The 'Vicarious Play,'" 118.

17. Ibid., 125.

18. For more on lynching in the American West, see Michael J. Pfeifer, ed., *Lynching beyond Dixie: American Mob Violence outside the South* (Urbana: University of Illinois Press, 2014); Michael J. Pfeifer, *The Roots of Rough Justice: Origins of American Lynching* (Urbana: University of Illinois Press, 2013); and Ken Gonzales-Day, *Lynching in the West: 1850–1935* (Durham, NC: Duke University Press, 2006).

19. The film is an adaptation of Walter Van Tilburg Clark's 1940 novel of the same name. The film adaptation was a Western with noir-like elements (particularly in its damning resolution).

20. Wood, "The 'Vicarious Play,'" 120–121.

21. Bernardi, "Integrating Race into the Narrator System," 91.

22. Wood, "The 'Vicarious Play,'" 122.

23. Compare *The Birth of a Nation*, for example, with *Gone with the Wind* (1939), a post-Code plantation film. With the latter, Producer David O. Selznick made sure to cut from the screenplay scenes justifying the Klan and lynching, both of which appeared in Margaret Mitchell's original novel.

24. Guerrero, *Framing Blackness*, 33.

25. In many ways, *Django Unchained* references the blaxploitation film, one of the recurring generic references in Tarantino's oeuvre. In many of his films, such as *Jackie Brown* (1997), the director calls on blaxploitation as an homage to 1970s popular culture more generally. In *Django Unchained*, Tarantino utilizes blaxploitation's powerful black male heroes and action sequences, but the political emphasis of the earlier films is diluted by multiple generic references. Is Django modeled after a blaxploitation hero? A Western hero? A spaghetti Western hero? A slave hero?

26. A similar audio/visual combination appears in Steve McQueen's *12 Years a Slave* (2013), in which Solomon Northup is hung by his neck and left hanging in the yard as a warning to other slaves. While the camera swings around his body in a medium long shot, the sound track consists mostly of the sounds of the rope and Northup's toes scratching against the ground in an attempt to ease the tension in the rope.

27. Terri Francis makes a compelling case for the connections between Django's scar and the scars on Gordon, an escaped slave and Union soldier whose photograph was used to support abolitionist causes. Francis, "Looking Sharp," 34.

28. Gates, "An Unfathomable Place," 51.

29. Ibid., 58.

30. In my opinion, the film is most successful at communicating the horrors of slavery in a scene in which Schultz and Django first approach Candie Land Plantation. They encounter a group of overseers and an escaped slave (one of the "Mandingos" forced to fight for the plantation owner). The slave's punishment for fleeing is to be ripped to shreds by the slave hunters' dogs. Although audiences see little of the violence, enough is shown—in combination with the sound of the man's agonized screams on the sound track—to communicate the man's gruesome fate. The scene is played for what it is: a rendering of the inhumane results of the plantation economy.

9

12 YEARS A SLAVE AND
THE BIRTH OF A NATION

Two Moments in Representing Race

Julia Lesage

IN CONSIDERING THE FILMMAKERS' POLITICAL INTENTION, I HAVE no evidence that *12 Years a Slave*'s director, Steve McQueen, or screenwriter, John Ridley, thought of *The Birth of a Nation* when developing their film. McQueen did say that he wanted his protagonist to be a freeman who was kidnapped and sold into bondage; as an "outsider," that man would learn the rules of survival along with the viewers. McQueen and Ridley read about US slavery but did not settle on a specific approach until the director's wife, Bianca Stigter, showed them Northup's 1863 autobiography, *12 Years a Slave*, filled with many concrete details about slave labor and daily life.[1]

Griffith had based *The Birth of a Nation* on a sentimental novel, *The Clansman*, by Thomas Dixon. The novel posits whites and blacks as two unequal species and is highly melodramatic, a kind of anti–*Uncle Tom's Cabin*.[2] To a certain degree, the two films' contrasting literary origins suggest the appropriateness of a very different visual style for each. That is, *12 Years a Slave* uses a realist narrative script and visual style, presenting many details of slave life. In contrast, *The Birth of a Nation* has a much more melodramatic script and suppresses references to the mores and economy of the antebellum South in favor of developing a new plotline about Southern white women under sexual threat from black men (the Southern "rape complex")[3] and white men regaining public space, all of which is not depicted realistically but metaphorically (as the film's title announces).

Deriving from his left-liberal politics and his greater distance years-wise, McQueen's contemporary film traces the story of what Griffith's conservative film, closer to the slave era, cannot face.

Metonymy and Metaphor

Briefly put, *12 Years a Slave* relies on a rhetoric of metonymy to draw meaning from its fictional world, while *The Birth of a Nation* delineates its fictional world in the service of a raced and gendered national metaphor. That is, *12 Years a Slave* draws on the conventions of "realist" cinematic narrative.[4] In such a narrative, audience expectations about cohesive and "readable" characters and spaces are adhered to. Also, costume, camera work (for example, long shot, close-up, tracking, shot duration, continuity editing, and mise-en-scène) are used in a predictable way to express meaning. In this perspective, realist meaning usually comes from metonymy, a rhetorical device in which the part—in cinema, a small visual detail or a camera move, such as a close-up—can express the meaning of the whole. In fact, it is the way the narrative accumulates density by building on and emphasizing one small embedded detail after another that makes it realistic.[5]

In contrast, and coming at the inception of Hollywood fiction film and shaping it, *The Birth of a Nation* uses a much more overtly melodramatic structure. It pays little attention to the kinds of structures that later realist films might delineate: versions of popular knowledge, especially about science, work processes, or psychological states; the war between the sexes (except for raced rape threat); and the lives of the working class. Rather, it takes for granted what Deborah Barker has described as the Southern rape complex,[6] in which black-on-white rape becomes a metaphor for the defeated South, and indeed this film probably was one of the main vehicles for regenerating that complex over many years. Because the film excises the structures of slavery and the antebellum mind-set of the slaveholding class from its narrative, the film narrative projects onto blacks that class's deepest fears: loss of civic control and white male impotency masked by this new emphasis on sexually aggressive black men. Metaphor works by *not* representing something directly—here, by not developing reference to details of antebellum slave economy and daily life, both for masters and slaves. Rather, the metaphor works by analogy (the rape of the South) and substitution of a comparator of a different order. Furthermore, the rape metaphor not only shaped a film narrative but also became what George Lakoff and Mark Johnson would call a "conceptual metaphor"—a common ideological mind-set that people in a given culture might use to organize their experience. Here the metaphor is about controlling public life and racial purity, including that of white women.[7]

To say that the recent film, like many other theatrical successes, relies on a realism based in metonymy and that the older film relies on a popular melodramatic structure to develop a politically expedient metaphor is not to isolate these aesthetic strategies as unique to either film. *12 Years a Slave* has many melodramatic moments of heightened emotion, and it, too, can be seen as delivering a "message" or metaphor for people; in fact, historical fictions often deliver messages for contemporary times. *The Birth of a Nation*, in turn, was hailed as a milestone of realist historical fiction, especially in its depiction of the Civil War. It uses metonymy to establish what Roland Barthes calls "the reality effect."[8] In practice, theatrical melodrama was long known for taking up current problems and staging them with realistic sets and costumes; the plot structures, however, remained very similar—beleaguered innocents, suffering victims, heroes, villains, and evil versus good.[9]

I turn now to an analysis of selected moments from these two films to describe how they tell their stories, reference history, and address an audience—or potentially have different effects on viewers depending on the viewers' own situations. Because of my background in both production and criticism, I have a particular interest in how cinematic and script tactics influence meaning, and this interest will be reflected in what I see in the films.

12 Years a Slave: Solomon Northup as a Free Man in the North

12 Years a Slave introduces protagonist Solomon Northup as a free black man in 1841 living in Saratoga, New York. Both he and his wife, Anne, work—he as a musician and she as a caterer. Early in the film, in a flashback, we see him walking with his family on a commercial street, tipping his hat and chatting to another black family and then crossing the street, the whole family well dressed and freely enjoying access to urban public space. The family enters Parker's store, where Anne Northup looks for a travel bag. A simply dressed black man enters the store and wonderingly looks around. His unfamiliarity with such a store and its goods seems to mark him as a slave. As the store owner approaches this man to greet him as a potential new customer, the man's master comes in and pardons himself for the intrusion. Solomon looks the master in the eye and responds cordially, "No intrusion," as an equal. The man says, "Good day, sir," deliberately addressing only Parker.

This brief sequence and our earlier view of Solomon's family's large two-story frame house present a somewhat utopian view of what a cook and a fiddler might afford at the time, but in fact it is what film viewers are used to seeing as a protagonist's "home." In this narrative, these domestic fantasies of home preoccupy Solomon after he has been kidnapped by slavers and is about to be shipped South. The film's early visual track—with its costumes and the characters' acts of shopping, walking around the city, taking a carriage, and freely talking with whites—establish as a concrete reality Solomon's way of life, which he will lose.

Following a freeman into slavery means that the narrative will focus on his loss of identity. Thus, these origin flashbacks of home are utopian because they are based on a memory of what Solomon has lost. They set up a contrast between the capitalist North and the agrarian slaveholding South. Students could well trace the film's presentation of salient differences in economy, law, geography, public and private space, gender relations, and personal and social psychology. In terms of the narrative message, the film's script was based on research, but in this historical fiction, such concepts— which the viewer may or may not tease out—are expressed metonymically, through contrastive detail.

Solomon's native concept of self is that of the bourgeois individual as it developed in the industrial North, along with ideas of entrepreneurship and the self-made, self-reliant man.[10] As that ideology is enacted legally in the North, Solomon and Anne can enter into contract labor as free agents, use their money for clothing and a home, have full legal rights over their family, and live in a thriving urban milieu with many stores to shop in and places to visit or work. They have the freedom to move through all public space, including traveling out of state. In particular, Solomon is proud of his craft as a violinist/fiddler, his family and his role as pater familias, his companionate marriage, his house, his family's personal appearance, and his ability to craft for himself and them a good life. Such moral autonomy means that he is free to grow, develop both material and inner resources, act, plan, create values, choose many aspects of his daily routines, and forge short- and long-term goals. To think of oneself as an individual means assuming certain things about time: the reliability of cause and effect and the efficacy of planning forward to one's own advantage. And because this vision of selfhood, a kind of possessive individualism, has become a dominant, if often uncommented on, ideology under capitalism, filmmakers commonly invest a protagonist with such traits.

What is unique about 12 *Years a Slave*, and I will elaborate on this later, is that the way of filming social space says something about the power relations depicted, and thus about gender and race as well as about class. As the film progresses, uncommented-on visual details have much to communicate about how the industrial North and the slave South defined basic values and took for granted different versions of society. In watching the store scene described above, for example, first-time viewers of 12 *Years a Slave* may not attend to the slave owner's facial expression after Solomon addresses him directly, but they cannot miss how that man hustles his slave out of the store. I draw attention to this kind of play between small gestures and emphatic acts, because such an aesthetic strategy delineates social space throughout the film.

Narrative Disjunctures

With a structure similar to a captivity narrative, 12 *Years a Slave*'s storyline has a double reversal: the capture and the rescue.[11] The film also contains two major "punctuation" scenes, each shot as a cinematic tour de force and each summarizing Solomon's experience as a slave at two different plantations—those of Ford and of Epps. Narratively, each succeeding section of the film has a different style and tone:

1. New England, also seen in flashback in section 2.
2. Capture in Washington, DC; boat passage to New Orleans; the slave market.
3. Ford's plantation, establishing the plantation household's mise-en-scène and themes. "The hanged man" scene.
4. Epps's plantation, introducing as major characters slave owner Master Epps and slave Patsey. Long, emotionally charged melodrama. Brutal beating of Patsey as film's climax.
5. Denouement and falling action. Rescue and return home.

The film has a disjunctive narrative structure. Little dramatic tension is carried over from one episode to another. And Solomon's release is not the climax of the film; when it does come, it is a surprise to both him and those around him. Furthermore, when he leaves the Epps plantation, all the characters he has known there drop from the film abruptly. In fact, for an author to treat the theme of the slave experience entails disrupting ordinary narrative causality. Sam Worley, discussing Solomon Northup's autobiography, makes this point: "Any hope of rational narrative form is shattered by his [Solomon's] kidnapping. His descent into slavery brings with it a vision of the world as a place of contingency, illusion, and disorder, neither inherently rational nor irrational."[12]

From the moment he is kidnapped, Solomon and the other slaves cannot predict or make any plans. They can hardly rely on cause and effect. They know the basic rules of the game—obeying orders, speaking little, effacing self—and these sometimes work. The slaves expect punishment for their lapses but also unpredictable beatings at the master's caprice. Solomon learns this hard lesson when he is kidnapped and thrown into captivity.

In Washington, DC, after spending an evening drinking with his new employers, Solomon awakens in a darkened room. With the camera shooting down from the ceiling, he lies as a small white-clothed figure in a black space, a fetus emerging into a new life as a slave. Step by step, elements of Solomon's identity vanish. First, he has lost his freedom to move about; he tests his shackles in anger and disbelief. Then, his legal rights, his bourgeois identity, his freedom. The dungeon's space is nightmarish and abstracted. It teaches one lesson, enforced by beating. A number of such darkened spaces, in which identity is questioned, are presented throughout the film. I consider them liminal spaces, and they are often exquisitely composed, their beauty balancing and giving some distance from the narrated existential anguish of Solomon struggling to maintain a sense of self.

One of the principle aesthetic strategies McQueen employs in *12 Years a Slave* is to use a noticeable, spectacular cinematic move to carry the narrative forward or to draw some social or emotional conclusion. On the one hand, such a visual style is what makes the film an art film—adding dignity to the subject matter and perhaps guaranteeing both the work's longevity and critical success. On the other hand, it allows the director to address himself in different ways to different audiences, especially to black and white viewers. Because he uses images without exposition to carry much of the narrative, viewers will fill in much of the story with what they already know about slavery, what they assume about people and social life.[13] Many critics have commented on how the film's cinematography characteristically sets up tableaux, similar to painting. As a director, McQueen also has a reputation for incorporating nudity and images of privation and brutality in a way that might make the audience uncomfortable.[14] But the beauty of the visuals—strikingly composed wide shots, long takes that seem to take extra time, close-ups that convey many emotions all at once, and thoughtful ways of placing the characters in social space—is not only metonymically appropriate but also gives the viewer a sense of control over, a moment for reflecting on, the terrifying historical moment and personal situations that the narrative represents.

The Hanged Man

A central sequence in the film has almost no dialogue except for its beginning and end, but it says much about the structures determining plantation life. Visually, the sequence traces the plantation household and the power relations within and outside it. The scene begins as Solomon is working as a carpenter building a small structure and his white slaver boss tells him repeatedly his work needs to be redone. As the slaver reaches for his whip to strike, Solomon beats him to the ground, and then whips the white man with the coiled whip until he is exhausted. The overseer of the plantation rides up, sends the slave boss off, and tells Solomon, "Do not leave the plantation or I cannot protect you. Stay here." As Solomon sits on the unfinished building, shadows lengthen and time passes until late afternoon. Three men, including the slave boss, ride up and bind Solomon, dragging him close to the big house and hanging him on a tree. The plantation overseer, pistols drawn, chases the three men off. Solomon remains hanged but has been lowered enough so that his toes now reach the mud below him. Close-ups of his feet show him struggling to gain purchase so as to be able to breathe. As time passes, the overseer paces the veranda of the big house, and a bit later Mrs. Ford comes out briefly to look. Solomon stays hanged in this position for a long time. Finally, Master Ford gallops up on horseback and with a machete cuts Solomon down. Next, in the interior of the big house, Solomon lies on the foyer floor with his head on a fancy white pillow. Solomon tells Ford who he really is, and Ford replies, "I cannot hear that." He explains that he has sold Solomon to a hard master, Epps, since no other slave owner would take this rebellious slave and that Solomon's life was in danger at Ford's. In addition, he has a debt for which Solomon is collateral. The slave lies half dead on the big house floor.

This section of the film is temporally prolonged, and for the most part it has only ambient sound. Sometimes the hanged Solomon is seen with the slave cabins in the background, other times with the big house behind his head. Shadows lengthen between shots. The camera holds on him in a long shot, his toes struggling to gain purchase to let him stand. In the background, slaves come out of their cabins to go about their work. Some look at him, others do not. Children play on the grass behind him. A close-up

Figure 9.1. Delineating the plantation household, the panoramic shot shows Solomon as the hanged man with the slave cabins in the background and the slaves going about their daily routines. *Screen capture by author.*

of Solomon's muddied face shows his extreme condition. Finally, at dusk, a long shot shows the hanged man tiny in the background (fig. 9.1). Then there is a return to the narrative action as Ford enters on horseback and cuts Solomon down.

McQueen says he wanted this scene to echo many other historical lynchings, but it does much more than that. Metonymically it lays out the structures and daily routines of the Southern plantation household, which, unlike a home in the North, was a unit of relatively self-sufficient production in which slaves did both field and domestic labor. Because slaves and masters lived in close proximity, labor relations often meshed with personal ones. As we see the layout of both the Ford and Epps plantations, there is a big house with a veranda around it and various buildings nearby: the slave cabins, a new building under construction, a kitchen garden, a cotton shed, other farm structures, a pigpen (Epps)—all just paces away from one another (fig. 9.2).

Within this space, the male plantation owner, represented by his overseer, had full legal rights over the household. And the slave system needed regular enactments of violence to manage its coerced labor force. Slaves expected random whippings. In addition, there were certain rhythms to slave life, which we see in the hanging scene—the slaves performed a double day's work, doing the plantation's maintenance chores and cooking for themselves after a day working under overseers and drivers. Also, as depicted in this sequence, slaves always had to demonstrate that they "knew their place." Avoiding violence meant reticence, keeping emotion

Figure 9.2. A quarter turn away reveals the master's house in close proximity to the slave cabins.

off one's face, sticking to the narrow paths and actions allotted to them. Finally, it was not proper for Solomon to declare his identity to Ford, nor later to reveal he knew how to read and write. He was chattel, an expensive commodity ready for trade (he originally cost Ford $1,200). Portraying a socially dehumanized protagonist, throughout most of *12 Years a Slave*, Chiwetel Ejiofor faced the difficult task of creating a character who must suppress both emotion and knowledge from his public face.

The Epps Plantation: Act Three

Solomon's time under Master Epps constitutes a long sixty-minute section of the film, ending in the climax of Epps (and Solomon) cruelly beating a female slave, Patsey, who suffers under Epps's rapine lust. This section of the film is more melodramatic than the rest of the film and contains more close-ups conveying heightened emotions. The melodrama also gains its force from its actors' star performances (Michael Fassbender as plantation owner Epps and Lupita Nyong'o as Patsey).[15] Socially, the section depicts the power of the plantation owner. The melodrama traces the relation between this man's absolute power and his personality and capriciousness. Interestingly as a matter of narrative choice, McQueen does not develop in the plot much about the slave community, life in the cabins, slave rebellion, or individual escape. Instead, this section of the film builds audience involvement in more traditional ways, eliciting identification with the beautiful victimized woman and her suffering the obsessive attention of the villainous but arrestingly portrayed Epps. In addition, in Solomon's interactions

Figure 9.3. In the weighing shed, Epps's lust for Patsey is public, not private, and affects everyone in the plantation household. *Screen capture by author.*

with Epps, the actors' bodies indicate the two men's degrees of power very finely, especially the master's flamboyant exercise of his least whim and his large gestures alongside the slave's reticence and compacted bodily stance. At other moments, Solomon's story advances as we witness his frustrated attempts to communicate back home. This part of the film juggles two temporal registers: the familiar cinematic build toward a climax and the narration of slave time—the felt experience of having no control over the flow of one's life.

Michael Fassbender has worked a long time with director McQueen. In this film, Fassbender vigorously plays the plantation owner Epps with a focus on that man's absolute power—how it shapes him and how it affects the whole household. In the slave South, the master's law was personal, not impersonal nor adjudicated, as in the North. Ideologically, slave culture assumed a natural hierarchy and order within the household, with slaves legally chattel. In practice, since slaves were expensive and tied up so much of a master's capital, the slave owner and his wife had to learn to manage rather than just use force on slaves; and this entailed their knowing the slaves as people to a certain degree. Furthermore, a slave owner's exercise of power within the household could easily lead to and be governed by personal sadism since his potential brutality, racism, and sexual use of slave women were taken for granted as part of normal masculinity within his class (fig. 9.3).

Several sequences portraying Epps's and his wife's conflicting relationships with the slave Patsey articulate the particular register of social power enacted intimately within the slave household. For example, one night a drunken Epps comes into the slave quarters holding a lantern. He tells the slaves to come to the big house to dance, and when he stares at Patsey, who seems momentarily lost in the dance, Mrs. Epps sees the lust in her husband's eyes and throws a heavy decanter at Patsey, hitting the slave square in the face. Patsey falls to the floor. Mrs. Epps then demands that her husband sell this slave and threatens to leave, but he dismisses her and says he'll keep Patsey rather than her.

The scene depicts layers of dependency and frayed tempers. The slave owner's wife as mistress of the plantation household had to live in close contact with the women her husband took sexually. In her relations with her household slaves, affection and hostility mingled; for example, she might commonly slap her domestic servants if she considered them lazy, bumbling, or uppity. This scene makes it clear that Mrs. Epps's social power derives from her husband. He rebukes her about her own place in the slave household, and she has to put up with his profligacy and drinking. Her world is very small, and she has a protected place within it, but only to the degree that she respects its hierarchy.

The climax of the film shows Patsey's brutal beating. In an interview with scholar Henry Louis Gates Jr., a consultant on the film, McQueen said that he had to film such a scene in the manner he did to do justice to the subject matter, slavery.[16] The prolonged sequence is choreographed in lengthy tracking shots that move from wide shot to close-up and back, showing both the characters' intense emotions and the relations among them. It ends with gashing skin and spattering blood that are difficult to watch. It then cuts to a scene in a slave cabin, showing Patsey's mangled back, the gathered slave community as mute witnesses, and an emotional exchange of looks between Patsey and Solomon.

It's Sunday, which slaves have off and during which they do chores such as their own laundry. A drunken Epps comes down angrily from the big house searching for Patsey. Patsey explains that she had gone to a neighbor's to get some soap, which Mrs. Epps had denied her, because picking cotton made her "stink so much" it made her gag. As Epps has Patsey tied to a pole for a beating, we hear Mrs. Epps voice commanding, "Do it. Strike the life from her." Epps cannot bring himself to beat Patsey, so he commands Solomon to do it. Then Mrs. Epps says Solomon is "pantomiming" and making a fool of Epps. Epps points a pistol at Solomon threatening to "kill every nigger in my sight" if Solomon does not proceed more vigorously. Solomon whips Patsey fiercely and then can do no more. A furious, cursing Epps takes over and beats Patsey until he is exhausted.

Figure 9.4. As Epps beats Patsey with uncontrolled rage, the image is organized to comment on relative social power. Mrs. Epps, fully lit, is egging him on to kill Patsey; the slaves stand as mute witnesses in the background with their faces shaded. The next scene takes place in the slave quarters, where lighting and framing reveal the slaves' personal and communal response. *Screen capture by author.*

The lengthy tracking shots in this sequence recompose the scene to delineate the different characters, the slaves in the background as witnesses, the big house, the people's faces, and the brutal action. Patsey's naked back is not shown until toward the end. At that point the camera has moved in to show a close-up of Epps's face; then a swish pan to Patsey's back with shreds being torn off at each stroke; then back to Epps swinging now in a circular motion, hitting her on every downstroke, the camera moving in closer and closer to his face (fig. 9.4). In the next location, the slave cabin, the camera also emphasizes interpersonal emotions and social life, slowly tilting up to frame the whole slave community together in the cabin, sad witnesses to this atrocity. Patsey looks up to Solomon and cries; the viewer would remember that she had earlier asked him to drown her to put her out of her misery. In a close-up, we see Solomon's anguish and a tear falling from his eye and down his cheek.[17]

This beating scene is justified by both the plot and the subject matter. It seizes audience attention. It is like a rape scene in that it shows Epps's sadism proceeding from his obsessive lust, but enacting it to the borderline between life and death. It is also a questionable cinematic practice. For a long time, media culture has depicted vulnerable women, naked women, violated women in a way that performs, either subtly or overtly, as a spectacle that reproduces the social enforcement of the gender binary, the subordination of female to male. Discussing the social response to a smutty story in a way that would be applicable to viewing the flaying of Patsey and Patsey's flayed back, Sigmund Freud said that even a disgusted listener would feel shame tinged with repressed excitement. That is the function of smut.[18] This sequence in *12 Years a Slave*, like rape and rape threat sequences, reenacts a common location in representation that is fantasized by both oneself and others.[19] Furthermore, the flaying of the body, or torture scenes more generally, within the context of a realist aesthetic has become part of the iconography of narrative cinema. Audiences have a certain learned behavior with which they view such material, expecting a frisson, knowing the story will then move on.

Even more problematic is tying this frisson to the beating of a black body. Abolitionists used the tactic of showing slavery's bodily toll by having former slaves display their scars, which predictably would both horrify and thrill white viewers. In this vein, Jasmine Nichole Cobb recognizes the achievements of *12 Years a Slave* but has reservations about the film's use of a classical realist style. Constant visual surveillance over their captive workforce was a necessity for slave owners, she points out, but the Reconstruction era extended such a white looking practice to a more general, watchful suspicion of blackness, which now underlies racism in the United States: "Exactness as tethered to the historical record will delimit a comprehensive view of slavery as a system that fixated upon the objectification of blackness. Slavery cultivated the habit of observing blackness, indeed, cultivated whiteness, in part, through the surveillance of blacks. Accuracy as an object in McQueen's *12 Years* demands a willful commitment to the fetishization of black visibility and suffering as essential elements of transatlantic slavery. Demanding that viewers witness slavery's sadistic theatrics, to take part in the subjecting experience, McQueen offers up a screen of subjection to contemplate ideas about humanity."[20] Cobb astutely describes contemporary racial discrimination's origins partially in slavery's visual regime, surveilling blackness. I will return to this point about the social effects of certain ways of representing race in both *12 Years a Slave* and, later, *The Birth of a Nation.*

Slave Women's Limited Agency

To its credit, *12 Years a Slave* not only develops Patsey as a victimized slave woman but also gives viewers a perspective on slave women's agency, however limited. For example, sold into slavery in Washington, DC, along with

Solomon is Eliza, the former mistress of a man who deceived her and her two children when she expected to be given their freedom. In New Orleans, Ford buys Eliza but not her children. Once at Ford's, Eliza will not stop openly weeping for her children, and thus, as a disturbance, she is sold elsewhere. Although some might hardly call such weeping an expression of agency, for Eliza it is a persistent expression of her identity. When Solomon irritatedly tells her at the slave cabins to stop wailing, Eliza says, "It's all I have to keep my loss present." She also presciently warns Solomon not to think of Ford as a "decent" master; if he tells Ford who he really is, Ford will value him no more than "prized livestock."

An even more interesting female figure is the slave Harriet Shaw, mistress of household at the neighboring plantation and a friend of Patsey's, who seems to have gone to Shaw's often to visit Harriet on Sundays. Played with wit and geniality by Alfre Woodard, Harriet has gained power on the plantation through her ambition and sexuality and can live like a genteel lady. "I knowed what it like to be the object of Massa's predilections and peculiarities," she says looking at Patsey, indicating she understands the kinds of sexual practices slaves have to endure.

And finally, one other glimpse into slave sexuality occurs toward the beginning of the film with a series of vignettes of Solomon enmeshed in slave life. He lies on the floor a darkened cabin sleeping with other slaves. A woman lying next to him looks at him face to face and places his hand on her breast; then moves his hand down to her crotch. He touches her without enthusiasm until she climaxes. She then turns her back to him and cries. He is left in his reveries, and we see a shot of him in bed with his wife.

These incidents are presented without narrative or editorial comment; it is up to the viewer to interpret them. In the first example, Eliza acts to her own detriment, and the viewer may agree with Solomon, but it would be hard to deny the accuracy of her perception of him. In the second example, Harriet Shaw is so comfortably placed and well dressed and speaks in such an assured way that a viewer can hardly condemn her for using her sexuality as she does. The placid scene, however, can change at any time since she is still only a slave. And, finally, the wordless scene of Solomon's masturbating a woman to climax alludes to one of the great mysteries of slavery: sexuality and sexual choice among the slaves. The written record contains evidence only of slave reticence on the subject, and the kind of situation here that the film invents fills in a historical gap. Although these filmed moments are open to many viewer interpretations, I assign to these three episodes what I interpret as brief glimpses into slave women's negotiated agency.

What We Are Left With

Solomon persists in trying to communicate with friends and family in New York. Finally, he is engaged in a carpentry project with a white laborer from Canada who agrees to contact people outside for him. But that carpenter finishes their task of building a gazebo outside the big house and leaves. Solomon is in despair. Suddenly, perhaps many months later, a carriage drives up; the local sheriff asks Solomon a few questions to identify him; and then the Saratoga storeowner, Mr. Parker, steps out of the carriage and embraces Solomon. They drive away, leaving the frustrated Epps and a wailing Patsey in the background. The camera shifts in rack focus from background to foreground, and all the people on the Epps plantation are left behind, never to be heard of again.

When I first saw the film, this scene made me so angry that I wanted to dismiss the whole film as Solomon's (bourgeois) story. "What about Patsey?" as a viewer I demanded to know. However, this scissor-like cutting off of the slave story is appropriate to both Solomon's autobiography and this film. From an existential perspective, Solomon has lived two different lives in two different worlds. Furthermore, the subsequent falling action of the cinematic narrative does not wrap everything up with closure for Solomon or in a happy ending.[21]

In a certain way as *12 Years a Slave* narrates the history of slavery, it also abstracts it. Because the director and scriptwriter attended to the historical record, the film delineates important benchmarks defining slave culture, drawing viewers' attention to slavery's key structural, social, and psychological elements. In addition, the film sets out clear distinctions between capitalist bourgeois culture (the viewers' culture) and antebellum slave culture, which gives viewers a point of identification and a nuanced way to contrast their world and that of the slave.

The use of a *fictional* narrative—one characterized in many instances by visual advancement without verbal explanation—allows this version of slavery to present a story about what slavery felt like, allowing for viewers' differing emotional responses and interpretations, especially among white and black viewers. Layers of meaning at the connotative level of the film are often artfully expressed by the actors in fleeting and mobile facial expressions and in bodily stance, sometimes expressed in the script as the slaves' need to dissemble. In fact, we know very little about what slaves felt, what meanings they assumed, and what conclusions they drew in any given situation. Slave autobiographies, like Solomon Northup's, give us a partial view, but only that.

Furthermore, although a feature film made in the dominant classical realist mode will be highly communicable to many viewers, this aesthetic has limits. As Jasmine Nichole Cobb warns, taking an antirealist position: "*12 Years* reveals the confining nature of 'accuracy' (read as: objective, empirical, realistic, verifiable) as a concern for screen representations of slavery. This value functions to duplicate the nineteenth century context for contemplating slavery and limits our ability to imagine new possibilities derived from slavery as a concluded event."[22] Cobb here presents a challenge to realist discourse as profound as other manifestos that have greatly affected film criticism and practice. I am thinking here especially about Laura Mulvey's "Visual Pleasure and Narrative Cinema,"[23] in which a feminist theorizes cinema's gender representation, and Bertolt Brecht's "Notes to the Opera *Mahagonny*,"[24] in which a communist theorizes realist drama's depoliticizing effect. Film theory in the 1970s and 1980s, especially in the United States and Europe, developed a critique about cinematic realism—namely, that feature fiction film's metonymic, cause-and-effect narrative style constructs a passive spectatorial response. Steve McQueen's films, including *Hunger* and *Shame*, seem to enter this debate in a contrasting way. That is, McQueen narrates in acute metonymic detail his characters' abjection and immerses us in their bodily states. His films often make audiences uncomfortable at the same time that the themes elicit social and political reflection. In that way, perhaps deliberately on the director's part, *12 Years a Slave* can be seen as entering into the long debate about realism and its political consequences.

I will now turn from metonymy in cinematic racial representation to consider metaphor and to look back at a US film that used metaphor in a devastatingly effective way.

The Birth of a Nation: An Introduction

To teach *The Birth of a Nation* after *12 Years a Slave* seems useful pedagogically. I never taught *The Birth of a Nation* because I was revolted by how the film had been presented to me as a masterpiece of early US feature fiction film. In addition, as a teacher I found daunting the idea of holding the students' attention, disgusting them with obligatory viewing of a racist film, and taking them step by step through the necessary background information. If I wanted to teach an exemplar of Griffith melodrama, I taught *Broken Blossoms* or *Way Down East*.[25] But now it seems that if *The Birth of a Nation* were taught after the students saw *12 Years a Slave*, it would become immediately clear to the class what the early film elides: depicting slavery, explaining the plantation household, and contrasting freed slaves' and former slave owners' daily routines.

Historically speaking, during the Reconstruction era, a plantation economy continued to underpin life in the agrarian South, and Southern states' enactment of Black Codes and Jim Crow laws put the freed slaves back into farm labor under old-style authoritarian control. Not defined as such in the film, the "birth of the nation" that the title refers to is the Southern elite's continued reliance on Jim Crow disenfranchisement of freed black men. In particular, the film script builds tension by presenting a version of Reconstruction history that fears out-of-control blacks will take over streets, public spaces, and legal institutions. What is accurate is that both cinematically and historically, the Ku Klux Klan used lynching and the threat of violence to teach freed men their "place," and the film contributed to that.

Also noticeable to today's students would be *The Birth of a Nation*'s strange use of sexuality, because the plot construction relies so much on rape threats to white women. For anyone who considers slavery's recent legacy at the time the film was made, such a misplaced emphasis indicates that the film's narrative is a projective fantasy, covering over the systemic function of rape within slavery and the role that free access to slave women played in white slaveholding men's definition of their own sexuality.

What may be less obvious is that by having all its main characters live in town, in contrast to residing on a rural plantation, the film is already using an idea of home that has permeated US urban society from the capitalist North. Nineteenth-century bourgeois capitalist ideology postulated the home as a space apart from paid labor, with separate spheres designated for women and men. A cult of true womanhood euphemistically was held out as the ideal for those now decisively relegated to the domestic sphere. This concept would be familiar to *The Birth of a Nation*'s audience, and one they would have taken for granted. In addition, many members of that audience would have accepted as a narrative trope an idea concomitant with the notion of separate spheres for men and women—the fragility of white girls and women and the danger awaiting them outside the circle of marriage and the family. This assumption naturalizes the film's rape threat narrative, rendering it unremarkable. For many of *The Birth of a Nation*'s early viewers, protecting white women and girls was a plausible way to organize social life and a plausible way to organize a film.

The Cameron family never lived in a plantation household sustaining most of its needs as a self-sufficient agrarian social unit. In the film this small-town setting seems unremarkable, but such a condensation has a usefulness in letting the film elide the former realities of slavery. The Camerons live in a two-story house in Piedmont, North Carolina, on the main street, facing a narrow front yard and a waist-high white picket fence bordering the sidewalk that's right next to the street. Much of the action in the second half of the film, narrativizing a mythic version of Reconstruction, takes place in front of this house on that sidewalk and street, in scenes that illustrate the progressively distressing social changes impacting the Camerons' lives. The house's conversion into a boardinghouse after the Civil War facilitates the plot development as it allows the powerful but ailing US representative, Austin Stoneman, to stay there with his children, Phil and Elsie (Phil and Elsie arranged this move since Phil had fallen in love with Margaret Cameron on a vacation there, and Elsie had already begun a relationship with a wounded Southern officer in a hospital in Washington, DC—namely, Ben Cameron). However, we see none of the labor performed by Cameron women or by former slaves in the boardinghouse; nor is there reference to the larger economic underpinnings of the Reconstruction South, still based on a plantation economy, nor what happened to the Cameron plantation or the landholdings of their peers.

In sum, *The Birth of a Nation*'s narrative elides reference to the social, psychological, and economic *structures* previously dominant in the antebellum slaveholding plantation household. Instead, the film uses this house in town as a visual prop in a fantasy drama with clear spatial parameters—the "good" Cameron house faces black disorder in the streets. The script's narrative excision—not developing its white characters as members of a previous slaveholding class—facilitates audiences' receiving the film metaphorically, as a fantasy that transforms remembrance. The film's trajectory connects older emotional structures characteristic of melodrama—for example, threat to white women—to a climax that metaphorically represents an invigorated masculinity for white Southern men that depends on the founding of the Ku Klux Klan. In this way, the film is a white fantasy about both gender and race.

Figure 9.5. The US militia takes over the sidewalks of Piedmont, pushing away the Camerons in front of their own house. *Screen capture by author.*

Struggles in the Streets

Three moments from the film demonstrate how *The Birth of a Nation* develops a subplot of a black threat on Main Street to delineate social relations and "explain," through visuals, why the South needs the Klan.

Stoneman has sent his protégé, the mulatto Silas Lynch, South to organize freed slaves and get out their vote. Lynch makes his headquarters in Piedmont. At one point, as Ben and young sister Flora Cameron come out of their house to go out on the street, a group of black soldiers comes down the sidewalk and pushes them back (fig. 9.5). The soldiers' leader tells Ben to give way; Flora cowers next to her brother. Silas Lynch then joins them at the gate to the Cameron house; he is well dressed in a top coat and hat, better dressed than Ben. Visually threatening, the soldiers and Lynch are all bigger than Ben, and they crowd him back toward the house. From his side of the fence, Lynch remonstrates, "This sidewalk belongs to us as much as it does to you, 'Colonel' Cameron" (fig. 9.6). As Lynch walks away, Ben grips his cane like a sword in suppressed fury (fig. 9.7).

Later, on Election Day, all the black men who step up to the ballot box are allowed to vote, while the leading white men of the city are disenfranchised.

Figure 9.6. Silas Lynch remonstrates: "This sidewalk belongs to us as much as it does to you, 'Colonel' Cameron." *Screen capture by author.*

Figure 9.7. Ben clutches his cane. He's the emasculated man who cannot defend his family and their right to public space. *Screen capture by author.*

Armed black soldiers supervise the proceedings. Near the ballot box are placards that we have seen blacks holding at other times; these signs proclaim: "Equal rights, equal politics, and equal marriage" and "Forty acres and a mule for every colored citizen." Several sequences later, black voters celebrating their electoral victory are depicted in a shot that is visually the reverse of an earlier one of the Confederate soldiers from Piedmont leaving their families and riding off to war. There the soldiers had ridden through the streets, away from the camera, cheered on by crowds of black and white townspeople lining the street. Here, in the postelection sequence, black soldiers march down the street toward the camera, with only black citizens cheering from the sides.

Finally, toward the end of the film, the black townspeople, dressed in finery, crowd together on the main street, filling it up, including the sidewalks. General rioting breaks out among them. A white man is pushed to the ground and beaten by a black soldier with a rifle butt. Another man, made to ride on a rail, is pushed up and down by the crowd, as is a white man who was tarred and feathered. In another shot, soldiers in the crowd assault a young black woman. These incidents are crosscut against images of white families sitting in fear indoors, some looking out of their windows to the street below. It is into this melee that the Klan rides, guns blazing as in a Western. The mob, including the soldiers, quickly turns and flees.

The way of filming social space here enacts Griffith's fantasy about Reconstruction power relations, emphasizing a fear of blacks and especially mulattoes and "race mixing." Griffith grotesquely choreographs Piedmont's social geography to threaten chaos when and if blacks overtly assert themselves as equal to whites in public space. Thus, in the first sequence described above, not only is Ben Cameron pushed off the sidewalk in front of his own house, a black soldier and a mulatto politician remonstrate with him face-to-face and eye-to-eye, standing up to him as an equal. To understand the degree of effrontery to the white Southern gentleman, one only has to recall the mores of the antebellum South, demanding that a slave "shrink" when addressing whites. In this scene, body position, mode of address, and way of looking are all challenges deliberately launched at Ben Cameron.[26]

The ballot box sequence makes the affront even more obvious because the action and mise-en-scène postulate systemic electoral abuse. Here, prominent armed black soldiers implement the electoral fraud. In addition to the film's depicting the US Army's military occupation of the South, the placards posted in this scene, as well as other references in the film to the

Freedman's Bureau and the Union League, explicitly address the politics of *The Birth of a Nation*'s Southern viewers; the terms point concretely to heavily contested aspects of and political organizing around Reconstruction. If rape threat (discussed in detail later) is postulated by *The Birth of a Nation* as the biggest threat to whites after Emancipation, then black suffrage surely is the next. This scene naturalizes and authorizes a later incident in the film that looks forward to the Jim Crow South. Toward the end of the film, the Klan members line up and face the small houses in the black section of Piedmont. It is another Election Day, and the masked, armed riders intimidate all the black men emerging from their homes, keeping these newly freed men from going downtown to the polls. The film's visual emphasis on street life—especially the scenes of white disenfranchisement and of an armed black population rioting—legitimizes the actions of the newly organized Klan. In turn, the Klan not only disarms the black men but restores the hierarchy of commonly accepted public behavior, including black deference to the white elite.

Such scenes mark the film as a projective fantasy. The film references little about a slaveholding South, and certainly almost none of the social and political process of Reconstruction. Rather, these scenes in public space trace the outlines of a fearful fantasy: "What now will the former slaves want to do to us—stand shoulder to shoulder with us and speak to us as equals, drive us from our streets and our civic life, mock us, take over our institutions, marry our daughters?" Much of this fantasy derives from inversion, fear of former slaves' vengeance; thus, the shot of a tarred-and-feathered white man implies, "They will do to us what we do to them." What gives this projective fantasy even greater emotional force in the film is the way it is tied to a sexual one—namely, that white women must be protected against the threat of black-on-white rape.

Rape Threat

Much of the narrative tension in *The Birth of a Nation* derives from the threat of rape that all the film's white female protagonists face, especially Flora and Margaret Cameron and Elsie Stoneman (fig. 9.8). Early in the course of the Civil War, as it is depicted in the film, Northern black troops ransack the Cameron house while the family seeks shelter in a root cellar below the kitchen; in that scene, the young Flora Cameron, held by her older sister Margaret, laughs hysterically, almost giving the family away. Later,

Figure 9.8. The metaphoric depiction of the "Southern rape complex. As he breaks down the door of the besieged cabin, a soldier grabs Margaret Cameron while her father pulls her away. *Screen capture by author.*

in a major plot development, a black soldier in Piedmont, Gus, stalks and meets up with Flora as she goes to get water from a woodland stream. Gus proposes marriage, and, frightened, Flora runs through the woods, chased by Gus, and she jumps off a cliff. As Ben Cameron holds Flora's limp body, she tells him Gus did it, and she dies in Ben's arms. Thus, avenging Flora's death was one of the first acts of the newly organized Klan, who lynched Gus and dropped his body in front of Silas Lynch's house.

The sexual threat to Elsie Stoneman is depicted in a more detailed and prolonged way and plays a major role in building the narrative tension leading to the climax. At this point in the film, Griffith uses crosscutting to tie together numerous narrative strands that will ultimately intersect, concluding with the Klan's rescue of Margaret and Elsie and the Klan's restoration of the family's personal safety and the town's social order. The Cameron family and Phil Stoneman had fled to a cabin in a country meadow, with Dr. Cameron escaping imprisonment. In town, Elsie goes to Silas Lynch to ask for help. He proposes to her and then, with her entrapped, he tells his henchmen to quickly prepare for a forced marriage. Elsie tries ineffectively to escape, faints, is placed in a chair, awakens and breaks a window, screams

Figure 9.9. Phil Stoneman barricades the door with his body and Dr. Cameron saves his last shot to kill his daughter rather than let her be raped. Visually and narratively, the cabin is a visual metaphor for the besieged white vagina. *Screen capture by author.*

outside for help, and then is tied back to the chair and gagged. At the same time, the Klan gathers in large numbers to ride to Piedmont to wrest control from the armed black soldiers. Spies from town tell them of Elsie's predicament, so they ride to her rescue, too.

Finally, in the farm cabin in a meadow where the Camerons have taken refuge with some Union veterans, they and some faithful servants fend off a massive attack by black soldiers. As the soldiers try to come in through the windows and beat down the cabin door, the families retreat to the back room. That room's doors are battered, and a soldier grabs Margaret. Dr. Cameron pulls her away as Phil Stoneman barricades the door with his body (fig. 9.9). In an extraordinary shot of that inner room, Dr. Cameron holds a pistol above the fainted Margaret's head, and the Union veteran holds his rifle butt ready to smash in Cameron's daughter's and wife's heads. It's made explicit that the men will fight to the death but will first kill the women and the girl to save them from rape. This scene is presented as a *tableau vivante*, a frozen moment of suspense crowded with detail. Such a rape threat moment in film functions in this way: "There is . . . a disruption of temporality and the time sense. Directorially, the scene isolates the rhythmic pulsations of the threat's narrative moment. . . . The formal treatment breaks up the sensual moment into its parts. The whole sequence functions like the fort/da where the future is made present in the anticipation of punishment and loss. Repetition and a kind of slowing down freeze, for a moment, the syntagmatic rush of the narrative."[27]

The location of the cabin is so free of other social context that the attack on it seems to occur less as a planned military action and more as an isolated pattern of men with rifles circling a cabin. Then the cabin is filmed from inside, in a crowded, claustrophobic mise-en-scène as it is being pierced by rifles, bodies, hands, and arms. In other words, just as the rape motif functions metaphorically in the film as a whole, here the stripped-down filmic geography turns the cabin metaphorically into something else as well—visually and narratively it is like a besieged vagina, with father and lover ready to kill their beloved rather than let her be raped.

Returning to the larger metaphoric connotations of the rape threat moment, we can fruitfully ask why it functions so predominantly as the emotional force for the film. It has a larger cultural function beyond its importance to this one script. As Deborah Barker describes it, such a scenario of black men raping white women exemplifies a "Southern rape complex." She describes the myth in this way:

> The Southern rape complex has been one of the most devastating and far-reaching "stories" to come out of the South. In the "southern rape complex," which assumes a black male rapist and white female victim, the victim is transformed into a symbol of a threatened white Southern culture while the black male symbolizes the threat. Rape, in the cinematic Southern context, carries with it a dramatic resonance associated with Southern history and issues of war, Reconstruction, and racial conflict, and has taken on almost mythic proportions in its justification of violence against black men. Not only is the logic of the southern rape complex integrally linked to the lynching of innocent black men, its distorting lens has also made white female sexuality socially unacceptable and rendered sexual violence against black women socially invisible.[28]

I would add another level to Barker's description. On a deeper psychic level, the metaphor allows viewers to displace and not acknowledge a key cultural and psychological adjustment imposed on whites, especially the former slaveholding class, after Emancipation—that is, the need to redefine both white male sexuality and [white] womanhood. In the antebellum South, both culturally and individually, white male sexuality included sanctioned, continual, and sometimes violent access to slave women's and girls' bodies, since slaves were legally chattel and not persons with bodily integrity or rights. A slaveholder had both a libidinous and economic investment in raping female slaves since any children born of rape among his slaves would become his chattel as well. Indeed, the slaveholder sometimes regarded inseminating slave women as a form of animal husbandry.[29]

In its inversion of slaveholding sexuality, then, it is no wonder that the Southern rape complex places such an emphasis on the evils of miscegenation.[30] In *The Birth of a Nation*, all sexual aggressors are black men, so that the script represses recent history and also any internal struggle white viewers may have with rehabituating themselves to very new structures of desire.

At the same time, the film also rearticulates a reduced concept of desirable womanhood distant from the multifaceted role of the white mistress of a plantation household. Posited in the characterizations of Elsie, Margaret, and Flora is a more Victorian kind of womanhood, one suitable to the (originally Northern) notion of separate spheres: that of the white, virginal, ethereal girl-woman, the angel of the hearth. Public space and the world of men are dangerous to this kind of woman. Like the freed slave in *The Birth of a Nation*, she has to be taught her place, dependent on the white man who will protect and rescue her. Her future is to bear his children and devote herself to them, and to create for him a well-run and loving refuge for him to escape to when he comes home from work. Buttressing such a vision of (bourgeois white) women's "place" is the metaphoric function of rape threat for the white women in the film. In addition, such a rape threat fantasy inverts and displaces so much of the psychic residue from slavery that it makes abuse of black women just disappear.

It is important to note how the film develops the story of Ben Cameron's recuperation of some of his lost masculinity following the South's loss of the war. In another moment similar to the one where he and Flora are jostled off the sidewalk by black troops, he encounters the future rapist Gus staring at the Cameron house. He emphatically orders Gus to keep away from there, and once again, Lynch remonstrates about blacks' rights in public space, at which Ben turns and walks angrily back toward his house.

After Flora's death, Ben sits by the river, the camera angling down on him as a small figure in despair. He had been organizing white men in the community, but now he has the inspiration to form the groups of costumed, masked riders that would be the Ku Klux Klan. To avenge Flora's death, the Klan lynches Gus. Later scenes establish the Klan as men of action mostly by depicting them on horseback, moving together as a mass group at great speed and using pistols to effect rescue and justice. After the Klan captures Silas Lynch, who was trying to abduct Elsie, they might lynch him, too. However, the film's seeming reestablishment of virility for Ben and his white peers comes at a cost; it requires masquerade and the regular performance of violence and intimidation to keep black men in their place. And it requires a view of white womanhood as sexually pure.

Thus, the whole film traces through its fantasy substructure the fragile masculinity of the former slave owners, in a storyline that masks these men's desperate grasp at personal and social potency. The Southern rape myth, reestablishing a frail white virility, itself has had a viciously powerful legacy. Robyn Wiegman summarizes its historical efficacy in the way that it underpins lynching: "Through the lynching scenario, 'blackness' is cast as a subversive (and most often sexual) threat, an incontrovertible chaos whose challenge to the economic and social coherency can be psychologically, if not wholly politically, averted by corporeal abjection and death. That lynching becomes during Reconstruction and its aftermath an increasingly routine response to black attempts at education, personal and communal government, suffrage, and other indicators of cultural inclusion and equality attests to its powerful disciplinary function."[31]

Conclusion: Thinking about History through These Two Films

Media culture in general attaches reduced, stereotyped meanings to race, gender, and social space, but some films have particular value as they try to delineate these contentious aspects of society through historical representation. In particular, historical fictions can illustrate for viewers precedents for current social problems and attitudes or usefully demarcate past social and economic structures that have left a formative trace in the present.

In that context, films about slavery and its aftermath have a special usefulness in the United States today, since the media and politicians generally avoid institutional analysis and historical reference when faced with outrageous incidents of interpersonal racial violence. Institutionally based, racially inflected injustice in the United States includes poor people's disenfranchisement, their lack of educational and employment opportunity, legal hostility to immigrants, inordinate imprisonment of people of color, and the legal murder of peaceful black men on the street. For those who want to take action around these issues, the two films analyzed in this chapter can help us better understand the history and economic, social, and legal structures underlying our political moment; inform what actions we might take; and trace what has shaped the resistance that we will likely encounter when trying to make social change.

For example, *12 Years a Slave* speaks to certain aspects of African American lives in our own times. The protagonist, an entrepreneurial individualist, enjoys the life of a free man with his family in the North, yet he is kidnapped and loses his identity when forced into the life of a slave. Impermanence and uncertainty have been introduced forever into his life. Back in the North, he cannot legally testify against his enslavers, finding he has no safety under the law. As Valerie Smith puts it, the film represents the "fragility of black freedom." Smith sums up the film's historical address to US viewers today: "Northup's twitching foot calls to mind as well Trayvon Martin, Renisha McBride, Jonathan Ferrell, and the hosts of other African Americans, largely invisible in the media, gunned down each year and whose shooters (whether law enforcement officers or civilians) go unpunished. How fragile indeed is black life in the Age of Obama."[32]

In contrast, because of its historical address and overt racism, *The Birth of a Nation* may seem to have fewer messages for activists today. But, in fact, it does teach an important structure underlying racist laws: the goal of white elites to control public space and the use of disenfranchisement in that process. It also shows how violence functions as a disciplinary admonition for both people of color and white women, especially in terms of "knowing their place." In addition, if viewers are taught to look for this, *The Birth of a Nation* provides much information about "marking"—how characterization, body type, costume, and physical range of action connote much of the film's message about race—and thus delineates a precedent for what Cobb refers to as the discriminatory marking of blackness today.

Film critics, and often media scholars, also often point out what a film does *not* show. Sometimes they do so in service of ideological analysis, other times to indicate how audience expectations and taste have variously shaped media production from one era to another. Also, media teachers, especially in writing assignments, often encourage students to further analyze one aspect of a film via social history, personal narrative, audience interviews, fan discourse, politically oriented analysis, and so on. As a result, the students also bring to the fore what the film does not show, and they fruitfully trace the implications of missing content.

If I were to prioritize one thing *missing* from *12 Years a Slave* and *The Birth of a Nation* that has great implications for viewers today, I would teach alongside these films material about the rise of the prison industrial complex in Reconstruction and how the privatized incarceration industry continues in modern form slave practices today.[33]

The historical tie between the US prison system and slavery has been traced by Angela Davis, who, throughout her intellectual career, has written about and worked as an activist against the prison industrial complex, which she sees as a continuation of slavery by other means. In our own times, prisons inordinately warehouse people of color and the prison population has grown to well over two million in the United States. From this perspective, *12 Years a Slave*'s story of Solomon Northup's loss of identity, impounded slave labor, and immersion in a culture of violence where every aspect of his daily life is controlled is also the story of contemporary imprisonment. Furthermore, Davis's analysis of the origins of modern US penal institutions in the Reconstruction South directly augments a reading of *The Birth of a Nation*, because her analysis lends new meaning to the film's depiction of out-of-control freedmen taking control of the town's streets and their violent containment by the Ku Klux Klan. Davis summarizes this history as follows: "In the immediate aftermath of slavery, the southern states hastened to develop a criminal justice system that could legally restrict the possibilities of freedom for newly released slaves. Black people became the prime targets of a developing convict lease system. . . . Thus, vagrancy was coded as a black crime, one punishable by incarceration and forced labor, sometimes on the very plantations that previously had thrived on slave labor."[34]

Whipping was common punishment on chain gangs, and these "leased" convicts could be worked to death. This was unlike the plantation owner's slave management, where, because of his capital investment, he needed to keep his labor force healthy enough to work. Furthermore, black convicts built the infrastructure for rising Southern industrialization, often laboring on railroad gangs or in mines. In this way, Davis's writing ties together both films discussed here, tracing the economic and legal bases for controlling freedmen, which *The Birth of a Nation* elides, and the dehumanizing slave-like conditions in prisons today, implying a contemporary extension of Solomon's experience in *12 Years a Slave*.

Because of the hegemony of bourgeois liberalism, it is often difficult for audiences to think systematically about US institutions and economic/political structures, and the ordinary script pattern of feature films, focusing on an individual in conflict or facing adversity, also discourages such thought. These two films, however, have much to teach about what is usually hidden from view.

JULIA LESAGE is Professor Emerita of English at the University of Oregon. She is Founder and Editor with Chuck Kleinhans and John Hess of *Jump Cut: A Review of Contemporary Media* (www.ejumpcut.org).

Notes

1. Solomon Northup, *12 Years a Slave*, as told to and edited by David Wilson (Auburn, NY: Derby and Miller, 1853).

2. Linda Williams, *Playing the Race Card: Melodramas of Black and White from Uncle Tom to O. J. Simpson* (Princeton, NJ: Princeton University Press, 2001).

3. I describe the Southern rape complex in more detail later in this chapter in the analysis of *The Birth of a Nation*. See Deborah E. Barker, *Reconstructing Violence: The Southern Rape Complex in Film and Literature* (Baton Rouge: Louisiana State University Press, 2005). Also dealing with the topic of the Southern rape complex extensively is Diane Sommerville, *Rape and Race in the Nineteenth Century South* (Durham: University of North Carolina Press, 2004). Especially useful is Sommerville's appendix: "Rape, Race, and Rhetoric: The Rape Myth in Historical Perspective," 223–261.

4. See David Bordwell, Janet Staiger, and Kristen Thompson, *The Classical Hollywood Cinema: Film Style and Mode of Production to 1960* (London: Routledge, 1985).

5. For a more detailed analysis of this process that draws on the work of Roland Barthes, see my essay: Julia Lesage, "S/Z and *Rules of the Game*," *Jump Cut: A Review of Contemporary Media*, no. 55 (2013), https://www.ejumpcut.org/archive/jc55.2013/LesageRulesOfGame/index.html. Originally published in *Jump Cut: A Review of Contemporary Media*, no. 12–13 (Winter 1976–1977): 45–51.

6. Barker, *Reconstructing Violence*.

7. George Lakoff and Mark Johnson, *Metaphors We Live By* (Chicago: University of Chicago Press, 1980). The film's plotline also illustrates Mary Douglas's argument in *Purity and Danger: An Analysis of Concepts of Pollution and Taboo* (London: Routledge, 1896) that societies that want to control social hierarchies and boundaries often do so through metaphors of sexual threat.

8. Roland Barthes, "The Reality Effect," in *The Rustle of Language*, trans. Richard Howard (Oxford: Blackwell, 1986), 141–148.

9. John L. Fell, *Film and the Narrative Tradition* (Berkeley: University of California Press, 1986).

10. For my argument in this essay about historical difference between regional concepts of the self in the United States, I am indebted to the writings of Elizabeth Fox-Genovese and Eugene D. Genovese—in particular, Fox-Genovese's *Within the Plantation Household: Black and White Women of the Old South* (Durham: University of North Carolina Press, 1988).

11. Captivity narratives were a common genre in the eighteenth and nineteenth centuries, written usually by white colonists captured by indigenous natives. Typically the captive would write about his or her captors as crude and alien.

12. Sam Worley, "Solomon Northup and the Sly Philosophy of the Slave Pen," *Callaloo* 20, no. 91 (1997): 243–259, at 246.

13. On the complexities of spectatorship for black independent cinema, see Terri Simone Francis, "Flickers of the Spirit: 'Black Independent Film,' Reflexive Reception, and a Blues Cinema Sublime," *Black Camera* 1, no. 2 (Summer 2010): 7–24.

14. McQueen's previous films *Hunger* (2008) and *Shame* (2011) contain many moments that provoke audience anxiety and discomfort.

15. The Internet Movie Database indicates that the film won 233 critical awards and 305 nominations. In 2013, it won Oscars for best motion picture, best adapted screenplay, best supporting actress (Lupita Nyong'o), best actor, best supporting actor (Michael Fassbender), and best costume design (Patricia Norris); http://www.imdb.com/title/tt2024544/awards?ref_=tt_awd.

16. Henry Louis Gates Jr., "Steve McQueen and Henry Louis Gates Jr. Talk 12 Years a Slave," three-part interview, *The Root*, December 24–26, 2013, https://www.theroot.com/steve-mcqueen-and-henry-louis-gates-jr-talk-12-years-a-1790899438.

17. McQueen talks about Ejiofor's spontaneous crying in this scene to Dan P. Lee, "Where It Hurts: Steve McQueen on Why *12 Years a Slave* Isn't Just About Slavery," *Vulture*, December 8, 2013, http://www.vulture.com/2013/12/steve-mcqueen-talks-12-years-a-slave.html.

18. Sigmund Freud, *Jokes and Their Relation to the Unconscious*, trans. James Strachey (New York: W. W. Norton, 1960), 163.

19. Julia Lesage, "The Rape Threat Scene in Narrative Cinema" (paper presented at the Society for Cinema Studies Conference, New Orleans, 1993), http://pages.uoregon.edu/jlesage/Juliafolder/RAPETHREAT.HTML. Julia Lesage, "Torture Documentaries," *Jump Cut*, no. 51 (2009), http://www.ejumpcut.org/archive/jc51.2009/TortureDocumentaries/.

20. Jasmine Nichole Cobb, "Directed by Himself: Steve McQueen's *12 Years a Slave*," *American Literary History* 26, no. 2 (Summer 2014): 339–346, at 343.

21. Miriam Petty, "Refusing the Happy Ending: *12 Years a Slave*," *Huffington Post*, October 21, 2015, http://www.huffingtonpost.com/miriam-petty/refusing-the-12-years-a-slave_b_4869602.html.

22. Cobb, "Directed by Himself," 341.

23. Laura Mulvey, "Visual Pleasure and Narrative Cinema," *Screen* 16, no. 3 (1975): 6–18.

24. Bertolt Brecht, "Notes to the Opera *Mahagonny* (1930)," trans. John Willett as "The Modern Theater Is the Epic Theater," in *Brecht on Theater*, ed. John Willett (New York: Hill and Wang, 1964), 33–42.

25. Julia Lesage, "*Broken Blossoms*: Artful Racism, Artful Rape," *Jump Cut: A Review of Contemporary Media*, no. 26 (1981): 51–55, updated in 2014, www.ejumpcut.org/archive/onlinessays/JC26folder/BrokenBlossoms.html.

26. In the Jim Crow South, a black man acting as a white man's equal would be punished. Martin Luther King Jr. developed a strategy of passive resistance partially in acknowledgement of this pattern.

27. Lesage, "The Rape Threat Scene."

28. Deborah E. Barker, "Moonshine and Magnolias: *The Story of Temple Drake* and *The Birth of a Nation*," *Faulkner Journal* 22, no. 1–2 (Fall 2006/Spring 2007): 142.

29. In a November 18, 2015, panel discussion on C-Span 2 about Katherine Franke's book *Wedlocked*, legal scholar Patricia J. Williams said this kind of rape was the story of her slave ancestors, who were bred to be fair-skinned house slaves; http://www.c-span.org/video/?400857-1/book-discussion-wedlocked.

30. In response to systemic abuses of rape and fragmenting of families, after Emancipation, one of the legal rights most frequently claimed by freed slaves was marriage, a public assertion of both marital and parental rights. Katherine Franke, in *Wedlocked: The Perils of Marriage Equality* (New York: New York University Press, 2015), discusses marriages in the postbellum South as a parallel to gay marriages today. She finds that, in addition to its many legal advantages, the state marriage contract imposes strict gender constrictions on marginalized communities that formerly have had many innovative, unlegislated ways to arrange sexual and familial households and affective bonds.

31. Robyn Wiegman, "The Anatomy of Lynching," in "African American Culture and Sexuality," special issue, *Journal of the History of Sexuality* 3, no. 3 (January 1993): 445–467.

32. Valerie Smith, "Black Life in the Balance: *12 Years a Slave*," *American Literary History* 26, no. 2 (2014): 365.

33. This essay was written before Ava DuVernay released her powerful documentary *13th*, about black incarceration, on Netflix. I do not have the space to analyze that film here but note that her analysis parallels that of Angela Davis, cited here.

34. Angela Davis, *Are Prisons Obsolete?* (New York: Seven Stories Press, 2003), 29.

10

ENGINEERING DIFFERENT EQUATIONS IN THE WAKE OF *THE BIRTH OF A NATION*

Blackface and Racial Politics in Bamboozled *and* Dear White People

Anne-Marie Paquet-Deyris

THE OBAMA YEARS SAW THE ISSUE OF RACE in the media dissolve into the era of the postracial, when race no longer seemed to be an obstacle to progress. For quite a few critics, such as Roy Kaplan in *The Myth of Post-Racial America* (2011) and David Leonard and Lisa Guerrero in *African Americans on Television: Race-ing for Ratings* (2013), however, such color blindness can result in bypassing direct confrontation with the persistent problems linked to race in contemporary US society.[1] Postracialism can thus deny problems that are still pervasive in American culture, making it impossible to resolve them.

In the current context of the treatment of racial stereotypes, D. W. Griffith's controversial 1915 film *The Birth of a Nation* still seems to be fully playing its part as a point of reference for present-day filmmakers. Griffith's blatant use of blackface and rewriting of US history have spurred several notable filmmakers, such as Spike Lee and Justin Simien, to recycle what Michael Rogin calls a "racial masquerade."[2] By flaunting racial stereotypes, Lee and Simien circumvent the great white narrative and address race directly instead of metaphorically; they also write every single character not outside but within his or her own racial background. Black characters are no longer removed from their own histories; rather, they are shaped, defined, and sometimes destroyed by them.

This chapter addresses the cultural, ideological, and sociopolitical aftereffects still wrought by *The Birth of a Nation*. I discuss the extent to which Griffith's controversial masterpiece influenced Lee and Simien to distinctly voice racial concerns and tensions and provide representational spaces on-screen in a provocative and reflective manner. How do the two filmmakers subvert the characteristic dynamic of black/slave/character to white/master/hero to instead embrace a wide variety of black stories, experiences, and perspectives? I explore the way in which, one hundred years after *The Birth of a Nation*—and somehow because of it—the two movies relocate America's problems with race to the very heart of the national debate and offer a kind of post-postracial screen model directly confronting racial history.

The Birth of a Nation as a Barometer

The impact of *The Birth of a Nation* is still so strong that the film's current reception summons very specific and passionate reactions about the staging of race and inequality today. French second-year students from Paris Ouest University who were studying the film recently were asked to comment on five specific clips and photograms from the film: (1) the opening intertitle about "the first seed of disunion"; (2) the sequence of the masters courting while the slaves are either working in the cotton fields or dancing for the masters in demeaning postures; (3) the sequence of the black representatives at the statehouse during Reconstruction cheering when intermarriage between blacks and whites is legalized; (4) the infamous pursuit into the woods and near-rape of the white Flora by renegade black soldier Gus; and (5) Gus's lynching by members of the Ku Klux Klan. The only version of the lynching scene in which the burning cross has not been excised is the 1915 uncensored print, as Jane Gaines underlined in her keynote address at the June 2015 conference at University College London whose theme was "a centennial assessment of Griffith's film."

The undiminished relevance of *The Birth of a Nation*'s controversial treatment of black people was obvious in most of the students' comments. They immediately reacted to mischaracterizations of black people in the film and in the Western world at large. They also made direct connections with the representations of Syrian and African migrants on television. Some of them criticized the way that European television channels covered the brawls between feuding gangs of African migrants in the French Calais "Jungle" in summer 2016 and the way police used tear gas and charged the migrants with dogs in order to dislodge and deport them to Britain.

If the filmic narrative is to them of primary importance, they also focused on the type of representational strategy used by the director, paying close attention to any form of bias. Most of the students readjusted the representation strategy with a mostly critical and corrective retrospective glance, voicing their concern in class, for example, when making a presentation on one of the film's sequences. They seemed to be instantly alert to the codedness of the representation of blackness and reacted to the use of blackface and its highly visual suggestiveness as a very visible distortion of racial representation—a physical signifier and signal that needs to be deciphered in light of *The Birth of a Nation*'s distorted discourse on race. Somehow, one hundred years later, exposure to Griffith's stereotypical portrayal of blacks enables the students to gauge the significance of the messages they receive from contemporary movies and media at large.

Similar to how the media are described in Robert Entman and Andrew Rojecki's pre-Obama book *The Black Image in the White Mind*, *The Birth of a Nation* seems to serve as "a kind of leading indicator, a barometer of cultural change and variability in the arena of race . . . encouraging audiences and media producers alike to become more critically self-aware as they deal with the culture's racial signals."[3] The students were also highly critical of the kind of paternalistic attitudes peddled by Griffith and most of the (white) critics who celebrated the movie when it came out. Rupert Hughes's "Tribute to 'The Birth of a Nation'" in the original 1915 souvenir program, is characteristic of this type of pervasive paternalistic discourse:

Hardly anybody can be found today who is not glad that slavery was wrenched out of our national life, but it is not well to forget how and why it was defended, and by whom; what it cost to tear it loose, but what suffering and bewilderment were left with the bleeding wounds. The North was not altogether blameless for the existence of slavery, nor was the South altogether blameworthy for it or for its aftermath. "The Birth of a Nation" is a peculiarly human presentation of a vast racial tragedy. There has been some hostility to the picture on account of an alleged injustice to the negroes. I have not felt it; and I am one who cherishes a great affection and a profound admiration for the negro. He is enveloped in one of the most cruel and insoluble riddles of history. . . . "The Birth of a Nation" presents many lovable negroes who win hearty applause from the audiences. It presents also some exceedingly hateful negroes but American history has the same fault and there are bad whites also in this film as well as virtuous.

It is hard to see how such a drama could be composed without the struggle of evil against good. Furthermore, it is to the advantage of the negro of today to know how some of his ancestors misbehaved and why the prejudices in his path have grown there. Surely no friend of his is to be turned into an enemy by this film, and no enemy more deeply embittered. "The Birth of a Nation" is a chronicle of human passion.[4]

Most whites shared the same paternalistic attitude, which partly explains the film's great commercial success. The "negroes" had been subjected to "a vast racial tragedy" that needed to be corrected, but this could only be achieved by accepting a very specific type of reformatted narrative that was "founded on Thomas Dixon's Story 'The Clansman' [and p]roduced under the personal direction of D. W. Griffith."[5]

Ninety-nine and eighty-five years later, respectively, filmmakers Spike Lee and Justin Simien actively reshaped this type of discourse on race relations by producing their own. As a direct consequence and in the wake of their film experiments, they also "reshap[e] White audiences' sensibilities, tastes and ultimately market demand."[6]

"Show and Tell": Blackness Visible

In Simien's *Dear White People* (2014), the first intertitle "Show and Tell" announces Sam's student film project, which is meant to shock. As one of the four main black characters struggling to define themselves in a mostly white Ivy League university, Samantha is framed early on as the most militant; she is a creative cinema student and host of the *Dear White People* radio show, where she vents her anger at white people. The viewer later learns, however, that she is biracial and has a white father. Sam makes it clear from the start that she identifies as an African American woman speaking and seeing from this specific vantage point. Early medium close-ups frame Sam pointing a camera at the spectator during her controversial radio broadcast or calling out the racial innuendos or outright aggressions experienced by African Americans in their daily lives. The story of the "race war [that went on] at Winchester University" seems to be told and shown from her own perspective in a metafilmic echo of Simien's (fig. 10.1).

These shots function in inverse proportion to Griffith's insistence on his own construction of black identity and stereotypes. He forms these constructions explicitly through title cards, as with the quotation from Woodrow Wilson's *A History of the American People* about crazed and insolent Negroes, and he refines the loyal stereotype visually with shots of the faithful mammy battling an "insolent and dangerous" black during Reconstruction.

Sam's critical and ideological stance—to publicly criticize the way white people look at black people and the state of race relations in general—highlights one of the most highly charged questions in twenty-first-century America: What does it mean to be black now, and who can claim

Figure 10.1. In Simien's *Dear White People*, Sam, black student of media arts. *Screen capture by author.*

"blackness"? Sam's short film *Rebirth of a Nation* stages white people in whiteface berating President Obama's reforms and how his health insurance plan caused havoc.[7] The film literally reimagines the original *The Birth of a Nation* and testifies to its continuing relevance to recent cultural and political developments. The film within the film first reverses and then displaces the unease black people feel when watching white actors in blackface wearing blackness like a costume that can be disposed of at will. The original intent of blackface minstrels to imitate and portray blacks as intellectually and culturally impoverished is thus turned upside down; white culture is now debased, and white Americans are dehumanized as they are placed in the position of victims of political and racial oppression. Discussing the "Racial Subtexts of Crime News" in *The Black Image in the White Mind*, Entman and Rojecki note the extent to which "the combined portrayal in front and profile shots yield an impression of guilt based on hundreds or thousands of previous, intertextual memories of the image in news and fiction."[8] Whiteface functions in *Rebirth of a Nation* the way blackface was meant to in the days of minstrelsy and in Griffith's film: the features of the white men and women are accentuated and stereotypical in their outrage, animalistic hatred, and despair at Barack Obama becoming president and at his subsequent health care reform (fig. 10.2).

The way whites are framed recalls Griffith's staging of malevolent blacks and angry mulattoes in *The Birth of a Nation*, whether it be Gus, the black "rapist" whose dark, threatening face disappears into the frame

Figure 10.2. Angry white man in Simien's *Dear White People.* *Screen capture by author.*

and incarnates a diffuse, insidious form of evil, or Silas Lynch and Lydia Brown, portrayed as "vicious" mulattoes. The two mulattoes in blackface are presented as being even more dangerous than blacks. As mixed-race people like Sam in *Dear White People*, they confuse the racial representational scheme and dream of a new social order. Because they literally cross the racial and social line and cannot be ascribed a specific positioning, they must be punished in a spectacular manner. In the end, Silas, for instance, is manhandled by Ku Klux Klan members so that viewers can only see the back of his head in the lower left-hand corner of the frame before he disappears offscreen.

By toying with these century-old images of blackness, Simien foregrounds what has changed—or not—in the system of representation of blackness. He exposes the constructed notion of race so that contemporary reverberations immediately become obvious and are compounded by the inscription on-screen of some Tea Party members' racial slurs and attacks on Obama, such as being "not that articulate," a "Communist! Fascist! Socialist!" who should "go back to Kenya!" (fig. 10.3).

In *Paint the White House Black*, Michael Jeffries foregrounds the type of metalanguage of race used in the public arena: "A quick Internet search for 'Tea Party racism' reveals countless verbal attacks, images and signs about Obama, who is derided as a socialist, terrorist, or Nazi and depicted variously as a topless African witch doctor in tribal garb, Hitler, the Joker, and an ape."[9]

Simien has Sam briefly play on "the African-male-as-ape overtones of 'classic' American films like *Birth of a Nation* (1915) and *King Kong* (1933)."[10]

Figure 10.3. In *Dear White People*, the inarticulate bulldog in Sam's *Rebirth of a Nation* short film. *Screen capture by author.*

Sam unexpectedly substitutes a close-up of a particularly "inarticulate" bulldog, circumventing the more widely used monkey image whose absence ironically becomes all the more noticeable. Furthermore, Simien fully captures the white spectators' deep sense of unease at such a reversal of the blackface minstrel show conventions: two blond boys can't even look at the screen; a bewildered brunette slides down in her seat; virtually no one dares to exchange afterward. The white teaching assistant's negative judgment about the film being "thematically dubious" duplicates what most black people (used to) think of the denigration of blacks in the days of minstrel entertainment. Representing the white male and female in whiteface as alternately hyperviolent and tragic victims plays into the negative stereotyping of blacks as hypersexualized and violent and as being therefore "legitimately" punishable for these very excesses in *The Birth of a Nation*. *Dear White People*, and specifically the short *Rebirth of a Nation*, bring to the fore in an ironically reverse way the "racial skew" and the ethnic offensiveness geared toward blacks.[11]

Exploring the roots of minstrel shows, Kris Collins shows how racial stereotyping stems from "one of white society's greatest fears, if assessed by its ruthless belittlement of blacks in minstrel entertainment, [which] was the social, intellectual and sexual advancement of African-Am. blacks into traditionally white cultural arenas."[12] The manipulation of an inverted racial subtext and the recycling of frightening and sensational visual images construct a sense of threat that dissociates blacks from these dangers while associating whites with them. Any distortion of racial representation is hence made ludicrously visible. The fact that we can barely distinguish on-screen that the protesters are white, mostly because they wear hoodies, visually underscores the coded representation of (usually black) rioters that goes all the way back to Griffith and extends up to the present, reverberating in demonstrations such as the ones that followed Trayvon Martin's shooting by George Zimmerman in a Florida gated community in 2012. The lumping together of these undifferentiated individuals mirrors the media's overrepresentation of violent crimes and their associations with blacks. It is also intended to make whites ponder the experience of being represented as part of a minority whose members seem to have no distinct identities—like the indiscriminate black crowds in *The Birth of a Nation* or the members of the Million Hoodie March in Manhattan on March 21, 2012, organized in memory of Trayvon Martin, who was wearing a hood at the time of his death.[13]

Similar to Spike Lee's approach in *Bamboozled*, Simien is intent on undoing the media constructs to which we are exposed and the way in which we—involuntarily or not—recycle them. In a British Film Institute interview entitled "*Dear White People*: 'All We Had during Awards Season Were Tragic Depictions of the Black Experience,'" Simien comments on the choice of comedy as a useful film genre and makes sure, just as in his opening sequence, that the audience picks up on the satiric intent of his film. The use of slow motion and silent era–like intertitles underlines the way in which comedy leads to a revision of the kind of messages we receive, are conditioned by, and eventually send back out:

> *You tackle so many controversial subjects. Why did it make sense to you to make it a comedy?*
>
> It's not a straightforward comedy, it has its dramatic moments, but I was just so taken by things like *Do the Right Thing* (1989), even movies like *Network* (1976) and *Election* (1999), that touch upon really deep, heavy subject matters but do it in a way that lulls you into being entertained. Satire has so much power because it gets you to laugh first before you realize you're laughing at yourself. . . .
>
> *Did you make Sam a filmmaker as a way of critiquing Hollywood?*
>
> All the characters have some form of self-expression; Lionel writes for the newspaper, Troy is a public figure on campus, Coco has her YouTube blog. I think the movie is saying something, not only about the cultural messages that we receive about ourselves, but the kind of the messages that we then put

back out into the culture because of how we've been conditioned. I got a lot of personal nerdiness out through her voice but I think of her as an observer. She's the kind of person who really takes the world in and attempts to blow that up.[14]

In addition to using comedy to radically circumvent the usual tragic mode used to focus on "the black experience"—in the singular and not the plural—Simien foregrounds the extent to which laughter offers a much wider representational spectrum. He also reinscribes himself in a line of directors using bitter irony as a—literally—spectacular weapon, reshuffling the *Hollywood Shuffle* model, after Robert Townsend's 1987 satiric film about African American actors in Hollywood. Unlike Townsend's hero, Bobby Taylor, who is limited to stereotypical black roles because of his ethnicity and competes for them even though he dreams of being able to get any part, Sam tries to resolve the problem of warring racial identities and painful social divisions for herself as a mixed-race person and for others by using race as a trump card. Her discourse on race curiously harks back, however, to Malcolm X's speech on the "Difference between Separation and Segregation" at Michigan State University in January 1963: "We don't go for segregation. We go for separation. Separation is when you have your own. You control your own economy; you control your own politics; you control your own society; you control your own everything. You have yours and you control yours; we have ours and we control ours."[15]

More than fifty years later, Sam still sounds like a Black Power activist. The camera ironically focuses on the survival guide of African Americans on an elite, mostly white campus she plays with while broadcasting *Dear White People* and later frames her throwing out any white student who ventures into Armstrong-Parker House, the traditionally black residence hall. Simien goes further in his demonstration of how radical identity and racial discourse are constructed than, for instance, *Mad Men*'s showrunner Matthew Weiner. The latter stages racism and sexual politics in a self-reflective mode. He plays with the white viewers' (mostly Don's and Pete's) relative malaise as they watch Roger Sterling's infamous blackface serenade to his fair young wife in season 3, episode 3, "My Old Kentucky Home." As Kent Ono remarks, "the show's embrace of the past is not only loving but also uncomfortable."[16] Weiner uses the more conventional inscription of blackface on-screen to "classicly" capture a white man whose face and hands are painted black. And Valerie Palmer-Mehta notes that Roger's song about "gay" "negroes" in summertime "underscores how this [late 1950s]

Figure 10.4. In *Dear White People*, the dominant black
perspective pondering the alien dimension of the "others."
Screen capture by author.

example of minstrelsy rationalizes racial oppression and dehumanizes its
victims" while attempting to emphasize for contemporary audiences how
much the notion of political correctness has evolved since the 1950s.[17] Such
a moment of self-conscious racial representation problematizes and lit-
eralizes one of the main critiques leveled at the show: "*Mad Men* reports
the past from the perspective of white people, as well as through the lens
and bodies of white people through how we view unfolding events.... The
show's strategies of whiteness, which invariably center on white perspectives, also structure overall attitudes about race, including the way people
of color are understood."[18]

The show's resonance, then, is not as extensive as *Dear White People*'s
Rebirth of a Nation precisely because the perspective is a white one as
opposed to a black one. In Simien and Sam's films, the black perspective is
ironically mediated through the vantage point of yet another young black
female wondering in the short *Rebirth of a Nation*, "What is wrong with
these White people?" (fig. 10.4).

Just as it does in *The Birth of a Nation*, the white man's gaze on "the
Africanist presence [which] was crucial to [his] sense of Americanness"
also functions as the dominant perspective in Spike Lee's 2000 movie *Bamboozled*.[19] The black bodies, however, are portrayed in such grotesquely stereotyped ways and blackface is flaunted at the viewer with such vigor that

this extreme representational strategy immediately deconstructs the manner in which present-day racism works. By investing the creatively gifted lead black character with authorial control, Lee reinvents the black stereotypes of the Black Buck–turned–Uncle Tom and the dancing coon Donald Bogle first theorized in his 1973 groundbreaking study *Toms, Coons, Mulattoes, Mammies, and Bucks.*[20] Lee makes them serviceable in a highly satirical fashion in the character Mantan's *Very Black Show* (also the French title of *Bamboozled*), which Mantan is creating for the TV channel he works for. So that the derisive intent of the recycling of such racially offensive stereotypes may not be missed, Lee has the opening sequence coincide with Delacroix's voice-over giving a definition of *satire*: the first meaning is "a literary work in which human vice or folly is ridiculed or attacked scornfully," and the second meaning is "irony, derision or caustic wit." The media-projected images recycled by "Dela" diversely affect people's perceptions of themselves and others. They acquire a life of their own and eventually escape his authorial strategy, which was originally to wrest control from his white boss and get him to fire him. Their destructive impact is finally materialized on-screen in a very literal way. Lee's spectacular variation on the old dancing coon stereotype ends up being recycled ad nauseam. Twelve years after the dancing Toms and coons of *The Birth of a Nation*, Al Jolson had already set a new trend in what Donald Bogle calls the "Blackface fixation"[21] when singing "My Mammy," "a classic example of the minstrel tradition at its sentimentalized, corrupt best."[22] Referring more specifically to Paul Sloane's 1929 film *Hearts in Dixie* (in *Bamboozled*, the name Lee gives Dela's assistant, Sloan Hopkins, may be an ironic reference to Paul Sloane), Bogle asserts that, "In the end, as the first all-Negro musical, *Hearts in Dixie* pinpointed the problem that was to haunt certain black actors for the next half century: the *blackface fixation*. Directed by whites in scripts authored by whites, the Negro actor, like the slaves he portrayed, aimed (and still does aim) always to please the master figure."[23]

Reminiscent of *The Birth of a Nation*'s representation of white patriarchy and dancing slaves and of Alan Crosland's 1927 first talkie, *The Jazz Singer*, Dela's creations in blackface, Mantan and his friend Sleep N'Eat, gradually invade the entire screen space, paradoxically hailed by enthusiastic audiences, black, white, Latino, and Asian alike (figs. 10.5 and 10.6).

The shots of the raving crowd and of ethnically diverse faces in blackface artificially creates a strange, literally *imagined* spectatorial community whose common identification seems to be shaped by the same mediated

Figure 10.5. Mantan and Sleep N'Eat acting and dancing in *Bamboozled*. *Screen capture by author.*

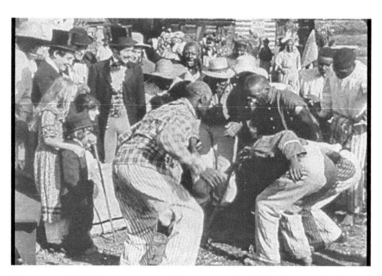

Figure 10.6. Griffith's inscription of white patriarchy: blacks dancing for the white masters. *Screen capture by author.*

Figure 10.7. In *Bamboozled*, the film and Dela's end. *Screen capture by author.*

images. The illusion is so powerful that Lee eventually replaces the live black tap dancers with objects that play even more into stereotyped images of black life: black collectibles finally take over his desk, haunt him in Donald Bogle's words, and destroy his life. The image thus materializes on-screen the way that historical legacies of racism can not only overdetermine one's identity but also become literally lethal (fig. 10.7).

Griffith's representation of the invasion of space by African American representatives (most of them white actors in blackface with some black extras) parallels the proliferation of black memorabilia that eventually invisibilizes the inscription of the African American artists and showrunners. Conversely, at the end of Griffith's film, the frame is purged of the black presence. To borrow from Linda Williams's keynote address titled "In the Shadow of *Birth of a Nation*: D. W. Griffith and Blackface Traditions," presented at the June 2015 conference at University College London, "the almost magical black disappearances" offscreen are matched in Lee's movie by the equally magical multiplication of the black figurines in the frame.

Bursting the Postracial Bubble?

Griffith first frames blacks as slow-witted, lazy figures or loyal house servants that would remain nonthreatening and subservient to whites and could therefore be regarded with paternal fondness. He then captures as sex-craved, aggressive, and ambitious beings that were to launch the new elaborate stereotype of the "brute Negroes"[24] of Reconstruction. Out of these set characters, Griffith mostly focused on the figure of the "rapist" in blackface to support the patriarchal cult of the pure, true, white woman. Conversely, Lee and Simien portray black people as self-assertive, fiercely independent, and creative. Samantha White in *Dear White People* and Pierre Delacroix, Sloan Hopkins, and the two tap dancers Manray and Womack in *Bamboozled* actually impose a new tone on the two filmic narratives. At the same time, they also recycle some black stereotypes—such as the black militant angry young (wo)man eager to please his/her followers— and hence toy with the same stereotypes that television and movies continue to project. As Simien underlines, however, what matters is to further the "conversation" about what many critics deem to be the pernicious myth of postracialism in an America where the intersection of race and class still very much matters. Asked by host Terry Gross on NPR's *Fresh Air* about the development of *Dear White People*'s specific tone, Justin Simien explained:

> After our first black president . . . everyone thought we were in a post-racial America and then that post-racial bubble [was] burst by the Birther Movement and horrible tragedies like Trayvon Martin, . . . [and] the blackface parties . . . that cumulatively awakened me to just how dangerous covert racism can be and how it's a lot more comfortable for us to stick our heads in the sand about it. But that did unleash an anger in me. It's just people's refusal to see or to at least be open to experiences different than them. . . . That's when the film took on a much more charged tone to it and became *Dear White People*.[25]

Lee's and Simien's narratives create interesting dissonances with Griffith's exclusory white national narrative, which boldly charted the possibility of a different America by rectifying the narrative of the Civil War and literally reconstructing Reconstruction. Tracing a line of continuity from *The Birth of a Nation* to their own narratives, Simien and Lee function in inverse proportion to postracial narratives in a so-called postracial era. In the January 18, 2010, "'Post-Racial' Conversation, One Year In" on NPR's *Talk of the Nation*, Ralph Eubanks defined postracial first as an American society where race is no longer an impediment to progress and second as a color-blind society where one is first and foremost an American.[26] In Lee's and Simien's movies, as in *The Birth of a Nation*, however, race is very much the great divide planting the seed of disruption that Griffith underscored in his film's first intertitle. In this sense, the two movies are also reflexive markers in film history, because they actively focus on the ways that racial identities are constructed and contested through engagement with film and media at large.

Unlike many recent films and TV shows (ABC's *Scandal*, for instance), race is not a vanished concept that is no longer a societal issue. On the contrary, it is the very centrality of race that allows Simien and Lee to articulate plural post-postracial discourses documenting racial crises (even though *Bamboozled* is not a post-2008 Obama-era movie). The directors placed black characters in the lead roles not to silence racial tension but to "orient public attention to questions of society and morality"[27]—and, as Ronald Jacobs states in *Race, Media and the Crisis of Civil Society*, to foreground the way that, "in the modern media age, a crisis becomes a 'media event.'"[28] It is significant that each crisis in each film is mediated through a number of characters' viewpoints and broadcast live on TV, the internet, or the radio. Simien, like Lee, captures the various degrees of response to these crises of different African American individuals, focusing in minute detail on their experiences, interpretations, and performances of blackness. Coco Conners, for instance, a sophomore in economics at Winchester University, shapes her own narrative of identity politics on her blog and web videos by advocating assimilation and upward mobility. Her strategy to fit in directly contradicts Sam's. One opening shot shows Sam watching the news report about the race war triggered by Garmin Club House white students when they organized a blackface "Unleash Your Inner Negro" party for Halloween (fig. 10.8).

The flashback technique Simien uses to chronicle the development of the crisis on campus enhances what Ronald Jacobs calls "important elements for the different narratives of civil society and nation" and the way in which a "crisis produces a particular type of narrative lingering, which emphasizes not only the tragic distance between is and ought but also the possibility of heroic overcoming."[29] Samantha very much embodies the "distance between is and ought." She is only one of the multiple (stereo) types held up to critical scrutiny in *Dear White People*. As a complex illustration of varied types of racial consciousness in the Obama era, Sam is a locus of resistance to white patriarchal culture. Her second student film chronicles the blackface party crisis at Winchester. Called "Black Faces" in some ironic echo of the theme of the party, it no longer references Griffith's *The Birth of a Nation* but focuses on the students' differing versions of a real incident. Duplicating Simien's strategy, it gives a platform to the plurality of voices at play beyond Sam's own, as black and female. It reflects the ways that race affects Americans in real places and instantly draws her

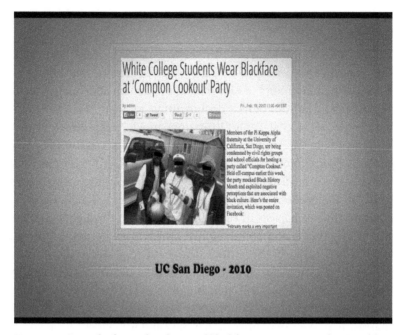

Figure 10.8. From the fictional to the actual blackface parties: *Dear White People*'s epilogue. *Screen capture by author.*

peers' critical acclaim. In the final shots however, Sam's angry ideological stance comes to an abrupt end when she publicly joins hands with her white boyfriend, Gabe, whom she had so far met in secret. The great black/white divide in American society is rendered temporarily irrelevant, the simple gesture dissolving the boundaries of race. This inverted variation on Griffith's unnatural biracial couple, Silas and Elsie, and visual echo of loving (white only) couples at the end of the film functions as yet another ironic comment on the final title cards in *The Birth of a Nation*, "Liberty and union" and "City of Peace."

In *Dear White People*'s epilogue, the shots of race-themed parties at major universities immediately impose a refiguration of the happy couple and their short-lived inscription of some postracial bliss. Rooted in the long tradition of using irony in African American culture mainly theorized by Henry Louis Gates Jr. in *The Signifying Monkey*, the visual contrapuntal effect achieved by such a stark contrast functions as "a metaphor for textual revision,"[30] for some new type of script "expos[ing] race not as resolved but as repressed."[31] The point seems to be that even if it provides an outlet to discuss the current state of race, there is no real resolution. The "distance" Ronald Jacobs refers to has been appreciated differently according to each individual student's perspective and seems to fit the least controversial version of the term postracialism as defined by Lawrence Bobo in his essay titled "Somewhere between Jim Crow and Post-Racialism." To Bobo, postracialism signals a merely hopeful trajectory for social trends and change to come.[32] Moreover, it seems that the concept can be apprehended in temporal terms. This moment in identity politics translates as a potentially dangerous place on the way to another state of interpersonal relations. As Tessa Thompson, who plays Samantha White, remarks, "I feel like we're in a space where we want to feel like we're post-racial until we're at a standstill about talking. Until there's these eruptions like the Trayvon Martin case, like what happened with the [Los Angeles] Clippers"[33] (when team owner Donald Sterling made racial remarks and, as a result, was banned from the NBA in 2014).

The films *Bamboozled* and *Dear White People* and their respective moments in interracial history provide specific representational spaces for such a conversation to unfold. It is a conversation that has been continuously developing and has steered away from Griffith's fantasy and revisionist exploration of racial and sexual politics and social justice in the newly unified white nation at the end of *The Birth of a Nation*. An additional meaning of "distance" could relate to the way the characters are very much written inside their racial references so that the presence of their black bodies is no longer a mere token erasing blackness, as seems to be the case in many portrayals of blacks in film and on television. In his *Sight and Sound* article "Black Like Us," Ashley Clark emphasizes that "*Bamboozled* and *Dear White People* are definitely new millennium texts in the way they deal with the production and effects of new media (dissemination of information on the internet plays a key role in both narratives). Yet tonally they hark back to a gaggle of weird, acidly humorous films that posed thorny questions about race in the turbulent aftermath of the Civil Rights movement, and the assassination of Martin Luther King, Malcolm X and Robert Kennedy."[34] Playing on the notions of mediation and amplification of messages by the new technologies, Lee and Simien aim to generate some form of change.

A wide variety of discourses are being relayed by major African American figures representative of the different sections of the black community, thus working against the normative Hollywood modus operandi and the versions of black identity created by the media. Both filmmakers underscore how the new media record and distort reality and materialize on-screen the

Figure 10.9. The end of Sam's second short film *Black Faces*: "Dear White People, . . . you know what, never mind!" *Screen capture by author.*

camera eye filming the moments of crisis. As Manthia Diawara puts it in "The New Blackface," they manage "to stereotype the stereotype," enabling the performers and creators to "fill all the spaces that the old stereotype occupied and to be the star of the new show" (fig. 10.9).[35]

In *Dear White People*, the final shot of Sam's second short film frames her looking straight at the camera, challenging us, the spectators, to have that valuable discourse on blackness, "to at least ask the questions," as Simien told Ann Lee in the July 2014 British Film Institute interview.[36] Sam's defiant look and pause materialize on-screen what Michael Jeffries calls "a gathering place"[37] when referring to Obama's role in American society.

To paraphrase the title of Denzel Washington's 2007 film, Sam has turned into a "great debater," bringing the possibility of such a postracial conversation into the public arena, mirroring Lee's and Simien's strategies when they went mainstream. Sam's suggestive silence at the end functions as the exact opposite of Elsie's shout for freedom at the end of *The Birth of a Nation*. Elsie's predetermined discourse was meant to impose a national identity not so much forged from within as violently imposed on the racial Other. Sam's script includes diversifying stories and testifies to her mastery of the media.

ANNE-MARIE PAQUET-DEYRIS is Professor of Film and TV Series Studies and African American Literature at Paris Nanterre University. She is editor with Marie-Hélène Bacqué, Amélie Flamand, and Julien Talpin of *The Wire: L'Amérique sur écoute*.

Notes

1. H. Roy Kaplan, *The Myth of Post-Racial America: Searching for Equality in the Age of Materialism* (Lanham, MD: Rowman & Littlefield Education, 2011); David J. Leonard and Lisa A. Guerrero, eds., *African Americans on Television: Race-ing for Ratings* (Santa Barbara, CA: Praeger, 2013).

2. Michael Rogin, *Blackface, White Noise: Jewish Immigrants in the Hollywood Melting Pot* (Berkeley: University of California Press, 1996), 121.

3. Robert Entman and Andrew Rojecki, *The Black Image in the White Mind: Media and Race in America* (Chicago: University of Chicago Press, 2000), 205.

4. Rupert Hughes, "A Tribute to 'The Birth of a Nation,'" in *The Birth of a Nation Original Programme* (New York: Epoch Producing, 1915), 9–12, New York Library Digital Collections, digitalcollections.nypl.org/items/510d47da-5b30-a3d9-e040-e00a18064a99#.

5. *The Birth of a Nation Original Programme*, 1.

6. Entman and Rojecki, *The Black Image*, 189.

7. Sam's short film within the film (24:33–25:50) also echoes Simien's own internet tests and adjustments when getting ready for the screenplay and movie. It will eventually evolve into an altogether different short at the end.

8. Entman and Rojecki, *The Black Image*, 82.

9. Michael Jeffries, *Paint the White House Black: Barack Obama and the Meaning of Race in America* (Stanford, CA: Stanford University Press, 2013), 32.

10. Ibid., 8.

11. Entman and Rojecki, *The Black Image*, 78.

12. Kris Collins, "White-Washing the Black-a-Moor: *Othello*, Negro Minstrelsy and Parodies of Blackness," *Journal of American Culture* 19, no. 3 (1996): 94.

13. "Shooting of Trayvon Martin," en.wikipedia.org/wiki/Shooting_of_Trayvon_Martin.

14. Ann Lee, "*Dear White People*: 'All We Had during Awards Season Were Tragic Depictions of the Black Experience,'" British Film Institute, July 14, 2015, www.bfi.org.uk/news-opinion/news-bfi/interviewers/dear-white-people-awards-season-tragic-depictions.

15. Malcolm X, "Difference between Separation and Segregation," speech, Michigan State University, January 1963, ccnmtl.columbia.edu/projects/mmt/mxp/speeches/mxt14.html.

16. Kent Ono, "*Mad Men*'s Postracial Figuration of a Racial Past," in *Mad Men, Mad World: Sex, Politics, Style, and the 1960s*, ed. Lauren Goodlad, Lilya Kaganovsky, and Robert Rushing (Durham, NC: Duke University Press, 2013), 300.

17. Valerie Palmer-Mehta, "Men Behaving Badly: Mediocre Masculinity and *The Man Show*," *Journal of Popular Culture* 42, no. 6 (2009): 1061.

18. Ono, "*Mad Men*'s Postracial Figuration," 315–316.

19. Toni Morrison, *Playing in the Dark. Whiteness and the Literary Imagination* (New York: Vintage Books, 1993), 6. Referring to the Americanness of *Huckleberry Finn*, Morrison also foregrounds the "interdependence of slavery and freedom, of Huck's growth and Jim's serviceability within it" (55).

20. Donald Bogle, *Toms, Coons, Mulattoes, Mammies, and Bucks: An Interpretive History of Blacks in American Films* (New York: Continuum, 1996).

21. Ibid., 27.

22. Ibid., 26.

23. Ibid., 27.

24. Ed Guerrero, ed., *Framing Blackness: The African American Image in Film* (Philadelphia: Temple University Press, 1993), 15.

25. Terry Gross, "'Dear White People' Is a Satire Addressed to Everyone," *Fresh Air*, NPR, October 16, 2014, https://www.npr.org/2014/10/16/356494289/dear-white-people-is-a-satire-addressed-to-everyone.

26. Ralph Eubanks, "'Post-Racial' Conversation, One Year In," *Talk of the Nation*, NPR, January 18, 2010, www.npr.org/templates/story/story.php?storyId=122701272.

27. Ronald Jacobs, *Race, Media and the Crisis of Civil Society: From Watts to Rodney King* (Cambridge: Cambridge University Press, 2000), 9.

28. Ibid., 9.

29. Ibid., 9.

30. Henry Louis Gates Jr., *The Signifying Monkey* (New York: Oxford University Press, 1988), 88.

31. Samantha Menard, "The Myth of Post-Racial Television" (unpublished paper, University of Long Island, 2014), 51.

32. Lawrence Bobo, "Somewhere between Jim Crow and Post-Racialism: Reflections on the Racial Divide in America Today," *Daedalus* 140, no. 2 (2011): 13.

33. Ed Rampell, "'Post-racial' *Dear White People* Comedy Premiering," *Mississippi Link*, October 9, 2014, 17.

34. Ashley Clark, "Black Like Us," *Sight and Sound* 25, no. 8 (August 2015): 35.

35. Manthia Diawara, "The New Blackface," in *Blackface*, ed. David Levinthal (Santa Fe, NM: Arena Editions, 1999), 15.

36. Lee, "*Dear White People.*"

37. Jeffries, *Paint the White House Black*, 156.

11

RACE, SPACE, SEXUALITY, AND SUFFERING IN *THE BIRTH OF A NATION* AND *GET HARD*

David C. Wall

As Anna Everett, in *Returning the Gaze: A Genealogy of Black Film Criticism*, makes clear, whatever may be said of D. W. Griffith's *The Birth of a Nation*, its "secure place in the annals of American and international film histories" is assured.[1] But how do we continue to make sense of this film—one of the key canonical texts of world cinema—especially at this particular historical moment, one hundred years after its first release? Formed by the adjudicating processes of assessment and investment that are the product of history and ideology, cultural canons inevitably both reflect and refract broader cultural discourses; and *The Birth of a Nation*'s continued presence and importance in the field speaks to the ongoing cultural and ideological labor in which it is engaged. In considering why it still matters, and the ways that we make sense of it as we try to describe, understand, and interpret, we need to think also of how its own sense-making structures work in relation to the multiple domains in which the film is situated. In other words, we must consider *how* it means as much as *what* it means.

Mainstream film studies and criticism—historically and institutionally white, of course—have routinely downplayed *The Birth of a Nation*'s overt and ugly racism in the promotion of its formal technique and artistic quality. This lenticular approach to the film suggests that its content and form are entirely separable elements of the cinematic experience and that we can simply choose to isolate one or the other. But, of course, this is a chimera. It is the effervescent dynamism of *The Birth of a Nation*'s structural qualities that so convincingly articulates the film's racial consciousness. The routine relegation of racial representation as a mere adjunct to the film's form is perhaps a paradigmatic example of the way in which the ideological structures of film studies as an academic discipline still attempt to coerce the viewer-critic into a presumptive sympathy with a white subject. However, notwithstanding the enormous amount of writing on *The Birth of a Nation* that lays claim to what, in a different context Benedict Anderson referred to as a "halo of disinterestedness,"[2] it is clear that, as James Snead puts it, in D. W. Griffith's *The Birth of a Nation*, "film form and racism coalesce into myth."[3] The film's formal elements are not separable from its political and ideological assertions. In short, its aesthetic is its racism.

We should keep in mind that this text is a living thing—not merely an artifact of the past but something constantly at work in the present, still laboring to assert its discursive and ideological claims, sitting as it does in constant conversation with much more recent texts. To quote Snead again, the mythifications of race are "political in nature . . . [and] continue to assert their presence today."[4] So we, as contemporary spectators, cannot, in any meaningful sense, remove ourselves from the history of this film or those subject positions we occupy that inform and inevitably shape our responses to it any more than we can remove ourselves from the multitude of discursive networks of history, race, and visuality that we (and the film) inhabit.

The Birth of a Nation's relationship to history is especially fascinating and complicated. The film makes a constant and committed effort to offer itself up as factual history as well as dramatic enactment and epic entertainment. In its strategic deployment of character, narrative, and plot, the film labors to provide a collective memory for its white audience rooted not in nationality or region but in race. Considering the contingent histories of its multiple (and constantly multiplying) contexts, we can think of *The Birth of a Nation*'s relationship to history in three distinct and inextricably related ways: first, the film claims to "document" the past as it purports to depict a history of things, events, people, and places as they actually were in the past; second, it is itself a document of history in that it is the product of the historical and cultural moment from which it emerges; and, third, it sees itself as an engine of history in that it has a clearly articulated political function.[5]

Considering how important history is, then, to Griffith's project, the apolitical approach of removing the aesthetic from the ideological is an even more remarkable strategy. Its presence and power in the service of whiteness has not emerged over time; this is no revisionist assessment but rather is present from its very inception. The National Association for the Advancement of Colored People's protests against the film along with an attendant "intense furor" resulting in "censorship, demonstrations, and race riots,"[6] were a corollary to the resurgence in interest and membership of the Ku Klux Klan that emerged in the wake of the film's release. As well as clearly indicating, as Ed Guerrero puts it, "how deadly serious the new medium, barely twenty years old, had become as a tool to create and shape public opinion and racial perceptions,"[7] that controversy reveals just how conscious the contemporary audience was of the absolute centrality of race to the film's significance.

Guerrero's emphasizing of the medium's newness is also critically important as cinema becomes a collision point for race and modernity. This new and dynamic technology of seeing and being constitutes perhaps the crucial arena of visuality to which black America both has access and is made subject/object of. In short, there is no cinematic technique, there is no aesthetic, there is no film without its racial representations. Without its black bodies, *The Birth of a Nation* does not exist. The extracinematic codes, then, that Snead's Barthesian reading of *The Birth of a Nation* argues both structure and support the construction of the racial subject in the film might be just as usefully considered as critical elements in the network of what Ella Shohat and Robert Stam refer to as that wider "orchestration of ideological discourses"[8] that constitute culture through the scopic regimes of race and space. And what we see codified in *The Birth of a Nation* we see reiterated repeatedly throughout the history of American cinema.

In choosing to read *Get Hard* (dir. Etan Cohen, 2015) in relation to *The Birth of a Nation*, I assert that those same scopic regimes remain in play in contemporary American film. Indeed, part of the purpose of the centennial symposium, "From Cinematic Past to Fast Forward Present: D. W. Griffith's *The Birth of a Nation*," held at Indiana University in 2015 and from which this volume is derived, was to demonstrate the profound and continued presence of Griffith's film across the landscape of American culture. It takes little effort to identify myriad films that, whether consciously or not, draw on the racial representations that coalesced in Griffith's epic. From *Judge Priest* (dir. John Ford, 1934) to *Guess Who's Coming to Dinner* (dir. Stanley Kramer, 1967) to *Django Unchained* (dir. Quentin Tarantino, 2012), American film unavoidably speaks race through the visual grammars of blackness cemented by *The Birth of a Nation*. In this respect, *Get Hard* is an especially interesting correlative text. Its release exactly one hundred years after *The Birth of a Nation* offers a neat historical confluence, but a greater significance resides in the film's central assertion that blacks are both the cause of (and corrective to) white suffering, along with a concurrent deployment of blackface as the central narrative conceit. Though *Get Hard*'s parsing of race is designed (I think) with the intention of playing with, and even subverting, those long-standing tropes and stereotypes, its failure in this task results in an inevitable retrenchment of racist imagery that, notwithstanding its intentions, proves no less pernicious than that in *The Birth of a Nation*.

My reading of these films is informed implicitly, if not explicitly, by Russian critic Mikhail Bakhtin's concept of the dialogic. Bakhtin has generated a veritable industry of scholarship since his works were introduced to the West in the 1960s and 1970s. The breadth of his thinking and range of analysis is extraordinary, but, as Martin Flanagan points out, it is dialogism that "provides the closest thing there is to a dominant metaphor in the Bakhtinian oeuvre."[9] In *The Dialogic Imagination*, an analysis of novelistic language in general and Dostoevsky in particular, Bakhtin asserts a fundamental argument that all meaning derives from dialogue—that is, the interaction between two actors or agents in history. Acknowledging that my description of Bakhtin's analysis here is necessarily superficial, it is important to at least gesture toward the complexity of his thought in this arena. Dialogism goes beyond merely a sense-making process of conversation, so to speak, and reaches to the very depths of the structures of subjectivity. Seeing the subject rooted in language puts Bakhtin in the company, of course, of many other linguists and philosophers of the twentieth century. But he moves beyond merely seeing identity rooted in language to understanding it as dialogue itself and, thus, a product of otherness at its most fundamental level. As Michael Holquist puts it, "in dialogism consciousness is otherness."[10] Further, "there is an intimate connection between the project of language and the project of selfhood: they both exist in order to mean."[11]

Critical to the project of dialogism, then, is an acknowledgement that understanding/sense making is a process—a constantly renegotiated settlement of meaning—rather than a terminal point of arrival. Approaching film this way forces an acknowledgment that our own relationship to the text is an ongoing process of discursive engagement rather than simply the passive consumption of product or the critical assessment of an object entirely external to ourselves. Our relationship to, and membership in, the discourse communities that surround the production, dissemination, and consumption of *The Birth of a Nation* and *Get Hard* mean that we play a crucial role in the constant recreation and redefinition of the text, just as it plays a role in ideologically making claims on us. The plethora of events, symposia, and conferences addressing the centenary of *The Birth of a Nation*'s release stands as compelling evidence for this.

Just as characters work dialogically within the frame of the film, viewers are also structured by their dialogic relationships to the events and utterances—in the broadest sense of that term—that they experience on the screen (as well as all that they experience beyond it.) As individual characters in the films are socially and cinematically constituted subjects, viewers are also socially and cinematically constituted subjects. So, while we as subjects are, of course, present and conscious in reality—in Bakhtin's own oft-repeated assertion, "there is no alibi for being"—at the same time, our subjectivity and selfhood are products of the roiling polyphonic discourses into which we are interpolated and through which we are individuated. Alterity—the inevitable, unavoidable, and constant dialogic presence of the other—is fundamentally constitutive of that self. While the febrile dynamics of alterity can help make sense of the ways in which the cinematic text plays a crucial role in the construction of the subject in a general sense, it seems peculiarly appropriate as a framework for reading *The Birth of a Nation*, which is already so overtly and profoundly structured on disgust toward and desire for a racial Other. However, while accepting that we make meaning of the text as much as we take meaning from the text, finding ourselves on ground that is always contestable and indeed always contested, no film is simply an inchoate or empty eruption waiting for us to pour meaning into it. Indeed, every text asserts a claim to an "official" reading, even though that claim is always doomed to failure.

I will turn to a discussion of *Get Hard* shortly, but first I want to consider *The Birth of a Nation* in terms of what Cedric Robinson refers to as its "neurotic sexuality,"[12] for it is *The Birth of a Nation*'s articulation of racial anxiety through that neurotic sexuality that most profoundly links it to *Get Hard*. There is not one moment in *The Birth of a Nation* when the residue and trace of white desire for the black body is not present, ghost-written through every frame. It may have been the case that, as Robert

Lang suggests, Griffith made the film in large part as a propaganda effort against miscegenation,[13] but as Martin Flanagan points out, "texts are perhaps at their most energetically meaningful when their contradictions are exposed."[14]

Notwithstanding the film's apparent desperate aversion to the idea of racial mixing, it gives itself up to a phobic fascination with the very thing it purports to disdain. A couple of well-known examples are instructive here. Consider the visual grammar of the infamous sequence in which Flora Cameron is pursued to her death by Gus, stroked as it is with an erotic charge derived from the excitement of the chase. Consider, too, the equally famous scene toward the end of the film with the "little party in the besieged cabin" as the film returns again and again to the threatened white female body and the tantalizing teasing possibilities of sexual violation and transgression. Fear and fascination here are always intertwined as what is socially marginal always becomes symbolically central. As Peter Stallybrass and Allon White put it, "disgust always bears the imprint of desire."[15] So, as the film consistently stakes its claim for the inviolable and fundamental purity of whiteness, it betrays an equally insistent fascination with a racial messiness that abjures purity, with an abjection pervading the margins where the racial system teeters constantly on the brink of collapse. The carefully demarcated spaces of whiteness—the cabin, the street, the Camerons' house, Flora's innocent body—are continually ruptured, and the boundaries repeatedly transgressed. In the process, these spaces become "privileged sites of male exchange, racial violence, erotic investment, and spectatorial interest."[16]

I would argue that one of the reasons for *The Birth of a Nation*'s success and endurance is that it extends to the deepest recesses of white subjectivity—not only in how it represents and portrays blackness on the screen but in its profound dialogical reliance on the structures of white desire for the black body. As Robert Lang notes, "the film's obsession with miscegenation is the key to its structure and meaning as melodrama."[17] And further, as Susan Courtenay argues, it is the compelling and irresistible fantasy of the "conjured threat of the black rapist" on which the film's entire "purifying project" is founded.[18]

This irresistible fantasy, though articulated in less explicit or overt ways, is no less consistent in much more recent American film. From *The Last King of Scotland* (dir. Kevin Macdonald, 2006) to *Cop Out* (dir. Kevin Smith, 2010) to *Django Unchained*, the same fascination with the black body that is so redolent of *The Birth of a Nation* adumbrates mainstream representations of race. The broad landscape of twenty-first-century Hollywood images of blackness functions as a reworked canvas for the "purifying project" to which Courtenay refers. And those same scopic registers that are at work in *The Birth of a Nation* continue their visual and cultural labor in *Get Hard* as the spatial and racial boundaries between white and black, rich and poor, free and imprisoned, gay and straight, are tantalizingly and continually collapsed and reconstituted. The implied gaze at this complicated and compelling spectacle of race, romance, disgust, and desire is perforce white, heterosexual, and male.

In addressing what she terms the "birth of the 'great white' spectator," Courtenay situates a fascinating link between *The Birth of a Nation* and early twentieth-century newsreel films of the great black heavyweight boxer Jack Johnson. The contradictory impulses of fear and fascination that the Johnson footage elicited in its white audiences speaks to a fundamentally voyeuristic relationship to blackness that of course existed prior to the emergence of film.[19] (Indeed, we might argue that the entire history of white visual representations of the black body is predicated on that desirous impulse to voyeurism.) Eastman Johnson's famous *Negro Life at the South* (1859) is only one emblematic—albeit especially telling—example in its mapping of the visual tropes and encodings that shape race as a profoundly scopic experience, validating the "white gaze" as it does.[20] But we also should consider the limitless range of advertisements, cartoons, blackface performance, antislavery propaganda, board games, book and magazine covers, and on and on and on. Every image is stroked with desire for the black body, placed ubiquitously as the visual property of the white gaze. Whether in abjection, subjection, trauma, service, or even death, the image of the black body is always and everywhere available for the enjoyment of the white spectator.

Even though the roiling ambivalence of disgust and desire that is the constant companion of these images was nothing new, the exciting technology of cinema allowed for these visual discourses to be constituted and disseminated in wholly new and modern ways. And as well as widening the arena for the subjection of the black body for a white audience, Courtenay argues that both the Jack Johnson newsreel films and *The Birth of a Nation* performed a critical function in serving up powerful cinematic "inscriptions" of "white suffering" and "agony." Further, "the image of a black man beating a white man has everything to do with the production of the image of a black man desiring a white woman."[21] White masculinity, then, is predicated on a nexus of anxiety where race, sex, violence, and desire collide.

Further, the profound linkages between the white spectator, the black body, and the act of violence serve as a network through which the fear of black sexual violence becomes reconstituted as a site of desire for that black body. At this moment of "profound representational struggle in American cinema,"[22] the white spectator is never merely watching a black image on the cinema screen but is being constantly dialogically constructed and individuated by that image. And white suffering is a critical element of that desire, as a node of discursive instability, in which the white subject may play with the compelling possibilities of that which it finds equally fearful and fascinating. From blackface through popular white appropriation of cultural and musical styles and language, those performative possibilities imply a dizzying set of complicated and contradictory narratives of resistance, rejection, and even liberation.[23]

As the landscape of visual culture is structured in relation to all other cultural and social domains, spatial nodes are critical to understanding the construction of the black body as a visual object. Built into the very possibilities that those bodies might represent is their spatial, as well as racial, circumscription; as the body is defined by those spaces to which it is granted or refused access, space is always and inevitably racialized. The boundaries of the cinema frame contain the black body just as it is contained within the carefully demarcated spaces of the cotton field, the big house, the slave quarters, or the ghetto. Part of the anxiety implicit in the scene in which Gus chases Flora Cameron—and which Griffith's celebrated cinematic technique creates—is the black body roaming, out of control, through space previously controlled by an ever-present—even if sometimes only implied—whiteness. The black body roaming free is an uncontrolled body, and the uncontrolled black body is deeply threatening. And so space itself allows for the scopic regimes of cinematic spectatorship as well as functioning as the literal and metaphorical center of a visual racial registry where fear, violence, and desire collide.

A brief sequence early in *The Birth of a Nation* demonstrates how even the most apparently innocent image is striated with this desire. The Northern Stoneman family are visiting their Cameron cousins in the South. As the Stonemans are shown around the Camerons' estate, an increasing affection develops between Phil Stoneman and Margaret Cameron. "Over the plantation to the cotton fields," the intertitles tell us, "By way of Love

Figure 11.1. The young white lovers walk together across Griffith's bucolic landscape. *Screen capture by author.*

Valley," we follow the young lovers as Griffith employs several cinematic techniques to draw viewers in to the burgeoning romance, not least a scene of pastoral, prelapsarian innocence as they stand together in the far distance of a picturesque landscape (fig. 11.1).

As we move through the frames of the film, we move through the development of this romance as the lovers walk on, all of which demands a discursive set of exchanges that are structured in terms of both race and space. The narrative of white romance—white desire—is given a rather odd charge by its acting out at the point of the laboring black body. As the lovers walk in long shot across Love Valley, the scene fades to a short documentary-like sequence of close-up and medium shots of slaves picking cotton. As Griffith lingers on those real black bodies working in the field, the white lovers enter the frame. With the whites now in medium shot, the background is filled with black slaves. In this brief sequence, Griffith structurally links white romantic desire to the black laboring body. The space of romance is simultaneously the space of racial violence and abjection, and the spatial relationship established between the white and black bodies in this sequence is a perfect visual embodiment of the broader social structures of race. Those white and black bodies are present simultaneously and yet entirely separated; the laboring black body is relegated to the rear of the scene as the carefree young white cousins wander throughout, always facing out toward us, standing with their backs to reality and, perhaps, to history. This sequence not only emphasizes that white desire is fundamentally predicated on the marginalized black body but also reinforces the spatial demarcations of race while showing the permeability of those boundaries.

This burgeoning romance occurs at the beginning of the film and thus serves as the foundation for the suturing of North and South through their shared foundational whiteness. It also asserts the essentially benign nature of white power. The spaces occupied by these happy and laboring black bodies is neat, controlled, and well ordered, precisely because they are being carefully husbanded by the gentle, guiding hand of white paternalism. But as the narrative progresses and the Reconstruction period begins, the film portrays the breakdown of the spatial order as a direct consequence of the breakdown of the racial order. From the notorious scene in the statehouse to the white residents of Piedmont being accosted in the streets by newly liberated blacks, from the infamous black Gus rape sequence to the besieging of the Camerons' cabin toward the film's end, the spatial ordering of blackness is defined by criminality and chaos.

This visual encoding of racial power as spatial power becomes a standard Hollywood trope from *The Birth of a Nation* to the present day, and Etan Cohen's *Get Hard* is merely one of the latest iterations of Griffith's spectacle of space and race. Considering *Get Hard* in dialogic relation to *The Birth of a Nation*, we can identify how the films mean in similar ways and draw them together through a consideration of the way space, race, and the black body are all utilized as critical elements in the experience of looking. Fundamentally, their shared structures of meaning are predicated on the establishment and maintenance of boundaries and markers—both literal and figurative—that allow for the constant renewal and relegitimation of the scopic regimes of whiteness so that space itself becomes the site at which, through which, and from which the film is asking us to understand it. As the white gaze is defined by a scopophilic obsession with the black body, we might expect those spaces to not only speak whiteness but also be eroticized in some way. Desire for the black body can be thought of, then, as a suturing element for a white gaze that links space and race. More than this, characterized by that same neurotic sexuality that Cecil Robinson identifies as pervading *The Birth of a Nation*, *Get Hard* utilizes space as critical to the construction and performance of race as it situates white suffering at its discursive and ideological center.

Starring Will Ferrell as multimillionaire financial wizard James King, framed for embezzlement and sentenced to ten years in federal prison, *Get Hard* opens with King's white body in the agony of despair. Establishing the centrality of white suffering for the ensuing narrative, King fills the frame, weeping and wailing, his body in heaving spasms. Then the film flashes back to "one month ago"; an aerial long shot shows a Bel Air street sign as a black SUV enters the zone of privileged whiteness below. The camera then tracks through James King's house, arriving ultimately in his bedroom via a montage of interiors that serve as banally predictable signifiers of wealth (expensive furniture, housekeepers, gardeners, a wine cellar) and slightly more subtly coded signifiers of whiteness. At the same time, the sound track plays Iggy Azalea's "Fancy." This jarring eruption of "blackness" into such a carefully controlled and contained white space gestures toward the oncoming and imminent collapse of cultural and racial boundaries on which the film's narrative is predicated. But, of course, Iggy Azalea is not black. A white Australian performer who has adopted the language and style of contemporary African American rap, her presence points to the complexity of race as performance that adumbrates the film.

The configuring of race and space continues throughout the lengthy opening and credits sequence as a series of juxtapositions contrasts the material circumstances of the lives of the two main characters. Cuts of Bel Air and the unidentified "ghetto" shift from King's mansion to a rundown city neighborhood street (with the predictable cop car driving slowly by) and then to the interior of the house of Darnell Lewis (Kevin Hart), where we see him on the phone discussing a mortgage problem. We then see Lewis's daughter entering school through a metal detector as yet another cop drives by. This spatialization of race through stereotypical signifiers of blackness, criminality, and violence is linked to the legitimizing presence of white authority. The two domestic circumstances are also contrasted: King's is wealthy, well ordered, clean, quiet, highly controlled, and sterile; Lewis's is messy, chaotic, noisy, and yet warm and loving. The high/low dichotomy of their lives is perhaps best encapsulated by the sequence of split-screen images of the two men arriving simultaneously at the same workplace. In the upper half of the screen, James King strides into the building's foyer and up the escalator. In the screen's bottom half, Darnell Lewis drives his battered flatbed truck into the basement (fig. 11.2).

Figure 11.2. James King strides purposefully up the stairs while Darnell Lewis drives into the basement parking garage. The image reflects the film's spatial articulation of racial hierarchy. *Screen capture by author.*

The first physical contact between the two characters comes when King goes to collect his car, which has been left with Lewis's cleaning company (which operates out of the basement of King's office building). There is some brief confusion when King assumes that Lewis is trying to mug him. With the confusion sorted out, King asserts that he would have reacted in exactly same way had Lewis been white. This comic scene reveals the film's effort to consciously engage with contemporary discourses around cultural representations of race. This effort is demonstrated even more clearly in the film's theatrical poster (fig. 11.3). The image of Will Ferrell having his hair put into cornrows by Kevin Hart is a self-conscious and comic gesture toward the presence and power of visual stereotypes. Its visual charge comes from a comic inversion whereby a white middle-age businessman is sporting "black" hair. This series of significations can be read as a twenty-first-century movie winking knowingly at its audience as it lays claim to a sophisticated understanding of the workings of race as performance. But in other ways, the movie is merely the stage for a blackface performance in the grand tradition of minstrelsy.

During the early years of cinema, conventions of blackface performance were carried over from other arenas of entertainment. No less than in vaudeville or music halls, performers and audiences were never seduced

Figure 11.3. Blackface part 1: *Get Hard* theatrical release poster.

into thinking they were seeing black performers. Indeed, the point for white spectators was that they were quite deliberately and purposefully enjoying whites performing their fantasies of blackness. Like other films of the period, *The Birth of a Nation* employs both white and black actors, but the principal black characters are always played by whites. In *The Birth of a Nation*, Gus (played by Walter Long) metonymically embodies the entire structure of white fascination with black sexuality as obsessive, repressed, and denied, and phobic in its return. To have a black actor in the role would demand an acknowledgment of that fascination. But a white actor allows for the portrayal to be shifted through a second-order representation so that blackness and black male sexuality become a dominant fetish for a white—especially male—gaze. Blackface in film allows a safe space for white fantasies of transgression and desire, because the overt and explicit nature of blackness as performance always allows for the arresting of the fantasy at a point of complete abandonment and the terror that whiteness may disappear forever. As that is true for Walter Long as Gus, it is true for Will Ferrell as James King.[24]

While the film's knowing allusion to "blacking-up" asserts a consciousness of the operative discourses of race, it simultaneously—and perhaps much less self-consciously—articulates the freedom with which whiteness may choose to shift through the sets of visual significations and codifiers of blackness at will. In doing so, *Get Hard* employs the kind of complex and contradictory visual and narrative strategies seen in all interracial buddy films. The film's racial awareness must be situated in, and lay claim to, the violence of history so that it may then be allowed the fantasy suturing of those racial antagonisms. In other words, for the gags about stereotyping to work, the narrative must acknowledge the realities of the racial discourses outside the frame. At the same time, the narrative wants to sit outside a history in which all mainstream Hollywood systems of representation are designed to please, tease, and titillate the white eye. The ambiguity surrounding the labor of these multivalent racial, ethnic, and cultural signifiers points to the complexity of demarcations that are both fluid and flexible.

The confrontation of the boundary is always a process of pleasure as well as policing. As the film's narrative unfolds, we follow James King's body as it is constantly being reconstituted at the boundary of black and white. And it is at those critical boundary points of rejection and reconstitution that King ultimately seeks and finds his redemption, for if it is anything, *Get Hard* is a film about salvation. And that salvation is realized through his performance of blackface.

In this moment, there is a fascinating further correspondence around blackface as a performative strategy to be made with *The Birth of a Nation*. In Griffith's film, the faithful black servants, who offer a form of racial, political, and even transcendental salvation to the whites, are performing blackface in a number of complicated ways. Within the frame of the film, a certain performance of blackness is defined and demanded by the whites. Reliant for their own (literal and figurative) white existence on the black bodies surrounding them, the Stonemans and Camerons need blackness to be performed in very specific ways and along a spectrum from the "faithful souls" to the animalistic black Gus. But without the frame of the film, that same cultural labor, undertaken by both black and white actors, is being performed for the film's white audience. *Get Hard* struggles with this complex process in its self-reflexive and self-conscious invocation of the problematics of blackface. Though making a sincere attempt at a kind of metarendering of race that would deplete blackface of its aggressive power, the film can never escape the form's troubled history. In this sense, as a product of Hollywood, *Get Hard* cannot be seen as anything but in direct conversation with *The Birth of a Nation* and the broader history of racial representation in American cinema. And that history tells us, time and time again, that white bodies under threat are rescued by blacks. Moving beyond Griffith, however, there is a significant difference in that James King is redeemed not only by the presence and faithful service of Darnell Lewis but also by his own abjection and suffering as part of the process of his *becoming* black.

Knowing that he will be unable to cope with the ten-year stretch in prison that he is imminently to begin, King employs the services of Lewis to "teach" him how to survive in prison. But survival in this context really functions as a second-order metonymic signification. What King actually wants is Lewis to teach him how to be black, because it is through the codifications and discourses of blackness that King believes he will be able to avoid suffering and trauma. But there is a complicated paradox at work here. The suffering to which Lewis subjects King by way of toughening him up—getting him hard—for prison becomes a mode of resistance and redemption. But, of course, it is merely the playing out of suffering and trauma, the fantasy gesture of a white body choosing to subject itself to those disciplinary and carceral processes to which the real black body in history has been unwillingly and ubiquitously consigned.

The demeaning and debasing of the white body by a powerful black figure recalls that earlier fascination that was folded into both the spectatorial experience of watching the Jack Johnson newsreels and the sense of white victimhood that pervades *The Birth of a Nation*. As Darnell Lewis turns James King's house into a prison, suffering is then spatialized with the tennis court now the "yard" and the wine cellar now the "cell." This triangulation of race, space, and trauma struggles to elide the fundamental paradox at the heart of white fear of and fascination with black bodies. James King is terrified of being black, of being made subject to the demeaning, dehumanizing traumas and agonies of a black body; and yet he is simultaneously demanding that he be made subject to those very same processes of abuse and abjection.

Blackface as a central comic conceit is made explicit in the film, most notably when Lewis decides to take King to meet his gang-banging cousin Russell in the "hood." Explaining that Russell is "very suspicious of outsiders. You walking in there they're probably going to think you're a cop off the bat," the following telephone conversation takes place:

DL: "I need you to do something for me so that we don't create any dangerous situations."

JK: Blackface?

DL: What the fuck was that?!

JK: I'll see you tomorrow. [he hangs up quickly]

DL: James! James! Don't do nothing stupid. Just dress casual.

This exchange sets up the visual gag for the next scene, when, the next morning, Lewis arrives at King's house to collect him. A close-up of Lewis's incredulous face as King exits his house cuts to a brief sequence shot and edited like a music video. With Nicki Minaj's "Beez in the Trap" playing on the sound track, King walks in slow motion toward Lewis's car, his gardener and ground staff dancing in the background. Dressed, as he explains to Lewis, "like L'il Wayne," King is, indeed, in blackface (fig. 11.4).

The blackface issue is raised again when the two men arrive at Russell's house. With King sitting low to the floor surrounded by various members of the Crenshaw Kings, Russell sits opposite (in every sense) embodying a supposedly authentic black heteromasculinity. King explains: "I need

Figure 11.4. Blackface part 2: Will Ferrell as James King as Li'l Wayne. *Screen capture by author.*

protection and I'm hoping to join the Crenshaw Kings," to which, through riotous laughter, Russell replies: "I've seen white people before but you motherfucker, man, you white as mayonnaise." He laughs. "Oh shit, maybe in blackface, who knows?" Causing King to look subtly in admonishment at Lewis, Russell's reference to blackface asserts again the film's self-conscious employment of race as a cultural signifier. But this is within the context of a scene that otherwise confirms and affirms the structures of a scopic regime that is committed to negotiating scenes of normative blackness as hostile, violent, drug-ridden, hypersexualized, and hypermasculinized. And even in this blackest of black spaces, encoded in the most aggressively banal and predictable significations of the ghetto, the white body will always assert order and control over the black body. It will always demand the authority to make the space its own. Because whiteness always demands something of blackness—nurturing, rescuing, labor—the black body is thus always to be available for the use of whites. By the end of this scene, King has asserted his racial and spatial authority as he begins to reconstitute the gang structure along the lines of a hedge fund company.

Later in the film, hopeless that his innocence will ever be proven and having argued with Lewis, King returns to the Crenshaw Kings. Once more in blackface, though now dressed in dark clothes without any of the comic edge supplied by the lurid colors of his previous incarnation, King is at the

Figure 11.5. Blackface part 3: Will Ferrell as James King as
stereotype thug. *Screen capture by author.*

point of becoming a member of the gang (fig. 11.5). Though this scene still
relies on the comic inversions of blackface seen previously, it takes a far
more serious turn. Russell asks: "You ready to get put on the hood?" to
which King replies, "I'm rollin'!"

The scene cuts immediately to a party with a montage sequence of King
drinking, smoking, dancing, fooling around with a young woman, and finally
being handed a gun. In voice-over, Russell explains: "Once you step through
this threshold, motherfuckers are ready to kill for you. I mean a whole fraternity of motherfuckers is gonna have your back. But there's only one way
outta this. That's when your casket drops into the ground. So from this day
forward you have eternal protection until your eternal demise." A cut shows
Russell looking intently into King's face. Pointing to the front door, Russell
says: "We're dead-ass serious about what we do. And if you go through that
threshold and make it back we're gonna be dead-ass serious about you."

This talk of threshold returns space, spatiality, and the boundary to the
critical center of our analysis of race and identity. James King is in blackface, playing out a white fantasy of "nigga" blackness. But once he completes
his initiation—once he steps through the threshold and moves beyond the
boundary—his whiteness will be forever compromised. Having given up all
hope, King is prepared to take that final step, to embrace suffering and cede
his whiteness. For King, fulfilling the narrative and visual logic of Hollywood, to be black is to have no path to redemption. But fulfilling that other
well-worn narrative path of Hollywood, at the final moment of exchange,
King is rescued by his faithful black friend as Lewis reaches Russell's house
in time to dissuade King from his course of action: "James, you've got a

choice right now. You've got the right path, you've got the wrong path. Make the right decision James." King does, and he leaves with Lewis. Once they are in the car together, King reverts from the heavy-handed, hard-drinking, dope-smoking gangsta to the panicky, fearful milquetoast he was previously. Having been saved by the good and faithful Lewis, King reassumes the coded visual and linguistic signifiers of whiteness. Indeed, it is, in fact, King's whiteness that Lewis has redeemed.

Just as the bounded space within *The Birth of a Nation* is traversed by whites at will, so too in *Get Hard*, as demonstrated by King's moving in and out of the "ghetto," there is no space that is not ultimately available to the white body, even if it demands blackface as payment for entry. However, there is one moment when King's whiteness has nowhere to retreat and becomes fully feminized and fully victimized. As part of his reconfiguring of the Bel Air mansion as a prison, Lewis has turned King's tennis court into a prison exercise yard, in which King becomes wholly subject to the disciplinary violences of a reconfigured racial authority. As Lewis literally acts out a conflict between a black and a Latino prisoner, King is pushed from one to the other and determined solely by his whiteness, refused any control of space that is constructed as a field of sexual as well as racial collapse and reconstitution.

His moment of safety comes when he is adopted by a third character, a gay character, who claims King as his own sexual property. James King's overriding and repeated anxiety—the critical node of his abjection and suffering—is to be made the victim of sexual assault. Stuck in the prison yard, King's whiteness is no longer the determining factor in the legitimacy of occupation of space—it can no longer assert its unexamined authoritative presence either to occupy spaces it chooses to or to demarcate the occupation of space by others. It is in this disruption of space that we see enfolded the disruption of whiteness and heteromasculinity; to lose control of space is to lose previously held racial and gendered power. Predicated on the profound linkage between space, power, and sexuality, the loss of spatial authority carries with it the loss of racial and sexual authority. In that sense we might read King's sexual anxieties as second-order significations over the loss of racial and spatial authority. The singular and obsessive fear of sexual assault is mediated through the critical boundary of race, for the certainties of race collapse through the realization of and subjection of the self to sexual desire. The film begins with, and returns unendingly to, this neurotic fear revealing (and reveling in) its fundamental fascination. When

James King first encounters Darnell Lewis and tells him that he will be going to San Quentin, Lewis reacts in horror:

> You know what, let me give you my statistical analysis. You going to San Quentin, there's a hundred percent chance you're going to be somebody's bitch. Ten years of this [he slams one hand into the other repeatedly]. You know what that is? That's a big ass black man on your pale white ass [he repeats the gesture even more aggressively] ugh, ugh, ugh, ugh. You [he gestures to King and affects a whiny, high-pitched voice]: "No, I don't want any more, stop, that's enough!" Too late, he done tagged the next guy in. [He gestures even more rapidly and aggressively with his hands.] That's like a rabbit. You don't want him no more, so now here comes the guy who wants to rub your face. Guess what, you can look forward to ten years of it.

Sometime later, having tried in vain to teach him to fight, and with only twelve days before he is incarcerated, Lewis decides that there is only one other option for King: "I got a plan. You're gonna learn how to suck dick." Over lunch at "LA's number one gay hook-up scene," Lewis explains that, "bottom line, we're talking about survival," and therefore King must go to the bathroom and "politely" ask someone, "Do you mind if I give you a little head?" Exhibiting that dizzying combination of neurotic fear and phobic fascination, the film has King on his knees in a bathroom stall with a pickup from the restaurant. In an extended slow-motion sequence, with his eyes tightly closed and his mouth gaping open, King moves his head toward the man's groin. Inching ever more slowly forward, the teasing possibility of the transgression of this final boundary is drawn out for as long as possible. Inevitably, however, at the very last moment, King turns his head away in horror. Returning to the table and admitting his failure, Lewis demands loudly of King: "Are you ready to get hard?" to which King replies, "I am ready! I am ready to get hard! I'm gonna show you how hard!" Lewis responds: "That's what I want to hear so let's go home and get hard!" Having been granted the pleasures and possibilities of a transgression ultimately refused, it is not difficult to imagine that the standing applause given to King and Lewis by the other diners as they leave the restaurant is really an eruption of congratulatory relief demanded of the audience by the film itself.

As the boundaries (both figurative and literal) of race, space, and sexuality are structured, threatened, dismantled, and reconstituted, their visual encoding constitutes the social and discursive parameters of whiteness, blackness, and heteronormativity. As the contradictions in Griffith's film rupture its drive for textual purity, *Get Hard* labors to convince viewers of its knowing postracial sensibility while mired in the trammeled racial representations it purports to undermine. But more than this, these texts live, work, breathe, and speak whiteness together. I am, of course, not suggesting that *Get Hard* was explicitly influenced by *The Birth of a Nation* or that it is even in any way self-consciously responding to it or is overtly racist in that sense. Indeed, by playing with recognizable tropes and discourses, *Get Hard* attempts to situate itself as beyond the vulgarities of Griffith's unreconstructed racism. But there is a mutually constitutive reciprocity between the texts that is constituted by the film's relationship to the spectator, the history of film, and indeed the entire history of Western culture. In other words, these objects are being constantly reconstituted as they turn toward and away from each other, as they encounter reflections, refractions, and resonances. It is clear that the narratives of race critical to *The Birth of a Nation* are present in any number of ways in contemporary cinema—indeed across contemporary culture—without those links having to be in any way deliberate or necessarily obvious. As with *The Birth of a Nation*, a critical sense-making structure in *Get Hard* is the spatialization of race in service to a scopic regime that asserts the normativity of the white, heterosexual gaze. By getting spectators to look (and in the looking, of course, is everything), sexuality, race, and power collide in the demarcation of space. There is no way to avoid our interpolation into the communities of meaning that surround the text. It is not so much that we approach the text to read it dialogically, but that dialogism structures the text. It is our job to unpack the dialogical processes in order to understand the broader relationships between the social, the political, and the aesthetic. The "singular [generic] text" can only be fully understood when situated in relation "principally to other systems of representation."²⁵ These texts make claims to certain meanings that we can assess, understand, interpret, and reinterpret.

Finally, and perhaps most significantly, both *The Birth of a Nation* and *Get Hard* are movies that assert white suffering as their dominant visual, discursive, and rhetorical trope. The presence and function of blackface speaks to deep anxieties over the white body being demeaned, dehumanized, beaten, and abused. The attendant tropes of white victimhood can be read in different ways. For instance, for *The Birth of a Nation*'s audience in 1915, it might be surrounding discourses of post–Civil War Southern resentment; for *Get Hard*, we might point to debates surrounding affirmative action. But it is all too easy to see the fundamental shared structures of whiteness that inform both of those broader discourses. Constructed through the arrangement of spaces of trauma (battlefields of the South, the prison cell and prison yard), both films triangulate race, space, and suffering. Equally, there is always present a profound fascination for those spaces in which whiteness may play out in fantasies of abjection, promising the compelling vision and experience of boundary collapse. What the assault on the decorous boundaries of white life in both *The Birth of a Nation* and *Get Hard* conveys—beset as the films are by the specters of racial abjection and sexual violence—is that there is no redemption without suffering. Though *Get Hard* might grant the modern eye a set of images that allow for the playing out of white fantasies about being black that *The Birth of a Nation* could only hint at, both films share the most profound assertion that it is white suffering—not black—that is at the heart of the American experience.

DAVID C. WALL is Associate Professor of Visual and Media Studies at Utah State University. He is editor with Michael T. Martin of *The Poetics and Politics of Black Film: Nothing But a Man*, and editor with Michael T. Martin and Marilyn Yaquinto of *Race and the Revolutionary Impulse in The Spook Who Sat by the Door*.

Notes

1. Anna Everett, *Returning the Gaze: A Genealogy of Black Film Criticism* (Durham, NC: Duke University Press 2001), 59.

2. Benedict Anderson, *Imagined Communities: Reflections on the Origin and Spread of Nationalism* (London: Verso, 1998).

3. James Snead, "Birth of a Nation," *White Screen/Black Images: Hollywood from the Dark Side* (New York: Routledge, 1994), 39.

4. Ibid.

5. This idea is explicated more widely and in relation to history film generally in Michael T. Martin and David C. Wall, "The Politics of *Cine-Memory*: Signifying Slavery in the History Film," in *A Companion to the Historical Film*, ed. Robert A. Rosenstone and Constantin Parvulescu (Chichester, UK: John Wiley), 445–467.

6. Gerald R. Butters, *Black Manhood on the Silent Screen* (Lawrence: University Press of Kansas, 2002), 66.

7. Ed Guerrero, *Framing Blackness: The African American Image in Film* (Philadelphia: Temple University Press, 1993), 15.

8. Ella Shohat and Robert Stam, *Unthinking Eurocentrism: Multiculturalism and the Media* (New York: Routledge, 1994), 180.

9. Martin Flanagan, *Bakhtin at the Movies: New Ways of Understanding Hollywood Film* (Basingstoke, UK: Palgrave Macmillan, 2009), 5.

10. Michael Holquist, *Dialogism: Bakhtin and His World* (London: Routledge, 2002), 18.

11. Ibid., 23.

12. Cedric Robinson, *Forgeries of Memory and Meaning: Blacks and the Regimes of Race in American Theater and Film before World War II* (Chapel Hill: University of North Carolina Press, 2007), 98.

13. Quoted in ibid., 104.

14. Flanagan, *Bakhtin at the Movies*, 183.

15. Peter Stallybrass and Allon White, *The Politics and Poetics of Transgression* (Ithaca, NY: Cornell University Press, 1988).

16. Susan Courtenay, *Hollywood Fantasies of Miscegenation: Spectacular Narratives of Gender and Race* (Princeton, NJ: Princeton University Press, 2005), 62.

17. Robert Lang, "*The Birth of a Nation*: History, Ideology, Narrative Form," in *The Birth of a Nation*, ed. Robert Lang (New Brunswick, NJ: Rutgers University Press, 1994), 17.

18. Courtenay, *Hollywood Fantasies*, 64.

19. As well as the complicated visual spectacles of race that blackface minstrelsy embodied and demanded from both performer and audience, every element of popular and material culture of the nineteenth century—from advertising to postcards to children's games to food products to sheet music and on and on—featured black bodies in myriad states of subjection, abjection, and transgression. This ubiquitous presence in American visual culture throughout the period (and onward to the present day, we might add) is testimony to its compelling fascination for the white spectator.

20. See my longer discussion of Eastman Johnson's painting in David Wall, "Transgression, Excess, and the Violence of Looking in the Art of Kara Walker," *Oxford Art Journal* 33, no. 3 (2010): 277–299.

21. Courtenay, *Hollywood Fantasies*, 50.

22. Ibid.

23. There has been much critical work over the last couple of decades in this area, but readers unfamiliar with the broader arguments around the complexity of blackface as a cultural and racial modality should begin with the groundbreaking Eric Lott, *Love and Theft: Blackface Minstrelsy and the American Working Class* (Oxford: Oxford University Press, 1993).

24. This argument that blackface historically provided a complex arena for whites to act out a myriad of social, cultural, and racial anxieties and ambivalences has been asserted and complicated by any number of writers over the last couple of decades, not least in Lott, *Love and Theft*.

25. Robert Stam, *Film Theory* (Walden, MA: Wiley-Blackwell, 2000), 203.

12

ANGER OR LAUGHTER? THE DIALECTICS OF RESPONSE TO *THE BIRTH OF A NATION*

Chuck Kleinhans

IN 1980, SPIKE LEE MADE A TWENTY-MINUTE FILM as his first-year MFA project at New York University (NYU). The film, titled *The Answer*, was an angry response to *The Birth of a Nation*, and it caused controversy.[1] The film depicts an unemployed black screenwriter/director who agrees to write and direct a remake of D. W. Griffith's famous 1915 work. But when he realizes he can't do it, his decision prompts the Ku Klux Klan to burn a cross on his lawn. The final image shows the writer running out, knife in hand, to confront the racists. Lee states that, in his time at NYU, *The Birth of a Nation* was taught as a masterpiece, and, most pertinently and egregiously, the faculty validated it but never mentioned that the film promoted a Ku Klux Klan revival that directly contributed to the lynching of many black people. *The Answer* obviously prefigures Lee's satiric feature *Bamboozled* (2000), in which black creative media folks produce a program based in buffoonish racist stereotypes, which turns out to be, against their plans, spectacularly successful.

I explore two aspects of this situation, using it as the hinge of a diptych to consider, on one side, the critical standing of Griffith's epic, which has stirred angry responses since it was first exhibited, and, on the other side, comic satiric responses to the film, the Ku Klux Klan, and contemporary media racism. In addition to dividing the essay in this way, I use the endnotes to create another layer of critical commentary. Thus, a relatively fluid and quick discourse in the main body will be complicated and elaborated by a different layer of consideration.

One: *The Birth of a Nation* at Fifty in Bloomington, Indiana

My Blu-ray copy of *The Birth of a Nation* has the following promotion tag on the back cover: "One of the greatest American movies of all time!"[2] I dispute that. While *greatest* is obviously a flexible and highly subjective term, and easily recognized by most Americans over a certain age as advertising hyperbole, it remains widely used and granted at least passive consent in art criticism. I want to ask why the term can be used so casually and to point out the political and ideological flaw in still using it. I suggest that we simply laugh at *The Birth of a Nation* and dismiss this pretension of its universal quality.

I say this not to be critical of the historical research that has been done on the film. Historical research into the text itself and into the film's context and reception is absolutely useful, necessary, and important. Nor do I argue that the film is not significant in film history for its often-noted innovations: feature length, epic spectacle, road-show presentation, intervention in popular imagining of history, and (some) changes in acting style and narrative crosscutting. The fact is that it was (more or less) the first film to bring these elements together.

What I address here is different: Is this precise film in any way meaningful (or threatening) in the United States today? Does it deserve an angry response? And my answer to both questions is no. The film is laughable, and it is worth dismissing by ridicule. I know that some people think the film is still dangerous, despicable, and worthy of censorship—or at least "trigger warnings." But I hope to persuade them that *The Birth of a Nation* is long past its sell-by date as effective race propaganda. The world has moved on. Not that racism isn't still a major issue and problem in the search for justice in the United States; but it is present and enacted and expressed and opposed in very different ways today. It is very present in the recent ebb and flow of 2016 presidential campaign politics, when issues involving race and nationality are being worked out in a diverse set of issues: police violence against black people, Islamophobia, deportation of undocumented immigrants, and so forth. In this larger framework, the residual issues of the US history of slavery, the Civil War, and the unfinished work of Reconstruction have a different nature and resonance. At its most visible, this racist nostalgia appears as the new lost cause of flying the Confederate battle flag and maintaining monuments and place names of the Confederacy. But that should not distract us from the central organizing goal of stopping police violence on black people in the short run and creating social and economic justice in the long run.

But I want to return to the term *greatest* and pull it apart a bit. How is it that such a racist film became commonly labeled "one of the greatest," or a "masterpiece," or a "landmark"? Of course, the film's owners and promoters would understandably use such terms to attract the public to screenings. But how is it that the field of film studies has frequently fallen into the same pattern? To answer that question, I look not at the centennial of *The Birth of a Nation* but at the fiftieth anniversary, in 1965.

Several things were going on at that time that we might not be aware of today. First of all, many people who cared about film and film history at that point were old enough to have actually seen earlier screenings of the film, or to remember Griffith's funeral in the immediate post–World War II era. And this actually makes a difference. In a time when people did not have ready and personal access to films of the past (as we do today with video recordings, DVDs, and streaming), they relied on their own knowledge and memory of screenings they had attended. This was the (perhaps golden) age of the film society—a nonprofit cultural enterprise, typically in college communities, organized to make important films from the past available as examples of film art.[3] And it was the dawn of the college-level film course, with the introductory courses usually organized around "masterpieces" and historical surveys of important films.

Today we can see the mid-1960s as a watershed moment in film studies.[4] An older generation had faced the uphill struggle of getting movies recognized as an authentic art. Largely they did this by evoking an old-fashioned rhetoric of art world concerns, which admitted that, in literary critic Edmund Wilson's terms, there were "classics and commercials," and that most cinema fell in the latter camp. But, the proponents argued, some films were indeed art, and masterpieces, modern classics. Thus, a canon of worthy works was a major articulation of this belief.[5]

As film studies expanded in the 1960s, moving from the former platform of journalistic film reviewing to the prospects of the academy, the older model was revised in terms of slightly different norms. To establish film within the academy, the field had to face the already validated arts, particularly literature and visual arts, and make a convincing case that film (1) was an art form unto itself, (2) contained important works, and (3) was made by recognized artists. The doctrine of authorship provided an important scaffolding to this construction. Against the fact that feature narrative film was very much an industrial product, financed as an entertainment business, aimed at making a profit, and based in a collaborative art process, authorship allowed for genius or master artists. D. W. Griffith was easily interpreted in this way because he had achieved notable works over a long span of time. He had also clearly advanced cinematic narration and drama in a sequential pattern that showed development. In this frame, *The Birth of a Nation* was validated as not just a major or notable work (which it certainly is in Griffith's career) but with the attached honor of being a masterpiece or classic—that is, as art. Understanding this casual slide from one category to another and receiving validation in the process depends on sorting out several factors.

First, there is a confusion between historical development and art. Art history, in particular, has tended to project an evolutionary model of aesthetics. Each successive art movement was taught as facing and overcoming and transcending the limits of the previous age or movement. The same pattern (though to a lesser degree in actual practice) was apparent in literary history. It is thus easy to see why the technologically dependent and narratively and performatively shaped development of cinema would be read as one based in progress, in an evolutionary or developmental model. *The Birth of a Nation* clearly is a big step up from Griffith's earlier biograph films. But is that formal change one that produces an increase in art?

That depends on how we understand *art*, and the set of dominant assumptions about art in the intellectual milieu of the mid-1960s was different than the general consensus today. We are now on the other side of the art/society divide. The effect of the Cold War on US cultural and intellectual life was to validate a formalist and rather pure Kantian ideal of what constituted art—divorced from the social, the political, the historical. This formalist choice to regard the artwork as separate from its social origins and social effects allowed for the validation of a remarkable and fairly complex text such as *The Birth of a Nation* as a distinct and valuable artwork, linked to its creator/author but divorced from its political agenda and social effect, and from real audiences.

Of course, actual screenings of *The Birth of a Nation* in the museum, cinematheque, film series, or classroom framework almost always included some notice of and apology for the film's extreme racism (or at least this was the case in the North).[6] But discussion of the film, especially by those who were teaching it in the college curriculum, almost always oscillated between saying the film was racist but historically important (though that "history" was often taken as meaning history of cinema rather than political or cultural history) and saying it was a major work of cinematic art (with art understood in the Kantian sense of disinterested and autonomous appreciation).[7] In contrast, consider the measure that Spike Lee bluntly used in his NYU experience: "Well, they never talked about how this film was used as a recruiting tool for the Klan and responsible for Black people getting lynched."[8]

My own approach to this is deeply embedded in my personal history in terms of film studies and the progress of civil rights in the 1960s.[9] Thus, it was especially interesting to me that the instigating event for this essay, a conference on the film's centenary, took place at Indiana University in Bloomington, where I arrived in fall 1966 to pursue graduate work in comparative literature. It just so happened that comparative literature was the home of film studies at the university at the time, with leading roles played by professors Harry Geduld, Ron Gottesman, and Charles Eckert.[10] And early on, they addressed Griffith and *The Birth of a Nation*—most notably in the then pioneering series of "Focus On" handbooks, which included Geduld's *Focus on D. W. Griffith* (1971) and, commissioned by Geduld and Gottesman, Fred Silva's *Focus on The Birth of a Nation* (1971).[11]

Geduld first mentions *The Birth of a Nation* as Griffith's "most controversial film" without specifying what the controversy was. A few paragraphs later, the film is mentioned as "his greatest commercial and (arguably) his greatest artistic triumph." The book's critical commentary section begins with the director's wife's account of how the film was made, an excerpt from Nicholas Vardac's book on the transition from stage to screen emphasizing cinematic technique, a second article on technique, and then an assortment of negative criticisms of the film from a National Association for the Advancement of Colored People pamphlet of the time. So the volume definitely recognizes the controversy surrounding the film. Geduld's way of handling (or finessing, some might say) the matter is to summarize the film in the antepenultimate and penultimate paragraphs of his introduction as: "the first film to reveal the vast potentialities of the motion picture as a vehicle for propaganda. It was the first film to be taken seriously as a political statement and it has never failed to be regarded seriously as a 'sociological document.' . . . *The Birth of a Nation*, while it heightened a perversion of history and the dogma of racism to the level of art, also indicated the rich possibilities inherent in applying the techniques of the motion picture to the imaginative interpretation of documentary material."[12] Personally, the phrasing is too delicate for me, because I dispute the argument of "art," but inescapably Geduld acknowledges the problem, as would any thinking academic in the civil rights era. But the book's back cover blurb still identifies the film as a "classic" (in quotation marks).

Silva's introduction to *Focus on The Birth of a Nation* uses a similar rhetoric. He refers to seeing "Griffith's masterwork not only as an outmoded, biased account of Reconstruction, filled with unquestionably racist attitudes, but as a genuine cinematic achievement." And, although he asks the question, "Can a work of art be judged successful apart from its content?" he implicitly answers it by assuming such a separation is possible.[13] He also repeatedly returns to excuses for the white South: "Griffith presented the values of a conquered people who viewed the rubble of what they had conceived as a civilized, moral way of life. The permanent values of the land, the humanistic possibilities of the aristocracy, the importance of place, the tragic impact of the Civil War, and the heightened sense of melodrama." Most glaringly, Silva expresses concern for the white South ("conquered") while utterly ignoring the black South (most obviously and literally freed, granted human status and civil rights). This kind of rhetorical slippage can seldom go unremarked on today.[14]

Race in Bloomington

In addition to thinking of *The Birth of a Nation* in relation to the emergence of academic film studies and the notable pioneering work done at Indiana University in the era of the film's fiftieth anniversary, it is worthwhile to think about the situation of race relations in Bloomington and at Indiana University at that time. After all, knowledge is always situated. What was the situation in the mid-1960s?

When I arrived as a graduate student in comparative literature in 1966, the campus was only a few years beyond finally integrating the barber shop in the Memorial Union so that African American students could get their hair cut there, and "reserved" signs in the large student union cafeteria were finally removed, allowing black students to sit anywhere in the space. Frankly, Bloomington was much more a "mid-Southern" environment than a Northern one. Although Indiana University had one of the first Afro-American studies programs in the United States, the university faculty and student body in no way reflected the demographics of the state of Indiana. Only through direct student agitation and action was change initiated: a long paper by the radical left Students for a Democratic Society documented racial exclusion in the fraternity and sorority system. Subsequently, black athletes on the football team made demands and conducted a boycott, resulting in a losing season for the team and a win for progressive change as the administration insisted that the Greek system remove its exclusion clauses.[15] Similarly, a sit-in by the Afro-American student organization blocking the pending "Little 500" bike race in 1968 and a further blockading of Ballantine Hall during negotiations with administrators produced some major positive changes, including expanded admissions of African American students.[16]

However, such progress was balanced by the daily discrimination black people faced in Bloomington. Robert Johnson, a sociology graduate student and head of the Afro-American student group, was repeatedly threatened with firearms and attempts to run him off the road when driving around town with his white girlfriend. The Klan was an active presence, even filing for a permit for a major demonstration (which was denied due to a judge's conclusion that it would likely lead to a violent confrontation). Nearby Martinsville, on the main highway halfway to Indianapolis, had been a stronghold of the Ku Klux Klan in the 1920s and 1930s and was well known as a town where black people could not stop to buy gas for their cars.[17] In 1968, a black woman selling encyclopedias door-to-door there was stabbed to death. In Bloomington, a small Afrocentric store, Black Market, opened up on Kirkwood Avenue in 1969 and was firebombed over the Christmas break. Professor Orlando Taylor, the head of Afro-American studies, was arrested for participation in the Ballantine Hall affair along with activist students and subsequently left the university.[18]

In this context, it's possible to understand why *The Birth of a Nation* could be shown on campus in classrooms and in film club screenings with only the most token acknowledgement of the film's racism. It was an ongoing struggle to have African and African American perspectives in the curriculum and in the classroom.[19] So, another fifty years later, we can measure some progress in discussing the politics of *The Birth of a Nation* at a conference on campus. The Klan seems to have disappeared from Bloomington, though local racist incidents still occur—such as a sophomore yelling "white power" while trying to forcibly remove a Muslim woman's hijab in fall 2015. And given the opportunity, my taxi driver, while taking me from the campus site to the hotel for visiting attendees, frankly voiced his racism and xenophobia toward the recent surge of Chinese students at the university along with some mundane anti-Semitism.

In summary, the motivation to professionalize and academicize film studies combined with other factors to override the logical intellectual extension of the pragmatic world of the US civil rights era into intellectual life for most liberal and all conservative intellectuals of the period. Only the radicals and activists attempted to move the fulcrum point. The first major academic study of *The Birth of a Nation* appeared in 1964, a special ninety-five-page issue of *Film Culture* publishing the erstwhile efforts of Seymour Stern, who had a hagiographic approach to Griffith. Stern was also a vehement denier of any racism in the film or in the director himself, having carried on since the early 1940s a vendetta against "communists" who critiqued the film's politics and (according to Stern and others) ran the Film Department at the Museum of Modern Art.[20] Thus, a virulently racist film could be easily passed off as "one of the greatest," "a masterpiece," "a classic."

Two: Laughing at *The Birth of a Nation*

Today it's easy to understand Spike Lee's anger at *The Birth of a Nation*'s critical reputation as a prestigious work at NYU in 1980. Lip service liberalism rested on several factors: the historical delay created by generational difference; stunted development of the film studies field, which had been distorted by the effects of postwar anti-leftism in the academy and cultural circles; and a confusion of the film's historical position with its aesthetic and cultural value. Since then, things have changed. The Ku Klux Klan is a fragmented shadow of what it was in the 1920s, sometimes appearing in headlines as a shorthand but insignificant as a player in white supremacist activity and a general right-wing racism. In terms of media image, the visual embodiment of race in *The Birth of a Nation* is now totally out of date, to the point of being discredited and laughable. One mark of that is today's active satiric ridicule of the Klan and of distended old-school racism. Visual culture has changed, and cultural norms and expectations have changed as well. In today's contested terrain, racism is unquestionably present, but it takes different cultural forms, and this fact makes Griffith's film a ridiculous relic. My charge against *The Birth of a Nation* in today's world is that the film is laughable due to its antiquated acting style, its extreme prejudice about African Americans and Southern white womanhood, and its melodramatic staging of battlefield bromance.

In terms of actor performance, the film's histrionic and presentational acting style is so foreign to today's audience that almost everyone's reaction can only be distanced, alienated, and unsympathetic (which directly contravenes the film's goals of heroic spectacle and melodramatic pathos). I acknowledge the excellent work that has been done in specifying the gradual development of acting style from nineteenth-century stage melodrama to early dramatic film and the move toward what we now call the classic narrative film of the 1920s.[21] But I would note that when figures such as Tom Gunning, Ben Brewster and Lea Jacobs, and Roberta Pearson make their case about the "maturation" of acting style or its increasing realism (relative to what preceded it), this is true of the narrow and finely examined time-specific progression they address. But that doesn't make *The Birth of a Nation* transparently readable or even "gradually adaptable" a century after its premiere.[22]

Shifts in cultural perception make the film's foundational attitudes grossly offensive to ordinary viewers. I will only sketch the most obviously cringe-worthy aspects here. First, all the film's depictions of African Americans are instantly recognized as racist: happy field slaves, docile house slaves, inherently evil mulattoes, rampaging uniformed soldiers, and menacing rapists. I am not saying we are in a postracial era; rather, I assert that the visual culture representations of black people have decisively changed. The blackface images in *The Birth of a Nation* and the minstrelsy presentation of actual African Americans present in the film are today blatantly marked as absurd and dated, fit only for ironic scorn. This current view is the result of numerous factors, such as the presence of star athletes in major sports; the importance of African Americans in the entertainment industry, especially music, and entertainment media; and, of course, the presidency of Barack Obama. Black "positive images" exist now in the general (and mostly white) public consciousness in a way they didn't a few decades ago. This is not to say that racist images of blacks don't still appear, only that they are different.

Further, Griffith's images of helpless females linked to a cult of virginity have no credibility. In a time of the female action hero, decades of final girl characters, and even child-marketed self-willed girls and princesses, no one can transparently accept the film's premises about Southern white womanhood. Those assumptions, part of a strange psychosexual pattern in Griffith's creative output (as well as in his personal life, it seems), were out of date when the film was released.[23] And they only became more out of touch over time, never matching the mainstream of twentieth-century girlhood and young adulthood in the United States. By the time of World War II, the meme of Southern white womanhood decisively changed in the popular imagination, as seen in the film version of *Gone with the Wind* (dir. Victor Fleming, 1939). Scarlet O'Hara's transformation from superficial girl to determined, self-willed woman shifted mass understanding of the Southern belle while maintaining, to be sure, the narrative and trope's saturated racism (discussed below). Today, as the United States approaches "majority minority" demographic shifts, finds biracial and multiracial families and individuals unremarkable—at least in urban areas and certainly in the mass media—and demonstrates clear changes in generational attitudes to interracial personal relations, few can accept the film's hysterical racist fears.

Finally, the bromance of North and South, climaxing in the battlefield death scene of Tod Stoneman and Duke Cameron dying in each other's arms, goes on so long that the "comrades in death" scene not only invites but emphatically underlines a homoerotic subtext, unspeakable in 1915 but obvious today. Griffith's masculinist sentimentalism becomes grotesque and thus laughable.

Similarly, the narrative device of last-minute rescue remains a staple of Hollywood action melodrama, but *The Birth of a Nation*'s version of the Klan riding to salvation for whites and pure vengeance seems grossly unrealistic.[24]

Mocking the Klan

We live in a time of expansive satiric and ironic humor political commentary. Following on the long run of *The Daily Show with Jon Stewart* and *The Colbert Report*, combined with the expansion of YouTube in the millennium years, snark has become the common currency of political discourse, even extending its vulgar forms into the Republican Party's presidential candidate debates in 2015–2016. Who would have foreseen Donald Trump asserting his penis was a good size in a national televised debate after a rival ridiculed Trump's "short fingers"?[25] In a similar vein, news in February and March 2016 that the best known former KKK leader endorsed Trump, who in turn stalled on rejecting the gesture, brought forward a new round of comic satire mocking the Klan as did, for example, a *Saturday Night Live* fake commercial.[26] Various "Voters for Trump" extol their candidate with a final reveal of what they've been up to: painting "White Power" on the

Figure 12.1. Still from *O Brother, Where Art Thou?* Screen capture by author.

side of a building, ironing a Klan robe, and gathering wood for a Klan cross burning.

Another example of humor undermining white racism appears in *O Brother, Where Art Thou?* (dirs. Ethan and Joel Coen, 2000). After earlier adventures and mishaps, the three white escaped-convict heroes stumble upon a Ku Klux Klan lynching. They spot the victim as a black musician friend whom they had met earlier. Determined to save the musician, they intervene and run off, in the process killing an earlier adversary. The Coen brothers present a nighttime cross burning and the Klansmen in rigid formation, itself a cinematic echo of Leni Riefenstahl's interpretation of Hitler's Nuremberg rallies. In a classic set of revealed and mistaken identities, "the boys" are read as black when they are revealed at the rally because their faces are covered with dirt from the previous scene. The Klan leader is shown as none other than Stokes, the "reform" candidate for governor, and their previous nemesis, Big Dan, exposes them (fig. 12.1). Running off with their buddy, the boys throw the Confederate battle flag high in the air. With the leader's cry of "Don't let that flag touch the ground" (the mark of defeat in battle), Big Dan steps forward and heroically catches the flagpole with his bare hands. Triumphant in his achievement, the moment is short-lived when the boys cut the cable holding the giant burning cross, which then falls on the hero.

In the next scene, at a political rally for the incumbent candidate Menelaus "Pappy" O'Daniel, his opponent Stokes arrives and explains that he was just at the failed lynching. He is undercut by the boys, who are performing live "Man of Constant Sorrow," which, unbeknownst to them, had become a hit recording with constant airplay. In a double-recognition scene, The Klan leader spots the musicians as the "miscegenators" who ruined the lynching, and he tries to rally the crowd against them. But those present

Figure 12.2. Still of Dave Chappelle as Clayton
Bigsby, a secretive white supremacist, performed
during a skit in the first episode of *Chappelle's
Show. Screen capture by author.*

defy the Klansman because they love the Soggy Bottom Boys' music, and
they ride the Klansman out of town on a rail. Popular culture art triumphs
over racism.

The Klan was ridiculed in the first episode of the first season of *Chappelle's Show* on Comedy Central in 2003. Dave Chappelle performed his
most notorious sketch, a mock PBS *Frontline* investigative documentary
depicting Clayton Bigsby (Chappelle), a secretive white supremacist author
(fig. 12.2). When the *Frontline* team arrives to interview the recluse, they
discover he is a black man, blind since birth, raised in a Southern school
for the blind in which he was told he was white. Having imbibed environmental racism, Bigsby spouts the most jingoistic slogans of white power
and racist ranting. The film crew follows him to a book signing for his new
volume. Along the way, they stop for gas at a rural outpost where a gang
of white good old boys try to intimidate Bigsby because he is black, but
uncomprehending, he joins in their racism. Next, Bigsby's vehicle pulls
alongside some white teens in a convertible playing loud hip-hop music,
and he yells at them to turn off the music. "Did he just call us niggers?"
one guy exclaims, and they erupt in celebratory high-fiving. Arriving at the
meeting, Bigsby dons a Klan robe and hood and appears before his supporters calling for "white power." When one of Bigsby's most enthusiastic followers asks him to remove the hood so they can see their hero, he does so.
The reveal stuns the audience. One fellow's head explodes. The report ends
with the deadpan observation that Bigsby did finally accept his identity as

Figure 12.3. Still of the vigilante gang from *Django Unchained. Screen capture by author.*

an African American, but then divorced his wife of nineteen years "because she was a nigger lover."

Quentin Tarantino inserted an anachronistic sequence in this 2012 feature *Django Unchained*, set just before the Civil War. After the bounty hunter pair, white King Schultz and freed slave Django, murder three outlaws who worked as overseers, the plantation owner hunts them down and conducts a night-rider raid on their wagon. The sequence presents both hard-charge riding and flashbacks to the initial assembly. In a characteristic Tarantino scene, that gathering shows men pointlessly arguing about the sacks they will wear over their heads: whether they fit, that the poor eyeholes obscure their vision, that they are badly made, and so on (fig. 12.3). The vigilante gang appears petty, laughable, and inept, not fearsome and bold. The point is sealed when they surround the wagon and Shultz detonates an explosive charge, killing and injuring the night riders.[27]

In a short sketch from the Comedy Central show *Key and Peele*, the African American pair are strolling in a park when a blond woman's small terrier aggressively barks at them (fig. 12.4).[28] The woman apologetically explains that this is her new shelter dog that goes after all dark-skinned people. Key smiles and nods, saying they are not offended because "we can't know what the dog has been through." Cut to a year earlier, and the dog is revealed as the leader at a Klan cross burning, barking out "white power!" in subtitles (fig. 12.5).

These four examples show the ability of comedians today to mock and dismiss the Ku Klux Klan, significantly without dismissing racism itself. They are not asserting that we have reached a postracial plateau. Rather,

Figure 12.4. Still from Comedy Central's *Key and Peele*. *Screen capture by author.*

Figure 12.5. Still from Comedy Central's *Key and Peele*. *Screen capture by author.*

they neatly maneuver and make the menace look ridiculous. But it is important to understand that this tactic depends on the vastly decreased prestige and power of the Klan, the foolishness of the group's costumes and self-aggrandizing righteousness, and the critical distance that today's audience has from the Klan.[29] The move depends on a formal shift, a distance, and a critical separation that allows for snarky wit. And it's not always possible to achieve that.

A case in point: a sketch from the final season of *Key and Peele* in 2015, in the wake of notorious police assaults on and shooting of black men. Key, in whiteface, plays a trigger-happy cop who shoots black men he encounters: a guy holding a Popsicle and so forth. Finally, the black chief of police, played by Peele, arrives on the scene, where Key is explaining his murders as excusable mistakes. Key sees the chief, pulls out his gun, and shoots him, again excusing the "mistake." The sketch is too true to be funny. The performers were no doubt completely aware of this—"too soon," as the world of professional comedy would say. Which underlines the point that a gap is needed for effective satire. This sketch has outrage but no laughs (nor should it).[30]

Another example of the gradual evolution of social norms and understanding that underlines *The Birth of a Nation*'s racist imagination can be identified when we recognize that satiric ironic humor always has power only in relation to the social space and time in which it appears or reappears. Things have changed, for example, since *The Birth of a Nation*'s fierce images of a black man menacing a Southern white woman, as is evident in the notorious example of Kanye West's 2009 interruption of Taylor Swift's acceptance speech for best female video at the MTV Video Music Awards ceremony.[31] It was an initially serious moment in which West went onstage, took the microphone away from Swift, and then claimed the award should have gone to Beyoncé: "I'm sorry, but Beyoncé had one of the best videos of all time!" The episode has become a standard joke about Kanye's over-inflated ego and sense of masculine privilege. Several years later, Swift (or more likely someone faking her) managed a neatly snarky retort when Kim Kardashian gave birth to West's child by tweeting: "Yo I'm happy for you imam let you finish but Beyonce had one of the best labors of all time."[32]

An Emerging Form

Today, while a general discussion is taking place regarding youth's presumed narcissism especially framed by new digital social media technologies, another activity is emerging. These new platforms and devices increase the possibilities of grassroots communication and thus increase the potential for dissenting and critical voices to be heard. I'm referring to the online world of YouTube, bloggers, and the remarkable presence of people making strong antiracist statements in a snarky comic form.[33] Particularly with the growth and development of the Black Lives Matter movement, there is a wider range of dissenting and activist discourse especially by black women. Much of this is very serious, very political, and often polemical, but an important part of this discourse frequently uses sarcastic comedy. One example: one of the best known moments of the 1939 film

Gone with the Wind is Scarlett O'Hara's confrontation with Prissy. Scarlett's cousin Melanie goes into premature labor during the Atlanta campaign. Scarlett, in hysteric mode, tells the slave servant to get the doctor, but Prissy fears the dead, dying, and injured at the field hospital and doesn't carry out the errand. On the servant's return, Scarlett realizes she will have to go. The scene of her arrival provides a major turning point: the Confederacy is clearly doomed with so many casualties, the doctor must tend them, and Scarlett realizes she will have to take control. On returning to the house, she orders Prissy to prepare for the imminent birth only to hear the slave's famous line, "I don't know nothin' about birthin' babies!" Scarlett then slaps Prissy.

The moment has been reproduced in mash ups and other forms.[34] YouTube comments often include arguments. A basic racist response claims Prissy is stupid (or "retarded"). But there's also an incredibly sharp and sarcastic response that celebrates Prissy's self-election out of the dilemmas of white women dealing with imminent pregnancy. One of these responses, by YouTube user TheAdelaidehall, states: "Melanie is moaning & groaning in painful agony, Scarlett is so stupid she believes Prissy can 'birth babies', Prissy takes her time, sings & quite frankly doesn't give a damn about either of those two white bitches . . . I call that attitude! Go Girl! (Love Prissy)."

I argue that in terms of style, presentation, and overt politics, *The Birth of a Nation* is no longer effective race and gender propaganda. Thus, we don't need to fear it. Anger is not the best response; dismissive laughter is. But on a deeper and underlying level, the film did speak to and of and for white anxieties (through the entire class range) about twentieth-century modernity. And those psychic formations rest in material conditions that have only become more accelerated in our current neoliberal era.

Among the distresses of twentieth-century modernity dramatized in *The Birth of a Nation* are the destructive force of war on combatants and civilians; economic collapse; the middle classes losing ground; and the immense expansion of state power and state legitimization witnessed in bureaucratization, large-scale surveillance of individuals, and a feeling that the state, a distant state (today called Washington, DC), controls our lives. Surveillance is not just the National Security Agency's collection of internet and phone data but also in trigger warnings and admonitions about appropriate Halloween costumes or "check your privilege" remarks. Added to this is the privatization of life caused by capitalist social organization with the commercialization of private life and runaway expansion of consumer culture. All this is experienced as the collapse of traditional cultural and moral hierarchies. Thus, the appeal of nostalgia: "Make America Great Again." The three-period division of *The Birth of a Nation* dramatizes this theme: a pastoral antebellum South that is prosperous and ordered; the disorder and conflict of the Civil War and its aftermath; and the conflicted end of Reconstruction and a return to the ordered past.

These broader ideological formations are still with us as witnessed in the 2016 presidential campaigns. They also appear in various specific conversations, such as debates over women's reproductive health rights, including abortion; in arguments on gun violence and regulation; and in discussions of police violence against minorities. We are in the process of an epistemic shift. We might call this a postmodern sensibility in which there is, to use one example, a lack of confidence in authority. But this cuts both left and right in its result. The right looks to simple slogans voiced by humorless dogmatic speakers. And it calls on nostalgia for an imaginary past. The left looks a different way: toward a progressive and expansive future, sometimes sloganeering, but often ironic. That gap provides the ground for a conflicting negotiation: mockery, snark, and sarcastic satire flourish in this evolving field. Without easy access to the levers of power, speaking truth, even if rueful or ironic, remains a democratic option. Thus we return to the perennial issue of comic satire: Is it subversive or adaptive? And the answer is, it is always contingent, always based in the specific intersection of text, context, and audience.

On this ground we see in *The Birth of a Nation* a racist nostalgia for an ordered past depicted as the happy plantation life of the antebellum South. The Civil War then becomes the turning point, and Reconstruction embodies all the fearful anxieties, such as Northern carpetbaggers running the government and imposing laws. Lives are controlled by seemingly arbitrary or corrupt state decrees (surely the basis for the vast grassroots support for Kim Davis in summer 2015)[35] as bedrock ideological formations such as heteronormativity seem overthrown. In the film, changed power relations are presented as disorder and pose the most danger to Southern white womanhood in the two dramatic cases of Gus and Little Sister and the cabin scene. Within the film, the rise of the Ku Klux Klan is seen as the only solution to the disorder. While a grassroots vigilante mass movement of night riders is no longer plausible, certainly we see considerable acceptance among a significant number of US whites of militant, military, and sweeping violence—in the promised swift deportation of eleven million undocumented people and registration for US Muslims, as promised by Donald Trump in early 2017, and in the extralegal execution of Trayvon Martin by a self-appointed vigilante amateur cop and in the military-style police occupation of Ferguson, Missouri. These are not laughing matters. They summon us to action. And one handy tool to maintain a sensible balance in the struggle is using our comic sense.

CHUCK KLEINHANS was Associate Professor Emeritus of Radio/ Television/Film at Northwestern University. He was Editor with Julia Lesage and John Hess of *Jump Cut: A Review of Contemporary Media* until his death in 2017.

Notes

1. The film is not available for viewing. Lee and others have described it. The filmmaker has claimed variously that on viewing it as part of evaluating first-year students, the faculty voted to kick him out for disrespecting *The Birth of a Nation*. His version was disputed by faculty who said some teachers did want to weed out Lee, but others advocated for him and he was continued. They offer different reasons: that Lee was brash and obstreperous, that the film was an overreach of his skills at the time, and so forth. John Colapinto, "Outside Man: Spike Lee's Unending Struggle," *New Yorker*, September 22, 2008, 56–57. Cinema at NYU is divided into two departments. Lee was enrolled in the film production program. There was also a well-known and well-regarded film history and criticism program. It is not clear whether Lee is referring to faculty in both programs or which specific professors were involved.

2. *The Birth of a Nation*, directed by D. W. Griffith, Kino Classics 3-disc ed. (New York: Kino Lorber, 2011). The quote is attributed to the American Film Institute, and, although no specific source or author is given for the blurb, I have no reason not to take it at face value. To its credit, after this come-on, the following text describes the film as controversial and opposed by the NAACP from its premiere on. Of course, it remains testimony to the pervasive dismissal of concerns about racism that both institutions—the American Film Institute and the commercial distributor Kino Lorber—validate the film's "greatness."

3. A few museums and cinematheques should be mentioned here, such as New York's Museum of Modern Art and Henri Langlois's Paris Cinémathèque Française. In the United States, the Museum of Modern Art had the extraordinary significance of distributing films to the network of film societies in the postwar era. In the 1960s, *The Birth of a Nation* was available in 8 mm and Super 8 mm versions from Blackhawk Films, which served the amateur consumer market. These were typically shortened versions.

4. A useful survey of US and UK film studies is Lee Grieveson and Haidee Wasson, eds., *Inventing Film Studies* (Durham, NC: Duke University Press, 2008), which, unfortunately, ignores McCarthyism and Cold War ideology in shaping the field. An important historical perspective on the 1960s film discipline is found in the introductory chapter of Dana Polan, *Scenes of Instruction: The Beginnings of the U.S. Study of Film* (Berkeley: University of California Press, 2007).

5. In general, in the US postwar era, conservatives tended to dismiss the entire range of mass culture for not matching their standards for "high art." Liberals and leftists tended to split, with some deploring popular culture while others viewed it as a social phenomenon worth taking seriously or an expressive form linked to the popular consciousness, particularly with pop music and media connecting to youth and dissent.

6. Museum and film society screenings at this time typically included a page of program notes on the film—a framework that would include notice of the most offensive parts. I am not accounting here for the film's screenings by Ku Klux Klan and similar white supremacist organizations that did use the film for propaganda purposes and recruiting. Tom Rice, *White Robes, Silver Screens: Movies and the Making of the Ku Klux Klan* (Bloomington: Indiana University Press, 2015), provides a detailed account of the Klan's relation to the film in the first half of the twentieth century. Since the Klan did not have prints, it connected with the original and revival screenings for recruiting and promotion of the organization. I believe the film is no longer serviceable for that purpose, as I argue later in this essay.

7. For the brief against Kant, a thorough introduction is Pierre Bourdieu, *Distinction: A Social Critique of the Judgment of Taste*, trans. Richard Nice (Cambridge MA: Harvard University Press, 1984).

8. Spike Lee, interview with Pharrell Williams, "Spike Lee Shows NYU The Answer | Ep. 9 Part 1, Segment 4/4 ARTST TLK | Reserve Channel," October 8, 2013, www.youtube.com /watch?v=4q5PX4joOyg. The remarks begin at six minutes into the segment, immediately after a naked blonde white woman serves beverages to the two black artists.

9. I should make it clear that, although I began teaching university film classes in the late 1970s, I never taught *The Birth of a Nation*. Partly this was because I seldom taught film history per se, and never the silent era. I have taught some of Griffith's melodramas in classes on melodrama. Although teaching *The Birth of a Nation* can be the occasion for many "teachable moments" about its racist ideology, in general the film presents distinct problems in its epic length and in the need to create a fuller historical context of US history, particularly of slavery, the Civil War, and Reconstruction. Given the effective elision of these matters in the US high school curriculum, *The Birth of a Nation* needs much more framing and elaboration than other films of the era for the college classroom. So, for pragmatic pedagogical reasons, I wouldn't include it in a survey film history class. Other Griffith films could serve the purpose. On the other hand, for a topic-focused course—on the history of racism in US cinema, for example, or the historical epic genre—it deserves a substantial consideration. Julia Lesage's recent suggestion to teach the film *after* teaching *12 Years a Slave* (2013) is an excellent strategy.

10. I knew all three, and became close friends with Eckert, but for various reasons I never actually took a film class.

11. Handbooks were an important critical and pedagogical tool in early film studies. They were useful and fairly inexpensive textbooks that brought together materials on films and filmmakers, sometimes scripts, often initial journalistic reviews, notable interviews, and later scholarly and critical commentary. The Focus On series combined biographical, critical, and historical approaches and provided a casebook collection—diverse essays around a common text such as a short story or critical essay supplemented by different critiques and commentaries—that could be the starting point for an undergraduate paper. It was designed to continue from the typical college introductory expository writing classes, which heavily used the casebook approach at the time. The all-in-one book was designed for the student to have basic materials for a compare-and-contrast essay that would develop his or her ability to study, evaluate, and balance different critical approaches to the same text. Commonplace in

literature departments, the Focus On series was the first casebook publication designed for the film curriculum.

12. The separation of art from sociology was a standard Cold War ideological move and so common as to be generally unremarked.

13. It's worth noting for today's readers that the issue of reactionary content and art was widely discussed in terms of fascist and other problematic art by intellectuals in the postwar era by figures such as Sartre and de Beauvoir, and it continued in the work of Sontag on Leni Riefenstahl and Kristeva on Céline. The Frankfurt School and other Central European exiles and thinkers contributed to the discussion in looking back at Weimar Germany and in exploring the postwar question of art after the Holocaust.

14. Silva goes on to invoke various (white) Southern writers: the Southern Agrarians, William Faulkner, Robert Penn Warren, Allen Tate, and John Crowe Ransom. I'd argue (or hope) that today no intellectually honest critic could fail to not also mention a distinguished line of African American intellectual and literary figures who offer a quite contrasting view of US history and legacy.

15. The situation is more complex than my sketch here can indicate. Perhaps the best short summary is in Mary Ann Wynkoop, *Dissent in the Heartland: The Sixties at Indiana University* (Bloomington: Indiana University Press, 2002)—although as a participant at the time, I find it very thin and overly reliant on established press versions, official documents, and administrators as authorities. The grassroots experience and the activist side is not well represented. Some oral history has been collected but, again, mostly from the establishment point of view. I worked on the consecutive underground press papers of the era, *The Spectator*, *No Spectators*, and *Common Sense*, which provide an alternative view, as well as the local annual *Disorientation* pamphlet produced by the New Left–based New University Conference chapter.

16. Wynkoop tends to separate the antiwar left from the black movement, whereas I see them as running together with extensive informal ties. The Klan and other armed whites were a known presence in the area. Marching in an antiwar demonstration from campus to the courthouse square (where the draft board office was located), one could see white men brandishing guns on the roofs of buildings on Kirkwood Avenue.

17. Although it probably was not formally enacted into law, Martinsville was known as a "sundown" town—one in which any black person's life was at risk after sundown. Discrimination there extended to anyone "different," as hippies also discovered in trying to buy gas in Martinsville.

18. Taylor and the others were found innocent of the charges at trial years later. The Black Market firebomber was eventually apprehended and revealed as a member of the Ku Klux Klan, as was the Martinsville killer. With rampant hysteria in the Indiana legislature and drum beating by the Indianapolis newspapers, in the public eye there was no differentiation between student activism, African American, feminist, antiwar, counterculture, gay, and socialist movements. It was also true that progressive forces were so small in numbers that in order to have a party, all those different trends would mingle, unlike the bigger and more divided or sectarian fields of urban politics of the time. The campus did have the unusual situation of one year electing a member of the Black Panther Party as president of the student government with the head of Students for a Democratic Society elected as vice president.

19. Gottesman did make an effort, including Ralph Ellison's *Invisible Man* in his introductory survey of US literature course (and inviting me, an all-but-dissertation, to lecture on it for the class). Following Taylor's departure, Robert Johnson was installed as interim chair of Afro-American studies, and he asked me to teach a special section of the

comparative literature introductory course for black students arriving under the new "group" program. I hesitated, asking whether it wouldn't be better to have a black teacher. He replied there was no one available, so wouldn't it be better to have me teach it than to not have it offered? My department agreed with the plan, and I redesigned the content with African, Afro-Caribbean, and African American literature.

20. The details are explained in Janet Staiger, *Interpreting Films: Studies in the Historical Reception of American Cinema* (Princeton, NJ: Princeton University Press, 1992), 134–152. It is also discussed in Melvyn Stokes, *D. W. Griffith's* The Birth of a Nation: *A History of "the Most Controversial Motion Picture of All Time"* (New York: Oxford University Press, 2007), 254–258. I discuss the involvement of Stern's contemporary in Chuck Kleinhans, "Theodore Huff: Historian and Filmmaker," in *Lovers of Cinema: The First American Avantgarde 1919–1945*, ed. Jan-Christopher Horak (Madison: University of Wisconsin Press, 1995), 180–204. In 1939, while working at the Museum of Modern Art, Huff prepared a shot-by-shot description of the entire film that circulated first in mimeograph and that was later, a decade after Huff's death, turned into a museum publication: Theodore Huff, *A Shot Analysis of D. W. Griffith's "The Birth of a Nation"* (New York: Museum of Modern Art, 1961). It appears to be the first such detailed breakdown of a motion picture and thus helped institutionalize the film's prestigious place in film studies.

21. The recognized histories are Tom Gunning, *D. W. Griffith and the Origins of American Narrative Film: The Early Years at Biograph* (Urbana: University of Illinois Press, 1991); Ben Brewster and Lea Jacobs, *Theatre to Cinema: Stage Pictorialism and the Early Feature Film* (Oxford: Oxford University Press, 1997); Roberta E. Pearson, *Eloquent Gestures: The Transformation of Performance Style in the Griffith Biograph Films* (Berkeley: University of California Press, 1992). Their analyses are relative and incremental for the short span they study (at most a decade and a half). I am using the baseline of a century.

22. By "gradually adaptable," I mean that the average audience could quickly learn the pertinent conventions and come to accept them. This viewer adaptation often works with films using a broad comic mode, such as Chaplin or Keaton, but it is impossible today for a serious dramatic or epic mode. The kind of acting we witness in *The Birth of a Nation* to ordinary viewers (who are not film buffs or professors of cinema fluent in the historic range of cinema) seems ludicrous. At best, such acting is accepted by the ordinary public in convivial recreations of nineteenth-century melodramas reenacted at tourist venues anchored in sentimental views of the US Western frontier and other archaic amusements. It might be possible for those predisposed to the film's racism to read it as a historical docudrama, antiquated in form but presenting "what really happened."

23. Michael Rogin argues that the film's obsession with protecting white womanhood from African American men not only was directed at controlling black sexuality but also functioned at controlling white females. Michael Rogin, "'The Sword Became a Flashing Vision': D. W. Griffith's *The Birth of a Nation*," in *Ronald Reagan, the Movie and Other Episodes in Political Demonology* (Berkeley: University of California Press, 1987), 190–235.

24. From our more distant vantage point, we can see the direct descent from *The Birth of a Nation*'s cavalry charge and Klan riders to subsequent Hollywood Westerns with the US cavalry or sheriff's posse riding to the rescue. But these tropes are dated with more psychological and lone-hero Westerns of recent decades. Perhaps the last big cinematic charge was Francis Ford Coppola's air cavalry episode in *Apocalypse Now* (1979), itself a heavily ironic and satirically over-the-top scene.

25. Obviously, the precedent had been set nearly two decades earlier when Republicans promoted the Starr Report investigation of the Clinton-Lewinsky scandal with the final report, printed in almost every newspaper in the country, detailing oral sex, ejaculate on clothing, and penetration with cigars in the Oval Office. Suddenly a generation of middle-schoolers became intensely aware of fellatio and manual stimulation as commonplace erotic activity with the widely noted result that teen boys were now expecting girls to perform fellatio.

26. "Voters for Trump Ad," *Saturday Night Live*, March 6, 2016, www.youtube.com /watch?v=QgopO9VG1J8. Opening the same show was a parody of Trump defending his penis size in "CNN Election Center Cold Open," *Saturday Night Live*, www.youtube.com /watch?v=Y1hEyiE2q-w.

27. In an interview, Tarantino revealed his disgust at the fact that John Ford, who worked on *The Birth of a Nation*, was one of the film's Klan riders. Ford appears, uncredited, as a rider who lifts his hood to see clearly. Subsequently as a director, Ford became famous for his ride-to-the-rescue scenes, particularly in his cavalry films. Quentin Tarantino, "Tarantino 'Unchained' Part 1: 'Django' Trilogy?" interview by Henry Louis Gates Jr., http://www .theroot.com/tarantino-unchained-part-1-django-trilogy-1790894626.

28. "Racist Dog," *Key and Peele*, season 2, episode 2, October 3, 2012, www.cc.com/video -clips/djbfk9/key-and-peele-racist-dog.

29. However, this should not obscure real-life political facts such as the disturbing presence of Steve Bannon as chief strategist in the Trump White House. Before joining the Trump team, Bannon headed the alt-right (i.e., white nationalist) Breitbart News web empire.

30. There is, though, an effective thought exercise here: When in the future and how could the same narrative be played out in an effective laugh-producing comic form? The sketch premiered in season 5, episode 1, on July 8, 2015. One year earlier, the police killing of unarmed Michael Brown in Fergusson, Missouri, sparked widespread protests and birthed the Black Lives Matter movement. US police average about one hundred killings of unarmed black citizens every year. As those tragedies continue unabated, it is hard to see how they could become the subject of farce.

31. "Kanye West Ruins Taylor Swift's VMA Moment 2009," September 15, 2009, www.youtube.com/watch?v=z4xWU802cvA. Swift is associated with Southern heritage (she moved to Nashville at age fourteen) and her earlier genre, country music.

32. Of course this "feud" serves the long-term business interests of both parties by keeping them in the celebrity entertainment news. In February 2016, West released a recording with attendant publicity in which he claimed credit for making Swift famous (patently absurd) and saying he would willingly have sex with her (with the implication that she would like this and she should be complimented by his attention). Swift took the high road, responding in a Video Music Awards show message telling her young women fans to ignore haters and follow their own dreams.

33. This continues my interest in ephemeral media, a basic characteristic of our digital new media moment. I address this in *Jump Cut* essays on fan blogging; for example, Chuck Kleinhans, "There's a Sucker Born Every Minute. Audiences Blog about *Sucker Punch*," www.ejumpcut.org/archive/jc53.2011/ckSuckerPunch/index.html. Here my interest is in the streams of comments that collect in response to blog clips and YouTube items. These threads quickly turn to trolling behaviors but also heavily use comic sarcasm to score political points in arguments. While they "disappear" in the most topical blogging (even more effervescent

on Twitter and similar platforms), they are also trace evidence of individuals formerly excluded from this curious corner of the public sphere, now being somewhat empowered to express themselves on issues of the moment or day.

34. Gremlinbitch87, "Prissy," February 18, 2011, www.youtube.com /watch?v=PAV3OfHo4n4, contains TheAdelaidehall comments. Clarence Fisher, "Gone with the Women," September 6, 2009, www.youtube.com/watch?v=hE7w7KaKbmM, mashes the slap scene in *Gone with the Wind* with Butterfly McQueen scenes in *The Women*.

35. Davis, an elected official, a county clerk in Kentucky, in defiance of a federal court order, refused to issue marriage licenses to gay couples. She became a celebrity hero to the Evangelical Right.

INDEX

12 Years a Slave, 24, 206n26, 207, 209, 211, 212, 215, 219, 222, 223, 234, 235

Aborigines' Protection Society, 82, 83, 96
African Americans on Television: Race-ing for Ratings, 239
African Film Productions, 96, 110, 112
African Methodist Episcopal Church, 78
African National Congress, 123
Afrikaner, 22, 107, 108, 109, 110, 114, 115, 117, 118, 119, 121, 123–24
Airport, 62
Aitken, Roy and Harry, 56–57, 58, 61, 65, 76
AME Church, 78
Anderson, Benedict, 260
Anglo, Saxon, 3, 10, 18
Anglo-Boer War, 110
"Anglo-Celt," 82
Answer, The, 282
Anti-Slavery Society, 82, 83, 96
Argo, 184
Arizona Colored Women's Clubs, 40
Aryan, 10, 146
Assassination of Lincoln, The, 54, 55, 56
Astor Place Riot, 38

Bakhtin, Mikhail, 167, 262, 263
Baldwin, Davarian, 2, 10
Ballantine Hall, 288
Bamboozled, 25, 26, 239, 248–49, 250, 251, 252, 253, 255, 282
Banks, Lee, 38
Barker, Deborah, 208, 231
Barthes, Roland, 209
Basil Corporation, 76, 78–79
Battle of Blood River, 112, 117, 120, 123, 124, 127
Battle of Gettysburg, The, 172
Baudrillard, Jean, 177, 184
Beaudine, William, 67
Beloved, 184
Bergman, Ingmar, 58
Beyoncé, 296

Big Daddy, 197, 201, 202
Bi-racial. *See* Mulatto
Bioscope, The, 81
Birth of a Movement, ix
Birth of a Nation, The [2016], 184–85, 208
Birth of a Nation, The [1915], ix, xn3, 1, 2–3, 6–9, 17, 18, 19, 20, 21, 22, 24, 25, 26–27, 33, 34, 35, 38–39, 41, 42, 43, 47, 50–52, 53, 54, 55, 56, 57, 58, 59, 60, 61, 62, 63, 64, 65, 66, 67, 68, 69, 70, 71, 72, 76, 77, 78, 79, 80, 81, 82, 83, 84, 86, 87, 88, 89, 90, 91–92, 93–95, 96, 97, 98, 99, 107, 112, 115, 116, 117, 118, 119, 120, 129, 130, 131–33, 137, 138, 140, 142, 143, 145, 151–52, 153–54, 157, 164, 167, 168, 170, 171, 172, 176, 179, 180, 181, 184, 185, 193–94, 195–96, 197, 200, 201, 202, 207, 208, 219, 222–24, 225, 228, 232, 234, 235, 239, 240, 241, 243, 244, 245, 246, 248, 249, 250, 252, 253, 254, 255, 256, 259–61, 262, 263, 264–65, 266, 268, 272, 273, 274, 277, 279, 280, 282, 283, 284, 285, 286, 287, 288, 289, 290, 296, 297, 298; beyond *Birth,* 184–85, 240–42; at Bloomington, 283–89; filmic manifesto, 6; genres, 7, 10, 23, 24, 132–33, 193, 194, 195, 200–1, 203, 204, 205n7, 302n24; historical memory, 6–7; historical omissions, 10–11, 13; nontheatrical market, 46–53; protests against, 16–18, 33–39, 40–41, 288–89, 300n18; role of Black women against, 39–40, 43; reception in Australia, 87–92; reception in Britain, 81–83, 85, 88; reception in Canada, 76–81; reception in Caribbean, 98; reception in France, 80, 83–86, 93, 98, 105n112; reception in Germany, 92–95, 98; reception in South Africa, 95–97, 107–22, 123–34; reception other abroad, 98; sexual paranoia, 92–95; small gauge, 52–61; social class hierarchy, 13–16; transnational, 21–22

Birth of a Race, The, 17
Bitzer, Billy, 62
Bivens, James T., 33, 40
Black Beast, 14
Black Buck, 14, 248, 249
*Black Camera, An International Film
     Journal,* 49
Black Cinema House, ix
Black Codes, 223
Black Empire, 7, 14
Blackface, 120, 139, 239, 243, 245, 247, 248, 249,
     251, 253, 256, 265, 266, 270, 271, 272, 273,
     274, 275, 277, 281n19, 281n23, 281n24, 290
Black Film Center/Archive, ix, x, xi
Black Hawk Films, 47–48, 56, 61, 62, 65,
     74n36
Black Horror Campaign, 93
Black Horror on the Rhine, 22, 92, 93
Black Image in the White Mind, 241, 243
Black Like Us, 255
Black Lives Matter, ix, 2, 43, 296, 303n30
Black Power Movement, 201, 247
Black Reconstruction, 131
Black Scourge in Europe: Sexual Horror Let
     Loose by France on Rhine, 92
Black Shame Campaign, 94
Blaxploitation, 155, 192, 193, 204
Blight, David, 131
Bloedrivier Heritage Site, 123, 129, 130
Bloomington, Indiana: Afro-American
     Studies, 288–89; Indiana University
     campus protests, 287–89; race relations
     1960s, 287–89
Bobo, Lawrence, 255
Bogle, Donald, 249, 251
Bonilla, Yasimar, 192
Booth, John Wilkes, 177, 179
Boston Daily Globe, 42
Boston Guardian, 16
Bourdieu, Pierre, 13, 15, 29n21
Bourke-White, Margaret, 124, 126
Boussenot, Georges, 85
Bow, Clara, 67
Brabin, Charles, 69
Bradley, David, 52–53, 56–57. *See also* David
     Bradley Collection

Brecht, Bertolt, 222
Brewster, Ben, 290
British Board of Film Censors, 81, 82
British Film Institute, 71, 81, 246, 256
Broken Blossoms, 223
Brown, Lydia, 151
Brown, Michael, 138–39
Brown, Samuel A., 41
Brownlow, David, 59
Brownlow, Kevin, 152, 169
Building a Nation, 115, 116, 117, 118, 120, 124,
     127, 128
Bureau of Censorship in Montreal, 97

Caddoo, Cara, 17, 18, 19, 20, 33–45
Cameron, 14, 15, 146, 160, 183, 196, 199, 224,
     227, 228, 229, 232, 268, 273; Ben, 63, 168,
     225–27, 229, 232; Duke, 168, 291; Flora, 8,
     62–63, 94, 150, 151, 169, 182, 194, 202, 225,
     228–29, 232, 240, 264, 265, 266, 298
Canadian Observer, The, 77, 78
Candace, Gratien, 98
Capitalism, 10, 13, 28n15, 210
Capra, Frank, 130
Card, James, 58
Caribbean, 3, 17, 38, 86, 98
Carnes, William G., 36
Carpetbagger, 14
Cecil Theater, 39
Central Commission of Control, 22, 83
Chamberlain, Lord, 83
Chappelle's Show, 293
Charlottesville, 20
Charney, Mark, 175
Chase, Calvin. See *Washington Bee*
Chesnutt, Mary, 183
Chicago Defender, 39, 41
Chicken Thieves, 14
Cicero, 201, 202
Cine-memory, 6–7, 10, 173–74
City of Peace, 254
Civil rights movement, 184, 255
Civil War, 3, 25, 63, 77, 81, 82, 84, 88, 132, 138,
     141, 164, 165, 172, 174, 176, 194, 209, 224, 228,
     252, 283, 287, 294, 298; post–Civil War, 279
Civil War Battle Scenes, 54, 55, 56

Clansman, The, 17, 65, 69, 141–42, 149, 164–65, 179, 207, 242. *See also* Dixon, Thomas
Clark, Ashley, 255
Classic Film Collector, 53, 59, 60
Clinton, Hillary, 131
Cobb, Jasmine Nichole, 219, 222, 234
Cohen Brothers, 292; Ethan, 26, 268
Colbert Show, The, 291
Cold War, 285
Collins, Kris, 245
Colonial Office, 83
Colored Protective Association, 43
Colored Women's Clubs, 40, 45n24
Coltrane, John, 21, 50
Committee on Racial Equality, 68
Commonwealth Immigration Restriction Act, 88
Confederacy, 43, 63, 118, 130, 176, 227, 283, 292, 297; flag, 43
Confessions of Nat Turner, The, 185
Congress [US], 2, 4
Conners, Coco, 253
Coon, 14
Cop Out, 264
Corbucci, Sergio, 192
Courtenay, Susan, 264–65
Cowboy Justice, 198
Cripps, Thomas, 34, 120
Crisis, The, 39, 82
Crisp, Donald, 63
Crosland, Alan, 249
Crowley, Michael H., 42
Cuba, 3
Cuniberti, John, 46
Currier and Ives, 173
Curse of a Nation, The, 90

D. W. Griffith: Father of Film, 152, 169
Daily Herald, 92
Daily Show with Jon Stewart, 291
Daly, Lucy. See *Pickaninnies*
David Bradley Collection, 21, 57
Davis, Angela, 235
Davis, Kim, 298, 304n35
Davis, Peter, 7, 22, 95, 96, 107–34, 123, 124, 130
De Mille, Cecil B., 67, 198

De Voortrekkers, 22, 95–96, 111–112, 113, 114, 115, 116, 118, 120, 129, 130, 133
Dear White People, 25, 239, 242, 243, 244, 245, 246, 247, 248, 252, 253, 254, 255, 256
Declaration of the rights of Man, 86
Defender, 38
Denver Silent Film Festival, ix, x
Deschin, Jacob, 46, 48, 49
Diagne, Blaise, 85
Dialogic Imagination, The, 262
Diamond Fields Advertiser, 97
Diawara, Manthia, 169, 256
Die Bou van 'n Nasie. See Building a Nation
Die schwarze Schmach [Black Slave, The], 93–94
Die Vaderland, 117
Django Unchained, 24, 155, 191–92, 193, 194, 195, 196, 197, 200, 202, 203, 204, 206n25, 206n30, 262, 264, 294
Dixon, Thomas, 16, 40, 65, 88, 92, 140, 141–43, 145–46, 148, 149, 155, 157, 160, 161, 164–65, 171, 175, 182, 183
Do the Right Thing, 246
Dostoevsky, 262
Dragstrip Riot, 52
Drawing the Global Colour Line, 129
Du Bois, Nina Gomer, 83
Du Bois, W. E. B., 82–83, 131
Duke, David, 52
Dunn, James L., 33, 36–37
Dunnahoo, Tom, 59
DuVernay, Ava, 184, 238n33

Eckert, Charles, 286
Edenic State, 95
Edison Company, 197
Educational Screen, 53, 54, 58
Ejiofor, Chiwetel, 215
Election, 246
Emancipation, 228
Emancipation Proclamation, 173
Emanuel African Methodist Episcopal Church, 43
Enlightenment, 3, 28n9
Enforcement Acts, 169
Enright, Ray, 69
Entertainment Films, 48

Entman, Robert, 241, 243
Envision Freedom: Cinema and the Building of Modern Black Life, 17
Epoch Producing Corporation, 88
Essex Film Club, 59
Eubanks, Ralph, 252
Eureka, 71
Everett, Anna, 259
Everson, William K., 49–50, 68–69, 70

F. C. Pictures Corporation, 54
Faithful Souls, 14, 15, 95, 119, 120, 145, 149. *See also* Uncle Tom
Fassbender, Michael, 215, 216
Fehrle, Johannes, 192
Ferguson, 299
Ferrell, Jonathan, 234
Ferro, Marc, 17–18
Fiedler, Leslie, 141
Film Classic Exchange, 54
Film Culture, 289
Film Forum, ix, x
Film Society of the School of Visual Arts, 49–50
Films in Review, 66
Fire and Desire: Mixed Race Movies in the Silent Era, 153
Flanagan, Martin, 262
Fleming, Victor, 198
Focus on D. W. Griffith, 286
Focus on The Birth of a Nation, 286
Ford Theater, 63
Forgeries of Memory and Meaning: Blacks and Regimes of Race in American Theater and Film Before World War II, 153
Forman, Tom, 198
Forrest Theatre, 37, 39, 43
Fortress Europe, 10
Foskey, Clara, 33, 39–40
Foster, Lugenia, 33, 40
Foster, Stephen, 139
Francis, Terri, 192
Frederickson, George, 152
Freedman's Bureau, 4, 228
Freemon, Django, 191. See also *Django Unchained*
Frency, 62

Fresh Air, 252
Freud, Sigmund, 219
From Cinematic Past to Fast Forward Present: D. W. Griffith's *The Birth of a Nation* Centennial Symposioum, ix, 18–19, 261
Frontier, 132
Frontline, 293

Gaines, Jane, 95, 153–54, 158, 159, 240
Garner, Eric, 139
Garvey, Marcus, 85
Gates, Henry Louis Jr, 194, 203, 217, 254
Gator and the Pickaninny, The, 14
Geduld, Harry, 286, 287
George Eastman House International Museum of Photography and Film, ix, x, 58
Get Hard, 26, 261, 262, 263, 265, 268, 269, 271, 272, 273, 277, 278–79, 280
Gill, Brendon, 152
Gill, David, 59, 169
Gish, Lillian, 62, 63, 66, 177. *See also* Stoneman: Elsie
Glory, 184
Golden Dawn, 69
Gone with the Wind, 148, 291, 297
Gottesman, Ron, 286
Graham, Wesley F., 37, 42
Gramsci, Antonio, 20
Granville, Augustus, 42
Grassroot Experience, 21, 50
Gray, Freddie, 139
Great Migration, 168–69
Great Moments from Birth of a Nation, 53, 56–57, 61–65
Great Trek, 109, 112, 117, 124
Greengrass, Paul, 180
Griffin, Sean, 13
Griffith, D. W., ix, 2, 6–7, 10, 13, 14, 15–16, 21, 22, 23, 25–26, 33, 34, 35, 37, 41, 42, 50, 59, 60, 62, 63, 64, 65, 67, 69, 70, 76, 82, 84, 88, 89, 93, 94, 96, 98, 107–8, 119, 123, 129, 130, 131, 132, 133, 140, 141, 142, 144, 145, 146, 147–49, 151, 152, 153, 155, 157, 160, 161, 164–70, 171–72, 174, 175, 176, 178–82, 183–84, 185, 194, 196–97, 200, 203, 208, 223, 227, 229, 239, 240, 241, 243, 246, 250, 251–52, 253, 254, 255, 260–61, 264,

265, 266, 267, 268, 273, 278, 282, 284, 285, 286, 287, 289, 290, 291; audiences, 7–8, 168
Griggs, John, 57–59
Griggs Moviedrome, 48, 53, 59
Gross, Terry, 252
Guardian, 36
Guerrero, Ed, 24, 193, 201, 261
Guerrero, Lisa, 239
Guess Who's Coming to Dinner, 261
Gunning, Tom, 290
Gus. *See* Rape: Gus
Gutsche, Thelma, 114

Habitus, 13–14
Haiti, 3
Hall, John B., 42
Hammond, Michael, 81
Hampton Collection, 67
Hampton, John, 67–68
Hansen, Miriam, 168, 177–78, 180
Hart, Kevin, 269, 272
Hawaii, 3
Hays, Will, 96
Hearts in Dixie, 249
Hees, Edwin, 95
Hemmings, Sally, 183
Herb Graff Collection, 56, 58
Heston, Charlton, 52
Hill, Estelle E., 42
History of the American People, A, 170, 172, 242
Hitchcock, Alfred, 62
Hitler, 52, 244, 292
Hodes, Martha, 176
Hollywood, 7, 13, 39, 46–47, 48, 61, 63, 69, 96, 107, 184–85, 201, 208, 246, 247, 255, 265, 272, 273, 276
Hollywood Shuffle, 247
HollywoodSoWhite, ix
Holquist, Michael, 262
Home Movies, 53
Houénou, Kojo Touvalou, 85, 98
House of Bondage, The, 6
Howard, Lillian, 37
Howe, Lawrence, 18, 24, 164–87
Hughes, Rupert, 241

Hulu, 71
Hunger, 222
Huns, 82

Image Entertainment, 71
Imperialism, 10
In the Clutches of the Ku Klux Klan, 91
Independent Lens, ix
Indiana University: African American and African Diaspora Studies, ix; American Studies, ix; Center for Research on Race and Ethnicity in Society; Cinema and Media Studies, ix; College of Arts and Humanities Institute, ix; Media School, ix; New Frontiers in the Arts and Humanities, ix; Ostrom Program, ix; Poynter Center, ix; IU Cinema, xi
Indianapolis Freeman, 38, 41
Inglourious Bastards, 180, 203
Intercontinental Marketing Corp., 54–56
International Slavery Museum, ix
Intolerance, 51, 67
Ivens, Joris, 107

Jacobs, Lea, 290
Jacobs, Ronald, 253, 255
Jarvie, Ian, 165, 166
Jazz Singer, The, 249
Jefferson, Thomas, 182
Jeffries, Michael, 244, 256
Jezebel, 14
Jim Crow, 3, 4, 38, 39, 65, 132, 149, 223, 228, 255
Johnson, Bennie, 39
Johnson, Eastman, 265
Johnson, Herbert, 41
Johnson, Jack, 265, 274
Johnson, Mark, 208
Johnson, Robert, 288, 301–2n19
Jolson, Al, 249
Jones, Raven W., 42
Journal, Le, 85
Judge Priest, 261

Kansas City Silent Film Festival, ix, x
Kaplan, Roy, 239
Kardashian, Kim, 296

Kaufman, J. B., 42
Keaton, Buster, 180
Kennedy, John F., 177, 255
Kerr, Leah, 49
Key and Peele, 294, 295–96
Killiam, Paul, 59
King, James, 269–70, 271, 272, 273, 274–75, 276, 277, 278
King Kong, 244
King, Martin Luther, Jr., 184, 255
King, Rodney, 140
King, Sergeant, 36
King of Kings, 67
Kingsley, James H., 42
Kino, 71
Kleinhans, Chuck: dedication, 25–26, 282–304, 300n9
Klinger, Barbara, 61
Ku Klux Klan, 7, 8, 9, 17, 19, 24, 25, 28n5, 51–52, 64, 67, 81, 91, 94, 130, 145, 148, 151, 152–53, 157–58, 169–72, 177, 182, 183, 191–92, 193, 194, 195, 196, 197, 199, 200, 201, 202, 203, 204, 223, 224, 225, 227, 228, 229, 232, 235, 240, 244, 261, 282, 291–92, 293–95, 298, 300n6, 301n16, 301n17, 301n18; at Bloomington, 283–87
Kuhlman, Erika, 93

La Presse, 80
Lake, Marilyn, 129
Lakoff, George, 208
Lamar, Howard, 132
Landry, Lawrence, 59
Lang, Robert, 263–64
Last King of Scotland, The, 264
Lattimore, Dr., 35
Lawson, Lillian, 36
Lee, Spike, 25, 26, 239, 246, 248, 249, 251, 252, 255, 256, 282, 286, 289, 299n1
Legree, Simon, 141
Leonard, David, 239
Leopard Spots, The, 69, 141, 164
Lesage, Julia, 24–25, 207–38, 300n9
Lewis, Darnell, 269, 270, 271, 272, 273, 274, 275–76, 277, 278
Liberty and Union, 254

Lichtenstein, Alex, 7, 23, 123–34
Life, 124
Life on the Mississippi, 175
Lincoln, 176
Lincoln, Abraham, 16, 63, 81, 84, 146–47, 172–73; assassination of, 174–82
Lincoln Motion Picture Company, 18
Little Sister, 54, 63; Little Colonel. *See also* Cameron: Ben, Flora
Litwack, Leon F., 92
London Film Productions, 96
Lost Angeles Times, 67
Lott, Eric, 38, 139
Lunn, Arthur, 37
Lynch, Silas, 7, 9, 14, 62, 94, 141, 145, 151, 182, 225, 229, 232, 254
Lynching, 3, 5, 38, 157–58, 159, 197, 198–99, 200, 201, 202, 203, 204, 232–33, 240, 292

Mad Men, 247, 248
Madmen of Mandoras, 52
Mahagonny, 222
Maingard, Jacqueline, 95
Malcolm X, 247, 255
Mammy, 14, 148, 149
Mandingo, 193, 200, 202
Manifest Destiny, 3
Marsh, Mae, 62. *See also* Cameron: Flora
Martin, Michael T., ix–xii, 1–29, 173–74
Martin, Trayvon, 139, 234, 234, 246, 255, 299
Marxism, 13
Mask of Fu Manchu, The, 69
Massey, Stephen, 33, 40
Massood, Paula, 24, 191–206
McBride, Renisha, 234
McDonald, Laguan, 139
McMurry University, 56
McQueen, Steve, 24, 25, 207, 208, 212, 214, 215, 216, 217, 219, 222
Melodrama, 24, 137, 138–39, 140, 151, 161, 162, 183, 193, 194, 264
Mexicans. *See* Wetbacks
MGM, 52
Micheaux Film Corporation, 18
Micheaux, Oscar, 23, 139, 153–54, 155, 156, 157, 158, 160, 161, 162

Million Hoodie March, 246
Minot Films, 58
Miscegnation, 7, 23, 94, 97, 119–20, 141,
  183, 184, 197, 201, 227, 244, 254, 264, 292;
  miscegenous sexual assault, 151, 182–83.
  See also Rape
Mississippi Burning, 184
Monroe, Mary E., 37
Mont Alto Motion Picture Orchestra, xi, x,
  xn3. *See also* Saur, Rodney
Montgomery Business Men's League, 38
Morrison, Toni, 183
Motion Picture Association of America, 200
Motion Picture Producers' Association, 96
Motion Picture Production Code, 200–1
Movie Classics, 57
MTV Video Awards, 296
Mulatto, 7, 14, 15, 64, 79, 94, 141, 145, 183, 291;
  mulatta, 151, 242
Mulvey, Laura, 222
Museum of Modern Art, ix, 50, 54, 68
Muslims, 1
*Mutual Film Corp. v. Industrial Commission
  of Ohio*, 152
My Mammy, 249
My Old Kentucky Home, 247
Myth of Post-Racial America, The, 239

Nat Turner Rebellion, 185–86
Nation, 92
National Assembly, 22, 85, 86
National Association for the Advancement
  of Colored People, 16, 17, 34, 50, 82–83, 96,
  131, 151–52, 261, 286
National Association of Colored Women's
  Clubs, 40
National Party, 110
Native Americans, 3, 132, 133
Native Son, 169
Nazi, 98, 118, 203, 244
Negro Life at the South, 265
Network, 246
Newsome, Bree, 43
New York Times, The, 47, 48, 68
Nigger, The, 90
Nixon, Richard. *See* Southern Strategy

Norman Manufacturing Company, 18
Northup, Solomon, 25, 209–10, 211, 212, 213,
  214, 215, 234, 235
Notes on the State of Virginia, 182
Nyong'o Lupita, 215

O Brother, Where Art Thou?, 292–93
Obama, Barack, 1, 27n2, 234, 239, 241, 243,
  244, 253, 256, 290
Occupy Movement, 2
O'Hara, Scarlet, 291, 297
Old Dominion University, ix, x
OscarsSoWhite, ix
Our American Cousin, 176
Ox-Bow Incident, The, 198

Packard Humanities Institute, 67
Paint the White House Black, 244
Palmer-Mehta, Valerie, 247
Paquet-Deyris, Anne-Marie, 25, 239–58
Parade of the Clansman, 149–50
Parker, Alan, 184
Parker, Nate, 184–85
Parson, Neil, 114
Pax Britannica, 108
Pearson, Roberta, 290
Peebles, Samuel, 66–67
Peer Gynt, 52
People's Baptist Church, 33
Philippines, 3
Photoplay Productions, 59
Pickaninnies, 14
Picturisation of History, 164, 185
Plaatje, Sol T., 83, 96–97, 98, 107
Plantation Genre, 193, 197, 201, 203
Plastic Age, The, 67
Playing the Race Card, 140
Popular Photography, 56
Posey, Jane W., 42
Postracialism, 1–2, 239, 251, 252, 255
Preller, Gustav, 114
Prinn, Carl T., 42
Prologue to the Birth of a Nation, The, 59
Psycho, 62
Puerto Rico, 3
Puller, Aaron Williams, 33, 35–36

Pullman, Bill, 198
Pulp Fiction, 203

Raack, R. J., 165–66
Race, Media and the Crisis of Civil Society, 253
Racial Other, 181–82
Rand Daily Mail, 97, 129, 133
Rape, 25, 54, 62, 94, 151, 159, 182, 194, 208–9,
    218, 219, 228–33, 238n30; Gus, 8, 9, 62, 63,
    94, 149–51, 152–53, 158, 169, 182, 199–200,
    202, 229, 232, 240, 243–44, 264, 266, 268,
    272, 273, 298
Ray, Charles P., 39
Rebirth of a Nation, 243, 245, 248
*Reconsructing Patriarchy After the Great
    War. See* Kuhlman, Erika
Reconstruction, 81, 130, 131, 143–44, 154–55,
    164, 169, 170, 175, 181, 182, 194, 196, 223, 224,
    227, 228, 233, 235, 240, 242, 252, 268, 287
Reel Classic DVD, 71
Reid, Wallace, 63
Republican Party, 291
Requiem, 193
*Returning the Gaze: A Genealogy of Black
    Film Criticism*, 259
Reynolds, Henry, 129
Rhineland Horror Campaign, 93
Rhodes, Cecil, 118
Rice, Tamir, 139
Rice, Tom, 4, 51
Ridley, John, 207
Riefenstahl, Leni, 292
Riot in the Master's Hall, 181
Robinson, Cecil, 268
Robinson, Cedric, 153, 160, 161, 263
Rogin, Michael, 2, 146, 167, 239, 302n23
Rohauer, Raymond, 58–59
Rojecki, Andrew, 241, 243
Rolprentinsetsels, 126, 129
Romantic racialism, 144–45
Rosenstone, Robert, 165, 166
Ruggles, Wesley, 67

Sadoul, Georges, 84
Sambo and Aunt Jemima: Comedians, 14
Sanders, Pharaoh, 21, 50
Saturday Night Live, 291

Sauer, Rodney, x
Savage Other, 119, 120
Scandal, 253
Schlesinger, I. W., 111
Schoeffel, John B. *See* Tremont Theater
Schultz, King, 191, 197, 202
Scott, Walter, 164
Seaton, George, 62
Selma, 184
Selman, David, 69
Shaka Zulu, 129
Shame, 222
Shaw, Harold, 129
Shaw, Robert Gould, 184
Sherlock Jr., 180
Shohat, Ella, 261
Sight and Sound, 255
Signifying Monkey, The, 254
Silent Movie Theatre, 67
Silva, Fred, 286, 287
Simien, Justin, 239, 242, 244, 246, 247, 248,
    252, 253, 255, 256. *See also Dear White
    People*
Simpson, O. J., 140, 151
Sinclair, William A., 37
Slavery, 6, 10, 119, 130, 132, 144, 148, 154, 204,
    207, 211–12, 213, 214, 215, 216, 217, 218, 219,
    220, 221, 222, 223, 224, 227, 232, 235; slave
    women agency, 219–21
Sloane, Paul, 249
Slow Fade to Black, 34
Smith, Guy Crosswell, 86
Smith, Valerie, 234
Snead, James, 260
Sorlin, Pierre, 172
South Africa, 22, 23, 95–97, 98, 107–122,
    123–30, 132–33
Southern Rape Complex, 25
Southern Strategy, 1
Spaghetti Western, 192, 203
Sparrows, 67
Spielberg, Steven, 176
Square Shooter, 69
Stage and Cinema, 114–15
Stam, Robert, 261
Star, 97
Stephenson, Adele: jacket cover, 5, 30, 190

Sterling Donald, 255
Sterling, Rod, 247
Stewart, Jacqueline, 49
Stokes, Melvyn, ix, 2, 21–22, 46, 73n15, 76–106, 151–52
Stone Film Library, 54, 55
Stoneman: Austin, 14, 84, 151, 182, 183, 196, 224; Elsie, 9, 14, 62, 94, 141, 148, 149–51, 177, 178–79, 183, 194, 228, 229–30, 232, 233, 254, 256; Phil, 147–48, 177, 178–79, 224, 230, 266, 273; Tod, 291
Stowe, Harriet Beecher, 88, 91, 140, 144, 147, 155, 161
Striker, Wallace, 37
Styron, William, 185
Sully, 180
Sunday Times, 117
Supreme Court, 2
Swart gevaar, 118
Swift, Taylor, 296

Talk About a Stranger, 52
Talk of the Nation, 252
Tarantino, Quentin, 24, 155, 180, 191, 192, 193, 194–95, 203, 204, 294, 303n27
Tarbox, Charles, 54
Taubman, Paul, 58
Taylor, Orlando, 288
Theodore Huff Memorial Film Society, 69
They Built a Nation, 22–23, 124, 126–29, 130, 131–32. See also *Die Bou van 'n Nasie*
They Saved Hitler's Brain, 52
Thompson, Leonard, 132
Thompson, Tessa, 255
Thornton, Dr., 35
Thunderbird Films, 59, 60
Toms, Coons, Mulattoes, Mammies, and Bucks, 249
Toronto Daily Star, 78
Townsend, Robert, 247
Tremont Theater, 33, 40, 41
Trinity Baptist. *See* Graham, Wesley F.
Trotter, William Monroe, 16, 36, 37
Trump, Donald, 1, 27n1, 291, 299, 303n29; "Make America Great Again," 298
Twain, Mark, 175, 176
Tyler, Texas Black Film Collection, 49

Uhrich, Andy, 20, 21, 46–75, 130
Uncle Tom, 14, 23, 88, 91, 138, 139–44, 151, 155, 157, 162, 249; Mammy and Jake personages, 147–48
Uncle Tom's Cabin, 145, 155, 160, 193, 194
Underground Railroad, 77, 78
Union Congregational Church, 80
Union League, 228
United 93, 180
Universal Studios, 62
University College London, ix, x
Up from Slavery, 131

Vardac, Nicholas, 286
VCI Entertainment, 71
Very Black Show, 249
Vickers, Jon, xi
Virginia Film Festival, ix, x
Virginian, The, 198
Volk, 110
Voortrekkers, 123, 124, 125, 126, 128, 132. See also *De Voortrekkers*

Walker, William, 152–54, 162
Wall, David C., xi, 6, 26, 173–74, 259–81
Waller, Gregory, 48
Walsh, Raoul, 63
Walthall, Henry, 62
Washington Bee, 41
Washington, Booker T., 131
Washington, Evelyn B., 42
Watermelon Contest, 14
Watkins, W. H., 38
Way Down East, 223
Weiner, Matthew, 247
Wellman, William A., 198
Wetbacks, 1
White House, 2
White Roles, Silver Screens: Movies and the Making of the Ku Klux Klan. See Rice, Tom
White Supremacy, 15–16, 22, 27n2, 43, 98, 132, 142, 145, 146, 160, 185
Why We Fight, 130
Wiegman, Robyn, 233
Wilentz, Sean, 38
Williams, Linda, ix, 14, 23, 24, 137–163, 251
Wills, Gary, 51

Wilson, Edmund, 284
Wilson, Woodrow, 16, 170–71, 172, 242
Wister, Owen, 198
Within Our Gates, 23, 137, 139, 153–54;
    storyline, 155–58
Wood, Amy Louis, 196, 198
Woodard, Alfre, 220
Worley, Sam, 212

Wright, Richard, 169

Yale Film Study Center, 56, 58. *See also* Herb
    Graff Collection
YouTube, 296, 297

Zimmerman, George, 246
Zulu's Heart, The, 22, 108, 119, 132–33